Richard Rorty

Richard Rorty

The Making of an American Philosopher

NEIL GROSS

The University of Chicago Press Chicago and London

NEIL GROSS is assistant professor of sociology at Harvard University.

The University of Chicago Press, Chicago 60637
The University of Chicago Press, Ltd., London
© 2008 by The University of Chicago
All rights reserved. Published 2008
Printed in the United States of America

16 15 14 13 12 11 10 09 08   1 2 3 4 5

ISBN-13: 978-0-226-30990-3 (cloth)
ISBN-10: 0-226-30990-8 (cloth)

Library of Congress Cataloging-in-Publication Data

Gross, Neil, 1971–
Richard Rorty: the making of an American philosopher / Neil Gross.
p. cm.
Includes bibliographical references and index.
ISBN-13: 978-0-226-30990-3 (cloth: alk. paper)
ISBN-10: 0-226-30990-8 (cloth: alk. paper)
1. Rorty, Richard. I. Title.
B945.R524G76 2008
191—dc22
[B]

2007039954

⊗ The paper used in this publication meets the minimum requirements of the American National Standard for Information Sciences—Permanence of Paper for Printed Library Materials, ANSI Z39-48-1992.

Contents

Preface for My Fellow Sociologists

Colleges and universities play vital roles in contemporary American life. There are more than 4,200 institutions of higher education in the United States today, enrolling 17.5 million students annually, and more than a quarter of American adults now earn bachelors degrees.[1] For children from middle- and upper-middle-class families, attending college has become a nearly universal experience—an indispensable juncture in the life course during which students are exposed to new ideas, make lasting friendships, begin to discover who they are as young adults, and build bridges to the rest of their lives. Going to college isn't just important for social reasons, however. The wage premium associated with a college degree has been growing, such that, increasingly, it is access to a college education that separates the haves from the have-nots.[2] It is in large part for this reason, and despite exorbitant growth in the cost of college tuition, that students are flocking to colleges and universities in record numbers. Beyond the credentialing function that colleges and universities serve,[3] and beyond the direct employment they provide to several million people—along with significant multiplier effects and the spread

1. National Center for Education Statistics, 2006, *Digest of Education Statistics*, Washington, D.C.

2. See, for example, David Card and Thomas Lemieux, 2001, "Can Falling Supply Explain the Rising Return to College for Younger Men? A Cohort-Based Analysis," *Quarterly Journal of Economics* 116:705–46.

3. Randall Collins, 2002, "Credential Inflation and the Future of Universities," pp. 23–46 in *The Future of the City of Intellect: The Changing American University*, Steven Brint, ed., Stanford: Stanford University Press.

of local knowledge networks that sustain entire communities[4]—the university sector has also become crucial to the economic growth of the nation as a whole, with technology transfer to industry now a major source of innovation[5] and an increasing proportion of economic activity revolving around the knowledge work performed by those with collegiate and postcollegiate training.[6]

At the heart of this institution lies the faculty: 630,000 full-time professors, along with 543,000 adjuncts, among whom are included many of the world's leading scientists and thinkers.[7] Social scientists know a great deal about the American faculty. Because of institutional record keeping and the fact that the professoriate is routinely subjected to social surveys, we can trace the changing social background of professors, their distribution across fields and institutions, their salaries and benefits, their orientation toward teaching or research, their social and political attitudes, the correlates of their productivity, and more. In light of the growth over the last two decades of the interdisciplinary field of science studies,[8] we also know much about the research activities of professors in the physical, biological, and engineering sciences: about how the institutional terrain they navigate is structured by political-economic forces, about the interaction of social networks and materiality in the production of scientific knowledge, and about the social processes by which observational reports of the empirical world come to be transformed into scientific facts.

Basic demographic and attitudinal information aside, however, there is a key segment of the American professoriate about which we know relatively little: humanists and social scientists. Humanists and social sci-

4. See, for example, Christopher Berry and Edward Glaeser, 2005, "The Divergence of Human Capital Levels across Cities," Harvard Institute of Economic Research Discussion Paper 2091; Sean Safford, 2004, "Searching for Silicon Valley in the Rust Belt: The Evolution of Knowledge Networks in Akron and Rochester," MIT Industrial Performance Center Working Paper 04-001; Jason Owen-Smith and Walter Powell, 2004, "Knowledge Networks as Channels and Conduits: The Effects of Spillovers in the Boston Biotechnology Community," *Organization Science* 15:5–21.

5. Jason Owen-Smith and Walter Powell, 1998, "Universities and the Market for Intellectual Property in the Life Sciences," *Journal of Policy Analysis and Management* 17:253–77.

6. Walter Powell and Kaisa Snellman, 2004, "The Knowledge Economy," *Annual Review of Sociology* 30:199–220.

7. Jack Schuster and Martin Finkelstein, 2006, *The American Faculty: The Restructuring of Academic Work and Careers*, Baltimore: Johns Hopkins University Press, 41. These figures are for 2003.

8. See David Hess, 1997, *Science Studies: An Advanced Introduction*, New York: New York University Press.

entists, though they may come to be the object of historical attention, are almost never studied systematically by those in science studies, who tend to regard the natural sciences as representing the hard cases for demonstrating that knowledge production is a social enterprise. Important questions therefore remain unanswered. How do humanists and social scientists select projects on which to work? What factors help to determine which theories, approaches, and methods they end up using? Under what conditions do intellectual movements in the humanities and social sciences arise?

Although the most significant organizational transformation in the American research university in recent decades involves the growth of the life and engineering sciences, the humanities and social sciences continue to be of considerable importance. Nine of the twenty largest disciplinary fields in which bachelors degrees are awarded today are in the humanities or social sciences,[9] humanists and social scientists together make up approximately a quarter of the full-time faculty,[10] and humanities fields in particular thrive at the undergraduate level at elite colleges and universities,[11] whose students may carry the ideas of humanists with them into politics, the judiciary, the media, the corporate boardroom, and other sites of social power. Although knowledge of literature and the arts and the ways of understanding these associated with the humanities may be a less valuable form of cultural capital in the United States today than in the past,[12] the theories of humanists like Freud and Foucault still

9. This count, based on data from the National Center for Education Statistics, excludes interdisciplinary majors.

10. Schuster and Finkelstein, *The American Faculty*, 447. As of 1998, humanists made up 16.1 percent of the full-time faculty, social scientists 11.4 percent. The proportion of faculty members in the humanities is shrinking, however. Using international data, David Frank and Jay Gabler find that "the relative emphasis allotted to teaching and research in the humanities sharply declined during the [twentieth century] from about one-third of total university faculty to less than one-fifth [while].... The relative precedence of the social sciences in the academic core sharply increased, from less than one-tenth of overall faculty to almost one third." See David Frank and Jay Gabler, 2006, *Reconstructing the University: Worldwide Shifts in Academia in the 20th Century*, Stanford: Stanford University Press, 64–65.

11. Roger Geiger, 2006, "Demography and Curriculum: The Humanities in American Higher Education from the 1950s through the 1980s," pp. 50–72 in *The Humanities and the Dynamics of Inclusion since World War II*, David Hollinger, ed., Baltimore: Johns Hopkins University Press.

12. Richard Peterson and Roger Kern, 1996, "Changing Highbrow Tastes: From Snob to Omnivore," *American Sociological Review* 61:900–907.

circulate widely within the ranks of the increasingly important "creative class,"[13] while also serving as ideational resources for movements aimed at political or cultural change.[14] The social sciences have even greater social significance—particularly economics and psychology, with the former directly influencing public policy and economic decision making nationally and internationally,[15] and the latter providing vocabularies that shape people's understanding of everything from politics[16] to practices of love and intimacy.[17]

In light of this importance, our lack of social-scientific understanding of how humanists and social scientists make knowledge represents a serious lacuna. In recognition of this fact, a handful of scholars—most working outside science studies—have recently begun to explore the topic. Important theoretical contributions have come from Andrew Abbott, Pierre Bourdieu, Charles Camic, Randall Collins, Michèle Lamont, and Robert Wuthnow, among others[18]—sociologists all—who have con-

13. Richard Florida, 2004, *The Rise of the Creative Class and How It's Transforming Work, Leisure, Community, and Everyday Life*, New York: Basic Books.

14. On the importance of Foucault to the gay and lesbian rights movement, for example, see David Halperin, 1995, *Saint Foucault: Towards a Gay Hagiography*, New York: Oxford University Press.

15. Marion Fourcade-Gourinchas and Sarah Babb, 2002, "The Rebirth of the Liberal Creed: Paths to Neoliberalism in Four Countries," *American Journal of Sociology* 108:533–79; David Harvey, 2005, *A Brief History of Neoliberalism*, New York: Oxford University Press; Margaret Somers and Fred Block, 2005, "From Poverty to Perversity: Ideas, Markets, and Institutions over 200 Years of Welfare Debate," *American Sociological Review* 70:260–87.

16. James Nolan, 1998, *The Therapeutic State: Justifying Government at Century's End*, New York: New York University Press.

17. Anthony Giddens, 1992, *The Transformation of Intimacy: Sexuality, Love, and Eroticism in Modern Societies*, Cambridge: Polity.

18. See Andrew Abbott, 2001, *Chaos of Disciplines*, Chicago: University of Chicago Press; Pierre Bourdieu [1984] 1988, *Homo Academicus*, Peter Collier, trans., Stanford: Stanford University Press; Charles Camic, 1983, *Experience and Enlightenment: Socialization for Cultural Change in Eighteenth-Century Scotland*, Chicago: University of Chicago Press; Randall Collins, 1998, *The Sociology of Philosophies: A Global Theory of Intellectual Change*, Cambridge: Harvard University Press; Michèle Lamont, 1987, "How to Become a Dominant French Philosopher: The Case of Jacques Derrida," *American Journal of Sociology* 93:584–622; Robert Wuthnow, 1989, *Communities of Discourse: Ideology and Social Structure in the Reformation, the Enlightenment, and European Socialism*, Cambridge: Harvard University Press. There have been some notable recent empirical studies as well, including Bethany Bryson, 2005, *Making Multiculturalism: Boundaries and Meaning in U.S. English Departments*, Stanford: Stanford University Press; Marion Fourcade, 2006, "The Construction of a Global Profession: The Transnationalization of Economics," *American Journal of Sociology* 112:145–94;

cerned themselves with understanding the social processes confronted and enacted by humanists and social scientists, in the contemporary academy and during prior historical periods, as they formulate and advance knowledge claims.[19]

It is to this literature that my book about Richard Rorty aims to make a contribution. As I describe in the introduction, the book is a case study in this nascent research area, which Camic and I, writing of scholarship that also examines the knowledge-making practices of natural scientists, have termed "the new sociology of ideas."[20] My goal is to develop, on the basis of immersion in an empirical case, a new theory about the social influences on intellectual choice, particularly for humanists—that is, a theory about the social factors that lead them to fasten onto one idea, or set of ideas, rather than another, during turning points in their intellectual careers. Where the most important theoretical work in the area stresses the strategic dimensions of such choice—the ways in which it

Marion Fourcade-Gourinchas, 2004, "Politics, Institutional Structures, and the Rise of Economics: A Comparative Study," *Theory and Society* 30:397–447; Grégoire Mallard, 2005, "Interpreters of the Literary Canon and Their Technical Instruments: The Case of Balzac Criticism," *American Sociological Review* 70:992–1010; James Moody, 2004, "The Structure of a Social Science Collaboration Network: Disciplinary Cohesion from 1963 to 1999," *American Sociological Review* 69:213–38; Joachim Savelsberg, Lara Cleveland, and Ryan King, 2004, "Institutional Environments and Scholarly Work: American Criminology, 1951–1993," *Social Forces* 82:1275–1302. There was also a small bubble of activity in the sociology of the social sciences and humanities in the late 1960s and 1970s, though some of this work departed from the assumption of contemporary researchers that sociology can help explain, not just the quantity, but also the content of intellectual work. Key studies in this vein, many carried out under the influence of Robert K. Merton, include Joseph Ben-David and Randall Collins, 1966, "Social Factors in the Origins of a New Science: The Case of Psychology," *American Sociological Review* 31:451–65; Diana Crane, 1972, *Invisible Colleges: Diffusion of Knowledge in Scientific Communities*, Chicago: University of Chicago Press; Alvin Gouldner, 1965, *Enter Plato: Classical Greece and the Origins of Social Theory*, New York: Basic Books; Nicholas Mullins, 1973, *Theories and Theory Groups in Contemporary American Sociology*, New York: Harper and Row. For discussion, see Charles Camic, 2001, "Knowledge, the Sociology of," pp. 8143–48 in *International Encyclopedia of the Social and Behavioral Sciences*, vol. 12, Neil Smelser and Paul Baltes, eds., London: Elsevier.

19. I use the terms "knowledge" and "knowledge claims" to mean the arguments advanced by humanists or social scientists, regardless of their epistemological status or content.

20. Charles Camic and Neil Gross, 2001, "The New Sociology of Ideas," pp. 236–49 in *The Blackwell Companion to Sociology*, Judith Blau, ed., Malden: Blackwell. In this piece, Camic and I discuss the features that distinguish recent work in the area from earlier scholarship carried out under the banner of the sociology of knowledge.

is shaped by thinkers' desires to amass status and prestige in the "intellectual field"—I argue that intellectual choice may also be influenced by the "intellectual self-concepts" that thinkers hold: the narratives of self to which they subscribe that characterize them as thinkers of such and such a type, as "activist" or "Christian" intellectuals or, in the case of Richard Rorty, as "leftist American patriots."

Why attempt to develop a sociological theory around the case of a single intellectual? I have both epistemological and practical reasons for doing so. On the epistemology side, I subscribe to the view, advanced by sociologists such as Peter Hedström, Barbara Reskin, Arthur Stinchcombe, Richard Swedberg, and Charles Tilly, that the goal of sociology is not to identify universally valid covering laws of social life but is rather to tease out the hidden social mechanisms and processes that make particular outcomes more likely for interactions and events occurring at a micro-, meso-, or macrolevel.[21] Too often work calling for the study of social mechanisms proceeds from methodologically individualist assumptions linked to some version of rational choice theory, and, in the hands of Hedström, one of the most vocal advocates of the study of mechanisms, social mechanisms turn out also to be tied to a simplistic conception of belief at odds with what cultural sociologists, cognitive psychologists, and others understand to be the nature of cognition and meaning.[22] Correctly conceived, however, as the intervening processes by which, on the basis of institutionalized meaning structures and in the absence of countervailing factors, X would make Y more likely, social mechanisms are the holy grail of sociology. The question is how to identify them.

I believe the social-scientific research enterprise must encompass two interrelated but distinct phases: a phase of theory building, in which the goal is to develop theories about the mechanisms generative of particular

---

21. Peter Hedström and Richard Swedberg, 1998, "Social Mechanisms: An Introductory Essay," pp. 1–31 in *Social Mechanisms: An Analytical Approach to Social Theory*, Peter Hedström and Richard Swedberg, eds., Cambridge: Cambridge University Press; Peter Hedström, 2005, *Dissecting the Social: On the Principles of Analytical Sociology*, Cambridge: Cambridge University Press; Barbara Reskin, 2003, "Including Mechanisms in Our Models of Ascriptive Inequality: 2002 Presidential Address," *American Sociological Review* 68:1–21; Arthur Stinchcombe, 2005, *The Logic of Social Research*, Chicago: University of Chicago Press; Charles Tilly, 2001, "Mechanisms in Political Processes," *Annual Review of Political Science* 4:21–41.

22. As in Paul DiMaggio, 1997, "Culture and Cognition," *Annual Review of Sociology* 23:263–87; Ann Swidler, 2001, *Talk of Love: How Culture Matters*, Chicago: University of Chicago Press. I discuss these issues in Neil Gross, 2007, "A Pragmatist Theory of Social Mechanisms," unpublished manuscript.

outcomes, and a phase of systematic empirical investigation, in which an attempt is made to assess the causal significance of the theorized mechanisms across a large number of cases. Theory building should be kept analytically separate from systematic empirical investigation, in my view, because the task of developing an adequate conceptual vocabulary for understanding the social universe and then deploying that vocabulary to explain social phenomena is sufficiently complex that trying to simultaneously devise rigorous, large-scale empirical tests of those same theories often dumbs them down, retarding theoretical progress. In this sense, I agree with Stephen Turner, who argues that sociological theory is a mature field and that when its autonomy from systematic empirical research is compromised, it is forced to backtrack.[23] Unlike Turner, I believe this autonomy can only be relative. Although much valuable theoretical work involves clarification of key concepts—work that often requires more meditation upon texts and ideas than engagement with empirical materials—such work is but preliminary to the task of identifying operative mechanisms. Identification of this kind must proceed on the basis of a deep familiarity with the empirical phenomenon the theorist is trying to explain, lest it be implausible and not adequately tied to the institutionalized meaning structures and processes actually at play. I am thus opposed in principle to armchair theorization of the kind practiced by game theorists and others and believe the theorist of mechanisms must develop her or his theories through immersion in empirical cases. Such immersion, however, should not be confused with the effort to test theories systematically, which requires a very different orientation toward empirical data and is, of course, equally important. In fact, the second reason theory building must be only relatively autonomous from systematic empirical testing is that theories should only command widespread agreement if they pass empirical muster—which is to say that theories must ultimately feed into systematic research—while the ways in which theories fail to pass muster must be factored into attempts at theoretical respecification or refinement. But this is not to say that theoretical work in itself should not count as a contribution to knowledge. With the important qualification that theory must have a solid empirical foundation and that theorists and systematic empirical researchers must be engaged in dialogue, my view is that sociology will only make explanatory headway if the value of

23. Stephen Turner, 2004, "The Maturity of Social Theory," pp. 141–70 in *The Dialogical Turn: New Roles for Sociology in the Post Disciplinary Age*, Charles Camic and Hans Joas, eds., Lanham: Rowman and Littlefield.

a division of labor between theorists and empirical researchers is recognized. This requires that theory and empirical research be evaluated according to different criteria: theory should push inquiry along in new, interesting, and promising directions, while the main question that should be asked of systematic empirical research, informed by theory, is, are its findings correct? The failure of sociology—in particular, American sociology—to recognize the value of this kind of epistemological pluralism is one of the main reasons we have not made as much progress as a social science as some would hope.

But even if we grant that theory should be developed through empirical immersion, the question remains of what form that immersion should take. Whether the units of analysis are nation-states, institutions, social movements, or individuals, empirically informed theorization could proceed through the study of multiple cases or single cases. Studying multiple cases is extremely useful, for it allows the theorist to leverage insights through comparison. Theories developed through immersion in single cases, by contrast, risk reifying the idiosyncratic or exceptional—though this danger seems greatest to those who confuse simplistically *generalizing* from a single case with the procedure of using a single case to *think through* some social phenomenon. Nevertheless, this risk may be justified if the phenomenon is so complex, or so hidden from view, that anything less than full attention to a single instance of it would result in inadequate and superficial understanding. Knowledge making in the humanities and social sciences is a phenomenon that meets this criterion for justified risk, because the activity that constitutes the object of explanation—the production of a body of ideas—is a complex affair involving polysemous symbolic output and because intellectuals, along with their biographers and other historians, as discussed in the introduction, typically downplay the mundane social processes involved in knowledge making in favor of a discourse of creative genius, leaving few traces in autobiographical recollections or standard historical treatments of the bread-and-butter social interactions involved. My interest in this study is in individual academicians and the social processes to which they are subject as they go about formulating their ideas and staging academic careers. Accordingly, in order to overcome the resistance to sociological analysis that intellectual life presents, I focus on the case of a single intellectual, reconstructing from scratch the details of Rorty's biography and career through 1982, the year he published *Consequences of Pragmatism*, a book of follow-up essays to his groundbreaking 1979 work, *Philosophy and the Mirror of Nature*. I use this reconstruction to help develop and lend prima facie plausibility to the theory of intellectual self-concept. Attempting to produce such a reconstruction for multiple intellectuals would have involved a considerable sacrifice of depth for breadth, and the resulting treatment of each—along with the associated sociological insights—would have been more superficial.

As to why my unit of analysis is individual academicians rather than some higher order social aggregation such as academic departments or intellectual networks or disciplines, the answer is that what is true of sociological theory more generally is true also of the sociology of ideas: the most robust theories are those committed to specifying the nature of the "micro-macro link"[24] and that build up from an understanding of individual-level social action. One does not have to be a methodological individualist to recognize that meso- and macrolevel social phenomena are constituted out of the actions and interactions of individual persons and that understanding individual-level action—its nature and phenomenology and the conditions and constraints under which it unfolds—is helpful for constructing theories of higher order phenomena, even though the latter have emergent properties and cannot be completely reduced to the former.[25] Knowledge of individual academics and the social processes they confront as they make their intellectual and career choices is therefore important not only for its own sake—inasmuch as it helps to explain the emergence of their ideas—but also as a preliminary to developing theories of broader sociointellectual dynamics.[26]

My methodological rationale for studying Rorty as opposed to some other humanist or social scientist is threefold. First, as I describe in more detail in the introduction, Richard Rorty was one of the most prominent American intellectuals of the second half of the twentieth century. While this may mean that his is a somewhat exceptional case, it also means that Rorty was at the center of a great many important discussions and held key positions at leading American institutions. His life thus opens a window into the main centers of knowledge making in late twentieth-century American academe in a way that studying a less influential, less well-positioned, and less prolific thinker would not. Second, although Rorty's

24. See Jeffrey Alexander, Bernhard Giesen, Richard Münch, and Neil Smelser, eds., 1987, *The Micro-Macro Link*, Berkeley: University of California Press.

25. See R. Keith Sawyer, 2005, *Social Emergence: Societies as Complex Systems*, Cambridge: Cambridge University Press.

26. For an attempt to build up from such microlevel theorizing, see Scott Frickel and Neil Gross, 2005, "A General Theory of Scientific/Intellectual Movements," *American Sociological Review* 70:204–32.

autobiographical recollections, like those of most other intellectuals, must be read with sociological skepticism, he kept detailed records of his everyday experiences, particularly during his formative years, in the form of correspondence with his parents and friends and was kind enough to give me access. In an era when a declining number of intellectuals write and save such letters and when privacy concerns often lead those who do to keep them out of the public eye, the Rorty case represents a rare empirical treasure trove. Third and finally, Rorty underwent a number of major intellectual shifts over the course of his early career, so studying him is an opportunity to examine multiple instances of intellectual choice, with diverse outcomes, spread over the life course.

I have a practical reason for writing about Rorty as well. As I make clear in the introduction, my aim in this book is not only to engage in theory building but also to encourage those who are interested in intellectual life but who are not sociologists to take the sociology of ideas seriously as an intellectual project. The only way to convince nonsociologists of the value of this enterprise is to focus on a thinker like Rorty in whom many are interested and to proceed nonreductively—that is, in a way that pays sufficient attention to the ideas themselves and to the sociointellectual contexts in which they were generated, so that those interested more in the ideas than in the sociology will not dismiss the project out of hand. In order to meet this requirement, the book presumes some familiarity with philosophy and tries not to overly simplify Rorty's thought.[27] One downside of this strategy is that sociologists unfamiliar with philosophy or American intellectual history may have a difficult time with some of the material. I encourage any such readers to focus on the introduction, chapters 9 and 10, and the conclusion—the sociological take-home messages are contained therein. I hope that intellectual historians, philosophers, and other readers, for their part, will also venture into these more sociological chapters, but they should do so with the knowledge that the chapters are written first and foremost for a sociological audience.

A further reason for going into such detail with the intellectual history is more accidental. During the course of my research, which took me to archives in Eugene, Rochester, and Stanford, among other places, I discovered a rich body of historical material about Rorty, his family, and his many friends and colleagues that I suspect will be of intrinsic interest to

---

27. Despite these efforts, there are no doubt aspects of my philosophical discussion with which some philosophers will quarrel. Some such quarrelling is to be expected as the natural reaction of a disciplinary community to social-scientific scrutiny.

scholars of American intellectual life. Although I could have advanced my sociological arguments well enough with reference to a smaller sample of this material, I would be failing in my duty as a scholar were I not to ensure that this information made its way into print. The resulting book is unorthodox for a sociologist, but as a long-time student of the classical American pragmatist philosophers Charles S. Peirce, William James, John Dewey, and George Herbert Mead, I have come to believe that form must follow function.

By using the Rorty case to develop better, more explanatory theories about the social influences on intellectual choice, I hope to stimulate further research—of both a theoretical and systematically empirical nature—into a phenomenon of great importance in the knowledge society: the development by intellectuals of their ideas.

Acknowledgments

Sociologists of science have long insisted that research is a cooperative enterprise, and this book is no exception to the rule. It would not
have been possible to write the book in anything like its current form
had Richard Rorty not opened up his files to me and granted me carte
blanche to write whatever I saw fit with the materials I found. Before he
died, I had the chance to thank him for his openness and integrity and for
letting me peer inside his life, but I wish to record my gratitude here as
well. My greatest intellectual debt is to Charles Camic, who supervised
my doctoral dissertation at the University of Wisconsin–Madison. Camic
has continued to be generous with his time over the years, giving me feedback on nearly everything I have written. He has profoundly shaped the
way that I think and the way that I write, and I am a better sociologist for
it. There is no one in the discipline I admire more. Many other scholars
also took the time to read and comment on drafts of the manuscript or
discuss the project with me, and I thank them for their excellent suggestions. I am particularly grateful to Jeffrey Alexander, Gianpaolo Baioc-
chi, Matteo Bortolini, Robert Brandom, Randall Collins, Nathan Glazer,
Julian Go, Peter Hare, Gilbert Harman, Steven Hitlin, Hans Joas, Robert
Alun Jones, John Lachs, Michèle Lamont, Donald Levine, Amélie Rorty,
Mitchell Stevens, John Summers, Jonathan Turner, Stephen P. Turner,
Alan Wald, Robert Westbrook, Christopher Winship, and Stephen
Vaisey. Their comments have helped me avoid many embarrassing errors
of fact and interpretation. I take full responsibility—of course—for any
errors that remain. Presentations I made at Boston University, New York
University, Princeton University, the Yale Center for Cultural Sociology,

and as the Coss Dialogues Lecturer at the 2005 meeting of the Society for the Advancement of American Philosophy helped me hone my argument. Barry Glassner was the one who encouraged me to take the single chapter of my dissertation that was about Rorty and expand it into a full-blown monograph. I have also benefited from outstanding research and editorial assistance and wish to express my gratitude to my research assistants Anthony Smith, Colin Koopman, James Maguire, Robert Owens, and Stephen Zafirau, and to Stephen Larsen for helping me whip the manuscript into shape at a crucial juncture. Mary Quigley provided excellent administrative support. Internal grants from Harvard paid the bills. Special thanks are owed to David Cutler, dean of the social sciences, who helped me finance a research junket in Palo Alto; and to Robert Sampson, chair of the Sociology Department, who helped soften the financial blow when computer disaster struck.

During the years it took for this book to reach completion, my wife, Jessica Berger Gross, has been my inspiration and my muse. Jessica and I grew close during the dark days that followed the death of my father, and, save for the demands of our careers, we have been inseparable ever since. I am thankful every day for her lovely spirit, for her talents and charm, and for what she has taught me about life and about myself.

Finally, I would like to honor the memory of my parents, Herbert and Sonya Gross, whose intellectual curiosity—and kindness—are qualities I will always admire. I count myself blessed to be their son.

Archival Sources

ACCF American Committee for Cultural Freedom Archives,
      Tamiment Library/Robert F. Wagner Labor Archives, New
      York University (New York, N.Y.)
IAS   Institute for Advanced Study Archives (Princeton, N.J.)
JRC   James Rorty Collection, University of Oregon Library,
      Department of Special Collections (Eugene, Ore.)
RRP   Richard Rorty's Papers, Stanford University (Stanford, Calif.)
WRC   Winifred Raushenbush Collection, American Baptist
      Historical Society, Colgate Rochester Crozer Divinity School
      (Rochester, N.Y.; the American Baptist Historical Society
      collection will be transferred to Atlanta in 2008)

Introduction

In 1965, Richard Rorty, an associate professor of philosophy at Princeton University, published an article titled "Mind-Body Identity, Privacy, and Categories" in the *Review of Metaphysics*. Rorty's aim in the article was to defend "identity theory"—the position, originally formulated by J. J. C. Smart, an analytic philosopher teaching in Australia—that "empirical inquiry will discover that *sensations* (not thoughts) are identical with certain brain-processes."[1] Opponents of identity theory, like the University of Rochester's James Cornman[2] and Pittsburgh's Kurt Baier, had recently argued that for identity theory to be true, all the attributes potentially associated with sensations and other mental events—such as their being "dim or fading or nagging or false" or involving "after-images"[3]—must be features of brain processes as well. But statements asserting as much would inevitably commit a "category mistake" in that they would postulate things being true in the realm of the physical that are appropriate semantically only for the realm of the mental. How could this objection be avoided?

Rorty outlined two possible responses. The first, which he termed the "translation" approach and which he associated with Smart, insisted on a strict definition of identity and sought to show that sentences involving seemingly mentalistic attributes could in fact be translated into

1. Richard Rorty, 1965, "Mind-Body Identity, Privacy, and Categories," *Review of Metaphysics* 19:24–54, 24. Here and throughout the book italicized words or phrases in quotations reflect emphases in the texts cited.

2. Cornman moved to the University of Pennsylvania in 1967.

3. Cornman, quoted in Rorty, "Mind-Body Identity," 25.

physicalistic language. The second, which Rorty developed and championed, he called the "disappearance" approach. On this approach, the "relation" between brain processes and sensations is not one of "strict identity, but rather the sort of relation which obtains between . . . existent entities and non-existent entities when reference to the latter once served (some of) the purposes presently served by reference to the former."[4] Rorty's argument was that philosophical ideas develop within particular historical-linguistic contexts. That our way of speaking about sensations developed in a context where we were not in a position to observe brain processes led to certain linguistic idiosyncrasies, and it is no more incumbent upon the identity theorist to show that statements concerning brain processes are compatible with these idiosyncrasies than it is incumbent upon the philosopher of psychology to ensure that everything that may be said of "demoniacal possession" may also be said of "hallucinatory psychosis."[5] But if it were one day discovered that sensations are nothing but brain processes, wouldn't it mean that all those who continue to refer to sensations in their everyday speech hold false beliefs? In response to this problem, Rorty marshaled philosopher Wilfrid Sellars's arguments about the nature of epistemic discourse. The truth or falsity of sensory reports is always relative to reporters' knowledge of the vocabularies in which they issue them, Rorty claimed. That one vocabulary has superseded another does not render reports issued in the earlier vocabulary false, especially if its use continues to serve a purpose, which it would in this case, as it is more convenient to report on pain and other bodily events in terms of sensation than to create a whole new quotidian language around the findings of brain science. The semantic objection to identity theory therefore carries no weight.

Seventeen years later, in 1982, Rorty—now Kenan Professor of the Humanities at the University of Virginia—published an essay in the *American Scholar,* the magazine of the Phi Beta Kappa Society, into whose ranks he had been inducted in college. The essay was called "Philosophy in America Today," and a revised version of it appeared later that year in Rorty's first essay collection, *Consequences of Pragmatism.* The essay told the story of the revolution that had taken place in American philosophy starting in the late 1930s with the immigration, from Austria and Germany, of the logical positivists. The positivists sought to usher in an era in which philosophical investigation would support the activities of scientists—natural and

---

4. Rorty, "Mind-Body Identity," 26.   5. Ibid., 27.

social—by, among other things, clarifying the meaning of key terms like "causality" and "verification." This clarifying work, they thought, should itself be carried out in a scientific spirit, with attention to logical rigor, a focus on problems capable of solution, and a willingness to disregard any idea that did not help advance these aims. All forms of speculative philosophy, especially metaphysics, were proscribed, and the history of philosophy downgraded. The positivists' emphasis on rigor and problem solving fit with the culture of the American university at the time, Rorty suggested, and this helped the positivists and their students—who modified their program—to capture most of the major American philosophy departments midcentury, where analytic philosophy, eventually construed to include both "ideal-language" and "ordinary-language" approaches, came to dominate. In this intellectual climate, Rorty wrote, "a graduate student … in the process of learning about, or being converted to, analytic philosophy, could still believe that there were a finite number of distinct, specifiable philosophical problems to be resolved—problems which any serious analytic philosopher would agree to be *the* outstanding problems."[6] It was believed, furthermore, that analytic philosophy, in its various forms, offered the conceptual tools necessary to solve these problems.

These beliefs, according to Rorty, were now relics from the past. The work of thinkers within the analytic tradition such as W. V. O. Quine, Sellars, and the later Ludwig Wittgenstein had called into question many of its key dogmas. At the same time, Thomas Kuhn's contributions to the history of science were making analytic philosophers aware that the "linguistic turn"—a phrase coined by Gustav Bergmann and which Rorty used as the title for a popular 1967 edited volume of analytic writings—was not the end of philosophical history but referred to just another paradigm, destined to be transcended as its anomalies accumulated. And in fact, Rorty argued, that was exactly what was happening in contemporary philosophy. The result was fragmentation of the field. Today, "any problem that enjoys a simultaneous vogue in ten of the hundred or so 'analytic' philosophy departments in America is doing exceptionally well."[7] Outside the analytic tradition, new philosophical voices, including those of contemporary Continental thinkers, were demanding to be heard. Many analysts decried this state of affairs, still clinging to positivist hopes for a

6. Richard Rorty, 1982, *Consequences of Pragmatism: Essays, 1972–1980*, Minneapolis: University of Minnesota Press, 215.

7. Ibid., 216.

rigorous and scientific philosophy that could solve problems definitively. But Rorty was no longer among them. Years earlier he had been a hard-nosed analyst himself, engaged in rarefied debates in the philosophy of mind. Now he encouraged his fellow philosophers to take a "relaxed attitude" toward the question of logical rigor, to stop drawing arbitrary boundaries between philosophy and other humanities fields, to open up more to the history of philosophy, to put the social and political concerns raised by Continental philosophers back on the table, and to cease worrying whether philosophy has a coherent paradigm. In philosophy, Rorty remarked, "we should let a hundred flowers bloom."[8]

The difference between these two texts in terms of orientation, problematic, and tone is pronounced.[9] The first was written by an analytic philosopher focused on a sharply delimited technical debate and proceeded from the common analytic assumption that "one cannot make a judicious assessment of any proposed thesis until one understands its constituent concepts."[10] The second was written by a philosopher who was decidedly postanalytic in the sense given to that term by John Rajchman and Cornel West in their 1985 volume on the subject.[11] Rajchman and West understood analytic philosophy to be "a specialized occupation with precise formal problems, one that eschewed public debate, disclaimed the requirements of literary or historical erudition, dismissed phenomenological and existential thought, and found little scientific and nothing philosophical in either psychoanalysis or Marxism."[12] Postanalytic philosophy, by contrast, of which Rorty was taken to be a leading representative, rejected these assumptions, not on a priori grounds, but because "technical work" in the analytic tradition had called them into question, leading philosophers to reengage with the concerns of other humanists. What accounts for the change in Rorty's outlook?[13]

8. Ibid., 219.

9. This is not to say that Rorty's argument in the earlier text cannot be reconciled with his argument in the latter. Both proceed from historicist assumptions that I describe in later chapters.

10. Avrum Stroll, 2000, *Twentieth-Century Analytic Philosophy*, New York: Columbia University Press, 8.

11. John Rajchman and Cornel West, eds., 1985, *Post-Analytic Philosophy*, New York: Columbia University Press.

12. Ibid., ix.

13. My argument is not the conventional one that Rorty went from being an analyst to being a pragmatist. As I show subsequently, he was interested in pragmatism from the start of his career, converted to analytic philosophy only after graduate school, and continued working in a modified analytic style after *Philosophy and the Mirror of Nature*. What

At one level, the goal of this book is to answer this question, while along the way documenting Rorty's journey from being an intellectually precocious adolescent on the school yards of rural New Jersey to becoming "the most influential contemporary American philosopher," as he was dubbed in a feature-length profile in the *New York Times Magazine* in 1990.[14] Drawing on extensive archival research, including an examination of thousands of pages from Rorty's personal files and family dossier,[15] the book reconstructs the facts of Rorty's early biography from his childhood until the publication of *Consequences of Pragmatism* in 1982, which followed closely on the heels of his 1979 book *Philosophy and the Mirror of Nature,* published when he was forty-eight. It identifies patterns of growth, change, and stability in his thought over the first quarter century of his intellectual career and relates these to his life experience.

At another, more fundamental level, however, the book is not just about Rorty. This is so because it treats the facts of Rorty's life not as constituting an ultimate object of explanation but as a means toward a larger explanatory goal: understanding some of the social processes that intellectuals encounter and navigate as they develop their ideas. In both its agenda and theoretical orientation, the book breaks with the three most prominent intellectual-historical approaches of the day.

* 2 *

The first of these approaches might simply be called humanism. On display in many popular intellectual biographies, the aim of a humanist approach to intellectual history is to weave a coherent narrative of a thinker's life and work around the notions of character and personality, to explain a thinker's ideas by situating them in the context of the life from which they arose. The vogue of psychohistory has long since passed, so for most of those scholars who write in a humanist vein, character and personality figure mostly as commonsense notions reflecting general insights about how people with different tendencies and dispositions navigate the complexities and dilemmas of the human condition, with all the

did change was his orientation. Increasingly he used the term "pragmatism" to signify the position at which he had arrived.

14. L. S. Klepp, 1990, "Every Man a Philosopher King," *New York Times Magazine,* December 2, 56.

15. I note here that throughout the book I have reproduced quotations from letters, diaries, and other unpublished materials as written, without correcting or calling attention to errors and variant spellings.

drama this entails. Thus it is that Richard Parker, in his biography of John Kenneth Galbraith, can orient his narrative around the progressive development of Galbraith's "later, mature character," his "partly innate, partly imposed attributes" of having "a cultivated and self-conscious singularity of thought and style, a certain circuitousness of career, and a marked distancing" with respect to "conservative colleagues,"[16] and that Ray Monk can explain Bertrand Russell's abandonment of philosophy and movement into political writing in the 1920s by pointing to a "transformation in his outlook and personality that had begun several years earlier with the release of his own instincts."[17] To call these and other similar works humanist is not to saddle them with philosophical baggage. Some are almost postmodern in their recognition of the fractured intellectual self and of the multiple and complex contexts that sustain it. Yet texts in this vein are marked by a belief in our common humanity, in the fellowship of intellectuals and nonintellectuals, with the resulting tendency to narrate stories of intellectual lives and careers by invoking the same tropes of the human condition as can be found in fiction, poetry, drama, and memoir. In such narratives, life and work are inseparable. The most abstract philosophic thesis may represent an expression of a thinker's underlying personality; a barbed rejoinder to another intellectual may be overdetermined by the dynamics of friendship, jealousy, lust, or disdain; and those whose intellectual work has real effects in the world—giving rise to political movements, restructuring economies, inventing weapons of war—must come to terms with their power and influence. The aim of the typical humanist account, however, is not to think in general terms about the nature of such connections. Its goal is to bring life and work together as part of the project of taking a measure of a particular intellectual's life, asking after its significance and broader meaning, with special reference to questions of creativity and virtue, the ethics of intellectual and political engagement, the dilemmas of authenticity, the dangers of corruption and self-aggrandizement, and the value of the ideas themselves.

A second approach, by contrast—the contextualist—downplays character and personality and focuses instead on reconstructing authorial intentionality. Understanding a text, scholars working in the tradition of Quentin Skinner and J. G. A. Pocock argue, means understanding what its author was trying to do in writing it: what kinds of argumentative moves

16. Richard Parker, 2005, *John Kenneth Galbraith: His Life, His Politics, His Economics,* New York: Farrar, Straus and Giroux, 5–6.

17. Ray Monk, 2000, *Bertrand Russell 1921–1970: The Ghost of Madness,* London: Jonathan Cape, 4.

she or he was attempting to make, against whom, and with what intended effect.[18] Understanding in this sense requires that historians abjure sweeping and progressive histories of an intellectual field that tell tales of its great figures speaking with one another across the ages. Rare is it that authors orient themselves toward such conversations, contextualists insist. More typically, their interlocutors are their contemporaries: other intellectuals or contributors to a given discourse at the time with whom they wish to register agreement or disagreement. On the grounds that it is these, more local conversations that establish the range of meaningful intellectual positions authors could have occupied, contextualists urge intellectual historians to keep their noses to the ground, reconstructing long-lost concerns and disputes in authors' immediate environments—some involving what would now be regarded as minor figures—that may have been salient for them. Identifying institutional, political, and cultural factors relevant to textual meaning is allowed by contextualists, but causally explaining the content of an intellectual's work—or its shifts over time—by reference to such factors is not. For Skinner and other contextualists, intentionality is the only sure determinant of human action, and there is reason to be wary of most claims of "influence," whether the entity said to be doing the influencing is an individual or society.

Less popular among intellectual historians than either humanism or contextualism is a third approach: poststructuralism. Championed in intellectual history by thinkers such as Dominick LaCapra, Mark Poster, and Hayden White, poststructuralism dismisses contextualism for its concern with historical objectivity, characterized as an illusory goal; for its belief in the singularity of authorial intentionality, which poststructuralism suggests to be multiple, fragmentary, and evanescent; for its unwillingness to connect up past and present by harnessing history to current critical aims; and for its focus on the author as creator rather than as a site for the unfolding of larger cultural structures.[19] Instead poststructuralists sug-

---

18. See James Tully, ed., 1988, *Meaning and Context: Quentin Skinner and His Critics*, Cambridge: Cambridge University Press. J. G. A. Pocock, 1989, *Politics, Language and Time: Essays on Political Thought and History*, Chicago: University of Chicago Press.

19. See Dominick LaCapra, 1983, *Rethinking Intellectual History: Texts, Contexts, Language*, Ithaca: Cornell University Press; Mark Poster, 1997, *Cultural History and Postmodernity: Disciplinary Readings and Challenges*, New York: Columbia University Press; Hayden White, 1973, *Metahistory: The Historical Imagination in Nineteenth-Century Europe*, Baltimore: Johns Hopkins University Press. On the affinities between poststructuralist intellectual history and the new historicism of Stephen Greenblatt and others—an intellectual movement largely confined to departments of literature—see Patrick Brantlinger, 2002, "A Response

gest that the best way to understand an intellectual text—or to explain the emergence of a set of ideas—is to analyze these larger structures: linguistic structures of alterity and exclusion that are given expression and simultaneously subverted in the cases analyzed by LaCapra; Foucauldian epistemes, or the taxonomies and assumptions—linked to power and political economy—that give sense to discourses and make inquiry possible, as considered by Poster; and the "deep" discursive structures, permitting different types of historical narration, that White tracks across the *longue durée* of the nineteenth century.

* 3 *

Each of these approaches—humanism, contextualism, and poststructuralism—has served as a historiographic frame for some excellent scholarship. Because of them we know a tremendous amount about the life and times of the most prominent figures of world intellectual history and some of their less influential counterparts. Yet we should not be blind to the problems with all three. Humanism, for its part, holds itself out as an intellectual enterprise in which explanation is driven more by the facts of the case and the narrative trajectories these suggest than by any a priori theoretical scheme. But implicit theorizing is unavoidable, and, as is true of most commonsense efforts to understand the human world, the facts typically picked out as important in humanist accounts are those relating to individuals: the parents, teachers, friends, lovers, rivals, and others who influenced or otherwise interacted with the intellectual in question. Interaction of this sort is indeed important, in intellectual life and beyond—society could scarcely exist without it. But many humanist accounts pay no systematic attention to the sociological structuring of such interaction and underestimate the causal significance of social factors such as the configuration of educational institutions or the state of academic labor markets in shaping the content of an intellectual's ideas.

Contextualists, for their part, tend to be more interested in explaining particular cases in terms of contingent historical circumstances than in identifying more general causal processes by which the ideas of intellectuals take shape. Yet the social sciences have been effective at identifying such processes outside the intellectual sphere, which calls into question

to *Beyond the Cultural Turn,*" *American Historical Review* 107:1500–511. More generally, see Elizabeth Clark, 2004, *History, Theory, Text: Historians and the Linguistic Turn,* Cambridge: Harvard University Press.

whether, as some contextualists would insist, human life is more contingent than determined. We understand reasonably well, for example, how exposure to higher education leads to the development of more liberal social and political attitudes;[20] we know that in most capitalist societies social class is an important determinant of health behaviors and outcomes;[21] we have a good sense for why some social movements for political change succeed while others fail;[22] and we can predict with reasonable levels of accuracy who will mate with whom, at least at the aggregate level.[23] Debates continue over how casual relationships in the social world can be reconciled with the reality of human agency,[24] but in light of current levels of knowledge in the social sciences, it is not credible to maintain that there are no general social processes that have a causal effect on human affairs. With regard to intellectual history—a realm we can believe exempt from social causation only if we succumb to what Pierre Bourdieu called the "scholastic illusion"[25] that knowledge producers are cut from a different cloth than others—this raises questions contextualists cannot answer. What processes drive the formation of authorial intentions? What factors, other than the contingencies of history, structure particular sociointellectual contexts? In his foundational 1969 essay, "Meaning and Understanding in the History of Ideas," Skinner took issue with historians and social theorists—especially Marxists—who would reduce ideas to their ideological function, and rightly so. Opposition to such reductionism, however, need not entail antipathy to the project of social-scientific generalization. There are, as we shall see, many causally significant social processes operative in the world of knowledge and ideas that have nothing to do with ideology, false consciousness, or class bias, and about these contextualism has little to say. In advancing this criticism, I do not mean to deny that

20. See Ernest Pascarella and Patrick Terenzini, 1991, *How College Affects Students: Findings and Insights from Twenty Years of Research*, San Francisco: Jossey-Bass.

21. See, for example, Mesfin Mulatu and Carmi Schooler, 2002, "Causal Connections between Socio-Economic Status and Health: Reciprocal Effects and Mediating Mechanisms," *Journal of Health and Social Behavior* 43:22–41.

22. Doug McAdam, Sidney Tarrow, and Charles Tilly, 2001, *Dynamics of Contention*, New York: Cambridge University Press.

23. Edward Laumann et al., 2004, *The Sexual Organization of the City*, Chicago: University of Chicago Press.

24. Mustafa Emirbayer and Ann Mische, 1998, "What Is Agency?" *American Journal of Sociology* 103:962–1023.

25. Pierre Bourdieu, 2000, *Pascalian Meditations*, Richard Nice, trans., Stanford: Stanford University Press.

important intellectual and moral purposes may be served by narratives stressing contingency, particularity, and context or that there may be a valid distinction between explaining an idea and understanding it. What I do wish to insist is that insofar as contextualist accounts ignore general social processes and mechanisms that shape ideas—or treat these only in an ad hoc manner—they cannot provide fully adequate explanations.

Given this view, it might be expected that my sympathies lie with poststructuralism. They do not. For though in principle poststructuralism is the most open of these approaches to the notion that the content of an intellectual's work may be a product of larger social and cultural structures and forces, it fails to be specific in its understanding of the relationship between structures and ideas. How exactly do entities such as epistemes function to stamp the ideas of individual thinkers? Or, to take a case analyzed by White, how does one get from "the theory of the tropes and of the relationships between them that [Giambattista Vico] took over ... from classical poetics"[26] to the view of history Vico actually held? How did this theory get inside Vico, so to speak? Why Vico and not someone else? Was it the only factor to have influenced his thought or career? More generally, what is the ontological status of such cultural structures? What explains their origin, diffusion, and institutionalization? How does this vary from period to period and intersect with more mundane considerations such as opportunities for academic employment or the quest to secure intellectual reputations? The devil is in the details, and poststructuralism's neglect of fine-grained causal theorizing in the intellectual sphere is notable.

* 4 *

A more satisfactory approach to explaining intellectuals' ideas does exist, however. This approach Charles Camic and I have called "the new sociology of ideas."[27] Consisting of scholarship informed by the theoretical contributions of sociologists such as Pierre Bourdieu and Randall Collins,[28]

26. Hayden White, 1978, *Tropics of Discourse: Essays in Cultural Criticism*, Baltimore: Johns Hopkins University Press, 216.

27. Camic and Gross, "The New Sociology of Ideas."

28. There are others in this group, although Bourdieu and Collins are my main interlocutors. A case could certainly be made for considering Bruno Latour a key sociologist of ideas, and at least one important study in the sociology of philosophy proceeds from Latourian assumptions. (See Martin Kusch, 1995, *Psychologism: A Case Study in the Sociology of*

the new sociology of ideas differs from the old sociology of knowledge—
that developed by figures such as Émile Durkheim, Karl Mannheim,
Robert K. Merton, and members of the Frankfurt School—in a crucial
respect. Where older approaches explained the ideas of intellectuals as reflections of broad social and cultural tendencies and "needs"—advanced
capitalism's need to legitimize itself philosophically, for example—new
sociologists of ideas seek to uncover the relatively autonomous social log-
ics and dynamics, the underlying mechanisms and processes, that shape
and structure life in the various social settings intellectuals inhabit: academic departments, laboratories, disciplinary fields, scholarly networks,
and so on. It is these mechanisms and processes, they claim, that—in
interaction with the facts that form the material for reflection—do the
most to explain the assumptions, theories, methodologies, interpretations of ambiguous data, and specific ideas to which thinkers come to
cleave. Although there is disagreement among new sociologists of ideas
as to what the operative mechanisms and processes are, the consensus
in the field is that they are "social facts" in roughly the sense Durkheim
intended when he used that phrase to identify sociology's unique object
of study:[29] they are external to the individual (although they also help to
constitute her as a social actor), and they both enable and constrain her
intellectual and career choices.

It is from the standpoint of the new sociology of ideas that I approach
the development of Rorty's thought. Yet there are two ways this could
be done. One would be to write a more or less conventional intellectual
biography focused on telling the story of Rorty's life but drawing occasionally on concepts and theories from the new sociology of ideas to
make sense of key developments. On this approach, the new sociology
of ideas would remain in the background, informing the argument, but
would not itself be advanced in the process, except insofar as its utility
for another empirical case would be demonstrated. There is nothing ob-
jectionable to such an approach, but it is not the one I take. Instead, I use

---

Philosophical Knowledge, London: Routledge.) Actor-Network Theory opens up for analysis
many previously understudied aspects of knowledge production—in particular, those to
do with the construction of facticity and the importance for science of physical and biological objects. Latour has been less concerned, however, with developing causal models
that link the production of particular kinds of ideas to particular social contexts and is thus
less useful for my project than other theorists.

29. Émile Durkheim, [1895] 1982, *The Rules of Sociological Method*, W. D. Halls, trans.,
New York: Free Press.

Rorty's biography as a case study by means of which to push the sociology of ideas in new directions.[30]

In my view, the major theorists in the area—Bourdieu and Collins—have developed explanatory models that go far in helping us understand how social processes operative in thinkers' environments influence the content of their thought and the structure of their careers. For Bourdieu, writing especially of the French context, there is a close relationship between an academic's social background and the position she or he will eventually occupy in the world of ideas.[31] Intellectuals from socially or culturally privileged backgrounds have an advantage as they make their way through the educational system, and as aspiring professors they not only gravitate toward the most prestigious disciplines but are welcomed with open arms by leading figures, who recognize them as fellow elites. Struggling with other academics to win as much intellectual prestige as they can, they typically end up cleaving to theories, positions, and approaches defined as high status, while those from less privileged backgrounds are relegated to lower-status intellectual views. Exogenous shocks can sometimes shake up these processes of social reproduction and under certain conditions thinkers can break free from the habitus, or socially structured dispositions, into which they have been socialized. On the whole, however, ideas serve strategic functions for thinkers, helping to position them in academic hierarchies, and inequalities in the wider society translate into inequalities internal to the intellectual field.

For Collins, it is also the case that coming from a privileged social position confers an advantage in intellectual life.[32] But in his view the kind of privilege that matters most is access to high-status intellectual networks, which may be tied only indirectly to class background. Access to

---

30. The value of case study research for social science is well established. Despite their limitations, case studies "permit ... the grounding of observations and concepts about social action and social structures in natural settings studied close at hand; provide ... information from a number of sources and over a period of time, thus permitting a more holistic study of ... complexes of social action and social meanings; ... furnish the dimensions of time and history to the study of social life; [and] encourage ... and facilitate ... theoretical innovation and generalization." Joe Feagin, Anthony Orum, and Gideon Sjoberg, 1991, "Introduction," pp. 1–26 in Joe Feagin, Anthony Orum, and Gideon Sjoberg, eds., *A Case for the Case Study*, Chapel Hill: University of North Carolina Press, 7–8. Also see Charles Ragin and Howard Becker, eds., 1992, *What Is a Case? Exploring the Foundations of Social Inquiry*, Cambridge: Cambridge University Press.

31. Bourdieu, *Homo Academicus*.

32. Collins, *The Sociology of Philosophies*.

such networks gives an aspiring intellectual access to the symbols—the intellectual or cultural capital—most highly valued and indeed sacralized within them. This permits the intellectual to formulate ideas that will be well regarded by those whose opinions matter most from the standpoint of forging an intellectual reputation and establishing an academic career. Not everyone from favored network positions will end up being successful, however. Too many thinkers vying to take top billing in the "intellectual attention space" will keep new voices from being heard. But intellectuals, as social actors driven—like all humans—by their emotional needs and desires, do not allow this constraint to deter them from trying to formulate ideas that will win them as much attention as possible from their colleagues, maximizing their levels of "emotional energy."

Both of these theoretical frameworks are useful in explaining aspects of Rorty's life. For example, Rorty's parents were both intellectuals—writers and activists of some renown in New York City circles in the 1920s, 1930s, and 1940s—and his extended family included numerous academics, writers, and artists. When he entered the higher education system he was therefore endowed with high levels of intellectual and cultural capital, which gave him a leg up as a student. This Bourdieusian insight can be coupled with one derived from Collins: generally speaking, intellectuals endeavor to affiliate themselves with high-status intellectual networks that permit them access to the symbols necessary for securing high-status slots in the attention space. This helps make sense of Rorty's move, in 1961, from Wellesley to Princeton. The two institutions from which he received graduate training in philosophy—Chicago and Yale—were both holdouts against the increasingly analytic tendencies of the field. It was probably because of network connections between his nonanalytic dissertation advisor and a professor at Wellesley that he had gotten the job there, but while Wellesley was a respected liberal arts college, it did not have a top-ranked philosophy department. Rorty sought to be more at the center of the disciplinary action and so refashioned himself as an analytic philosopher, working to bring himself to the attention of the analytic community. These efforts proved successful, allowing him to convert what was to be a temporary position at Princeton into a tenure-track post and giving him new network connections that made possible his further ascent in the disciplinary status structure.

These examples notwithstanding, the approaches of Bourdieu and Collins have their limitations. First, neither theorist pays much attention to the fact that intellectuals, like all social actors, are reflexive and have idiosyncratic and strongly held conceptions of self.[33] As anyone who has ever attended a faculty party will know all too well, intellectuals talk frequently about themselves, telling themselves and others stories about their experiences, interests, values, dispositions, and orientations in conversation, correspondence, diaries, statements of research progress, grant applications, lectures, and so on. Despite his shy and self-effacing manner, Rorty often engaged in this kind of self-commentary. There is good reason to believe that such stories or self-narratives are not epiphenomenal aspects of experience but influences on social action in their own right. Indeed, few notions have been as important in social psychology as those of self and self-concept.[34] Social-psychological theory and research suggest that self-narratives influence action in at least three ways: prospectively it is in terms of such narratives that actors identify and orient themselves toward goals and life projects; actors engage in efforts to produce retrospective accounts of their behavior that preserve their identity over time; and in situ self-narratives influence the availability and emotional loading of cognitive schemas and scripts, affecting the thinkability of and propensity to engage in particular actions. To be sure, some of the self-narratives intellectuals construct revolve around their positions in intellectual status structures, as the theories of Bourdieu and Collins might lead us to expect. But many others have little to do with concerns over intellectual status or prestige. One self-narrative that was important to Rorty, for example—and that reflected the influence of his parents—centered on the identity "leftist American patriot." The biographical evidence suggests this narrative was important at a critical juncture, inclining him toward a renewed affiliation with pragmatism, seen as an inherently progressive and American philosophy. But there is no room in the theories Bourdieu and Collins develop for influences of this kind, and no attempt to think through how the quest for status and upward mobility in an intellectual field may intersect and sometimes

33. As discussed in chapter 9, both Michèle Lamont and Jeffrey Alexander have advanced versions of this argument. See Michèle Lamont, 2001, "Three Questions for a Big Book: Collins's *The Sociology of Philosophies*," *Sociological Theory* 19:86–91; Jeffrey Alexander, 1995, *Fin de Siècle Social Theory: Relativism, Reduction, and the Problem of Reason*, London: Verso.

34. For example, see Bruce Bracken, ed., 1996, *Handbook of Self-Concept: Developmental, Social, and Clinical Considerations*, New York: John Wiley and Sons; Glynis Breakwell, ed., 1992, *Social Psychology of Identity and the Self Concept*, London: Surrey University Press; John Hattie, 1992, *Self-Concept*, Hillsdale: Lawrence Earlbaum Associates; Hartmut Mokros, ed., 2003, *Identity Matters: Communication-Based Explorations and Explanations*, Creskill: Hampton Press.

compete with thinkers' cognitive and affective interests in remaining true to narratives of intellectual selfhood that have become more or less stable features of their existence.

Second, as several reviewers of Collins's 1998 book, *The Sociology of Philosophies,* pointed out—including philosopher Anthony Grayling writing in the *New York Times*[35]—empirical work done under the auspices of the new sociology of ideas, particularly in its Bourdieusian and Collinsian forms, can be reductive. When mechanically analyzed through the theoretical lens of habitus and field or "interaction ritual chains," the richness and complexity of intellectual life can be flattened beyond recognition. All sociological models are simplifications of reality. But in their haste to demonstrate the value of their theories, Bourdieu, Collins, and those who have adopted their approaches have sometimes offered readings of intellectual texts—their objects of explanation—at odds with prevailing interpretations or have glossed over biographical complexities that, if more thoroughly analyzed, might suggest the inapplicability of their models to the cases at hand.

This book attempts to remedy the lack of theorization of the self that presently characterizes the new sociology of ideas, while simultaneously demonstrating that the sociology of ideas need not be a reductive enterprise. I devote a chapter to developing more fully my critique that Bourdieu and Collins ignore the significance of intellectual reflexivity and self-narratives and lay out a theory of "intellectual self-concept" that could, if integrated into the theoretical tool kit of the new sociology of ideas, account for even more of the variation in intellectual and career choices and outcomes. My central empirical thesis is that the shift in Rorty's thought from technically oriented philosopher to free-ranging pragmatist reflected a shift from a career stage in which status considerations were central to one in which self-concept considerations became central. I argue that it was the self-concept of leftist American patriot that decisively influenced his later work, pushing him—along with other factors—back in the direction of pragmatism.

It is important to note, in stressing the role played by self-concept in my account, that although processes relating to self-concept are of a social-psychological nature, self-concepts themselves are thoroughly social. Not only are the identity elements of which they are composed social constructs that acquire their meanings in relation to other identi-

35. A. C. Grayling, 1998, "Family Feuds," *New York Times,* September 27, book review sec., 20–21.

ties and in particular discursive communities,[36] they are also, as I argue in chapter 10, the product of thinkers' sequential immersion over the life course in various institutional settings—the family, the church, the peer group, the graduate department, and so on—where, because of processes of institutional structuration, certain identities have come to be given positive cultural codings. Intellectual self-concept is therefore a proper object of sociological study, particularly when examined, as it is here, in conjunction with the broader social and cultural factors that otherwise shape the institutional contexts and intellectual fields in which thinkers are located.

* 5 *

But who is Richard Rorty, and what is so significant about his philosophy? Rorty was born on October 4, 1931, the only child of James Rorty and Winifred Raushenbush. James Rorty was the son of an Irish immigrant and would-be poet who had married a schoolteacher with early feminist convictions. The two ran an unsuccessful dry goods business in Middletown, New York. After an apprenticeship with the local newspaper, James Rorty enrolled in Tufts College, near Boston, graduating in 1913. He served in France during World War I and then launched a career as muckraking journalist, writing poetry on the side and working periodically as an advertising copywriter to pay the bills. A well-known figure on the New York intellectual scene, James Rorty was influenced by Thorstein Veblen and wrote books on topics ranging from the Depression to the advertising industry. Winifred Raushenbush, for her part, was one of the daughters of Walter and Pauline Rauschenbusch, the latter an immigrant from Prussia. Her father, a Baptist minister and eventually professor of divinity at the Rochester Theological Seminary—as his own father, a German immigrant, had also been—was one of the leaders of the social gospel movement at the turn of the twentieth century, which invoked Christian themes to rally people around the cause of progressive social reform. Her mother held the position of minister's wife. Raushenbush, who changed the spelling of her name to deemphasize her German heritage, graduated from Oberlin College in 1916, majoring in sociology. She moved to Chicago to take a job as a research assistant for the sociolo-

36. For discussion see Karen Cerulo, 1997, "Identity Construction: New Issues, New Directions," *Annual Review of Sociology* 23:385–409; Michèle Lamont, 2001, "Culture and Identity," pp. 171–86 in *Handbook of Sociological Theory*, Jonathan Turner, ed., New York: Plenum.

gist Robert Park, working with him on *The Immigrant Press and Its Control* (1922) and his Survey of Race Relations on the Pacific Coast. Later she became a freelance journalist like her husband, writing pieces for magazines and newspapers. Her specialties were sociologically informed articles on race riots and fashion.

Richard Rorty grew up in a rural community in northwestern New Jersey, where his parents bought a house to escape city life. He was a precocious child, and at the age of fifteen was sent off to the so-called Hutchins College at the University of Chicago, which had recently begun accepting high school students and educating them in the great books of the Western tradition, culminating in a bachelors degree three years later.[37] At Chicago Rorty gravitated toward philosophy and stayed an extra three years to complete a masters. His thesis advisor, Charles Hartshorne, had been a student of the philosopher Alfred North Whitehead, and Rorty's thesis was on Whitehead's metaphysics. He went on to Yale, where in 1956 he defended a doctoral dissertation under the metaphysician Paul Weiss, arguing that the concept of potentiality, treated extensively by Aristotle and the seventeenth-century rationalists, remained of central importance to those working in the tradition of logical empiricism. Insofar as this was so, dialogue between analytic and nonanalytic philosophers—especially nonanalysts knowledgeable about the history of the field—was called for.

While at Yale Rorty married Amélie Oksenberg, a fellow graduate student. As mentioned previously, his first academic position was at Wellesley, but he soon moved to Princeton. His wife found work at Douglass College, then the women's arm of Rutgers. Rorty was promoted to associate professor in 1965 and to full professor in 1970. In 1972 he and Amélie Rorty divorced, having had one son. He married Mary Varney, a philosopher who received her Ph.D. from Johns Hopkins in 1970. They would have two children together.

In the 1960s and early 1970s Rorty earned a reputation as a smart analytic philosopher who was also well versed in the history of philosophy. He was prolific and could frequently be found on the academic lecture circuit, promoting his ideas at conferences and colloquia. His 1967 volume, *The Linguistic Turn*, was a popular text to assign in graduate courses, and several of his articles, including "Mind-Body Identity, Privacy, and Categories," were cited frequently and discussed in the pages of prestigious analytic journals. But Rorty's dissatisfaction with the version of the

37. In fact he moved to Hyde Park a few weeks before his fifteenth birthday.

analytic project institutionalized at Princeton had been growing since he received tenure. He found most of his colleagues arrogant and too narrowly focused. Relations with them soured more after his divorce; Amélie had been a popular figure in the department. Rorty formulated a plan to leave and was wooed by a number of schools, including Hopkins. At the same time, he worked to put the finishing touches on a book that would lay out the philosophical position he had been slowly developing since graduate school. In 1979 he served as president of the prestigious Eastern Division of the American Philosophical Association and was at the helm when a group of nonanalytic philosophers staged a protest at the annual meeting and, in a contested election, seized control of the presidency. Rorty had the authority to rule the election null and void on the grounds that some nonvoting members had cast ballots but chose to let the results stand. That same year he published *Philosophy and the Mirror of Nature*, which took the academic world by storm.

In his earlier analytic work Rorty might have been seen as a philosopher of mind. By contrast, the goal of *Philosophy and the Mirror of Nature* was to undermine the notion that mind is something "about which one should have a 'philosophical' view."[38] Rorty's hope was to call into question a conception of philosophy as the discipline that grounds knowledge claims advanced in other fields by providing an understanding of knowledge itself, or what it means for the mind to know. In Rorty's account, it was Kant who set philosophy on this epistemological course. Kant's theory of knowledge saw mind as composed of intuitions and concepts. Intuitions, immediate representations of objects, are passively received from the world and must be synthesized—subsumed under general concepts—in order to contribute to knowledge. Judgments that result are true—that is, represent the world objectively—if this act of synthesis has been carried out correctly, and philosophy has as one of its major aims to understand what this entails. Although Kant's vision for philosophy was revolutionary, Rorty noted that it built on images and metaphors developed by earlier thinkers. Descartes, for example, trying to secure the indubitability of knowledge in an age of skepticism, conceived of mind as ontologically distinct from matter, and Kant retained this conception, seeking to explicate the relationship between mind and world. Kant also took over from Descartes and Locke the image of objective knowledge as consisting of an accurate mirroring of the world by mind, as well as

---

38. Richard Rorty, 1979, *Philosophy and the Mirror of Nature*, Princeton: Princeton University Press, 7.

the notion that there exists "a ... privileged class of representations so compelling that their accuracy cannot be doubted."[39] For Kant this class consisted of representations grounded in the a priori.

Rorty, however, depicted these notions as essentially mythological—guesses about mind that developed in a historical context where knowledge of the actual workings of the human brain was limited. In a memorable chapter, he made this point by offering an account of what knowledge might look like to an alien race for whom "neurology and biochemistry had been the first disciplines."[40] Content to speak of their own brain processes in a language of neural stimulation, the aliens had no occasion to develop the myth that the mental is a distinct ontological realm or that there exist mental representations qua images in the mind whose relationship with the external world must be explained. Yet Rorty's goal was not to use current theories in cognitive science to rethink epistemology. Rather, he argued that philosophers, many working in the analytic tradition, had recently begun to realize the limitations of Kant's foundationalist program, which Rorty saw as having been taken up anew in early versions of analytic philosophy. Key to this program, in its various forms, was the assumption that a distinction could be drawn between cognitive material supplied by the senses and that supplied by the mind itself, with the latter securing the indubitability of the former. But it was precisely the sharpness of this distinction that was under attack in contemporary philosophy. Pointing to the commonalities between Quine's critique of the analytic/synthetic distinction and Sellars's attack on the "myth of the given," Rorty concluded that there is no position outside historically situated language games from which to distinguish mind from world. He went on to argue that there was a convergence between this conclusion and the insights of Donald Davidson and Thomas Kuhn. Davidson's efforts to push the philosophy of language toward a strictly empirical theory of meaning suggest that such a theory is likely to shed no light on "the relationship between words and the world."[41] And Kuhn's work in the history of science illustrates that criteria for choice among scientific theories never "float ... free of the educational and institutional patterns of the day."[42] This latter point, according to Rorty, called into question the assumption crucial to "the whole epistemological tradition since Descartes" that science's "procedure for attaining accurate representations in the Mirror of Nature differs in certain deep ways from the procedure for attaining agreement about 'practical' or 'aesthetic' mat-

39. Ibid., 163.   40. Ibid., 71.   41. Ibid., 262.   42. Ibid., 331.

ters."[43] Criteria for choosing among scientific theories—like criteria for determining the truth of sentences or for distinguishing fact from theory, analytic from synthetic, or intuitions from concepts—can emerge only out of particular language games, and the project of trying to ground knowledge claims in representations outside all such games is a hopeless endeavor.

But what should philosophy become once the mirror of nature metaphor, and with it the notion of the "philosopher as guardian of rationality,"[44] is abandoned? Rorty's proposal was that philosophers should now take up the task of "edification," or the "project of finding new, better, more interesting, more fruitful ways of speaking"[45] about the world. Invoking Hans-Georg Gadamer's use of the concept of *Bildung*, or self-formation, Rorty argued that for "us relatively leisured intellectuals" it was already the case that our capacity to "'remake' ourselves as we read more, talk more, and write more"[46] tends to be more highly valued than the goal of achieving indubitable knowledge. In light of such a value—which Rorty depicted as a contingent cultural preference, not some essential feature of humankind—the most helpful task philosophers could take up would be that of "perform[ing] the social function ... [of] 'breaking the crust of convention,' preventing man from deluding himself with the notion that he knows himself, or anything else, except under optional descriptions."[47] Interpreting the social, cultural, and natural worlds in new and interesting ways and stressing precisely the contingency of experience and language, philosophers could contribute to a genre of discourse that would help prevent a "freezing-over of culture" in the form of interpretive stasis.[48] In this capacity philosophers would be doing what many writers, poets, artists and other cultural creators also do, but would come at it with a different vocabulary and set of sensibilities and talents.

Rorty did not see himself as the first philosopher to advance such an argument. Although most of the substantive claims of the book were composed in the style of analytic philosophy and with reference to analytic figures, *Philosophy and the Mirror of Nature* opened with Rorty's attempt to link himself up with John Dewey, Martin Heidegger, and the later Wittgenstein, whom he called "the three most important philosophers of our century."[49] All three had started their intellectual careers as foundationalists, but later each "broke free of the Kantian conception of philosophy."[50] Rorty saw Dewey, Heidegger, and Wittgenstein as fellow travelers on the

43. Ibid., 332–33. 45. Ibid., 360. 47. Ibid., 379. 49. Ibid., 5.
44. Ibid., 317. 46. Ibid., 359. 48. Ibid., 377. 50. Ibid.

historicist, holist, and edifying path. "Each of the three," he wrote, "reminds us that investigations of the foundations of knowledge or morality or language or society may be simply apologetics, attempts to eternalize a certain contemporary language-game, social practice, or self-image."[51] Their thought is therefore inspirational to those who wish to develop a post-Kantian philosophical culture. Despite his attachment to Dewey, however, and articulation of a conception of truth that arguably owed more to the tradition of classical American pragmatism than to any other, Rorty was not at great pains in the book to label himself a pragmatist, at one point passing up the opportunity to do so on the grounds that the term had become "a bit overladen."[52]

It was not in *Philosophy and the Mirror of Nature* but in the essays republished in *Consequences of Pragmatism* that Rorty fully identified his intellectual project with pragmatism. What unifies these essays is the project of tracing a dividing line in modern philosophy. On one side stand philosophers with a scientistic orientation: those who, with Kant, hope to get "the eye of the mind" to have an accurate, world-conforming understanding of such things as "The Nature of Being, the Nature of Man, the Relation of Subject and Object, Language and Thought, Necessary Truth, [and] Freedom of Will."[53] Viewing philosophy as a discipline with a clearly delineated subject matter in which knowledge accumulation is possible, scientistic philosophers, in Rorty's portrayal, have little interest in the history of the field, follow strict methodological rules, and, envying the success of physical and biological scientists, emulate them stylistically and orient themselves toward their concerns.

Such a scientistic orientation, Rorty argued, was currently dominant in U.S. philosophy, and he registered displeasure with the situation. Rorty did not agree that philosophy has any distinctive, transhistorical subject matter; that there is any method that can give philosophy a "metaphysical [or] epistemological guarantee of success";[54] that the ambition of philosophy should be to provide a foundation for "such merely 'first-intentional' matters as science, art, and religion";[55] that philosophical writing, following the conventions of science, should eradicate all traces of textuality; that intellectual history is important only if the arguments of philosophers past are directly relevant to current controversies; or that the standard for evaluating philosophical theses must be "truthfulness to experience or ... discovery of pre-existing significance."[56]

51. Ibid., 9–10.   52. Ibid., 176.
53. Rorty, *Consequences of Pragmatism*, 15, 31.
54. Ibid., 172.   55. Ibid., 19.   56. Ibid., 153.

Instead, Rorty held out as exemplary the work of those philosophers standing on the other side of the divide: those like Dewey, Heidegger, Wittgenstein, Foucault, and Derrida who are "dominated by a sense of the contingency of history, the contingency of ... vocabulary ... , [and] the sense that nature and scientific truth are largely beside the point and that history is up for grabs."[57] Thinkers such as these take pride in the "novelty"[58] of their work, abhor the "comforts of consensus" associated with normal science, find their humanity in "redescription, reinterpretation, manipulation,"[59] and believe it crucial to "develop ... attitudes towards the mighty [intellectual] dead and their living rivals."[60] Their writing glories in its "oblique[ness] ... allusiveness and name-dropping"[61] and eschews the notion of a single right philosophical method. Philosophers of this sort resist normalization by recognizing that "it is a mark of humanistic culture *not* to try to reduce the new to the old, nor to insist upon a canonical list of problems or methods, nor upon a canonical vocabulary in which problems are to be stated."[62]

Such philosophers, Rorty argued, are pragmatists, whether or not they see themselves working in the tradition of Charles Peirce, William James, John Dewey, and George Herbert Mead. On this understanding, a pragmatist is someone who holds three beliefs: first, that "there is no wholesale, epistemological way to direct, or criticize, or underwrite, the course of inquiry"; second, that "there is no ... metaphysical difference between facts and values, nor any methodological difference between morality and science"; and third, that "there are no constraints on inquiry save conversational ones."[63] It is therefore the pragmatist who, with Harold Bloom, "reminds us that a new and useful vocabulary is just *that,* not a sudden unmediated vision of things ... as they are,"[64] and the pragmatist who seeks not to ground her or his beliefs transcendentally but who "knows no better way to explain his convictions than to remind his interlocutor of the position they both are in, the contingent starting points they both share, the floating, ungrounded conversations of which they are both members."[65] Nowhere did Rorty explicitly claim this to be a description of pragmatism that Dewey or the other classical pragmatists would have endorsed, but he insisted that Dewey is a crucial philosopher to read if we want to become pragmatists in this sense of the term, for Dewey's work offers us "suggestions about how to slough off our intellectual past, and about

57. Ibid., 228–29. 60. Ibid., 65. 63. Ibid., 162–63, 165.
58. Ibid., 153. 61. Ibid., 92. 64. Ibid., 153.
59. Ibid., 152–53. 62. Ibid., 218. 65. Ibid., 173–74.

how to treat that past as material for playful experimentation rather than as imposing tasks and responsibilities upon us."[66] For this reason—and despite the fact that Dewey sometimes seemed interested in "metaphysical system-building,"[67] a project Rorty denounced—Dewey is the hero of *Consequences*. Although Dewey and Heidegger are, "with Wittgenstein, the richest and most original philosophers of our time,"[68] Dewey ended up where Wittgenstein only gestured: in a systematic philosophical effort to "break down the distinctions between art and science, philosophy and science, art and religion, [and] morality and science."[69] Dewey's historicism is to be preferred over Heidegger's because it revolves around "the problems of men,"[70] not the history of Being.

In subsequent books and essays, Rorty's almost single-minded concern was to sketch the contours of a pragmatist position on a wide variety of intellectual, cultural, and political matters. In *Contingency, Irony, and Solidarity* (1989), he argued that pragmatic ironism could be reconciled with the demands of liberalism. In the essays published as *Objectivity, Relativism, and Truth* (1991), he explored the implications of pragmatism's antirepresentationalism and indicated what "followers of Dewey like myself"[71] would say about, among other things, democracy and ethnocentrism. In *Achieving Our Country* (1998), he took the position that there was no better way for the American left to renew itself than by embracing the Deweyan pragmatism that had been central to early twentieth-century American progressivism. And in *Philosophy and Social Hope* (1999), he outlined a pragmatist perspective on morality, law, education, and religion. In all these texts, Rorty embraced a rhetorical style he saw as singularly appropriate for the pragmatist intellectual. Rather than "examin[ing] ... the pros and cons of a thesis," he sought to "redescribe lots and lots of things in new ways, until you have created a pattern of linguistic behavior which will tempt the rising generation to adopt it."[72] Although Rorty sometimes labeled these redescriptions those of the "liberal ironist," the "anti-representationalist," or the advocate of "postmodern bourgeois liberalism," pragmatism was their common denominator. His overarching intellectual goal, from the mid-1970s on, was to make the case with Dewey that "discarding [the old Platonic dualisms] will help bring us to-

---

66. Ibid., 87.   67. Ibid., 85.   68. Ibid., 51.

69. Ibid., 28.   70. Ibid., 53.

71. Richard Rorty, 1991, *Objectivity, Relativism, and Truth*, Cambridge: Cambridge University Press, 211.

72. Richard Rorty, 1989, *Contingency, Irony, and Solidarity*, Cambridge: Cambridge University Press, 9.

gether, by enabling us to realize that trust, social cooperation and social hope are where our humanity begins and ends."[73]

Rorty's ideas were celebrated in some quarters and denounced in many more. In the eyes of fellow antifoundationalists like Stanley Fish or Cornel West, Rorty's effort to highlight the poverty of the epistemological project did a tremendous service for the humanities by valorizing and legitimizing creative and politically inspired readings and interpretations of texts over those claiming objectivity. "Motivated by the ambitious project of resurrecting pragmatism in contemporary North American philosophy," West noted, Rorty's "great contribution" was to "strike … a deathblow" to analytic philosophy and the disciplinary enterprises it sought to underwrite "by telling a story about the emergence, development, and decline of its primary props: the correspondence theory of truth, the notion of privileged representations, and the idea of a self-reflective transcendental subject."[74] Others, like Robert Brandom—Rorty's former student—or Jürgen Habermas and Richard Bernstein, who both sought to combine pragmatism with strands of the Continental tradition, understood him to be "one of the most original and important philosophers writing today,"[75] an "outstanding" intellectual who "consistently argu[es] in an informed and astute way,"[76] a thinker who "forces us to ask new sorts of questions about just what analytic philosophers are doing"[77] and whose ideas must be taken seriously, even if his claims are sometimes overdrawn or just plain wrong. More common, however, were critics: those like Donald Davidson or Hilary Putnam who resisted being read as Rorty would have them be and who charged his version of pragmatism with relativism; others within the pragmatist community such as Susan Haack who rehearsed the same relativism charge and accused Rorty of misinterpreting and misappropriating classical pragmatism; and still others such as James Conant, Simon Critchley, Terry Eagleton, or Nancy Fraser who took issue with aspects of his political and moral philosophy. Championed or condemned, Rorty quickly became one of the

73. Richard Rorty, 1999, *Philosophy and Social Hope*, New York: Penguin, xv.

74. Cornel West, 1989, *The American Evasion of Philosophy: A Genealogy of Pragmatism*, Madison: University of Wisconsin Press, 199, 201.

75. Robert Brandom, 2000, "Introduction," pp. ix–xx in *Rorty and His Critics*, Robert Brandom, ed., Malden: Blackwell, ix.

76. Jürgen Habermas, 2000, "Richard Rorty's Pragmatic Turn," pp. 31–55 in *Rorty and His Critics*, Robert Brandom, ed., Malden: Blackwell, 32.

77. Richard Bernstein, 1992, *The New Constellation: The Ethical-Political Horizons of Modernity/Postmodernity*, Cambridge: MIT Press, 21.

most talked-about intellectuals of the late twentieth century. Between 1979 and 2005, *Philosophy and the Mirror of Nature* was cited nearly two thousand times in publications indexed in the Arts and Humanities Citation Index. At the peak of his popularity in the early 1990s more than fifty humanities articles were published each year listing "Rorty" as a keyword, and a comprehensive bibliography of the secondary literature on Rorty contains over 1,700 entries.[78] *Philosophy and the Mirror of Nature* was translated into seventeen languages, and *Contingency, Irony and Solidarity* into twenty-two. Perhaps the true measure of Rorty's fame—or infamy—however, was that he managed to cross over, escaping the confines of academic discourse and entering popular culture, where he became a whipping boy for conservatives eager to denounce academic and leftist excesses. Thus it was that David Brooks, reviewing *Achieving Our Country* for the conservative *Weekly Standard,* could declare that "while [Rorty's] stuff appears radical, if you strip away Rorty's grand declarations about the death of God and Truth and get down to the type of public personality that Rorty calls for, he begins to appear ... as the Norman Rockwell for the intellectual bourgeoisie in the age of the booming stock market."[79] In a similar vein, George Will devoted a *Newsweek* column to Rorty, proclaiming Rorty's work to have "the single merit of illustrating why the left is peripheral to the nation's political conversation."[80] For many both inside and outside the academy, Rorty had become the intellectual subversive he was depicted as being in a documentary run on BBC Four in 2003, provocatively titled *Richard Rorty: The Man Who Killed Truth.*

* 6 *

I present the Rorty case in two parts. The first is contextualist intellectual biography. Here I reconstruct the facts of Rorty's life and intellectual career through 1982. My goal in doing so is to lay out all the important pieces of the empirical puzzle, from the circumstances of his upbringing to his posttenure experiences at Princeton. To this end, chapter 1 reconstructs the life history and thought of his father, chapter 2 that of his mother. Their ideas, self-understandings, and social position, I later suggest, were significant influences on Rorty's intellectual and career trajectory. I go

78. Richard Rumana, 2002, *Richard Rorty: An Annotated Bibliography of Secondary Literature,* Amsterdam: Rodopi.

79. David Brooks, 1998, "Achieving Richard Rorty; Leftist Thought in Middle-Class America," *Weekly Standard,* June 1, 31.

80. George Will, 1998, "Still Waiting for Lefty," *Newsweek,* May 25, 86.

into considerable detail with regard to his parents' thought not only for this reason but also because theirs are important intellectual stories in their own right. Chapter 3 describes Rorty's years as an undergraduate at the University of Chicago, chapter 4 his time seeking a masters degree there in philosophy. Chapter 5 recounts his experiences in the doctoral program in philosophy at Yale. In chapter 6 I discuss Rorty's years as an instructor and then assistant professor at Wellesley College from 1958 to 1961. In chapter 7 I chronicle Rorty's efforts to secure tenure at Princeton in the early 1960s, and in chapter 8 I report the steps and events that led him away from the paradigm of analytic philosophy in the 1970s and to leave Princeton for Virginia.

In presenting these biographical twists and turns, I try to stay as close as possible to the archival and textual data. The second part of the book reexamines Rorty's intellectual and career moves, this time through a sociological lens. Chapter 9 lays the groundwork for doing so by introducing the two most important theorists in the area, Bourdieu and Collins, by mounting a critique of them for failing to account for the significance of intellectual self-conceptions, and by outlining the core elements of the theory of intellectual self-concept. Chapter 10 then deploys this theory, alongside those of Bourdieu and Collins, where applicable, to explain three key intellectual choices in the first half of Rorty's career: his decision to write a masters thesis on Whitehead's metaphysics, his movement into mainstream analytic philosophy in the 1960s, and his turn back toward pragmatism in the 1970s. Only if the relevant social processes and mechanisms are invoked can these choices be more adequately explained. In the conclusion I summarize the argument of the book, list the general theoretical propositions pertaining the mechanisms and processes of knowledge making in the contemporary American humanities to have emerged from the case study, and lay out an agenda for future research in the sociology of ideas.

* 7 *

Before proceeding, two caveats are in order. First, although I have arranged the biographical chapters chronologically and say a great deal in each about Rorty's experiences, it should be clear that this is not a traditional biography. Beyond rejecting the historiographic and theoretical assumptions implicit in most biographies—a rejection that has influenced my selection of materials, leading me to focus more on mundane social and institutional circumstances than on interesting characters or dramatic or memorable scenes—the book does not attempt to be comprehensive in its coverage of Rorty's life. Although the conclusion says something about the state of Rorty's reputation in the 1980s and 1990s— the period when his fame was greatest and his ideas the most controversial—my focus is on the first half of his career, on the development of his ideas rather than their diffusion,[81] and more generally on the social processes that shape the production of knowledge by academicians in the years before they become eminent scholars in their fields. Even for earlier periods of Rorty's life, however, there are essays of his I do not discuss, lines of correspondence I do not analyze, disputes I do not mention, and personal relationships and psychic dramas that factor not at all into the account I lay out. Readers expecting to learn the complete story of Rorty's life are forewarned: I do not tell it here.

Second, my goal in the book is not to provide an exegesis of Rorty's ideas or a critical philosophical examination of them. As a sociologist of ideas who aims to proceed nonreductively, I do spend a great deal of time with Rorty's philosophy, trying to get enough of a handle on it to explain its social origins. But my aim in doing so is explanation, not interpretation, and readers turning to the book in the hope that it will directly resolve interpretive disputes about Rorty may be disappointed. Nor do I ever take a position on the value or truth of Rorty's thought, except in the following limited respect. Despite the work Rorty has done to call into question the meaning, desirability, and possibility of objectivity, I

81. This is not to say that Rorty's ideas stopped developing after 1982. In fact, while the social and political philosophy articulated in *Contingency, Irony, and Solidarity* and later works was in many ways continuous with the epistemological position developed in *Philosophy and the Mirror of Nature*, its details were worked out only over the course of the 1980s and early 1990s. This is not the least important or controversial aspect of Rorty's oeuvre, and by bringing the book to a halt in 1982 I subject myself to the charge that I am only analyzing the development of one part of his philosophy. In the 1980s and 1990s, however, as Rorty's reputation grew, his life underwent dramatic change. Although he continued to teach at the University of Virginia, and was thus subject to some of the usual cadences and rhythms of life in the ivory tower, he could also be found jetting around the country and the world, having been asked to lecture or take part in conferences or meet with colleagues or reporters or would-be translators of his books in Argentina, China, Czechoslovakia, England, France, Germany, India, Portugal, Spain, and Trinidad, to name just a few of the countries stamped on his passport during these years. To have written about this period in his life, and the ongoing development of his thought therein, would have been to write about the life of an intellectual superstar and would have required the analysis of a very different set of institutional structures, social mechanisms, and processes than those I consider here. The resulting gain in comprehensiveness would have been offset by a loss of coherence.

remain committed to Max Weber's view that objectivity is an ideal for the social sciences.[82] At a dinner party not long ago, I was asked if my goal in the book was to offer a "send-up" of Rorty's philosophy. I cannot agree that this is something the sociology of ideas should aim for. As the explanatory sterility of "ideology critique" approaches to the sociology of knowledge illustrates, projects that seek to explain ideas as part of an effort at condemning them typically do not select their objects of analysis on the basis of their potential to contribute to theory development, are blind to the full range of social processes that undergird knowledge making, often impose arbitrary theoretical schemes that bear little relation to empirical reality, and have an impossible time gaining firsthand access to research subjects. The sociology of ideas should avoid these problems and cultivate a studious indifference to the assumptions, theories, claims, and position takings it wishes to explain, never allowing itself to account for an idea's success merely by pointing to its essential truth, or its failure by reference to its falseness, in line with the recommendations of the "strong program" in the sociology of scientific knowledge.[83] That, at least, is what I have endeavored to do here in explaining the development of one of the most controversial bodies of philosophical thought of recent memory.

82. Max Weber, 1949, *The Methodology of the Social Sciences*, Edward Shils and Henry Finch, trans., New York: Free Press.

83. See the discussion in Steven Shapin, 1995, "Here and Everywhere: Sociology of Scientific Knowledge," *Annual Review of Sociology* 21:289–321; David Bloor, 1976, *Knowledge and Social Imagery*, London: Routledge and K. Paul. This is not to say that sociologists of ideas may not take as their problematic the question of why certain tensions or even contradictions can be found in an intellectual's thought. What they should not do is explain such tensions or contradictions by reference to cognitive failure *alone*.

O N E

James Rorty

* 1 *

James Rorty and his wife Winifred Raushenbush were on the periphery of the group that would become known as the New York intellectuals—that loose-knit, multigenerational assemblage of radical writers, critics, and poets who broke with the Communist movement from the left in the mid-1930s, who affiliated themselves with and published their work in New York–based literary magazines such as *Partisan Review* and *Modern Monthly,* and who were key players in the larger culture of bohemianism that flourished in the city in the first decades of the twentieth century.[1] Although they had distinctive trajectories, the thought of Rorty and Raushenbush developed more or less in parallel with that of the group's more prominent members, so identifying the central themes and concerns around which the New York intellectuals converged—and the historical experiences that were formative for them—offers a point of entry into the ideas to which Richard Rorty was exposed as a child.

* 2 *

Who were the New York intellectuals? One strand of historical research on the group, epitomized by James Gilbert's classic 1968 book, *Writers and Partisans,* describes the emergence of literary radicalism in New York in the 1910s and 1920s, centered on the publication of "little magazines"

1. See Christine Stansell, 2000, *American Moderns: Bohemian New York and the Creation of a New Century,* New York: Henry Holt and Co.

like the *Masses,* the *Dial,* and *Seven Arts,* as the expression of a modernist impulse that saw American writers break away from bourgeois conventions and morality that seemed to them to hark back to a nineteenth-century puritanical mentality.[2] This act of rebellion was accomplished by means of a receptiveness to European ideas, especially those of Marx, Freud, Bergson, Nietzsche, and Darwin. But while such a receptiveness often involved literal or symbolic expatriation and was linked to the sense that American society made no place for members of its intellectual caste, it was "paradoxically" the case that in turning to Europe, American writers sometimes found a "new faith in America and a desire to rediscover it."[3] The openness of American society to a fundamental remaking—despite or because of its individualistic and capitalistic tendencies—was a theme that bound together writers as diverse in political outlook as the nationalistic literary historian Van Wyck Brooks and the poet, editor, and revolutionary Max Eastman and kept the energies of the New York intellectuals high through the passing of the heyday of the bohemian Village, the repression of radicalism during the Red Scare of 1919–20, and later the coming of the Depression, which confirmed for many the prescience of Marx.

This is not to say that all radical writers of the time saw themselves as sharing common ground. Gilbert, like all historians of the period, emphasizes internecine quarrel. The main cleavage would form in the late 1920s, as magazines like the *New Masses,* founded in 1926 by Joseph Freeman, Hugo Gellert, Mike Gold, and James Rorty, began to purge themselves of editors and contributors who were not members of the Communist Party and did not believe that art should be subordinated to proletarian politics—part of a larger process of polarization by which intellectuals in the New York area either affiliated themselves with the Party or distanced themselves from it. As described later, James Rorty himself suffered from such a purge.[4] Rorty would briefly flirt with the Party again in the early 1930s. As the decade wore on, however, his

2. James Gilbert, 1968, *Writers and Partisans: A History of Literary Radicalism in America,* New York: John Wiley and Sons.

3. Ibid., 59.

4. The immediate occasion was Rorty's effort to publish the work of the California poet Robinson Jeffers, who many Communists saw as having fascistic tendencies. See the discussion in Alan Wald, 1987, *The New York Intellectuals: The Rise and Decline of the Anti-Stalinist Left from the 1930s to the 1980s,* Chapel Hill: University of North Carolina Press, 55. For Rorty's assessment of Jeffers, see James Rorty, 1933, "Robinson Jeffers," *Nation,* December 20, 137:712–13.

Trotskyist sensibilities prevailed. This was true of other New York intellectuals as well after the extent of Stalin's atrocities became known. Increasingly they, like Rorty, sought to publish their work in venues not controlled by the Party.

The center of action for anti-Stalinist thinkers soon came to be *Partisan Review,* founded in 1934 by William Phillips and Philip Rahv and then reinvented in 1937. Emerging out the Party's own John Reed clubs—local organizations where writers could get together to discuss revolutionary literature—*Partisan Review* would quickly break out of this mold, as Phillips and Rahv came to insist that "a specific work of art ... could not be understood by ... the general ideology to which it might be linked."[5] This standard precluded the application of a political litmus test to the magazine's contributors, and as a result *Partisan Review* editors "published such writers as Auden and Robert Lowell with whom they disagreed on political or religious issues."[6] But these were just two of the many leading figures in American and European letters whose writing appeared on the pages of the magazine. Others included T. S. Eliot, Franz Kafka, Mary McCarthy, Allen Tate, Lionel Trilling, Delmore Schwartz, and Gertrude Stein.[7]

While *Writers and Partisans* makes much of the schism between the *New Masses* and *Partisan Review,* and thus chronicles the migration over time of a number of leftist intellectuals from support for the Communist Party to more diffuse versions of socialism, a second historical perspective, associated with books like Richard Pells's *Radical Visions and American Dreams* (1973), is concerned to trace an even more dramatic arc: the movement on the part of many New York thinkers from radicalism during the Depression era to conservatism in the 1940s and beyond. James Rorty and Winifred Raushenbush never lost their leftist leanings, but like many other New York intellectuals they eventually became fiercely anti-Communist. Pells does not fail to specify the events that helped bring about change in this direction: Stalinist show trials between 1936 and 1938 that American Communists defended; the relative success of the New Deal, especially the Tennessee Valley Authority, which was seen as an indication that a middle road could be found between free market capitalism and complete collectivization; the intransigence and dogmatism shown by American Communists when confronted with challenges and criticisms from their friends on the left; and the realization that, even in the midst of the

---

5. Gilbert, *Writers and Partisans,* 137.

6. Ibid., 192.   7. Ibid.

Depression, class consciousness of the kind needed to foment revolution was scarcely to be found on the American scene.[8]

But while these factors brought about a rightward tilt, Pells contends that a significant amount of the movement has to be explained as a function of internal ideational dynamics. The turn toward Marx in the late 1920s and early 1930s, he insists, did not happen out of thin air; the groundwork for it had been laid earlier by Progressivism. Pells rightly describes the Progressive movement as heterogeneous in its aims and composition, including in its ranks those whose concern was breaking up monopolies as well as those who sought greater efficiency and planning in the operation of major social institutions. This latter group, in particular, often turned to the philosophy of John Dewey to justify its political program.[9] Dewey's notion of social intelligence—of treating institutions as collective experiments designed to solve social problems—seemed a trenchant critique of a society reeling from the shock of modernity yet caught up in processes of "culture lag" and at the same time a positive goal toward which Progressive reformers could strive. When American intellectuals such as Sidney Hook began reading Marx, they did so through pragmatist lenses, treating alienation and lack of social intelligence as two sides of the same coin. But this, Pells argues, was inimical to radical social transformation, for it ruled out in advance any institutional model for American society that was at odds with the values pragmatism regarded as central, values seen by many intellectuals as aspects of the American cultural heritage worth preserving. It seemed impossible to imagine from this perspective, for example, how Soviet-style collectivism could be transplanted to the rugged individualist soil of the United States; how support for Stalinism or any of the ideological-cum-political tactics needed to orchestrate a revolution could be anything other than a blasphemy against the democratic tradition; how anyone with experimentalist sensibilities could buy into the theory of historical materialism; or how piecemeal reform of the system, but not revolution, could fail to be the more authentically American political option. If there was a rightward lurch in the late 1930s and after, therefore, it was because American radicalism was, from the start, a self-limiting enterprise.

A third strand of the historical literature on the New York intellectuals, by contrast, highlights the group's social background, reflecting its own self-image as portrayed in autobiographical narratives that began to

8. Richard Pells, 1973, *Radical Visions and American Dreams: Culture and Social Thought in the Depression Years*, New York: Harper and Row.

9. James Kloppenberg, 1986, *Uncertain Victory: Social Democracy and Progressivism in European and American Thought, 1870–1920*, Oxford: Oxford University Press.

appear in the 1970s and early 1980s.[10] What did the crowd of writers and thinkers who affiliated themselves with *Partisan Review* have in common, aside from their left-leaning anti-Stalinism? Although the fact that there were at least three generations of intellectuals involved makes this a difficult question to answer,[11] members of the first and second generations, as Stephen Longstaff has observed, generally came from one of two social backgrounds: either they "had been raised in privileged circumstances and had gone to elite schools" like Yale, Harvard, and Vassar, or they were Jews from working-class families who "hailed from the Lower East Side, Brownsville, Williamsburg, and their like in other cities."[12] In the view of scholars such as Alexander Bloom and Terry Cooney, it was the Jewish experience that was determinative of the outlook of the group. Raised in first- or second-generation immigrant families that stressed the value of education and saw it as the only path to social mobility, these aspiring scholars found community and social acceptance in the few institutions of higher education that would gladly accept Jews as students at the time.[13] At schools like City College, they encountered a social scene where status was conferred for both political and theoretical savvy, whether or not it was true, as Bloom has suggested, that "the intensity and competitiveness of the classroom often provided the natural arena for the streetsmart confidence they had developed in the immigrant neighborhoods."[14] If their politics ran to the far left of the political spectrum—and

10. On this "spate of memoirs" see Westbrook's review of Hook's *Out of Step*: Robert Westbrook, 1987, "Stream of Contentiousness," *Nation,* May 30, 244:726–30.

11. Neil Jumonville notes that "the first generation included members born between 1900 and 1915 who came to political maturity in the 1920s or early 1930s: Sidney Hook, Lionel Trilling, Dwight Macdonald, Philip Rahv, William Phillips, Meyer Schapiro, Harold Rosenberg, Lewis Coser, Clement Greenberg, and Mary McCarthy. The second generation was born between about 1915 and 1925 and came to political maturity during the Depression: Irving Howe, Alfred Kazin, Daniel Bell, Nathan Glazer, Irving Kristol, Seymour Martin Lipset, Norman Mailer, and William Barrett. A third generation arrived on the scene after World War II and included Norman Podhoretz, Susan Sontag, and Michael Walzer." See Neil Jumonville, 1991, *Critical Crossings: The New York Intellectuals in Postwar America,* Berkeley: University of California Press, 8.

12. Stephen Longstaff, 1991, "Ivy League Gentiles and Inner-City Jews: Class and Ethnicity around *Partisan Review* in the Thirties and Forties," *American Jewish History* 80:325–43, 327, 325.

13. See Jerome Karabel, 2005, *The Chosen: The Hidden History of Admission and Exclusion at Harvard, Yale, and Princeton,* Boston: Houghton Mifflin.

14. Alexander Bloom, 1986, *Prodigal Sons: The New York Intellectuals and Their World,* New York: Oxford University Press, 36.

it did—it was because many newly arrived eastern European immigrant families regarded socialism not as a foreign idea but as part of their ethnic heritage. Radicalism and Judaism went hand in hand, both in the cultural imaginary and in social reality. Therefore, as Cooney reports, "for young intellectuals growing up in the Jewish community, some knowledge of radicalism was hard to avoid."[15]

There were several other features of the social environment shared by the New York intellectuals that—according to this strand of historical analysis—also shaped their ideas and career trajectories. First, especially for those in the first generation, the fact that Jews were effectively excluded from teaching in academe meant that if they wanted careers as intellectuals, it was going to have to be as writers and journalists. Hook and then Trilling would eventually find positions at NYU and Columbia, respectively, and later those like Daniel Bell and Seymour Martin Lipset would successfully enter the academy as well. But as Russell Jacoby points out in his otherwise tendentious *The Last Intellectuals,* it is likely the New York intellectuals would never have existed as a distinct social group—fractious though it was—had the American academic profession, with the tendency of its labor markets to distribute personnel across the country, welcomed them with open arms.[16] And there was another consequence of this exclusion: as a group the New York intellectuals suffered none of the narrowing of intellectual horizons that would have come about had most of them been incorporated into "the disciplinary system"[17] in American academe, which was coming into bloom at the time. Thus it was their social position—as much as their "Marxist intellectual orientation, which … resisted the categorization and specialization of disciplines"—that helped account for their "holistic and interdisciplinary approach," their "intellectual generalism that discouraged distinctions between literature and politics, or art and social policy."[18]

Second, the larger message communicated not simply by the exclusion of Jews from the academy, but by rampant American anti-Semitism in all spheres of life, was that Jews remained outsiders to American society.

15. Terry Cooney, 1986, *The Rise of the New York Intellectuals: Partisan Review and Its Circle,* Madison: University of Wisconsin Press, 32.

16. Russell Jacoby, 1987, *The Last Intellectuals: American Culture in the Age of Academe,* New York: Basic Books.

17. Andrew Abbott, *Chaos of Disciplines,* 122.

18. Jumonville, *Critical Crossings,* 9.

While this might have led to ethnic particularism, in the case of the New York intellectuals it led in the opposite direction: toward an embrace of the "cosmopolitan values" associated with "the broad Western tradition in the humanities"[19] that would lend them a meaningful identity—as carriers of that tradition—as well as the intellectual means to mount a vigorous critique of exclusionary and anti-intellectual American middle-class culture, while at the same time generating distance from the perceived narrowness of the traditional Jewish community.

Third, perhaps because the intellectual combativeness that characterized life at City College spilled over into the New York intellectual arena more generally, valorizing passionate but otherwise rational discourse as the means by which intellectual-political life should be carried out, there emerged a natural antipathy in the group toward any cultural or political framework that would undermine such discourse. On this account, it is the intellectual and political inquisitiveness and debate orientation of the *Partisan Review* crowd that accounts for its hostility toward the American Communist Party, which was bent on suppressing dissent; its simultaneous opposition to the fascism of the Iron Curtain and to McCarthyism; and later its opposition to the New Left, which Trotskyists-turned-conservatives like Irving Kristol would characterize as flawed insofar as 1960s radicals failed to "take their own and others' beliefs seriously, and to think coherently about them."[20]

To be sure, many of the New York intellectuals did not fit the Jewish mold. What the non-Jews who were active around *Partisan Review* had in common with their Jewish compatriots, historians claim, was the sense of being cultural outsiders. This was born of different kinds of experiences. Mary McCarthy, for example, was orphaned as a young child, raised by wealthy grandparents, and swept up in the sexual revolution of the 1920s. She, Dwight Macdonald, and the other *Partisan Review* gentiles hitched their fate to the intellectual program of the group's core because "the Jews of their acquaintance seem[ed] to have such easy personal access, not simply to Marx, but to Dostoevsky, Freud, Nietzsche, Mann, Rilke, Kafka, and so forth.... If, as Rahv used to maintain (echoing Nietzsche), historical insight into the workings of the modern era amounted to a new faculty of mind, a sixth sense, so to speak, then this new faculty seemed more developed among Jewish intellectuals."[21] Although tensions within

19. Cooney, *The Rise of the New York Intellectuals*, 7, 14.

20. Irving Kristol, 1977, "Memoirs of a Trotskyist," *New York Times Magazine,* January 23, 57.

21. Longstaff, "Ivy League Gentiles and Inner-City Jews," 331.

the group over ethnicity and religion would occasionally surface, for the most part the non-Jews embraced the intellectual norms and style of their colleagues in a moment of imitation and "expansive philo-Semitism."[22]

Rorty and Raushenbush came to their radicalism by other paths. For Rorty, it was his parents' political iconoclasm, along with his father's thwarted literary ambitions, that drove him into radical politics and writing. For Raushenbush, it was her parents' zeal for social reform. Like others in the New York intellectual circle, though, they partook of the cultural practice of "arguing the world"[23] and made a home where radical social criticism, politics, and literature were bread-and-butter topics of discussion. Their ideas and beliefs—and the passion with which they argued for them—would not fail to impress their only child.

* 3 *

James Rorty was born in Middletown, New York, in 1890. As previously noted he was the son of an Irish immigrant, political refugee, and aspiring poet who, along with his wife, a former schoolteacher, ran a dry-goods business.[24] After high school, Rorty spent a year working for the local newspaper before financial help from his sister and her husband enabled him to move to the Boston area and enroll in Tufts College, from which he graduated in 1913. He moved to New York, taking a job at the H. K. McCann advertising agency. In 1917, after the war broke out, he reluctantly enlisted in the army ambulance corps, eventually winning a Distinguished Service Cross for his heroism as an ambulance driver on the Argonne front.[25] Returning to New York he found himself "living in the same rooming house as Thorstein Veblen, often attending Veblen's lectures at the New School for Social Research."[26]

Rorty's politics were already left of center. His radicalism had been bolstered during his time in the army, for the ambulance corps attracted many who were opposed to the war but did not feel they could mount legitimate conscientious objector claims. He described himself in an essay

22. Ibid.

23. This was the title of a 1999 PBS documentary about the New York intellectuals, material for which formed the basis for a book. See Joseph Dorman, 2001, *Arguing the World: The New York Intellectuals in Their Own Words,* Chicago: University of Chicago Press.

24. Daniel Pope, 1988, "His Master's Voice: James Rorty and the Critique of Advertising," *Maryland Historian* 19:5–15, 6.

25. "James Rorty, 82, a Radical Editor," *New York Times,* February 26, 1973, 34.

26. Pope, "His Master's Voice," 6.

published in 1920 as a "near-Socialist who is also almost a vegetarian."[27] That same year he married a social worker named Maria Lambin, later describing the marriage in his unpublished memoir "It Has Happened Here" as hastily contracted, and moved with her to California, where he again went to work as an advertising copywriter, composing poems and essays in his spare time and reporting on the San Francisco literary and artistic scene for the *Nation*.[28] Rorty and Lambin soon split, however, and he took up with Winifred Raushenbush.

The few references to James Rorty in the historical literature emphasize that he experienced bouts of depression, including several breakdowns and hospitalizations, over the course of his life—an effect, as he described it, of being "shell shocked" during the war[29]—so it is no surprise that many of his early poems and essays are attempts to make sense of his war experience and come to grips with his depression. He noted in his memoir that "the shell-shock from which I suffered for at least three years after my discharge came from fighting the Army, not the Germans, but it was the real thing nonetheless, as shown by much that I did and wrote during those years."[30] Typical of his writing on the war is a memoir fragment published in the *Nation* in 1920 in which Rorty described the experience of carrying a stretcher alongside a man so pious that Rorty presumed him to be Sunday school teacher. Where before the war what would have struck him about such a man was his "inarticulate, fearful ... parochialism," Rorty could now see a good-hearted fellow soldier. War was terrible, but it had the unanticipated consequence of revealing everyone's humanity.[31] Only a month later, this more or less upbeat tone was replaced by a more somber one, as Rorty composed a short story about a depressed writer contemplating having one of his characters commit suicide. The writer was "an interesting young man, a morbid young man, a despairing young man" whose "insides hurt him."[32]

Although these texts were focused inward, Rorty's writing in the early 1920s could not be considered apolitical. Indeed, his essays about the war

27. James Rorty, 1920, "Standing in the Need of Prayer," *Nation*, April 17, 110:515–16.

28. James Rorty, 1922, "Anything Can Happen in San Francisco," *Nation*, June 7, 114: 684–85.

29. Pope, "His Master's Voice." Also see James Rorty, 1936, *Where Life Is Better: An Unsentimental American Journey*, New York: John Day, 269.

30. James Rorty, undated manuscript, "It Has Happened Here," JRC.

31. James Rorty, 1920, "Priests and Priests," *Nation*, February 28, 110:261–62, 262.

32. James Rorty, 1920, "Starkweather Writes a Happy Ending," *Nation*, August 7, 111:154–55, 155.

were often overt indictments of militarism, as when he accused a general speaking to his troops before sending them back to the United States of trying to instill the tendency to support the military at all costs[33] or when he noted, "I don't like the army, because ... it turns out an extraordinary quantity of morally and spiritually diminished individuals—bullies and boot-lickers. It is hostile to individuality."[34] This view goes some of the way toward explaining the commitment to pacifism that Rorty developed after the war, when he "rejected an offer to return to work for McCann, went to his family's home in Middletown, and tossed his army uniform out the window."[35] Already evident in his condemnations of militarism, however, was a tension that would beset Rorty's work to the end: his sense that the sanctity of the individual must be preserved and at the same time his recognition that individualism is politically debilitating. Thus, while he could be reassured by his war experiences that "my countrymen are in their way as vivid, as rich in individual personality as the French," he could in the same breath regret the fact that because "the war is over ... the individual once more becomes a factor in the political algebra of our country."[36]

If these tensions lay not simply unresolved but unacknowledged, a plausible explanation is that Rorty had not yet found a coherent ideological system that could contain them. His main intellectual influence at this point was Veblen, to whose memory he would dedicate his 1934 attack on the advertising industry, *Our Master's Voice*.[37] But while deriving from Veblen in the 1920s a sensitivity to the ways in which social groups make bids for status, it was not until the 1930s that Veblen began to figure more systematically in Rorty's writing. Even here, the adoption was partial, for while he drew from Veblen an interest in conspicuous consumption and the social and cultural machinery set up to promote it, he paid little attention to Veblen's efforts to rethink modern economics by examining the tensions between business and industry. Accordingly, much of the social criticism in Rorty's early work took the form not of an in-depth analysis of the political, cultural, or economic situation but of efforts to undermine the pretensions of those he considered opponents

33. James Rorty, 1919, "The General Says Good-Bye," *Nation*, July 19, 109:83–84.
34. James Rorty, 1919, "Hail—or Farewell," *Nation*, September 13, 109:365–66.
35. Pope, "His Master's Voice," 6.
36. Rorty, "The General Says Good-Bye," 83–84.
37. James Rorty, 1934, *Our Master's Voice: Advertising*, New York: John Day.

of the left, from artists in San Francisco who privileged "decoration" over critical "probing"[38] to the American Legion, which staged dinners where, between courses of beefsteak, members "wiped our fingers on the butchers' aprons, stamped on the floor, lifted our heads, and bayed forth 100 percent Americanism."[39]

Side by side with Rorty's social criticism was his embrace of classical Romantic themes, expressed with particular force in his poetry. A 1926 poem to a "young woman who wanted to die,"[40] for example, suggested that life's goodness could barely be discerned through the haze of human consciousness and that salvation could only be found through a return to nature, while a 1927 review of the California poet Mary Austin noted in passing that "in New York and other great cities one meets people who live as though they recognized no kinship with forms of life outside the human family."[41] Typical of his work in this style is a poem from 1925, "Now That These Two":

> Now that these two have parted, let a word
> Be said for the yellow
> Bird that flew, and the billow
> That broke on the sand, and the tree in which they heard
> The patient wind consent
> To all they said, and meant;
>
> These will endure, even after his fashion the bird.
> How exquisite is man and how unique,
> How strangely strident, how oblique
> From nature's habit, who can look unstirred
> Upon the earth with veiled eye.[42]

Like his other poetry from this period, this piece is filled with a sense of the wonder, majesty, and transcendence of nature, of humankind's

38. Rorty, "Anything Can Happen in San Francisco," 684.

39. Rorty, "Standing in the Need of Prayer," 515.

40. James Rorty, 1926, "Words for a Young Woman Who Wanted to Die," *Nation*, September 8, 123:223.

41. James Rorty, 1927, "A Good Word for California," *Nation*, December 14, 125:686–87, 686.

42. James Rorty, 1925, "Now That These Two," *Nation*, September 16, 121:302. I am reproducing here only two of three stanzas.

alienation from it, and with a Romantic longing for return. As he put it in a 1921 letter to Leo Lewis, his drama professor at Tufts and a distant relation:

> It seems to me that the whole of our contemporary civilization needs to be smashed and danced on.... It seems to me that if it isn't smashed it will be impossible for life to continue with dignity and significance. I think we need to re-discover our relation with nature—that to me is the great gift of Whitman.... The sort of dream I dream for myself when I am most rapturous and least responsible is a dream of people waking up out of the trance into which their fears and their conformities have cast them and living directly and powerfully "with the calm insouciance of animals" as Whitman says somewhere.[43]

Rorty's nature poetry met with some acclaim. One of his poems won a prize from the *Nation,* and two of his collections, *What Michael Said to the Census Taker* (1922) and *Children of the Sun and Other Poems* (1926), also received critical praise. A reviewer for the *Nation* may have been right when he said that while Rorty "feels the physical universe as keenly and freshly as any poet does these days," "his first interest, like his last, [is] in man.... Mr. Rorty rings the great bell of dawn, or calls upon the flowers, or invokes the fog, or magnifies the moon in order that we shall know how excellent these are, and how freely they go about their business. Our lack of strength, or fear of freedom—these are Mr. Rorty's subjects."[44] Be that as it may, there could be no mistaking Rorty's strong personal attachment to nature or his belief that humankind is at its best when it is in communion with the natural. So strong were these attachments that only a few years after their return to New York City, James and Winifred fled the urban environment altogether, moving to the rural hamlet of Easton, Connecticut, where they played landlord for a summer to Diana and Lionel Trilling[45]—though they would regularly travel back and forth between Easton and the city. By 1932 Rorty would be described by the *New York Times* as a "poet ... former advertising man and now Connecticut farmer."[46]

43. James Rorty to Leo Lewis, September 14, 1921, JRC.
44. Mark van Doren, 1927, "First Glance," *Nation,* January 5, 124:16.
45. See the discussion in Diana Trilling, 1993, *The Beginning of the Journey: The Marriage of Diana and Lionel Trilling,* New York: Harcourt, Brace, and Co.
46. "Book Notes," *New York Times,* July 6, 1932, 17.

∗ **4** ∗

By the mid- to late 1920s, as Daniel Pope has noted, "Rorty's Veblenism assumed a Marxist patina."[47] Veblen's voice continued to echo in a 1928 essay on the social and cultural conditions facing American writers, where Rorty asserted that "'Keeping up with the Joneses' is not merely the great American theme; it is what Theodore Dreiser has called it, the 'American tragedy.'"[48] But Marx was now part of Rorty's vocabulary as well, if more his general emphasis on class conflict than the whole theoretical apparatus of historical materialism, which would appear later. Without at all suggesting that art should be a handmaiden of politics, Rorty asserted "the recurrent alliance of the artist with … the radical movement … which derives its … energy from the revolt of the submerged classes."[49] Where prewar magazines like the *Masses* were "edited" and "written" for and by "bourgeois liberals," the *New Masses* gave expression to a "revolutionary culture" that was also evident among American novelists, whose "mood is one of protest and rebellion."[50] During this same period of radicalization, and after his ousting from the editorial board of the *New Masses*,[51] Rorty became involved with the defense of Sacco and Vanzetti and was arrested in Boston for protesting their impending execution.[52] In a review of Upton Sinclair's 1928 book *Boston* he described the anarchists as "class rebels who fearlessly and unreservedly gave over their lives to fighting for liberty and justice."[53] Already by 1925 his poetry sometimes expressed revolutionary messianic themes, as in a piece titled "The Walls of Jericho" in which a watchman comes to realize that the masses are marching toward the walls of the city.[54] He noted in 1928 that America was obsessed by "acquisitiveness," "mechanical toys,"

47. Pope, "His Master's Voice," 8.

48. James Rorty, 1928, "The Post-War Social Mind: The Arts, Liberalism, and Labor," pp. 73–92 in *American Labor Dynamics in the Light of Post-War Developments: An Inquiry by Thirty-Two Labor Men, Teachers, Editors, and Technicians*, J. B. S. Hardman, ed., New York: Harcourt, Brace and Co., 89.

49. Ibid., 73.   50. Ibid., 76, 80, 84.

51. Apropos of this ousting, Rorty would later tell Diana Trilling that he had named his cat Mike after Mike Gold, one of the cofounders of the magazine, because his cat was so stupid. But see his humane tribute to his cat in James Rorty, 1931, "I'm an Animal Too," *Harper's*, June, 123–24.

52. Wald, *The New York Intellectuals*.

53. James Rorty, 1928, "Boston," *Nation*, December 5, 127:618–19, 619.

54. James Rorty, 1925, "The Walls of Jericho," *Nation*, December 16, 121:707.

and "sterile conquests"[55] and by April of 1929 could be found observing that "all history—indeed all of life—seems to me to be best described as a system of power-tensions."[56]

It was during the Depression, however, that Rorty's radical criticism attained full power. Rorty was almost forty when the bottom fell out of the U.S. stock market, and though he was of the view that "the sensorium" of the writer "dulls with age" such that those "who attained prominence just before and during the war years" had on the whole "become ... immunized against the impact of the real,"[57] there was no evidence he himself had suffered such a fate. To the contrary, while retaining its satirical edge, his writing was now informed by a coherent theoretical and political perspective that put questions of political economy front and center.

This was certainly the case in *Our Master's Voice: Advertising*. Rorty began, as was his habit, with a few autobiographical comments. "I was an ad-man once," he titled his first chapter. He recounted how he had drifted into the business after college, thanks to family connections. At that time he "was a Socialist already," though "not until some years later did he come to know Karl Marx and Thorstein Veblen."[58] He promised to base his account on what he had learned during his years writing copy. But the book was not to be merely a tell-all exposé. Although his semi-fictionalized account of episodes in the life of the American adman, which portrayed him as uninterested in anything other than selling the product, was inevitably what drew the attention of critics in the popular press,[59] at the heart of the book lay an attempt to situate modern advertising in its broader socioeconomic context.

Contrary to the claims of some social scientists at the time—Rorty singled out as a target economist Leverett Lyon, one of the founders of the American Marketing Association—Rorty argued that advertising was not about educating consumers but about promoting consumption, a charge Veblen himself had also leveled. If advertising consistently displays certain themes—namely, those of "emulative acquisition and social snobbism"—it is because these correspond to behaviors it is in the interests of capital to promote. Invoking ideas that could be found in both Veblen and

55. James Rorty, 1928, "Southwestern Poetry," *Nation*, September 26, 127:298.

56. James Rorty, 1929, "Some New Mosaic Tablets," *Nation*, April 24, 128:509–10, 509.

57. Rorty, "The Post-War Social Mind," 75.

58. Rorty, *Our Master's Voice*, 4.

59. See "Warns of Abuses of Advertising," *New York Times*, November 11, 1934, 39.

Marx, Rorty claimed that advertising was thus part of the "machinery of [capital's] super-government.... By this super-government the economic, social, ethical and cultural patterns of the population are shaped and controlled into serviceable conformity to the profit-motivated interests of business."[60]

Social scientists like Lyon who failed to see this sometimes hid behind claims of objectivity and value neutrality. But Rorty cited at length an unpublished manuscript by Sidney Hook, in which Hook observed that the "quest for objective truth from a neutral point of view, independent of value judgments ... has become the great fetich of American social science."[61] Hook argued that there are radically different ways societies can be organized, each attaching to different class interests, and that the attempt to identify general laws of social life inevitably presupposes that one of those forms of social organization— often that of the status quo—is the best. For this reason, objectivity is impossible, and social science must be held morally culpable for hitching its interests to those of capital, rather than producing analyses that take seriously the value of social equality. Rorty's own book, though informed by social theory, would be "presented not as sociology, but as journalism."[62]

Rorty was aware that Hook's analysis owed much to John Dewey and that his own theory of knowledge, such as it was, was indebted to pragmatism as well. An unpublished, undated manuscript probably written around the same time observed:

> The social scientist if he is to function in anything but a vacuum must be a scientist, plus a philosopher, an artist, an engineer, and a statesman—a Lenin, for example. This, incidentally, would appear to be approximating the view which our most eminent American Philosopher, John Dewey, expressed in a recent article in the *New Republic*. Dr. Dewey, in criticizing the austere devotion of social scientists to "fact-finding," pointed out that this is scarcely the procedure of the physical scientist, who progresses, not so

60. Rorty, *Our Master's Voice*, 31, 30. Although there are similarities between this claim and those of members of the Frankfurt School, it is important not to imagine an influence of the latter on Rorty. Little of the Frankfurt School's writing had been translated into English by 1934, and James Rorty did not read German (though his wife did). Moreover, I came across no references to work done by members of the Institute of Social Research in Rorty's writings or papers from this period.

61. Ibid., 238.   62. Ibid., x.

much by finding facts, as by conducting controlled experiments to prove or disprove a priori theories.[63]

Rorty's critique of putatively objective social science had special meaning for him, because his brother, Malcolm, was a leading economist, statistician, and businessman of the day. Fifteen years older than James, Malcolm Rorty graduated from Cornell in 1896 with degrees in mechanical and electrical engineering.[64] He entered the telephone business and worked his way up the corporate ladder, becoming in 1922 assistant vice president and chief statistician of the American Telephone and Telegraph Company. The following year he became vice president of the International Telephone and Telegraph Corporation. Although not trained formally as an economist, Malcolm Rorty wrote numerous economic monographs, most defending a laissez-faire approach to business. In one from 1921, for example, he insisted that "it is not necessary to deprive capital of a due reward, or savings of their incentive, in order to assure a just recompense to labor. Rather may the labor of today gain by granting freely to the stored-up labor of yesterday, which is capital, that fraction of the increased output from new industrial processes and machinery which is necessary to stimulate savings and thereby promote business enterprise."[65] But Malcolm Rorty was not an armchair ideologist. He considered it essential that business be run in accordance with the theories and findings of modern economics, and this required hard economic data: facts and figures about the present-day economy. With this end in view, Malcolm Rorty became a key business backer and cofounder of the National Bureau of Economic Research (NBER). Founded in 1920 under the direction of Wesley Clair Mitchell and with financial support from the Commonwealth Fund, the Carnegie Corporation, and other foundations, the NBER's mission was to engage in basic research that could indirectly inform economic policy making. "The manner in which the NBER was organized," Malcolm Rutherford notes in a recent article, "with its commitment to empirical investigation, its large board of directors drawn from many different universities, scientific associations, and business and labor organizations, and its system of manuscript review designed to remove any possibility of

63. James Rorty, undated manuscript, "Acceleration and the Death of Meaning," JRC.

64. See "Col. M. C. Rorty, 61, Engineer, Is Dead," *New York Times,* January 20, 1936, 19. Thanks to Stephen Turner for pointing out the Malcolm Rorty connection.

65. M. C. Rorty, 1921, "Notes on Current Economic Problems: II. Social and Industrial Organization," Pamphlet, RRP, 6.

bias, was explicitly designed to assure confidence in the scientific objectivity of its work."[66] Its first large-scale project was an investigation of "the size and distribution of the national income."[67] That the NBER was committed to objective social science, however, did not keep its findings from being appropriated for political and economic gain. Malcolm Rorty engaged in acts of appropriation himself, noting in an American Management Association pamphlet from 1930, for example, that the NBER's research demonstrated the truth of the "productivity theory of wages … the fact that substantial increases in real compensation for work done can come, in the long run, only from increases in the productive efficiency of labor."[68] The implication was not simply that employers should do their utmost "to assure healthful working conditions and just and considerate treatment of the mass of employees" but also that "the services of the labor union policeman"—understood to decrease productivity—"are no longer required."[69]

A Republican, Malcolm Rorty opposed the New Deal, and the political distance between him and his brother could not have been greater. A year before his death, he wrote to James with comments on the manuscript of *Where Life Is Better* (1936), James Rorty's book about the Depression. "My plan for annotations, or even a preface," he said, "seems impracticable, in view of the extent to which your reporting has been permeated by your own particular social and economic viewpoints."[70] James Rorty's political identity was on display for all to see.

* 5 *

Aside from the striking parallels between James Rorty's doubts about social-scientific objectivity and those eventually staked out by his son with regard to inquiry more generally, what strikes the contemporary reader about *Our Master's Voice* is how little concerned Rorty was with the Depression. With its references to the excesses of American consumerism, the book seems more an indictment of advertising in the 1920s than in the

---

66. Malcolm Rutherford, 2005, "Who's Afraid of Arthur Burns? The NBER and the Foundations," *Journal of the History of Economic Thought* 27:109–39, 112.

67. Ibid., 112.

68. M. C. Rorty, 1930, *The Organization of the Managing Group*, General Management Series No. 109, New York: American Management Association, RRP, 9.

69. Ibid., 9, 8.

70. M. C. Rorty to James Rorty, October 2, 1935, RRP.

1930s. In Rorty's magazine pieces, however, and especially in *Where Life Is Better,* the Depression—its causes, meaning, and implication for America's future—took center stage. It took some time for Rorty, like many writers and intellectuals, to realize the severity of the Depression and its discontinuities from preceding periods of American economic history.[71] In a 1930 review of a book about the settlement house movement, for example, he noted that the "'black winter' of 1929–30" was "less black ... than the winter that is now upon us," while also asserting that "the phenomenon of unemployment incident to a severe business depression such as the present" was less of a threat to "the very existence of our civilization" than the fact that so many factory workers had been laid off during the boom times of the 1920s.[72] By 1931, Rorty would still insist, reviewing a book about social work for the *New Republic,* that "unemployed workers" are "tightening their belts, losing their homes and their furniture, beating up their wives and children, getting drunk, getting sick, going insane and dying," but that "they were doing all these things long before the stock-market crash" and that the cause of their plight was industrial capitalism itself, not merely economic slowdown.[73]

One year later, while still maintaining that the problem of the Depression was systemic and not temporary, Rorty acknowledged its scope. He noted in an article in the *Commonweal* that "America has a headache. Capitalism has a headache."[74] A piece in the *New Republic* called for the legalization of birth control "as a common sense relief measure," given that "one of the chief terrors of the depression" is "that of unwanted and disastrous childbirth."[75] And a poem titled "Winter: 1932" asserted that Americans could now choose revolution, or more of the same: "Two winters, and now a third; soon you must choose /... A soft land, hardening; a cold land, burning / Deep at the core."[76] It was in that year that Rorty joined the League of Professional Groups for Foster and Ford, taking on a staff position with the organization and throwing his support behind the Communist Party candidates for president and vice president, respectively.

71. This was true despite the fact that he had been laid off from what had been a cushy position writing copy for the firm of Batten, Barton, Durstine, and Osborne at a salary of $150 per week.

72. James Rorty, 1930, "The Right to Work," *Nation,* December 24, 131:712.

73. James Rorty, 1931, "If Social Workers Struck," *New Republic,* August 5, 322.

74. James Rorty, 1932, "The Logic of Ballyhoo," *Commonweal,* March 23, 570–72, 570.

75. James Rorty, 1932, "What's Stopping Birth Control?" *New Republic,* February 3, 312–14, 314, 313.

76. James Rorty, 1932, "Winter: 1932," *Nation,* February 10, 134:172.

By 1933, Rorty was reporting from the front lines of the Depression. In an article that referred to the work of sociologist Nels Anderson, he bemoaned the fact that "our economic collapse had sent 200,000, or 300,000, or 500,000 homeless children out upon the highways."[77] In his own field, advertising, the "Golden Bowl" had not been "broken, but it has been badly cracked, and through that crack has leaked about half of the 1929 personnel of the profession."[78] The intellectual stratum, in his view, was faring about as well. A piece in *Our America,* a magazine he helped start, noted that "many of the 'left' intellectuals are relatively secure economically. They can still eat."[79] But that was not the case for millions of other Americans.

After the ad industry furor over *Our Master's Voice* began to die down— and after Winifred had almost fully recuperated from the difficult delivery of their son—Rorty set out in 1934 on a seven-month automobile trip across the country, one of the efforts of a number of Depression-era writers to "travel around America in search of the thoughts and aspirations of ordinary people."[80] In letters, Winifred begged him to abandon the trip—to return to Connecticut and take care of their young child, whom they affectionately called "Bucko." But beyond Rorty's ambition to produce a book that would secure his reputation, he had a political agenda important enough to him that he resisted Winifred's entreaties: in addition to documenting the misery caused by the Depression, he aimed to discover whether American workers had it in them to join in revolutionary activity. This was a crucial question to ask not simply from the standpoint of the left but from that of anyone interested in the nation's fate, for as Rorty saw it, "within the framework of the present social order there is no escape either in space or time for the great masses of American citizens."[81] He had previously called the New Deal a "capitalist alphabet soup,"[82] given the proliferation of agencies with complicated acronyms, and his travels now confirmed for him that "the New Deal ephemerae I set out to chase ... are a part of the dream; the fervor of fake 'reform' is almost an index of the disintegration of the system."[83] This meant there could

77. James Rorty, 1933, "Counting the Homeless," *Nation,* June 21, 136:692–93, 692.

78. James Rorty, 1933, "Advertising and the Depression," *Nation,* December 20, 137:703–4, 703.

79. James Rorty, 1933, "The Intellectuals Had Better Mean It," *Our America,* January, 1.

80. Pells, *Radical Visions and American Dreams,* 195.

81. Rorty, *Where Life Is Better,* 13.

82. James Rorty, 1934, "Call for Mr. Throttlebottom!" *Nation,* January 10, 138:37–39, 37.

83. Rorty, *Where Life Is Better,* 13.

be no escaping "the central dilemma of our time and country, namely, the failure of the capitalist mode of production for profit to finance consumption or to make possible a world at peace."[84]

His travels afforded him many adventures, some of which he wrote about for the *Nation* and other magazines before reworking them as book chapters. February, for example, found him poking about in California's Imperial Valley at a time when lettuce pickers were on strike. He was arrested on charges of suspicion, his car and belongings searched, and he was forcibly escorted to the Arizona border. In Arkansas, Rorty was run out of town by a preacher who resented his inquiries into charges brought by the Southern Tenant Farmers Union. But he met good people along the way as well. He encountered labor organizers, newspapermen, and even a few politicians in the Upper Midwest who seemed to him both genuinely compassionate souls and men of action who understood that nothing short of radical social transformation could pull the country out of its economic predicament.

They were, unfortunately, in the minority. In state after state, Rorty found the same thing: "that ninety-five out of a hundred Americans have not grasped [the] dilemma [of the failure of the capitalist mode of production], whether stated in Marxian, technocratic, Utopian, epic, coöperative, or any other terms."[85] There was a "plague" under way in "every city [Rorty] had visited. ... Its victims, most of them, did not even know the name of the disease from which they were suffering."[86] It was true, Rorty said, that there was more labor militancy around the country than one might imagine. But even among those who might seem naturally predisposed to socialism—participants in buyers and other cooperative associations, for example, which Rorty had long supported—there was little recognition that depression was an inevitable outcome of the contradictions and tensions inherent to capitalism.

Rorty put the blame for this squarely on the shoulders of those in the culture industry, who had filled Americans' heads with cheap entertainment, distracting them from the true causes of the crisis. "Hollywood specializes in the manufacture of the soothing, narcotic dreams of love," he wrote, while "in New York, NBC and Columbia specialize in the manufacture of cheerio radio optimism, pre-barbaric dance rhythms, and commodity fetishism intoned by unctuous announcers."[87] His indictment did not stop with those cultural producers who were knowingly working in the interests of capital. Once again he criticized academics for embracing

84. Ibid., 23.   85. Ibid.   86. Ibid., 117.   87. Ibid., 107.

notions of objectivity rather than putting their knowledge to use in the service of countering ideological distortions. In the course of his travels he visited the University of Chicago but concluded that "red-hunters" would be "wasting their time" there, for the sociologists at Chicago "and elsewhere … have accumulated vast quantities of valuable descriptive material" but "adhere to Veblen's earlier attitude: they are more interested in what is happening and in what is likely to happen then in *making* things happen."[88] As he had done in his 1934 book, he reiterated his Hook-inspired charge against social-scientific objectivity: "No science and no art begins and ends with fact-finding; … some sort of social philosophy must guide the collection of facts and control their interpretation and use."[89] Nor, he said, "was I able to impress" on the sociologists that "they were citizens as well as sociologists; that if they let the facts stew long enough, some sort of fermented action would ensue."[90] In this vein he made fun of sociologist Donald Slesinger, who had prepared a display for the Century of Progress exhibition in Chicago. Slesinger had gone "so far as to inform the visitors that there was a depression" but had not bothered to explain "how, or why. If the sociologists understood these latter points, which may be doubted, they were not permitted to tell."[91]

But if, because of the project of distortion undertaken by the entertainment industry and the negligence of intellectuals, rebellion against capitalism was not on the minds of the American masses, what was? Rorty's answer was war and fascism. Although he blamed the culture industry for its obfuscations, he harbored no illusions about the organic tendencies of American culture. "Americans," he wrote, "have always been a violent people: physically and emotionally violent and mentally soft and lazy."[92] Given these tendencies—alongside what he saw as the beating of the war drum by the Hearst-run media—it was no surprise that many of the people he talked to during the course of his travels saw another world war as the only way the country could recover from its economic malaise.[93] This interpretation of the situation—that calls for war reflected the needs of a capitalist system in crisis—alongside Rorty's longtime pacifism, would help explain his objections later in the decade to America's entry into war, despite his denunciations of European fascism.[94]

---

88. Ibid., 128–29.

89. Ibid., 129. In the acknowledgments section he thanks Hook for having read parts of the manuscript.

90. Ibid. 91. Ibid., 134. 92. Ibid., 22. 93. Ibid., 264–65.

94. See his signature, alongside that of Thomas H. Benton, Lewis Corey, Sidney Hook, Suzanne La Follette, Dwight MacDonald, Mary McCarthy, Philip Rahv, Norman Thomas,

It was not only fascism in Europe that worried him. Indeed, he predicted that, in addition to war, the most likely outcome of the Depression would be the rise of a dictator in the United States. He harbored no illusions about the capacity of America's democratic tradition to prevent such an occurrence. The "democratic dogma" of "we, the people," he noted, was an illusion: "We have instead an established system ... in the operation of which one class of the population has been encouraged ... to exploit the other classes."[95] This structural weakness, when combined with economic vulnerability and what Rorty saw as rural populism's tendency toward nationalism and anti-Semitism, rendered the likelihood of an American turn to fascism high. In a chapter on Huey Long, Rorty pointed out that Long had been able to garner the support of the New Orleans business community only because the rise of absentee ownership—a topic of considerable interest to Veblen—made it less important for business to care about its legitimacy in the local political arena. Insofar as this was so, "the logic of capitalism in its present period of decline" could not be separated from "the logic of fascism"—though Rorty was quick to point out that Long's ascent to power was also contingent on "his appeal ... to the century-old hatred of the Southern hillbillies for the plantation owners and for the new hierarchy of big business."[96] But that Long had fallen to an assassin's bullet did not mean the threat he represented had vanished. "Our domestic situation," Rorty concluded, "is that of a progressively deteriorating social and economic anarchy, with a definite drift toward fascism."[97] He held out some slim hope that those on the radical left could use the situation to their advantage, but the book ended on a pessimistic note.

* 6 *

Rorty's attention to the threat of fascism marked a turning point in his thinking. For, as previously indicated, by the early to mid-1930s he became acutely aware of the fact that, while the crises of capitalism might predispose America to the rise of a dictatorship, by no means was a turn toward

Lionel Trilling, and others on a 1938 letter criticizing the *Nation* for "aligning itself with those forces, both of the right and of the left, which are pushing this country toward war." "War and *The Nation*," *Nation*, January 22, 1938, 146:111. Rorty was also a speaker at a 1937 protest against the war held at NYU. See "Huge Peace Rallies Mark Student Peace Day," *New York Times*, April 23, 1937, 1, 3.

95. Rorty, *Where Life Is Better*, 169.

96. Ibid., 343–44.   97. Ibid., 380.

Marx enough to save a nation from such a fate. Reviewing several books about Russia in 1931, Rorty acknowledged that the Communist Party there had embraced dictatorship: "They preach the world revolution according to the Marxian formula and are working intermittently to bring it about.... The pyramided dictatorship of the Communist party is real and earnest."[98] All along Rorty had been sensitive to Communist demands for ideological purity, as when he helped translate for the *Nation* in 1932 poems from Russian children's books, whose propagandist nature was painfully obvious,[99] or when, that same year, he drafted a letter to the editors of the *New Masses* encouraging them to treat radical writers affiliated with various John Reed clubs as something other than "schoolboys" forced to follow "inflexible tactical rules" for producing "revolutionary literature."[100] As the decade progressed, however, Rorty's condemnations of Communism would no longer take a lighthearted tone. A pamphlet published in 1934, for instance, "Order on the Air!" argued that American business was using the radio waves for its own gain, while failing to give equal time to its opponents. In so doing it was exploiting the public resource of radio just as Hitler, Mussolini, and Stalin—whom Rorty lumped together—were doing.[101] At the same time, Rorty increasingly turned a critical eye to the American Communist Party. In a typical move, *Where Life Is Better* criticized radicals in the San Francisco Bay Area who, "although not members of the Party ... hewed to the Party line more strictly than Earl Browder himself. This was natural, since Mr. Browder is subject to the Higher Learning of the Comintern, with its disconcerting shifts of permanent infallibility."[102]

What had happened between the late 1920s and the early 1930s to draw Rorty's attention to the fascistic tendencies of actually existing Communism can be summed up in a word: Trotsky. The intricacies of splits and divisions within the American radical movement and Rorty's changing affiliation over time with different groups cannot be of concern here except in broad brushstroke. Suffice it to note that 1928 was a pivotal year in the history of American Trotskyism. It was in that year Trotsky was exiled to Alma Ata. In 1929 he was forced to flee Soviet territory altogether, commencing a series of temporary stays in Turkey, France, and Norway

---

98. James Rorty, 1931, "More Truth about Russia," *New Republic,* July 8, 213.

99. Lydia Nadejena and James Rorty, 1932, "Shock Brigades," *Nation,* November 23, 135:496–97. The translation was no blanket condemnation, however, and went so far as to praise the poems for their "simplicity, vigor, and graphic quality."

100. Letter to the Editors of the *New Masses,* May 12, 1932, JRC.

101. James Rorty, 1934, "Order on the Air!" New York: John Day Pamphlets.

102. Rorty, *Where Life Is Better,* 281.

before being granted asylum in Mexico. Trotsky's disagreement with Stalin concerned not the truth of historical materialism—though the two interpreted it somewhat differently—but rather the use of repression and violence to keep revolution afloat. Trotsky was not a pacifist. At the international level he saw pacifism as a bourgeois phenomenon, and domestically he recognized that the seizing of the means of production may require taking up arms against the bourgeoisie and its representatives. Yet he opposed violent purges against dissenters and saw the Soviet state under Stalin, with its entrenched bureaucracy and privileges for Party leaders, as a transitional phenomenon that would have to give way. In the United States, the emergence of a formally unified United Communist Party in 1920 could not conceal the reality of factional disagreements among Communist sympathizers. The dominant faction, aligned with Stalin and in fact directed by him, soon gained complete control, and in 1928 those whose sympathies lay with Trotsky, like Max Schachtman and James Cannon, were "expelled from the group they had helped found."[103]

In their radicalism, many of the New York intellectuals sided with Trotsky. But this is not to say that those who did were all of one mind. Max Eastman, for example, one of the founders of the *Masses* and for a time a colleague of Dewey at Columbia, was criticized by Trotsky himself, as well as by Sidney Hook, for his 1926 book, *Marx and Lenin: The Science of Revolution*, which tried to divest Marxism of its Hegelianism.[104] Just a few years later, however, Eastman would become one of Trotsky's more influential American champions, translating several of Trotsky's books and condemning Stalinism in works of his own like *The End of Socialism in Russia* (1937) and *Stalin's Russia and the Crisis in Socialism* (1940). Hook—who, like Eastman, sought a reconciliation between Dewey and Marx—had sharp philosophical and political disagreements with Trotsky and his American acolytes but ended up playing an instrumental role in the formation of the Dewey Commission that undertook an impartial investigation of Trotsky's life to counter the charges brought against him in Moscow.[105] Rahv, Macdonald, McCarthy, and most of the rest of the *Partisan Review* crowd also gravitated in a Trotskyist orbit. Although there was never a formal affiliation between the magazine and the American Trotskyist party—the Communist League of America, founded by

103. Ibid., 32.

104. See the discussion in Bloom, *Prodigal Sons*, 100–101.

105. See Sidney Hook, 1987, *Out of Step: An Unquiet Life in the 20th Century*, New York: Harper and Row, 218–47.

Schachtman and Cannon, later renamed the Socialist Workers Party—
the magazine often published articles that praised Trotsky and endorsed
his positions. As Bloom puts it, perhaps too unsympathetically, "Many
Partisan writers fastened onto Trotsky in an uncritical way, idolizing his
skills, overvaluing his contributions, and finding reflections of their own
calling in his actions."[106] This was especially the case, Bloom goes on to
note, after the magazine was revived in 1937, the year after Trotsky was
put on trial in abstentia by Stalin.

What did the New York intellectuals like so much about Trotsky? Despite lingering allegations that, as a Bolshevik leader, he too had blood
on his hands, Trotsky was seen by many as a humanist who was unwilling to suppress basic human rights for the greater good of Communism.
In addition, Trotsky made critiques of Soviet propagandist literature,
art, and cinema part of his brief against Stalin. More generally, though,
support for Trotsky was a way for New York intellectuals to signal their
opposition to Stalin, who, beginning in 1928, undertook a program of
collectivization of the peasantry in which as many as 10 million resistors
were murdered. Although the full extent of these purges was not known
at the time, their significance was hotly debated among the New York
intellectuals:

> If the Communists regarded the trials as a test of one's political ortho-
> doxy, their most vehement opponents saw the purges as a sign that the
> anti-Christ had taken over the Church. Non-Stalinist radicals excoriated
> the proceedings as a charade, a frame-up, and a betrayal of the October
> revolution. Even for those who did not think that Stalin had deliberately
> sacrificed the cause of international socialism to Russian national interests,
> the purges were profoundly disillusioning. The government-sanctioned
> bloodletting reduced the Soviet leadership, in the eyes of Oswald Gar-
> rison Villard, "to the level of Adolf Hitler."[107]

As Pells goes on to note, however, even in the wake of the purges there
was disagreement within the American left and among its principal publication organs over how to interpret their meaning. Did the purges reflect
some intrinsic defect of the Communist system, or were they merely the
effect of the USSR having been taken over by a brutal dictator? Were they
evidence, as Trotsky argued, of the weakness of the Soviet state and of

106. Bloom, *Prodigal Sons*, 112.
107. Pells, *Radical Visions and American Dreams*, 306.

its sham commitment to workers? Or were Stalin's opponents genuine enemies of the Communist cause?

Several liberal and left-leaning magazines, including the *New Republic* and the *Nation,* took the view that the Soviet state *was* moving in the direction of greater freedoms, while also holding out the possibility that Stalin may have had evidence of Trotsky's complicity in a German plot to overthrow the Soviet leadership. Rorty, whose own view was that Trotsky was a hero, wrote a pained letter to the *Nation* in response. "For nearly twenty years I have read *The Nation* and written for it," Rorty began. "During that period I have always felt that ... *The Nation,* when confronted with a situation involving fundamental issues of truth, justice, and moral and intellectual integrity, would deal with it honestly and courageously." He was therefore aghast that the magazine had not come out in support of Trotsky: "In a hundred years, you say, we'll learn the truth about the trials. Nonsense. Where these obviously cooked up confessions have involved persons and actions outside the Soviet Union they have already been shattered to bits by Trotsky and by the easily verifiable evidence." He charged the editors with having "failed—patently, grossly, disgracefully."[108] Rorty would publish a few additional pieces in the magazine over the next few years—mostly book reviews—but after 1939 his long-standing affiliation with the *Nation* ceased, just as Dewey broke off ties with the *New Republic* over its stance on the Moscow Trials.

Earlier, in 1934, Rorty had joined Hook and others in the formation of the American Workers Party, a short lived "authentic American party rooted in the American revolutionary tradition, prepared to meet the problems created by the breakdown of the capitalist economy, with a plan for a cooperative commonwealth."[109] The party, with revolutionary aims, was intended as an alternative to both the Communist and Socialist parties and eventually merged with the Trotskyist Communist League. By the late 1930s, however, in light of increasing evidence that American workers had little interest in radical social transformation, as well as the growing specter of fascism in Europe, a number of prominent intellectuals on the left, including Trotskyists and liberals like Dewey, turned their attention to a new organization, the Committee for Cultural Freedom.[110] Its widely published manifesto, with 142 signatories, including both James Rorty and Winifred Raushenbush, declared that "the tide of

108. James Rorty, 1937, "Harsh Words from a Friend," *Nation,* February 27, 144:252.

109. Hook, *Out of Step,* 191.

110. See the discussion below about the Committee's reincarnation in the 1950s.

totalitarianism is rising throughout the world. It is washing away cultural and creative freedom along with other expressions of independent
human reason ... the totalitarian idea is already enthroned in Germany,
Italy, Russia, Japan, and Spain."[111] In a clear reference to the Communist
Party, the manifesto called for the formation of a group that would be
"independent of control, whether open or secret, by any political group"
and "pledged to expose repression of intellectual freedom under whatever pretext." Independence from the Party was insisted upon not just on
strategic grounds but also on moral ones, for in the view of Committee
members, the Party and its tactics also reflected totalitarian tendencies.
Rorty's personal mistreatment at Party hands must have helped convince
him of this. Although he supported Foster and Ford in 1932, as mentioned
earlier, he was not at that point a Communist Party member. And indeed,
as Hook reports, had any of the intellectuals who took part in the League
of Professional Groups actually read Foster's book *Towards Soviet America*
(1932), where he called for the "liquidat[ion]" of all dissenting groups,
they would likely have balked. Rorty, Hook recalls, "was at heart a poet,
sickened by the commercialism of capitalist life and culture and up in
arms at the cruelties and injustices of the depression. He made his political choices on the basis of his moral empathy and his sense for the integrity and authenticity of the persons with whom he associated."[112] For him,
as for other League members, the "rejection of socialism was not intended
to express the rejection of democracy."[113] Precisely because of his unwillingness to affiliate with the Party, however, Rorty endured snubs at the
hands of Party functionaries. A review of *Our Master's Voice* in the *New
Masses,* for instance, noted that "Rorty hates the advertising business, the
capitalist system, Soviet Russia, and Communists, apparently with almost
equal fervor. He *loves* himself—and next to his own colossal ego, Thorstein Veblen is perhaps nearest to his heart."[114] The reviewer went on to
suggest that, while Rorty was right to worry about the role that advertising men might play in the eventual rise of fascism in the United States,
"one is justified in the faint suspicion that James Rorty may be among
them."[115] It is no wonder that, in the 1936 presidential elections, Rorty
switched positions, joining Hook in supporting the Socialist candidate
Norman Thomas.[116]

111. "Manifesto," *Nation,* May 27, 1939, 148:626.
112. Hook, *Out of Step,* 182.   113. Ibid., 186.
114. Frank Thompson, 1934, "Rorty's Revenge," *New Masses,* June 12, 25–26, 25.
115. Ibid., 25–26.
116. "Fantastic Campaign Deplored by Thomas," *New York Times,* October 24, 1936, 6.

Over the next few years, Rorty, like many of the New York intellectuals, would become deeply involved with the Committee for Cultural
Freedom, participating in activities it organized, such as radio debates
over the value of the Dies Committee, the 1930s precursor to McCarthy's
House Un-American Activities Committee. As he would McCarthy, Rorty
opposed Dies on the grounds that his investigation stifled legitimate dissent. It became easier logistically for Rorty to participate in these debates
because, in 1935, the Rortys sold their property in rural Connecticut and
moved to Brooklyn, where Richard Rorty would attend the Berkeley
Institute, a private school, before the family decided to move full time
to what had initially been the summer property they acquired in Flatbrookville, New Jersey.

* 7 *

Rorty turned fifty years old in 1940, but already his best work was behind him. Having turned his back on the *Nation* and the *New Republic,*
he now placed most of his magazine work in *Harper's,* the *Commonweal,*
and *Commentary.* It is significant that *Commentary,* started in 1945, saw as
its editorial mission to contribute to "new patterns of living, new modes
of thought, which will harmonize heritage and country into a true sense
of at-home-ness in the modern world."[117] A continuation of *Contemporary Jewish Record,* the magazine regarded its birth as "an act of faith in
our possibilities in America. With Europe devastated, there falls upon us
here in the United States a far greater share of the responsibility for carrying forward, in a creative way, our common Jewish cultural and spiritual
heritage."[118] Rorty had not converted to Judaism, of course. But while he
would continue to publish pieces that satirized American culture,[119] the
bulk of his writing was now taken up with social problems that he saw as
the moral responsibility of the United States to solve, given the resources at its disposal and its place of influence in the world. For Rorty as for
other *Commentary* contributors, there was reason to hope that the United
States *would* act to solve these problems. Increasingly when he spoke of
America he described it not as the home of an insipid individualism but as

117. Elliott Cohen, 1945, "An Act of Affirmation," *Commentary,* November, 1–3, 2.

118. Ibid., 2.

119. For example, James Rorty, 1948, "Night Hawks over Bronxville," *Harper's,* February, 127. The poem recounted the life and death of an adman—"the carpenter's son in a
Maine village"—who had spent his adult life in white-collar ennui and died "hurrying for
the 8:25."

a nation of great potential whose core principles of freedom were worth preserving and which stood as a bulwark against what Rorty now saw as the menace of Soviet Communism. A 1941 article, for example, urged that the American diet be transformed in accordance with the findings of nutrition science on the grounds that "if America is to be strong—strong enough to preserve the freedoms and graces of civilized life in the modern world—we must hasten to build, not only better bombing planes, but better human bodies; we must repair and guard our nutritional ramparts."[120] Similarly, in a long expose of the practices that had made *Reader's Digest* so successful, Rorty refused to endorse the charge that the magazine was engaged in fearmongering when it suggested that "a radical conspiracy is undermining the American way of life." From Rorty's point of view there *was* such a conspiracy afoot, and he recognized that the *Digest,* with its enormous circulation, was in a position to "successfully defend, during the economic and social confusion of the post-war years, whatever is humanly valid and viable in the so-called 'American way of life.'"[121] More dramatic still was a 1947 piece that called for the suppression of all Stalinist "fifth column apparatus" in the United States. "No threat to our tradition of civil liberties will thereby be entailed," Rorty insisted. "On the contrary that is by this time the only way we can defend the status of true liberals. That is the only way we can protect the traditions and the institutions of freedom against the insidious, disintegrating forces of totalitarian expansion."[122] These were the same themes that Rorty echoed in hundreds of anti-Stalinist scripts he prepared for the Voice of America, his new employer, and in pieces he wrote for the Post-War World Council, whose goal, as Richard Rorty has described it, was "to publicize what Stalin was preparing to do to central Europe, and to warn Americans that the wartime alliance with the USSR should not be allowed to carry over into the postwar period."[123] A letter from 1943 shows that Rorty's radicalism had

120. James Rorty, 1941, "Total Defense and Public Health: The Importance of Nutrition in the Present Crisis," *Harper's,* March, 375–85, 385.

121. James Rorty, 1944, "The Reader's Digest: A Study in Cultural Elephantiasis," *Commonweal,* 78–83, 83. At the same time, however, Rorty pointed out that the magazine was beholden to business interests and that its particular strain of anti-Communism, linked to laissez-faire ideals, was likely to promote "the helpless, obscurantist drift of big and little business which seems likely to plunge us into economic collapse after the war and into political totalitarianism."

122. James Rorty, 1947, "To a 'Friend of the Soviets,'" *Commonweal,* January 10, 322–23, 323.

123. Richard Rorty, 1998, *Achieving Our Country: Leftist Thought in Twentieth-Century America,* Cambridge: Harvard University Press, 62.

become muted even on his own self-understanding and that this was linked to his critique of totalitarianism. Writing to an unidentified correspondent, he noted,

> the softening of my radical intransigence in social matters ... has occurred. Possibly it is age. I tell myself that I am disillusioned with shallow formulae; that too often I have seen doctrinaire political movements yield the opposite of what they promised; that I have found the technique of power-building to be pretty much the same, whether the builder is a labor leader, a big corporation all-right-Nick, or the candidate for government or president. ... The desperate need is to escape from the inertias: technological, social, economic, political, which we have created. The best man is the freest man. The best society is that which is itself subject to the fewest compulsions, and which imposes the fewest compulsions on its members.[124]

By the early 1950s, Rorty's anti-Communism reached a fever pitch. In *McCarthy and the Communists,* a book written with Moshe Decter and sponsored by the American Committee for Cultural Freedom, Rorty asserted that "the enemy is Communism. Its ranks comprise Communists, pro-Communists, fellow-travelers, spies, and Communist agents. Its works include infiltration, subversion, and espionage in government and in all other areas of public life."[125] For Rorty, there could now be no question but that Communist "traitors"[126] should be rooted out of government. But he disagreed with McCarthy's tactics. Above all, he doubted McCarthy's motives. Were McCarthy truly interested in identifying Communists his investigations would have been more systematic. But that he often raised charges in a scattershot fashion and failed to follow up indicated that McCarthy was more interested in political gain than in genuine anti-Communist crusading. One of McCarthy's most serious problems was his "muddled thinking"; he seemed incapable of "tell[ing] a Communist from a liberal."[127] The issue wasn't simply that McCarthy had, as a result, targeted a number of left anti-Communists. As problematic, he and his colleagues had in some instances tread lightly when they should have brought down the axe. For example, representatives of the State Department trying to determine what magazines should be held in overseas libraries had approved the *Nation,* "whose content," Rorty not-

124. James Rorty to "Malcolm," March 7, 1943, JRC.
125. James Rorty and Moshe Decter, 1954, *McCarthy and the Communists,* Boston: Beacon Press, 18.
126. Ibid., 8.   127. Ibid., 7.

ed—remarkably—"for a long period betrayed a susceptibility to Communist apologetics."[128] His feelings about his former publication venue aside, on the whole Rorty did not think the best way to root out Communists was to suppress free speech. He supported programs designed to teach American school children about the realities of life in the Soviet Union on the grounds that a democracy that defends itself by using antidemocratic tactics like censorship not only undermines the very values for which it fights but loses a crucial weapon in its struggle, namely, the ability to convince people by exposing them to the higher quality of life and democratic freedoms that obtain in open societies.[129] From this point of view, McCarthy was not just an inefficient anti-Communist but someone whose fascistic tendencies threatened to undermine the fight against Communism. Rorty opened the book with a quotation from William James: "Democracy is still upon its trial," James had written in 1897. "The civic genius of our people is its only bulwark," and only two things can "save us" from "degeneration.... One of them is the habit of trained and disciplined good temper toward the opposite party when it fairly wins its innings.... The other is that of fierce and merciless resentment toward every man or set of men who break the public peace."[130] Both McCarthy and the Communists had broken the public peace, and the fight for democracy was necessarily a fight against them both.

The American Committee for Cultural Freedom of the 1950s represented a rebirth of the committee by the same name of the 1930s. The former had been started in 1951 by Hook and others and was the American offshoot of the Congress for Cultural Freedom, held for the first time in Berlin in 1950. The Congress gathered leading intellectuals from around the world who opposed Communism and wished to do their part to bring about its demise. A response to Soviet propaganda efforts—including conferences held in New York, Paris, and Prague in 1949 under the guise of the cause of world peace, but which actually "peddle[d] anti-Americanism" and "tried to re-invigorate sympathies for the great moral good of the egalitarian, anti-capitalist social ideal of which the Soviet Union remained the dynamic exponent"[131]—delegates to the Congress "included some of the most respected and some of the most notorious thinkers of

128. Ibid., 32.

129. See "Communism Course Urged for Schools," *New York Times*, April 22, 1962, 49.

130. Rorty and Decter, *McCarthy and the Communists*, iv.

131. Giles Scott-Smith, 2000, "'A Radical Democratic Political Offensive': Melvin J. Lasky, *Der Monat*, and the Congress for Cultural Freedom," *Journal of Contemporary History* 35:263–80, 266.

the period, for example Arthur Koestler, Ignazio Silone, Sidney Hook, James Burnham, Arthur Schlesinger Jr, Hugh Trevor-Roper, and Franz Borkenau."[132] Beyond denouncing totalitarianism, speakers and other participants formulated plans to help limit Soviet expansionism by exposing the public to art, literature, drama, philosophy, and other cultural products that would contain anti-Communist messages. Additional congresses and festivals were planned to showcase such works, and the decision was made to form independent committees on cultural freedom in each of the major democracies and to start new publication organs.

Only in 1965 was it revealed that financial support for the Congress—and for the American Committee, in particular—was provided by the Central Intelligence Agency. As Frances Stonor Saunders explains, "A central feature of the Agency's efforts to mobilize culture as a Cold War weapon was the systematic organization of a network of 'private' groups or 'friends' into an unofficial consortium. This was an entrepreneurial coalition of philanthropic foundations, business corporations and other institutions and individuals, who worked hand in hand with the CIA to provide the cover and the funding pipeline for its secret programmes in western Europe. Additionally, these 'friends' could be depended on to articulate the government's interests at home and abroad, whilst appearing to do so solely on their own initiative."[133] While there were often disagreements—political, intellectual, and personal—between the individuals and organizations who took part in this expansive network, some with knowledge of the real sources of funding, most without, all were committed to fighting the Communist threat. Publications that received support from the government or whose editorial staffs were intimately bound up with the Committee included *Partisan Review, Commentary, New Leader,* and the British magazine *Encounter,* the last funded by the British intelligence service.

Rorty was not a mover and shaker in the American Committee, but beyond having written a book under its sponsorship, he was on its censorship committee. In a 1955 letter, Sol Stein, the executive director of the organization and a former United States Information Service officer, asked Rorty to investigate instances where free speech was being suppressed in

132. Giles Scott-Smith, 2000, "The 'Masterpieces of the Twentieth Century': Festival and the Congress for Cultural Freedom: Origins and Consolidation 1948–52," *Intelligence and National Security* 15:121–43, 122.

133. Frances Stonor Saunders, 1999, *The Cultural Cold War: The CIA and the World of Arts and Letters,* New York: New Press, 129.

the name of anti-Communism, on the grounds that suppression of basic rights was anti-American.[134]

Not all participants in the Committee agreed that censorship was a bad thing, however. Indeed, one prominent faction consisted of hardliners who supported McCarthy. Although Saunders describes *McCarthy and the Communists,* published a year before the formation of the censorship committee, as "a belated and rather ambiguous contribution," she notes, "that it was published at all provoked James Burnham to lead a walkout of the conservative wing of the American committee."[135] But the organization's leadership appears to have supported Rorty and followed closely the book's sales. A series of postcards in the Committee's files from Ed Darling, editor at Beacon Press, to Stein—who was also a "consulting editor" at the Press[136]—kept track of the newspapers in which the book was receiving favorable reviews, and commented on its sales success: "It's temporary, men.... We clap our hands to our brow, but this does not allay the anguish of having to tell you: we are out of stock [of the paper edition] on *McCarthy and the Communists.* The first printing of 22,500 was a lousy guess."[137]

Rorty's intellectual productivity did not cease with the publication of the McCarthy volume. He continued traveling internationally and wrote articles about what he saw as miraculous food and ecological systems he observed abroad, in Honduras and elsewhere. These travels did not temper his enthusiasm for the United States, which he continued to view as a bastion of freedom. In a letter to Amélie Rorty, Richard Rorty's first wife, written while he and Winifred were on vacation in the Canary Islands, he said, referring to the novel by Graham Greene, "I too shall read the *Quiet Amer* by GG on return. Do not be over-impressed by foreign critique of the US. Even supposedly intelligent people are so limited in their knowledge and appraisals of other countries & peoples.... Have read *Freedom in Contemporary Society* [by] Samuel Eliot Morison.... Excellent. One of the glories of the US is the capable men who live long enough to be completely outspoken and yet have good sense and judgment."[138] With his wife, he became a champion of the cause of civil rights, building on her long-standing interest in race and on their joint work in the 1940s for

134. Sol Stein to James Rorty, December 28, 1955, ACCF.

135. Saunders, *The Cultural Cold War,* 208.

136. See Susan Wilson, *The History of Beacon Press,* available at http://www.beacon.org/ client/pdfs/03.bp0316.pdf, 32, accessed February 9, 2007.

137. Ed Darling to Sol Stein, September 10, 1954, ACCF.

138. James Rorty to Amélie Rorty, January 31, 1957, WRC.

the Brotherhood of Sleeping Car Porters. He continued to write poetry and plays, as he had throughout his career, and lamented the fact that most never found their way into publication. Near the end of his life, he suffered a recurrence of his mental illness. Claiming in some letters divine powers of prescience, in his more lucid moments he retrospectively characterized all of his life's work as consisting of inquiries carried out in the name of the science of ecology, which he now cast in theistic terms at odds with his earlier indifference to religion. In a draft of his memoir, he observed,

> During ... [his own life time] man's place in the universe has become increasingly defined. The world views of science and religion have tended to coalesce in terms of an expanding ecological process. What I believe is implicit in what I have done and what I have written. I believe that there is a God, and that His purposes are manifest in the infinite ordering of nature and the life process. In such a belief there is no room for either sectarianism or agnosticism. Life is positive, creative, infinite in scope and possibility, unsullied by fear or doubt. In this faith the writers and artists of my generation have worked and suffered.[139]

Rorty and Raushenbush moved to Siesta Key, Florida, in 1972. He died the following year.

139. Rorty, "It Has Happened Here."

TWO

Winifred Raushenbush

* 1 *

In one of her memoirs, Diana Trilling recalled what it was like meeting Winifred Raushenbush and James Rorty during the summer she and her husband rented a ramshackle cabin from them in Connecticut. She remembered James Rorty as "the cheeriest of Irishmen, always in a chuckle," but "Winifred ... was of a more somber disposition.... She was a tall rawboned woman who talked very little and joked not at all, but she was efficient at flattering Lionel and snubbing me.... Certainly she commanded a moral universe beyond my reach; it was the universe of country living as this is experienced by women of sensibility who in moving to the country from the city believe that they have been cleansed of all the falsities and contaminations of modern civilization."[1] Raushenbush may have mastered the fine art of what to do with garden peas—something Trilling recalls being chastised by her for not knowing. But it would be a mistake to repeat Trilling's characterization of the couple as one in which the husband was the radical writer and his wife a nonintellectual appendage. For though Raushenbush was relegated to the role of assistant for many of James Rorty's—and Robert Park's—books, she was every bit as radical as her husband, and her intelligence and writing as sharp. Unfortunately, the volume of her published work was far less than his, owing to their different ambitions and, mostly, different opportunities, so the content of her thought cannot be as fully reconstructed.[2]

1. Trilling, *The Beginning of the Journey*, 124.
2. This is indeed a problem, for the greater quantity of material available about James might lead readers to conclude that he had a greater influence on his son than did Winifred. Amélie Rorty has suggested to me that this was not the case and that Winifred's

* 2 *

Although James Rorty's radicalization in the years following World War I paralleled the experiences of many other New York intellectuals, there is no evidence that his break from conventionality represented, as it did for many of them, a painful personal step forward. His brother Malcolm may have held relatively conservative views on economic matters, but his parents had both been iconoclasts. Raushenbush's radicalism was more hard won. For while her parents were approving in principle of her social activism, they disapproved of the fact that it led her to violate and even flout conventional gender norms and did their best to rein her in.

Early investigations of Walter Rauschenbusch and the social gospel movement tended to emphasize the movement's roots among upper-middle-class Protestant elites in the Northeast. More recent inquiries have "studied the social gospel as the religion of the American working class."[3] Whichever perspective is correct, historians can at least agree that at the core of the movement was the belief that the institutions of American society should be Christianized. This involved not a right-wing vision of Christianity but a left-wing one. Those who preached the social gospel tended to believe, as Walter Rauschenbusch did, that "the American social order ... was full of unregenerate sections, particularly the business segment, which was the source of current troubles.... Capitalism split mankind, resisted the worker's struggle for freedom and dignity, created inequalities, and stifled love. Christianity, on the other hand, created unity and solidarity, promoted freedom for labor, and bred equality, dignity, and love."[4] Rauschenbusch had been drawn to socialism during his time as a preacher serving German immigrants in Hell's Kitchen during the depression of the 1890s. He read literally Jesus's call for Christians to renounce mammonism and argued that Protestantism had gone astray by aligning itself with the interests of "the business and commercial classes."[5] The kingdom of heaven, he argued, was not something to be wished for

---

more thorough intellectual style relative to that of her "iconoclastic, temperamental, and intuitive" husband impressed itself upon Richard.

3. Ralph Luker, 1999, "Interpreting the Social Gospel: Reflections on Two Generations of Historiography," pp. 1–13 in *Perspectives on the Social Gospel: Papers from the Inaugural Social Gospel Conference at Colgate Rochester Divinity School*, Christopher Evans, ed., Lewiston: Edwin Mellon Press, 2.

4. Peter Frederick, 1976, *Knights of the Golden Rule: The Intellectual as Christian Social Reformer in the 1890s*, Lexington: University Press of Kentucky, 147.

5. Ibid., 145.

in the afterlife but a set of ideals to be striven for today.[6] Although he re-sisted joining the Socialist Party on the grounds that the worker's move-ment was overly instrumental in orientation and insufficiently attuned to Christian concerns, he saw social gospel Christians and socialists as hav-ing interests in common. The author of numerous books, Rauschenbusch left his pastorship in New York in 1897 to take a job as professor of divin-ity at the Rochester Theological Seminary, and a decade later sold more than fifty thousand copies of *Christianity and the Social Crisis*.[7]

Supportive though he was, however, of curbing the social, economic, and political interests of big business, Rauschenbusch held contradic-tory views about gender.[8] On the one hand, believing the family to be the premier this-wordly site where God's love manifests itself, he supported the movement for women's suffrage on the grounds that only if women are enfranchised can true equality and democracy become possible in the domestic realm. On the other hand, he cleaved to a Victorian ideology of separate spheres. While allowing that women should have the right to vote, and thus to exercise some power in the public arena, Rauschen-busch's view—which he enshrined in his theology and practiced with his own wife Pauline—was that women's primary responsibility should be the home, where they could serve as domesticators and spiritual uplifters of their husbands and children.

Because he held such a view, he was frequently at odds with his daugh-ter. For not only did Winifred experience in college a crisis of faith; she was also deeply affected by the emerging feminist movement—though later she would reject the identity "feminist"—and saw its implications to go beyond the question of women's suffrage, to offer women new possibilities for action in both the public and private spheres. Indeed, Raushenbush subscribed to many of the ideals of "New Womanhood" as analyzed by historian Carroll Smith-Rosenberg and others.[9] Although she never had the kind of loving relationships with other women that were central to those profiled by Smith-Rosenberg—women like Jane Addams, M. Carey Thomas, and Julia Lathrop—Raushenbush partook

6. Richard Wrightman Fox, 1993, "The Culture of Liberal Protestant Progressivism, 1875–1925," *Journal of Interdisciplinary History* 23:639–60, 645.

7. Frederick, *Knights of the Golden Rule*, 156.

8. My discussion here is based on Christopher Evans, 2001, "Gender and the Kingdom of God: The Family Values of Walter Rauschenbusch," pp. 53–66 in *The Social Gospel Today*, Christopher Evans, ed., Louisville: Westminster John Knox Press.

9. Carroll Smith-Rosenberg, 1985, *Disorderly Conduct: Visions of Gender in Victorian Amer-ica*, New York: Knopf.

of a cultural discourse emerging in the 1890s that stressed the importance of women's access to higher education, the need for them to break away from the constraints of the bourgeois family, and the vital role they could play in the Progressive movement as intellectuals, activists, and organizers. As Christine Stansell has noted, the New Woman also figured prominently in bohemian New York.[10] Although not all who found their cultural niche there had the same commitment to social justice as did the New Woman, the latter was controversial precisely because her emphasis on autonomy and political efficacy challenged prevailing expectations of women's roles and sexuality, and such a challenging was at the core of the cultural project of bohemianism, however much tensions remained between "American moderns" committed to women's equality, and those for whom free love was merely license to be a philanderer.

Raushenbush's letters to her father from college show her grappling with the question of what vocation she ought to pursue. Becoming a schoolteacher was, at the time, one of the few acceptable forms of employment for young middle-class women, and she briefly considered engaging in this line of work. But as Evans reports, "As Winifred moved through college ... [at Oberlin] it was clear that her major love was sociology.... She read widely in the social sciences, commenting in her letters on the virtues of intellectuals like Havelock Ellis and Sigmund Freud and feminist leaders such as Olive Schreiner, Emma Goldman, and Charlotte Perkins Gilman."[11] Before moving to Chicago to work with Park, she served as an organizer for the Ohio Women's Suffrage Association and in this capacity traveled around the state. Her interest in sociology, no less than her work as a suffragette, concerned her father, not because he insisted she settle down and marry right away, but because he was fearful that her involvement in these occupational worlds would expose her to the dangers of illicit sex, which might ruin her reputation or force her into a marriage of convenience. His worries were not unfounded. Raushenbush was on the front lines of the sexual revolution of the 1920s and openly confessed her interest in sexual experimentation. She poked fun at her father and others of his generation for their prudishness. For these and other attitudes and behaviors—including an incident in 1916 when she brought a revolver into her parents' house in Rochester and waved it around[12]—she was rebuked by her father and charged with

10. Stansell, *American Moderns*.

11. Evans, "Gender and the Kingdom of God," 61.

12. See Casey Nelson Blake, 2000, "Private Life and Public Commitment: From Walter Rauschenbusch to Richard Rorty," pp. 85–101 in *A Pragmatist's Progress? Richard Rorty and*

reckless disregard, not simply of social propriety, but of common sense. More generally, as Casey Nelson Blake has suggested, and consistent with the arguments of Smith-Rosenberg, Stansell, and others, the differences between Walter and Winifred were the differences between a generation still wedded to an ethic of "self-control" and one that embraced an "ethic of self-liberation."[13] What distinguished the latter from more hedonistic strands of bohemianism was the recognition that self-liberation, in politics and personal life, should be measured and serve some higher purpose. Implicitly drawing the three-way connection between Dewey, Winifred, and her son, Blake notes that Raushenbush "adopted an experimental approach to personal conduct. The virtues of innovation, openness, and scientific inquiry that she saw as necessary to a socialist politics had as their counterpart an experimental ethic in private life."[14] That this was so represented a major point of tension between her and her parents.

* 3 *

Raushenbush's interest in controlled self-liberation is part of what drew her to Chicago sociology. For though social control, not freedom, was the watchword of the Chicago school, a core assumption informing its investigations of Chicago was that scientific inquiry into the processes through which social life evolves in a rapidly industrializing city—and not armchair moralizing—could provide the key to rational social reorganization that would make no attempt to turn back the clock, as reformers of a more Victorian mindset might, on detraditionalization. Although Park, the intellectual leader of the Chicago school in the 1920s and 1930s, had a former newspaperman's healthy suspicion of social reformers and their motives, he and his colleagues nevertheless saw the amassing of sociological knowledge not as an end in itself but as a means to overcoming the dislocations wrought by modernity. Like Georg Simmel, by whom he was much influenced, Park could see both the negative and positive sides of modernization and viewed urbanism as the preeminent social form through which it comes about. While disruptive of traditional customs, mores, and institutions, and thus requiring implementation of new strategies of community control to rein in centrifugal social tendencies, urbanism, in Park's view, also releases important artistic and other creative

---

American Intellectual History, John Pettegrew, ed., Lanham: Rowman and Littlefield, 95.

13. Ibid., 92.   14. Ibid., 95.

cultural energies, catalyzing social change and pushing society forward in progressive directions. Among these directions in the United States was the eventual reduction of discrimination against recent immigrants and African Americans, who, under pressure from the "race relations cycle," would come to assimilate to the norms and values of mainstream white society, at the same time that sociological research into the lives of racial and ethnic minorities would render less plausible ideologies of racial hatred. From an early age Raushenbush too found herself concerned with what W. E. B. DuBois called the "problem of the color line,"[15] and that this was an abiding concern of the Chicago school must have made it all the more attractive to her.

Almost nothing has been written of Raushenbush's time at Chicago. An appendix to *The Negro in Chicago* (1921) describes her as having been a "graduate student" there in 1918, as having "prepared material for a book on [the] foreign-language press by Professor Robert E. Park ... 1918–20" and as working to "prepare ... maps and graphs for [a] book by Professor W. I. Thomas, 1919."[16] Archival evidence suggests she did not aspire to become a professor. An entry in her diary from 1919 notes that "as for my ambitions, I'd like to collect and present graphically the actual industrial and financial interrelations in the world for the education of the workers, I'd like sometime to be living a simple wholesome life in which I had children and belong, with humor, to a group. I'd like to push an enterprise which gave me a sense of leadership.... Would I like to study still, geography, physiology, etc? ... No, being a woman I don't want to be a scholar."[17] That she was not bent on entering the academy, however—as much a function of her preferences for direct political action as a reflection of the conditions of possibility she would have faced on the academic labor market[18]—does not mean she was unaffected by her time in Chi-

15. W. E. B. DuBois, [1903] 2004, *The Souls of Black Folk*, Boulder: Paradigm.

16. "Appendix: Preparation of Report," in *The Negro in Chicago: A Study of Race Relations and a Race Riot*, Chicago Commission on Race Relations, ed., 1921, Chicago: University of Chicago Press, 655.

17. Diary entry, March 14, 1919, WRC.

18. On one version of her resume Raushenbush recorded that although she had done only one year of coursework at Chicago, in the early 1920s she was "offered [a] teach[ing] position at the University of Iowa. Recommended by Ellsworth Faris, who had taught there and who in 1925 became chairman of the sociology department of the University of Chicago. I accepted and was then turned down, the reason being my German name. My grandfather, Augustus Rauschenbusch came to the U.S. in the 1840s and was a professor in Rochester, N.Y., where my father and I grew up. I had earlier, in 1916 been offered a teaching job in sociology in an eastern Negro college. I was recommended by my Oberlin sociology

cago. An autobiographical document in her papers notes, "My intellectual life began with my migration to Chicago in 1917. I learned life from three sources: the war, the city, and the university.... The professors who affected me most were Robert Ezra Park, George H. Mead, and William I. Thomas. Dr. Park has supplied me with most of the useful concepts about society that I possess. Mr. Park also steered me into the field of sociological research."[19]

In another unpublished document, she described the nature of her apprenticeship with Park:

> Between 1919 and 1921 and again between 1923 and 1925, I worked as Robert Park's assistant on research jobs of which he was director: the first a study of the foreign language press, financed by the Carnegie Corporation, the second a survey of race relations on the Pacific coast financed by the Institute of Social and Religious Research. When, during this period, I occasionally murmured that I wanted to take a writing course at the University of Chicago, he pooh-poohed the idea. Later my husband, like Dr. Park, a one time newspaper reporter, took the same stance. Both men believed that writing was best learned by a newspaper apprenticeship. I did not get the equivalent of a reporter's training from Dr. Park, but what I did get was an apprenticeship in sociological research undoubtedly very similar in kind to that of many of his other students. Although our relation was that of employer and employee, he proceeded to educate me gratis.[20]

* **4** *

Above and beyond her leftist sympathies and appreciation for Chicago-style sociology, little evidence remains about the character of Raushenbush's thought in these early years. Entries in her diary show that she was much concerned, as her father had been, with the relationship between religion and socialism. But where he had seen redistribution as a religious imperative, Raushenbush suggested that religious fantasy and socialist utopianism were of a piece. "Since the birth of Christ," she noted,

---

professor, Herbert Adolphus Miller. My father did not wish me to take it, so I declined. As a consequence of these two episodes I turned to writing." Undated document, WRC. This story makes it sound as thought she might well have gone into academia had the circumstances been different.

19. The document, titled simply "Winifred Raushenbush," is undated. WRC.

20. Undated document, WRC.

"there have been two great outstanding phenomena, religion and social-ism, with which individuals, regardless of race or nationality, have allied themselves.... Primitive man invented heaven.... The socialists have in-vented Utopias, the heaven on earth.... Religion and socialism are both an affirmation of the possible happiness of mankind; they are the great succeeding faiths of European civilization."[21] While these diary entries suggest she was preparing to write a longer paper on the topic, the bulk of her recorded thoughts are of a more personal nature and describe the tribulations she faced in relationships with men.

When research for *The Immigrant Press* was complete, Raushenbush re-turned to Chicago and took a staff position with the Chicago Commission on Race Relations. The Commission was responsible for the publication of *The Negro in Chicago,* a book that examined the race riots that plagued the city during World War I. Her exact contribution to the volume is un-known, but she maintained an interest in race riots throughout her life. In 1921 she returned to New York and began working as a researcher on various projects, including one on community tensions in Hell's Kitchen and another in which she and several other researchers were asked by the Institute for Social and Religious Research, an organization funded by John D. Rockefeller, to rewrite a book on churches in St. Louis. The project continued through 1923, at which time she again went to work for Park on his Pacific Coast study, financed by the same organization.

Because it is impossible to know how much of *The Immigrant Press* might have been written by Raushenbush—Park acknowledges her "in-valuable" assistance[22]—her participation in the Survey of Race Relations, which resulted in the publication of two of her articles for the 1926 vol-ume of *Survey Graphic,* where the entire team's findings were compiled,[23] provides the earliest evidence of her own sociological thought. As Henry Yu tells the story in *Thinking Orientals,*[24] the Survey was first conceived by social gospel missionaries concerned about "anti-Asian agitation" on the Pacific Coast and who wished to gather data on the assimilability—and potential for conversion to Christianity—of the region's growing Asian population. Park was selected as research director and put his own stamp

21. Diary entry, February 1919, WRC.

22. On this point in particular—though his influence can be felt throughout the chap-ter—I thank Anthony Smith for his excellent research assistance.

23. These included an article by Emory Bogardus on "social distance" and an essay by Park titled "Our Racial Frontier on the Pacific."

24. Henry Yu, 2001, *Thinking Orientals: Migration, Contact, and Exoticism in Modern Amer-ica,* New York: Oxford University Press, 21.

on the project. Raushenbush was hired as a member of the research team in 1923 at $60 per week.[25] She traveled throughout the region conducting interviews.

Her articles for *Survey Graphic* were based on research she had done in California's Central Valley, as well as in San Francisco and Vancouver. Park's theorization of a race-relations cycle was linked to an ecological view of group interaction that put the emphasis on processes of competition and cooperation arising by necessity in spatial environments with finite resources. Evidencing her intellectual debt to Park, one of Raushenbush's articles, "Their Place in the Sun: Japanese Farmers Nine Years after the Land Laws," mobilized just such a perspective to examine patterns of interaction between whites and first- and second-generation Japanese immigrants in two rural California towns. In one town relations were strained: the Japanese had come to outnumber whites, and their predominance allowed them to erect their own autonomous social institutions such as schools, churches, and business and voluntary associations. Internal dissension among the Japanese, centered on religious and caste differences, had also lessened the community's ability to interact with whites in a coordinated fashion. As a result, while "the Americans and the Japanese have by this time lived together ... for thirty-two years ... these two racial groups have shared no common enterprise and during the last six years their contacts, instead of increasing, have become even more restricted than before."[26] Social distance, combined with Japanese monopolization of the town's limited farmland resources, led to racial strain, and the town had recently become a hotbed for anti-Japanese agitation.

In the second town, by contrast, race relations were much better. Whites didn't want more Japanese moving in, but they weren't particularly hostile to those that lived there already. Raushenbush attributed this to four things: first, the fact that the Japanese remained a small minority, forcing them into regular contact with whites; second, the relative fertility of the soil, which meant that, for both white and Japanese farmers, life was less hardscrabble than in the first town, funding more neighborly goodwill; third, that here "the Japanese have not made themselves offensive by being different: they do not have their women work in the fields, the men wear made-to-order tailored clothes and instead of flaunting the dome of a Buddhist temple against the California sky, the

25. Galen Fisher to Winifred Raushenbush, July 3, 1923, WRC.

26. Winifred Raushenbush, 1926, "Their Place in the Sun: Japanese Farmers Nine Years after the Land Laws," *Survey Graphic*, May, 141–45 and 203, 142.

community is almost solidly Christian"; and finally, the fact that Japanese community leaders had exercised "intelligence" in lending their support to town projects and causes that would benefit all residents.[27] In the second town, in short, the race-relations cycle had been allowed to play itself out, as evidenced by the growing number of young Japanese Americans who, though destined to remain "hybrids who must all their lives carry the burden of being Americans by birth and Japanese by blood,"[28] were showing signs of assimilation: mastering English, aspiring to go to college and enter the world of mainstream business, and even, in the case of one woman profiled, entertaining the thought of marrying a white man. Beyond invoking Park's theoretical framework, the article also employed the case study approach typical of Chicago school investigations, relying on numerous sources of data, including newspaper reports, interviews, and historical materials. Raushenbush's other piece in the volume also mobilized Park's ideas, comparing and contrasting San Francisco's Chinatown to that of Vancouver and showing how both had become ethnic ghettos that, while emerging for understandable reasons like prejudice, nevertheless stood as barriers against the full assimilation of the Chinese into American society.[29]

* 5 *

When the Survey drew to a close, Raushenbush returned to New York, this time with Rorty in tow.[30] Although both had, at this point, long since declared their allegiance to the left, James Rorty's radicalization in the late 1920s and early 1930s occurred not in isolation but in tandem with that of his wife, who, in the same document where she expressed her debt to Park, described herself as "a pacifist and a socialist.... Of the external events of my life time which have affected me most, I would rank the Sacco Vanzetti case first, the war, second, and the planlessness of America during the present depression, third."[31] Raushenbush's radicalization involved neither a newfound commitment to socialism—a position on which she had practically been reared—nor serious movement into the fold of the

27. Ibid., 144.   28. Ibid., 144.

29. Winifred Raushenbush, 1926, "The Great Wall of Chinatown: How the Chinese Mind Their Own Business behind It," *Survey Graphic*, May, 154–58 and 221.

30. Rorty and Raushenbush met in San Francisco, but the circumstances of their meeting are unknown.

31. Undated document, WRC.

Communist Party but rather a growing interest in producing radical social criticism that might lead people to demand reform of a capitalist system in crisis. This interest put her in some tension with her Chicago school training. She did not doubt the value of Park's approach so far as it went. As a book reviewer for the *New York Herald Tribune*, the *Nation*, and other publications, she continued to extol the virtues of Chicago sociology.[32] But Raushenbush, like Rorty, was growing impatient with academic social scientists—sociologists included—and accused them of too often retreating into professionalism and specialization rather than using their knowledge for the purpose of social transformation. She observed in 1931, for instance, that "the academician—that is, the social scientist—dodges the very simple preliminary task of the thinker—that of counting up all the factors in the situation on the fingers of his two hands. . . . He confines himself to the mole hill of his speciality or a field of mole-hills, and ignores the mole hills in adjoining acres. Ask him to consider any situation in its totality, as a good physician, for instance, must, and he hides modestly behind his coat lapel and declares that you are asking too much."[33] In a similar vein, she panned Paul Cressey's classic *The Taxi-Dance Hall* in a 1932 review on the grounds that "it was his function, as a social scientist, to orient . . . social workers"—who might intervene in the lives of the women and men there portrayed—"in relation to the contemporary world, the world of 1932," a task that he had "quite signally . . . failed to do."[34]

Raushenbush's efforts to bring together in a more satisfactory way Chicago sociology and radical criticism were on display in a 1931 essay on women's fashion. The placement of the piece, in a book that included a selection by Margaret Mead, was a testament to the social connections she and her husband had forged to figures in New York intellectual circles. One of the book's editors, V. F. Calverton, was the founder of the *Modern Quarterly*, a radical magazine started in the early 1920s whose "most frequent contributors by the end of the decade were confirmed Marxists like Max Eastman and Sidney Hook"[35] and which, alongside the

32. For example, Winifred Raushenbush, 1929, "Main Street Is Dying," *Nation*, March 6, 128:290; Winifred Raushenbush, 1929, "An All-American Annual," *Nation*, March 13, 128:323–24.

33. Winifred Raushenbush, 1931, "Labor Analysis and Research," *New York Herald Tribune*, October 4, Section XI:15.

34. Winifred Raushenbush, 1932, "Automat for the Lonely," *New York Herald Tribune*, July 24, Section X:7.

35. Pells, *Radical Visions and American Dreams*, 14.

New Masses, represented a key venue for literary radicalism.[36] Although Raushenbush's conception of the fashion cycle owed something to Park's interest in social processes—Simmel, by whom Park was influenced, had also been interested in fashion—her treatment of the topic remained eclectic, bringing together what can only be described as a feminist sensibility with a Veblenesque concern for status markers.[37] "One learns about a civilization by studying its gods," she opened the essay by declaring. "Without question the god of our American acquisitive civilization is Things."[38] For women, fashion is the primary outlet for such acquisitive tendencies. This in itself would be enough to warrant its condemnation on the grounds that a culture that worships things is "empty at the core."[39] But hers was not to be merely a critique of fashion's excessive materialism: at the core of her argument lay the more far-reaching claim that much of social life involves contestation over status. Fashion is wrapped up with such contestation not simply in the sense that through it people attempt to materially embody their class positions. No less sinister, from the point of view of women's collective interests, fashion is a vehicle through which women compete with one another as part of the process of trying to win over and keep desirable husbands. There is no little irony in this, Raushenbush pointed out, as most men are oblivious to the fashion choices of their mates. Nevertheless, the fit between the needs of women for status differentiation and the logic of the fashion cycle, which emphasized the "timeliness" of particular styles, worked to the advantage of the fashion industry. Citing the estimates of "New York fashion analysts," Raushenbush noted that, three years into the Depression, the average American family living above a "comfortable" income level was still spending anywhere between $600 and $2,400 each year on clothing, a fact she regarded as shameful.[40]

Raushenbush's eclecticism in the essay was not insignificant. It reflected tensions in her politics and thought. On the one hand, try as she might to denounce the entire apparatus of American consumer capitalism,

---

36. Jumonville, *Critical Crossings,* 6.

37. Veblen wrote on fashion himself. For discussion of sociological work on fashion in general, see Diana Crane, 2001, *Fashion and Its Social Agendas: Class, Gender, and Identity in Clothing,* Chicago: University of Chicago Press.

38. Winifred Raushenbush, 1931, "The Idiot God Fashion," pp. 424–46 in *Woman's Coming of Age: A Symposium,* Samuel Schmalhausen and V. F. Calverton, eds., New York: Horace Liveright, 424.

39. Ibid., 445.   40. Ibid., 436–37.

there was something unconvincing in her presentation. Implicit in the essay, and explicit in a number of other articles she wrote on fashion for women's magazines, was the sense that Raushenbush was an admirer of the aesthetic aspects of fashion, however critical she might have been of the institution. On the other hand, she evidenced great reluctance to espouse a strictly Marxian view, which would have reduced fashion to pure surplus value. This reluctance stemmed in part from a long-standing skepticism toward utopianism of any kind. Indeed, her radicalism involved no illusions that a revolution in the United States was imminent; the most that could be hoped for was gradual social improvement. In a review of Jane Addams's *The Second Twenty Years at Hull House,* for instance, she praised the tempering of Addams's utopian vision that had occurred in the years after World War I. Addams's "eventual philosophy," she noted, "is that social change occurs slowly.... Students of culture diffusion would probably corroborate her findings."[41] Much later, she would likewise describe the "personal point of view" that informed the draft of the novel she was working on during the Cold War as premised on the belief that "human society is not infinitely perfectible."[42] It was not utopian dreaming to which she objected so much as her sense that utopians consistently overestimated their capacity to impose their preferred political and social systems on societies whose cultures would be resistant. This was particularly true of utopians in the United States. Striking a chord that would later be important to her son, she said in a letter to her husband,

> the itch I feel in many Americans I talk to that they wish America could live up to this role they were taught as children to believe she had, as an initiator, an inventor. If the American transition could be made on quite different terms than communist or fascist overthrow Americans would be so pleased ... I am sure that the best revolutionary brains, Lenin etc. recognized that one must work with the national temperament and to work with it, must understand it. Not necessarily value it, but know it is an artist knows his wood or clay. What else is the artist's material? My picture of the N.Y. radicals is that they talk always about their tools, not sufficiently about their materials.[43]

41. Undated manuscript, WRC.
42. See her fiction diary from the fall of 1965, WRC.
43. Winifred Raushenbush to James Rorty, December 11, 1934, JRC.

It was to overcome this lacuna that she encouraged James Rorty to explore the nation's "temperament" in *Where Life Is Better*. She wrote to her husband with advice for the book: "To ring the bell, you will have to according to me … answer those vague but important questions that are in the minds of almost every American. What is going to happen? Do we have to copy Europe? What is American? What can we cherish and nourish ourselves on? … Or excellent and beyond price, say what America is to you, your history, your struggle with your conception of it, your feeling for it, if you have had a history and a feeling. I have."[44]

* 6 *

Given her son's birth in 1931 and the fact that James Rorty often found himself out of town on writing assignments, Raushenbush's written output declined in the 1930s, though she continued to review books, publish occasional articles, and provide research support for her husband. Later, while she was working on her novel, she would chafe at the role of housewife, but in the 1930s she was more ambivalent about it, at one point begging her husband to remove himself from concern over management of the household finances on the grounds that she was more than capable of taking on that as well as other responsibilities. In a letter from 1934, written while Rorty was on the road researching *Where Life Is Better,* she pleaded, "If you'll let me manage it, you'll save yourself trouble. If you could learn just one trick, Honey, and that is to yield yourself, at a certain point or for a certain time, to another person. To be the passive receptive person, getting nourishment. I could take a lot off your hands, if you could learn that trick."[45] From the vantage point of the present, what stands out from the letter is that Raushenbush's criticism of Rorty's gender conventionalism was not made to justify her release from domestic obligations but to demand a ratcheting up of them. Some of this, no doubt, was born of Rorty's precarious health at the time of his trip and of her desire to lighten his load. Some may have come in response to Raushenbush's diminished capacity after her son's birth—the birth was difficult for her and required a long recovery—and her sense that while she had been left to care for Richard, there was more she could be doing. But at least some of the impetus appears to have originated in her view that, while women are perfectly capable of functioning outside the private sphere and should be

44. Winifred Raushenbush to James Rorty, undated, JRC.

45. Winifred Raushenbush to James Rorty, December 12, 1934, WRC.

given space to do so, inherent differences between the sexes necessitate that women and men play different roles in relationships. In a letter to her husband—the year is not recorded, though the book to which she refers was published in 1932—she described her reaction upon reading the autobiography of Mary Austin. "Some aspects of middle western American life she states in a way no one else has," Raushenbush reported, "because to other people they are obvious and to her important folkways. She adds to the Middletown picture very much in a few of her observations. The American Olive Schreiner. A feminist is generally a woman badly treated by a man. Her writing about men supplies a corrective to my generation. We thot men and women more alike than they are. Her generation thot them more different. I have demanded things of you I should'nt have, because I thought them more alike than they are. I have a feeling that soon I shall come thru to some truth of my own about the best possible relation between the two."[46] In fact, far from chastising Rorty for off-loading household responsibilities onto her, when she expressed dissatisfaction with their relationship it was to rebuke him for letting his own workaholic tendencies rub off on her.[47]

It was not only in regard to her feminism, however, that Raushenbush's radicalism—nondoctrinaire though it was from the beginning—began to moderate as the 1930s wore on. Within a decade of her son's birth she returned to her desk, publishing in 1942 her first solo-authored book, *How to Dress in Wartime*. Where at least some of her previous work on fashion put social criticism front and center, *How to Dress in Wartime*, written for a mass audience, did not. It was an advice book. Just because American women can "expect severe privation before the war is over," "this does not mean that you must become dowdy.... There is neither virtue nor patriotism in dowdiness, in or out of uniform."[48] The line was not meant to be ironic. In chapter after chapter, the book explained that being a responsible consumer of clothes during the war entailed dressing not like a sack of potatoes but as fashionably as possible given fabric shortages. This was important because if women have "individual, colorful, and amusing

46. Winifred Raushenbush to James Rorty, November 21 (no year), JRC.

47. In a 1934 letter to James, Winifred noted that "your driving yourself so hard has had its bad effect on both of us. Because you tried to drive me hard too, and threw me quite out of my natural way of going at things." Winifred Raushenbush to James Rorty, December 7, 1934, JRC.

48. Winifred Raushenbush, 1942, *How to Dress in Wartime*, New York: Coward-McCann, xi.

accessories" and clothes, their "appearance will be morale-building for [themselves] and others."[49]

That the book was a fashion advice manual did not mean it was completely apolitical. Its references to the morale-building function of fashion indicated Raushenbush's support for the war effort, despite her earlier professions of pacifism. Even more striking was the sense—not evident in her earlier work—that one of the great things about American civilization was that it permitted freedom of individual expression in all matters, including one's choice of outfit, while simultaneously minimizing expressions of class difference. The effort to resist unappealing forms of standardization in clothing was thus also patriotic in that it would help the country stay true to its founding ideals. "If American life, not just in the past but in the present and future, has values that are so soundly conceived that they can sustain us and perhaps the world," she observed, "these values are going to be reflected in our clothes, for clothes are at once a mirror and a language. Have we, for instance, any right to our claim that we are a democratic country?" "Our clothes say yes," she continued. "Never before in the history of Europe and America have clothes been as democratic as they were in the United States during the last twenty years. Everybody wore the same cut of clothes, regardless of how these clothes differed in quality of fabric or workmanship."[50] Raushenbush was not suggesting that every American should dress alike—quite the opposite. But that middle- and upper-class women had equal access to similar styles, though not to the same brands or fabrics, could, in her view, go so far as to serve as one more indication that "the moral axis of the world no longer lies in Europe … [but] seems to rest here."[51] The distance between this assessment of America's moral worth and the one staked out in her 1931 essay on fashion could not have been greater and suggests that Raushenbush, like her husband, moved in the direction of a leftist patriotism over the course of the 1930s and early 1940s.

* 7 *

That Raushenbush's radicalism was softening only served to heighten her political involvement. Around the same time that *How to Dress in Wartime* came out she could be found involved in a variety of activist organizations linked to the nascent civil rights movement. In 1945, for example, she served "as secretary of both the Committee to Save Colored Locomotive Firemen's Jobs and the Committee Against Race Discrimination of

49. Ibid., 101.   50. Ibid., 158–59.   51. Ibid., 158.

The American Civil Liberties Union," while also serving on the board of an organization pressing for passage of legislation making permanent the Fair Employment Practices Committee established by Roosevelt. In these capacities she turned her talents as a writer and social thinker to pamphleteering. The first of her pamphlets, published in 1943, the same year her husband published his pamphlet "Brother Jim Crow," testifies to her long-standing interest in questions of race. Published by the ACLU and costing ten cents, the pamphlet's basic argument, laid out in a brisk fifteen pages, was that sociological research had identified the causes of race riots in the United States and that on the basis of this knowledge steps could be taken to prevent such riots during wartime. The pamphlet drew on a series of four articles she had written for the *New York Post* on the Detroit race riots of 1943. Citing not simply *The Negro in Chicago,* which Raushenbush called "probably the most scholarly, impartial, complete account of a race riot in existence,"[52] but also the work of Charles S. Johnson, another Park student, author of the pioneering study *Patterns of Negro Segregation,* and the man who would secure a post for Park at Fisk University after his retirement from the University of Chicago, Raushenbush pointed to a variety of social situations in which racial unrest was likely given the influx of African Americans into the military. On the basis of this theory, Raushenbush identified twenty-three American cities where "the racial tensions of World War II are acute."[53] She did not think, however, that the sociologist should stop at the identification of mechanisms leading to undesirable outcomes. Instead, she offered a series of straightforward steps citizens could take to help prevent race riots in their communities. These ran the gamut from working to ensure that local police forces and state National Guard units have enough personnel on hand; to making sure that young people, black and white, have satisfactory employment opportunities; to getting clergymen involved in diffusing racial tensions. Lending coherence to these recommendations were two assumptions: first, that such steps should be taken by citizen activists working together under the rubric of local public relations committees, acting in concert with politicians and policy makers but bearing the ultimate responsibility for bringing about the necessary changes; and second, that the root cause of racial unrest was "the too great disparity between our wartime professions of democracy and the actual facts of Negro life in the United

52. Winifred Raushenbush, 1943, "How to Prevent a Race Riot in Your Home Town," New York: American Civil Liberties Union, 12.

53. Ibid., 3.

States," a situation Raushenbush saw as exacerbated by "the overcrowd-ing and underservicing of wartime production centers."[54] Although her husband had, over the course of his career, advocated a great many social reforms as well, here was a difference between them: Raushenbush insist-ed that such change be effected from the bottom up, not simply through the banding together of writers and intellectuals to bring attention to an issue, as had been James Rorty's preferred strategy, but through the com-ing together of ordinary citizens guided by the dictates of conscience and social-scientific knowledge.

A similar political project was at work in "Jobs without Creed or Color," published in 1945 by the Workers Defense League. Where the pamphlet two years earlier noted the divergence between the situation faced by African Americans and America's professed wartime ideals of de-mocracy, Raushenbush could now frame her calls for ending employment discrimination by comparing it to the evils of the recently vanquished Nazism. "With victory over Nazism won," she began, "this country is today struggling with a new surge of power not unworthy of its great libertarian tradition, to rid its own house of the menace and the mean-ness of racism."[55] Here was precisely the sort of rhetorical framing Richard Rorty had in mind when, many years later, he insisted that his parents, like many of those in their social circle, had no "doubt that America was a great, noble, progressive country in which justice would eventually tri-umph. By 'justice' they all meant pretty much the same thing—decent wages and working conditions, and the end of racial prejudice."[56] Indeed, Raushenbush claimed that prejudice was unpatriotic, noting that African American railroad firemen who had protested efforts by Southern whites to bar them from employment had given "the only answer any self-re-specting human being and any liberty-loving American can make to the threat of annihilation."[57] In her view, however, the situation was not hope-less. Roosevelt had been forced to issue an executive order banning job discrimination under pressure from black strikers in 1941, whose march on Washington would have proved embarrassing to a nation rallying to fight German racism. While insufficient to solve the problem, the order had created the Fair Employment Practices Committee, and she urged her readers to write their congressmen and express their support for mak-

54. Ibid., 6.

55. Winifred Raushenbush, 1945, "Jobs without Creed or Color," New York: Worker Defense League, 5.

56. Rorty, *Achieving Our Country*, 59

57. Raushenbush, *Jobs without Creed or Color*, 7.

ing it a permanent federal agency. Beyond that, she encouraged people to volunteer in their hometowns, either as representatives for the FEPC or as liaisons who could teach those bearing the brunt of discrimination to file complaints with the agency.

* 8 *

Raushenbush published several additional pieces over the course of the 1950s, including a rare coauthored piece with her husband—rare in the sense that she shared the byline with him rather than working behind the scenes. The essay, appearing in *Commentary,* examined the conditions leading up to what was widely viewed as an anti-Jewish riot in Peekskill, New York.[58] Visiting the scene of the incident and interviewing community residents, Raushenbush and Rorty concluded that its cause wasn't anti-Semitism per se but the irresponsible actions of the Communist Party, which had a considerable presence in the town and generated tensions in the community that were displaced onto Jews. Despite its condemnations of the Party, there was little else in the essay to indicate that Raushenbush had become as virulent an anti-Communist as her husband.

But the piece was not the only indication of her anti-Communist leanings. Also important in this regard, and indicative of her deep concern with questions raised by the Cold War, was the novel she struggled with in the 1950s and 1960s. Her papers contain thousands of pages of manuscript drafts and fiction notes, reflecting her inability to settle on a single theme. At one point the title was to be "Nina and Stalin," at another the much less promising "Out of What Womb This Ice?" The book was intended as a work of political science fiction. In a letter she wrote seeking support from the Huntington Hartford Foundation in Pacific Palisades, California, she temporarily fixed the moving target and claimed that "the underlying theme of this novel is whether man can escape his technology and specifically how he can get out of the nuclear trap, a question [to which] as most honest men agree there is at present no clear answer. One of the major themes of the novel is the nature and changing character of American Russian relations."[59] Drafts of the book painted a brutal picture of Stalin and explored the possibility of détente now that the regime had changed. It never reached completion.

58. James Rorty and Winifred Raushenbush, 1950, "The Lessons of the Peekskill Riots," *Commentary*, October, 309–23.

59. Fiction diary, February, 16, 1963, WRC.

She still had a book in her, though—a biography of Park she was commissioned to write for the University of Chicago Press. Park had spoken highly of Raushenbush. In a letter written in 1940 and reproduced in a two-page document she wrote titled "What Park Said about Me," he recalled that "of all the persons I have worked with and loafed with, you have been the most congenial companion, the best pal. No, I should qualify that statement. There were two others. One was Tom Lacey, whom you never knew, and the other was W. I. Thomas, whom you did. But you were a grand loafer, so absolutely superior intellectually, so thoroughly undisciplined and spirited … but so alive to anything anywhere good or bad—that was humanly interesting."[60] It is not obvious that closeness to one's subject and good biography go hand in hand, but such appears to have been the thinking of the Chicago editors and of Park's former students, many of whom sent Raushenbush their recollections and anecdotes about Park, which the book compiled. Interestingly, Raushenbush did not see the biography as disconnected from her broader political agenda. Beyond the view that sociology should guide social reform, she now took the position that what was to be most appreciated about Park was his ecological perspective, a framework for understanding the natural and social worlds that could serve as a powerful antidote to Communism. In a speech she wrote for her husband, she credited Park with having done "the only pioneer[ing] work in human ecology" and went so far as to assert that only by building up from Park's contributions and accepting "survival … as the basic foundation for all thinking about the future" could the West hope to win its historic struggle. "There is one tool that we lack in our competitive struggle with the Communist world," she had him say. "That is an ideology as apparently clear and comprehensible as Marxism, combined with a blue print of the future that the West intends to create.… The ideology of the next decades, when the historic moment for its emergence arrives, will probably be built around the concept of human ecology."[61]

The biography, written late in her life and without the benefit of any intellectual-historical training, was not her best work. It recounted the basic facts of Park's life and career well enough but was so hagiographic in tone that it eschewed not only critical engagement with his ideas but also the task of developing and sustaining an original interpretive thesis. What the anonymous reviewer for the University of Chicago Press

60. Undated document, WRC.

61. Winifred Raushenbush, "A Note on Human Ecology," undated document, WRC. A handwritten note on the two-page document reads "Written for speech by JR."

said about one of the chapters—that it contained "many tantalizing bits without the meal to follow"[62]—was the story of the book as a whole. The review suggested major revisions. Raushenbush, apparently disinclined to accept the advice, sent the manuscript to Duke University Press, which agreed to publish it. It is an indication that her greatest intellectual debt was to Park—and not to the classical American pragmatist philosophers who would be so important to her son—that she also failed to follow through on one of the Chicago reviewer's most specific suggestions. "I don't learn anything from this biography about the intellectual influence of Dewey, James, and Mead on Park," the reviewer noted. "For one who has read Dewey on the public and public opinion, and his conception of human nature, it is easy to see some common concerns and perspectives. But these are not developed in the book. William James is mentioned with awe, but his ideas are not touched." Neither would they be in the final version of the manuscript. Duke published the book in 1979, and just in time: Raushenbush died later that year.

---

62. Anonymous review sent to Marlie Wasserman, Associate Editor, University of Chicago Press, August 3, 1974, WRC.

THREE

The Hutchins College

* 1 *

When Robert Maynard Hutchins assumed the presidency of the University of Chicago in 1929, nearly two decades before Richard Rorty would commence his college education there, he inherited an institution that had become synonymous with the research focus of the modern American university. Founded some thirty-seven years earlier with money from John D. Rockefeller, Chicago embraced both the research mission and the organizational template that Daniel Coit Gilman had copied from leading German universities such as those at Berlin and Göttingen in building Johns Hopkins. Under the leadership of its first president, William Rainey Harper, Chicago attracted an illustrious faculty, drawn by the chance to take part in the heady intellectual conversations that came to define everyday life in Hyde Park, by the high salaries Harper was able to offer, and by the vitality of life in Chicago during a period of rapid urbanization and social change—a vitality around which the university, despite its sequestration on the South Side, aimed to orient its research. It was in this context that John Dewey and George Herbert Mead were lured to Chicago from Michigan and that Dewey's brand of pragmatism, geared toward a reconstruction of intellectual practice in light of a changing social and political environment, gained popularity outside the philosophy department, becoming a "common frame of reference . . . that made it possible for discoveries in one field to be significant for inquiries in another field."[1] Chicago also acquired an excellent reputation among students, at

---

1. Darnell Rucker, 1969, *The Chicago Pragmatists*, Minneapolis: University of Minnesota Press, 162.

both the graduate and undergraduate level, in no small part because it offered them contact with some of the nation's leading intellectuals and scientists.

As Chicago's research focus became entrenched, however, more of undergraduate education came to be offered through specialized departmental majors, as was the case at other American research universities as well. In the first two decades of the twentieth century, a national backlash movement against this trend developed.[2] While champions of academic professionalization insisted that only training in specialized majors could prepare undergraduates for the complexity of the modern world, a number of advocates called for the reestablishment of a classical curriculum. The justification offered was that students were being deprived, under the new system, of a common conceptual vocabulary and frame of cultural reference. Linked to this argument was another. Advocates of specialization sometimes invoked Dewey, who had argued that the American educational system—particularly the primary school system—should be restructured along experiential lines so as to teach students skills and techniques for thinking. Did not the skills and techniques of the various sciences count as among those it would be useful to impart to the educated elite? And, given the rapid development of the sciences, was not a specialized education necessary to achieve this end? Against this view, at least some in the emerging general education movement held that what ought to be taught were timeless truths and moral virtues and that these were encapsulated in the great books that composed the classical canon. These texts should be returned to their central and rightful place in the college curriculum, it was argued. As Daniel Bell noted,[3] larger social forces underlay the rise of this movement. The demand for general education coincided with calls for Americanization of the nation's immigrant communities. In both cases white, upper-middle-class Protestant culture, which defined itself in part around knowledge of classical arts and letters, was being held up as ideal in the face of challenges to its hegemony. Columbia was the first university to heed these calls in a significant way. In 1920 "generalist" John Erskine began offering a multiple-year honors course in which students read the masterpieces of Western civilization, including a few recent authors, like William James.[4]

2. Anne Stevens, 2001, "The Philosophy of General Education and Its Contradictions: The Influence of Hutchins," *Journal of General Education* 50:165–91.

3. Daniel Bell, 1966, *The Reforming of General Education: The Columbia College Experience in Its National Setting,* New York: Columbia University Press.

4. Stevens, "The Philosophy of General Education," 168. A very different account of the

Hutchins took over the presidency of the University of Chicago during a time of institutional uncertainty: "The University ... looked back on a distinguished history, but was experiencing some uneasiness about its future."[5] Harper had died in 1906, and neither of the two presidents since then had brought much creativity to the post. The Depression loomed on the horizon, the university faced increasing competition from other institutions, such as midwestern state universities, which were solidifying their research focus, and many undergraduates had become "more interested in 'college life' than in intellectual development."[6] A plan was put into place before Hutchins's arrival to shake things up at the undergraduate level by requiring that all students take two years of common survey courses, but this change was insufficiently radical for Hutchins. Hutchins's own undergraduate work had been at Oberlin, and he went on to earn a law degree from Yale before becoming dean of the law school there at the age of twenty-eight. More politician and executive than intellectual, Hutchins relied for advice on intellectual matters on his friend Mortimer Adler, a philosopher who had received his undergraduate education at Columbia under Erskine and with whom Hutchins had collaborated "in a study dealing with the rules of the law of evidence."[7] An advocate of the Great Books approach to education and student of Thomas Aquinas, Adler was an outspoken critic of Dewey, who had moved to Columbia in 1905. He opposed Deweyan pragmatism because he was in favor of all that it denied: "the denial of metaphysics and theology as independent of empirical science, the denial of stability in the universe and certainty in human knowledge, the denial of moral values transcending adaptation to environment and escaping relativity to time and place, the denial of intellectual discipline in education and of the light shed by an abiding tradition of learning, the denial of a personal God, self-revealed, and of a Divine Providence concerned with man's supernatural salvation."[8] Under Adler's influence, Hutchins developed a plan not only to establish

---

social factors behind the general education movement is given in Donald Levine, 2006, *Powers of the Mind: The Reinvention of Liberal Learning in America*, Chicago: University of Chicago Press.

5. Hugh Hawkins, 1992, "The Higher Learning at Chicago," *Reviews in American History* 20:378–85, 379.

6. Ibid., 379.

7. Gary Cook, 1993, *George Herbert Mead: The Making of a Social Pragmatist*, Urbana: University of Illinois Press, 184.

8. Mortimer Adler, 1941, "The Chicago School," *Harper's*, September, 377–88, 382.

a classical curriculum at Chicago but also to transform the philosophy department there so as to lessen pragmatism's influence in the university.[9] The changes Hutchins was able to make in the composition of the philosophy faculty will be considered later, but most important for present purposes are the curricular changes he instituted. Within a decade students would be able to enter the university after their sophomore year of high school—Hutchins's view was that gifted students were ready for college-level work earlier than the American education system allowed for[10]—and take "four years of general education, consisting almost entirely of required courses and allowing no major or field of concentration."[11] Courses in the so-called Hutchins College were "developed and taught by an autonomous faculty of the University.... The principal materials employed in the College were original works or selections therefrom ('Great Snippets'), rather than textbooks, and the principal method of teaching was by discussion of these materials in preparation for examinations not set by the instructor."[12] These were comprehensive exams that covered all a student was expected to know about a subject. As was true of Erskine's honors courses, the college's curriculum did not neglect modern contributions to knowledge. It involved "prescribed courses in three areas: the social sciences, the humanities, and the natural sciences"; in each area students would take "a sequence of three related one-year courses,"[13] along with classes in English, mathematics, history, Western civilization, and a foreign language, followed by a capstone course called Observation, Interpretation, and Integration (OII). In the social and natural sciences, in particular, "most of the texts were modern in date."[14] Students in search of greater specialization were then "encouraged to stay on and complete a Master's degree in their field of choice."[15]

9. In his revisionist account of the general education movement, Levine argues that Hutchins and Dewey shared more common ground than is usually acknowledged. It is certainly true that Hutchins was no opponent of experimentalism in general.

10. Robert Hutchins, 1933, "The American Educational System," *School Review* 41:95–100.

11. Hawkins, "The Higher Learning at Chicago," 381.

12. F. Champion Ward, no date, "Principles and Particulars in Liberal Education," RRP, 4–5.

13. Manuel Bilsky, 1954, "Liberal Education as 'Philosophy,'" *Journal of Higher Education* 25:191–96 and 226–227, 192–93.

14. Ward, "Principles and Particulars," 5.

15. Stevens, "The Philosophy of General Education," 170.

* 2 *

The idea of the Hutchins College appealed to James Rorty and Winifred Raushenbush. Richard was an intellectually precocious child who was insufficiently challenged in school and sending him off to Chicago at the age of fifteen would be a way to give him a head start in his education. In contemplating such a move, James and Winifred must have struggled with their close attachment to Richard and their fear that fifteen was too young an age for a book-smart child to live alone. From the beginning, Winifred's philosophy of child rearing had been to treat Richard as a young adult with great potential: "I have no desire to wish or think Bucko anything more than he will prove to be ... but I have been struck in reading Lincoln to find that a superior child like Bucko has somewhat similar traits. Lincoln also had a keen memory, he was also notably friendly, he was also a man as well as a child. I shall continue to treat Bucko both as a child and as a man. First because I get better results. Second because I think he rates it. He thinks of himself that way. So did I, as far back as I can remember."[16] The affections she and her husband lavished on their son were repaid in kind. When James was on the road, researching *Where Life Is Better,* the title of which he borrowed from an earlier tract he'd written about California, Winifred's letters begging him to return home were matched in their poignancy only by a crayoned book cover scribbled by Richard, then five years old: "New York: Where Life is Better."[17]

As is often the case for children of parents with high levels of cultural capital, many of Richard's childhood activities involved youthful forays into the worlds of cultural and intellectual production. When he was six, Richard wrote a play about the coronation of Edward, Prince of Wales, which he performed for an audience of his parents and their friends.[18] At seven, he wrote to the Harvard College Observatory expressing his desire to become an astronomer and asking whether it was a problem that he was not currently studying the subject in school.[19] As a twelve-year-old he delivered a speech during commencement exercises for the Walpack Township School in New Jersey commemorating the life and accomplishments of the songwriter Stephen Foster,[20] and the following academic

---

16. Winifred Raushenbush to James Rorty, November 8, 1934, JRC.

17. Book cover, 1936, RRP.   18. Rorty, "It Has Happened Here."

19. See "Jeannie" to Richard Rorty, May 12, 1938, JRC.

20. Commencement program, Walpack Township School, June 11, 1943, RRP.

year he began editing the school's student newspaper, the *Minisink Valley News.*

As noted in chapter 1, Richard attended the Berkeley Institute, a private school in Brooklyn, for much of the time he and his parents lived in New York City. For this he had been granted a scholarship. Despite his parents' most-of-the-year residency in rural New Jersey beginning in the late 1930s, attempts were made, no doubt with the furtherance of his education in mind, to secure scholarships for him at other private New York City schools in the early 1940s.[21] These appear not to have panned out, which explains not only why he remained enrolled in rural schools but also why, when he accompanied his parents on long trips to New York during his middle schools years, he temporarily enrolled in public school there. Although his extracurricular experiences in New York were memorable—he recalls in his autobiographical essay "Trotsky and the Wild Orchids" how he worked one summer when he was twelve ferrying documents back and forth between his parents' offices at the Workers Defense League and the offices of the Brotherhood of Sleeping Car Porters—at the time he preferred the educational experience offered by the Walpack schools, making this the subject of his editorial in a 1943 edition of the student paper: "though we have but thirteen pupils and the city school has more than thirteen hundred, the excessive number of students can do nothing but count against them.... The lack of numbers is the country schools best gift."[22]

But it was not only on such personal experiences that he wrote. A piece published in January 1944, for example, when he was thirteen, cheered the success of current war efforts and argued that famine relief, particularly in countries like India, should be part of any postwar recovery plan because material deprivation can give rise to fascism, as had happened in Germany.[23] The following month, he expressed his support for farm relief in the United States, which, he said, required an expansion of the total acreage under cultivation as well as the development of new technologies, all with the aim of famine prevention.[24] In an undated edition of the paper, probably written around Christmas time, he observed, invoking themes that would have made Walter Rauschenbusch proud, that "in

21. In a letter dated June 29, 1944, Winifred wrote to the head of the Polytechnical Preparatory Country Day School in Brooklyn asking for a fellowship for Richard: "In the past when Richard has attended private schools, it has been with the help of scholarships since our limited means would not have permitted it otherwise." JRC.

22. *Minisink Valley News*, March 24, 1943, RRP.

23. *Minisink Valley News*, January 31, 1944, RRP.

24. *Minisink Valley News*, February 28, 1944, RRP.

more than one way can this war be compared to that which Jesus fought. Christ might be compared to an underground leader who fought to liberate the oppressed in the Roman-occupied country of Palestine.... His doctrine of liberty for the common man is what the Russians, the French, the Chinese, and we here in America fought for in our respective revolutions."[25] These writings, in both their relative sophistication and subject matter, evidence the influence of Rorty's parents. This was hardly a matter of their high income having allowed Richard to attend the best schools—they struggled financially throughout their lives.[26] Rather, the Rortys passed along to Richard their facility with writing, critical analysis, and political discourse.

Consider his competence with language. In May of 1946, before he had received notification of his admittance to Chicago, Richard, then fourteen, spent a week in Flatbrookville taking care of his parents' house and dealing with their correspondence while his father was in Tennessee working for the Tennessee Valley Authority (TVA) and his mother was in New York City. During that time he came across a letter James had written to Winifred in which James worried how they could afford to send Richard to college. Richard was quick to reply:

> I didn't quite understand your comments on my going to college. I thought that I had done everything in my capacity to do about the college thing. There is no reason in the world why I should not go to work for one or two years at any time. Reasonably, I think I may say that I should prefer not to. I don't think you *prefered* [27] working your way through college. I have tried to keep my marks high in high school and I think that I've done fairly well. I intend to continue doing so.... If you catch me being unrealistic about money, please tell me at once. I'm sure that I have been from time to time but that was because I did not sufficiently understand the state of our finances. I am still fourteen years old and I hope to improve in all these respects through these years.[28]

The writerly control exercised in the passage is remarkable: the sentiment that his father's fears are unfounded is glossed as a failure on the

25. *Minisink Valley News*, no date, RRP.

26. James once told his son that for him and Winifred "money making is not easy." James Rorty to Richard Rorty, June 6, 1950, RRP.

27. Spelling was apparently not Rorty's strong suit.

28. Richard Rorty to James Rorty, May 28, 1946, RRP.

part of his more rational son to "understand" them; the sentences are clean and precise and use pairs of stressed and unstressed words to emphasize the writer's points ("Reasonably, I think I may say that I should prefer not to. I don't think you *prefered* working your way through college."); and the vocabulary and phraseology employed ("I did not sufficiently understand") is certainly not typical for fourteen-year-olds, then or now.

In all likelihood, the passage reflected habits of sophisticated language use that Rorty had picked up from his parents and their social circle. The Rortys were of course writers, and their house was filled with words and usages of language socially defined as being of high symbolic value. Linguistic competence was on display in and encouraged by everything from household conversation to correspondence between family members to the books, manuscripts, and magazines that cluttered the residence. This gave Richard certain advantages, not least because it set up the expectation that he should be an adept user of language as well. While many children perform plays for their parents and friends, few do so before audiences that might well have included, as one of the Rortys' house parties did when Richard was a child, "Allen Tate, his wife Caroline Gordon, Robert Penn Warren and Andrew Lytle."[29] Likewise, few children inhabit a household where sophisticated political discourse is so much the order of the day: where Sidney Hook or A. Philip Randolph might come to dinner, or where John Frank, one of Trotsky's secretaries, stayed for several months in the early 1940s, hiding out from Soviet assassins. Even visits with extended family would have been occasions for Richard to learn how to use language well. When the Rortys went to Madison, Wisconsin, to visit one of Winifred's brothers and his wife, for instance—something Richard continued to do on his own after starting at Chicago—it was not to visit philistines. Paul Raushenbush and Elizabeth Brandeis Raushenbush were economists who had spearheaded the development of Wisconsin's unemployment insurance system; Elizabeth, whose undergraduate work had been done at Radcliffe, was a professor at the University of Wisconsin and daughter of U.S. Supreme Court Justice Louis Brandeis. Nor would Richard have failed to learn high-status ways of using English when he spent time with his uncle Carl Raushenbush, also an economist, or his wife, Esther, a professor of literature at Sarah Lawrence, who, in 1965, would be appointed the sixth president of that

29. Rorty, "It Has Happened Here."

college.[30] Similar examples could be multiplied on both sides of the family. His childhood thus involved constant exposure to settings in which propriety demanded and social approval rested in part on how well one could argue and turn a phrase.

But it was not simply in this way that Richard's linguistic acuity was honed; his parents also engaged in active efforts to teach him how to write well. In a revealing letter that James wrote to his twelve-year-old son in 1943, he expressed concern that he was taking Richard "too much for granted."[31] He asked what he might do to be a better father. "For example, could I help you more than I do to understand the kind of world you're growing up into? By talking more to you? By finding books I think you're ready to read?" All these point to conversations that might have the side effect of teaching Richard how to express himself well, but James's suggestions did not stop there. "The best kind of education ever invented," he continued, "is the apprenticeship system, by which an old workman teaches a young workman the craft. How about my trying to teach you the craft of writing that way?" Not hesitating to sing his own praises, he observed: "I'm supposed to be a good poet and a good prose writer; anthologists reprint my poems and prose, and teachers put quotations from my writings in their textbooks. . . . Maybe Winifred would do the same thing for you with history and anthropology."

Consistent with these efforts, the Rortys began to explore alternatives to Richard's education in rural New Jersey schools. His high school experiences proved to be not as rosy as his middle school ones: he recalls being bored in his classes and bullied on the school yard. James and Winifred wanted him to succeed, but they could not afford to send him to a private school and had become sufficiently wedded to the ideal of rural living that they would not relocate for the sake of his education. So they began to consider sending him to college early. A May 1946 letter from the assistant dean of St. John's College in Annapolis, Maryland, to Winifred shows that she had written to inquire if Richard could enroll there before he finished high school.[32] St. John's had approached Hutchins in 1937 after going bankrupt and asked him to chair their board. He agreed, installed fellow Great Books advocate Scott Buchanan (whom he later brought to Chicago for a short time) as dean, and remade undergraduate education at the school along Erskinesque lines,[33] also allowing—like Chicago—

30. "Educator of Women: Esther Raushenbush," *New York Times*, January 20, 1965, 28.

31. James Rorty to Richard Rorty, September 3, 1943, RRP.

32. W. Kyle Smith to Winifred Raushenbush, May 22, 1946, RRP.

33. Stevens, "The Philosophy of General Education," 172.

gifted students to enroll after their sophomore year of high school. The assistant dean told Winifred that she had written too late to secure enrollment for Richard for the fall and that in any event most of the slots in the entering class were being taken up by veterans, who had pushed the average age of enrollment to twenty-two. The University of Chicago, which Winifred knew intimately and where she remained friends with several professors, including anthropologist Robert Redfield and his wife, Robert Park's daughter, seemed a natural alternative, and the Rortys took advantage of their contacts to get more information about the university's suitability for their son. During one of their absences in 1945, for instance, James wrote to Winifred: "Richard well, ... long letter to Dan Bell about U of Chicago. Doesn't know what he wants to be. Thinks U of Chicago would help him decide. Specific questions. Capable letter."[34] Richard's letter to Bell and Bell's reply are lost, but the response must have been encouraging. In April of 1946, Richard spent a day at Hunter College taking Chicago's entrance exam, recounting to his father that "by the time I had finished the last test, two-thirds of the other students had gone home.... Altogether, they were the most intelligent bunch I've ever been in. Chicago will be very rosy if these are the sort of people who inhabit it."[35] He was admitted for the 1946–47 school year on partial scholarship. That the instruction his father had given him on how to write paid off is evident from another comment Richard made after completing the exam. He found the math portion of the test difficult and was confused by the way the reading comprehension questions were phrased. "Finally," however, "came the test in writing skills," he wrote to his father. "Your criticisms of my past efforts were invaluable here."[36]

∗ 3 ∗

Writerly abilities were not the only thing transmitted from parents to son. Richard also took on elements of James's and Winifred's political and intellectual identity. He has said as much in interviews: "I was just brought up a Trotskyite," he told Joshua Knobe in 1995, "the way people are brought up Methodists or Jews or something like that. It was just the faith of the household."[37] The correspondence he carried out with his

---

34. James Rorty to Winifred Raushenbush, November 30, 1945, WRC.

35. Richard Rorty to James Rorty, April 21, 1946, RRP.

36. Richard Rorty to James Rorty, April 21, 1946, RRP.

37. The interview transcript is available at http://www.unc.edu/~knobe/rorty.html, accessed August 29, 2007.

parents during his first year of college corroborates this autobiographical claim. No sooner had he arrived at Chicago then he asked his father to send him copies of any and all articles of his that were published in "New Leader, H. Events, Commonweal, Harpers, Commentary"—all liberal, anti-Communist organs—"and whatever pieces of yours come out anywhere after I left."[38] In a letter that must have crossed in the mail with the request, James told Richard that he was getting him a subscription to Isaac Don Levine's magazine *Plain Talk,* a militantly anti-Communist broadsheet dedicated to "enlightenment of public opinion on all the insidious influences and deadly dangers threatening civilization from Communist ideology and imperialism."[39] His father told Richard the magazine provided a "good running critique of current politics including communist politics."

During this time, Richard also became involved with the Student Federalist movement, a nationwide group of high school and college students—including many returning veterans—which formed after the war and advocated the creation of a world government sufficiently strong as to prevent future hostilities.[40] It was a popular group on campus. "Just went over to the Student Federalists to count the results of a poll they took," Rorty told his mother. "About 95% of the students here want World Government now and half of those who took the poll said they will join the S.F. It's quite encouraging."[41] Although the Student Federalist movement would, in the coming years, find itself under attack from McCarthyite forces, Richard saw it as the perfect political vehicle for young, liberal anti-Communists like himself. Earlier that month he'd written to his mother that the Student Federalists "seemed the only clear-headed liberal group on the campus. There are ten varieties of Marxists, and they all call the others pseudo-liberals. Some of us are thinking of organizing the official Pseudo-Liberal Club."[42] There's a joking quality to this pas-

38. Richard Rorty, postcard to James Rorty, September 28, 1946, JRC.

39. Isaac Don Levine, 1976, "Introduction," pp. xi–xiv in *Plain Talk: An Anthology from the Leading Anti-Communist Magazine of the 40s,* Isaac Don Levine, ed., New Rochelle: Arlington House, xii.

40. See the discussion in Gilbert Jonas, 2001, *One Shining Moment: A History of the Student Federalist Movement in the United States, 1942–1953,* self-published by iUniverse. Rorty told his parents in 1946 that he had been going to Student Federalist "meetings and lectures pretty regularly." Richard Rorty to parents, November 24, 1946, RRP.

41. Richard Rorty to Winifred Raushenbush, November 12, 1946, RRP.

42. Richard Rorty to Winifred Raushenbush, November 3, 1946, RRP.

sage, but it makes clear what Rorty saw his political identity to be.

He would soon begin taking on identity elements from the Chicago milieu as well. In "Trotsky and the Wild Orchids," Rorty notes that "when I got to Chicago in 1946, I found that Hutchins, together with his friends Mortimer Adler and Richard McKeon, … had enveloped much of the University of Chicago in a neo-Aristotelian mystique. The most frequent target of their sneers was John Dewey's pragmatism…. [The idea of] moral and philosophical absolutes [which they propounded] … sounded pretty good to my 15-year-old ears…. Further, since Dewey was a hero to all the people among whom I had grown up, scorning Dewey was a convenient form of adolescent revolt."[43] Rorty's conversion to the notion of philosophical absolutes—one of the centerpieces of Adler's philosophy—did not happen right away, however. Letters from his first year at Chicago evidence ambivalence and skepticism about the Hutchins program. He wrote to his mother in November of 1946 that "there is a new theory on campus that Dr. Hutchins died three years ago. No one ever sees him and when they do He doesn't look at all like the photographs. We think that the University (Adler) got up a clumsy double to keep the legend going. There is an older, alternative idea that Hutchins never existed anyway and that He was merely a Great Thought in the mind of Adler."[44] The next week, he expressed a similar view when he told his mother that he'd gone

to a talk last night by the Great Book Indexers. This is a bunch of people who sit around for eight hours a day and read the 437 Great Books and make an index of all the sentiments expressed in them. There are topics like "immortality of the soul," "degradation of labor," "consistency of beauty," etc. They have to take all the quotes that everybody from Homer to Freud ever said about anything. It's probably a very interesting job except for the one poor guy who is given St. Thomas Aquinas and nothing else to read. I learned that by five o'clock yesterday, Chicago time, exactly 102 Great Ideas have been thought up by Western Civilization.[45]

And at the end of the 1946–47 school year, when he'd signed up to take the college's required integrative course (OII) for the fall, he joked in

43. Rorty, *Philosophy and Social Hope*, 8–9.
44. Richard Rorty to Winifred Raushenbush, November 3, 1946, RRP.
45. Richard Rorty to Winifred Raushenbush, November 12, 1946, RRP.

a letter to his parents that the course was "soon, I hear, to be renamed Perspicacious Retrospection, Introspection, Induction, Deduction, and Integration."[46]

By the following year, this skepticism receded. Rorty recalls that during the summer following his first year at Chicago, he read Plato intensively in an effort to prepare for his OII course. This reading, along with the course itself, were turning points in the development of his youthful philosophical outlook. It was at this time that he began to move closer to the kind of Platonism he retrospectively associates with this period in his life. In truth, Plato was only one of many philosophers he read that fall for OII. Others included Aristotle, Aquinas, Bacon, Descartes, and John Stuart Mill. But OII was not meant as a philosophy survey course. Its curriculum and approach had been designed by McKeon, whom Hutchins brought to Chicago in 1935 from Columbia. Shortly thereafter he was made dean of the Division of Humanities. The goal of the course—initially called Organizations, Methods, and Principles of Knowledge, or OMP—was not to indoctrinate students into any particular substantive philosophy but to teach them how to approach the diversity of philosophies on offer in the Western tradition. Building on McKeon's metaphilosophy, the course offered students "a schematism, a classificatory means by which [they] may analyze the important differences among philosophers."[47] For McKeon, this schematization rested on the notion that "every [philosophical] argument has a *selection* of materials with which to work, *principles* from which to proceed, a *method* by means of which it can get from premises to conclusions, and an *interpretation* of what the method establishes."[48] McKeon allowed that each of the elements in this fourfold matrix might take one of four values. The task of the student of philosophy was to ascertain which combination of variables, and hence overall profile, a particular philosopher or philosophical system fit most closely and then to use this as a basis for understanding. Thus, although OII covered a great many philosophers from eras past, its treatment of them was noncontextualist. Taught to fit thinkers into a transhistorical classificatory matrix, "Chicago undergraduates learned history as the history of ideas, without the social, economic, and cultural background

46. Richard Rorty to parents, May 18, 1947, RRP.

47. Bilsky, "Liberal Education as 'Philosophy,'" 195.

48. David Depew, 2000, "Between Pragmatism and Realism: Richard McKeon's Philosophical Semantics," pp. 29–53 in *Pluralism in Theory and Practice: Richard McKeon and American Philosophy*, Eugene Garver and Richard Buchanan, eds., Nashville: Vanderbilt University Press, 38.

needed for a richer historicist understanding of the texts."[49] What they were to extract from these texts were timeless truths and insights into the connections between the branches of knowledge, "preparatory to [the student] working out an integration for himself."[50]

No evidence remains of Rorty's precise philosophical views during his sophomore year at Chicago, so it is impossible to know whether, at that point, he had become convinced of the value of McKeon's ideas specifically. Rorty did well in OII—he told his mother that he'd received an A in it, alongside an A in French.[51] But hints that the quest for timeless truths, whether its impetus derived from Plato or some other source, came to take on considerable importance in his thinking can be found in his correspondence. For example, in May of 1948 James Rorty signed a contract with H. A. Morgan, one of the TVA's directors and an entomologist by training, to coauthor a book to be called "A Mooring for Mankind" (the book was never published.) Morgan, an advocate of the grassroots approach to bureaucratic decision making and planning for which the TVA would become famous, was also an environmentalist and subscribed to the view—as James Rorty himself would increasingly—that man and nature are interconnected and that from this interconnection flow certain ethical and political imperatives. This thoroughgoing naturalism, consistent with Dewey's philosophy, now struck the young Rorty as misguided. He told his father:

> I'm not clear, really, as to what Morgan's doctrine is all about. If it is an attempt at an ethical philosophy of any comprehensiveness, it would seem to fail. Precisely because man has no evident guiding principle from nature, he has erected the great superstructure of thought and institution that now alienates him from it. It seems to me that this development was inevitable. Damn it, man is much more than an animal and he can't treat himself in the way that he has treated all the things of nature. To reduce him to the part that he actually plays in the biological scheme seems to me both impossible and valueless.[52]

That Rorty was becoming convinced there were timeless truths about human existence it was the job of the philosopher—not the environmentalist—to discover did not change his political sympathies. He remained

49. Stevens, "The Philosophy of General Education," 182.
50. Bilsky, "Liberal Education as 'Philosophy,'" 226.
51. Richard Rorty to Winifred Raushenbush, April 7, 1948, RRP.
52. Richard Rorty to James Rorty, May 14, 1948, RRP.

steadfastly anti-Communist. In March of 1948 he reported to his mother that he was getting along fine in his new job as a waiter at a campus facility. He was making good money for light work, he said. "It's enough to make a man a Wallaceite," he noted, referring to Henry Wallace, vice president for one of Franklin Roosevelt's terms and candidate for president in 1948 with the backing of the Progressive Party. "Speaking of which, this campus is getting filled with them. The student newspaper is somewhat more Communist than the New Republic and half the people I meet are wearing those damn blue and white Wallace buttons. I would be scared, except that I suppose this is the only place in the country where they're so thick, except maybe in New York."[53] But in an effort to bridge the distance between his Flatbrookeville and Chicago identities, he now insisted that political tracts have sound philosophical justifications. In this regard, he told his father in the fall quarter of 1947, when he was enrolled in OII, to disregard the plan James had mentioned the year prior of getting him a subscription to *Plain Talk*. He could make do with back issues his father had at home; besides, "though it occasionally has something interesting, I don't think that messy, loosely written propaganda can ever be necessary enough not to be a liability to a good cause."[54]

* **4** *

As Rorty struggled to sort out who he was intellectually, he faced another hurdle: depression. During his second November in Chicago, he told his father that "the whole process of my education seems considerably less fresh, various, and new than last year" and complained that having to prepare so hard for his comprehensive exams was only making matters worse.[55] He worried about his own performance and also whether the financial burden his parents had incurred by sending him to college was hindering their creative expression. He asked his father a few weeks later, "In another of your letters you ask me if there is any problem that I would let you help me with. Allright, there is, a problem which only you could help. It is about you and your work. I want to know whether you are doing the sort of things you want to do and whether I am a hindrance. Specifically, would you have gone down to TVA if you hadn't felt

53. Richard Rorty to Winifred Raushenbush, March 10, 1948, RRP.
54. Richard Rorty to James Rorty, November 4, 1947, RRP.
55. Richard Rorty to James Rorty, November 4, 1947, RRP.

that I had to have a good education, etc. Would you be staying there to do the Morgan book if you didn't still feel the same thing?"[56] It requires no leap of psychoanalytic faith to see a connection between his performance anxiety and sense of guilt at having caused his parents financial hardship: only a stellar academic record could justify their sacrifices. How frustrating, then, that he felt this goal to be elusive. Presumably reflecting on his own experiences, which he now felt had inadequately prepared him for college level work, he asked his mother: "Why doesn't somebody write inflammatory articles about the quality of education in the public schools.... Nobody except educators seems to think about it. After the fashion war is decided, maybe you could try it."[57] The following quarter, in a typical moment of self-deprecation, he told Winifred that while he had received As in OII and French, these grades were "just a point or so above a B."[58]

His parents, for their part, tried to reassure him, and encouraged him to fret less. "If I have any worry about you," his father wrote, "it is that you get a little of the happiness that youth can have."[59] Richard initially tried to downplay his parents' concerns: it would not do for them to sacrifice financially *and* be responsible for propping up his mental health. "I'm glad that you have so few worries about me," he wrote, "but don't let the few you have bother you. I'm certainly having as happy a youth as most people."[60] But by the fall of his third year at Chicago, he would no longer pretend that his distress was anything but serious. He told his father that he'd gone to visit a doctor, who'd said that whatever he was experiencing was psychological, not physiological, in origin. "Maybe he was right," Rorty allowed.

> I would like to describe the way I feel to you. I have just sort of stopped caring about my work, the future, Tanya [a young woman he was then dating], or anything else. This seems to be something more than a simple spell of depression, which I have occasionally and which go away again, both in duration and intensity. The most obvious consequence is that I, who participated actively in discussions and always was well ahead in my work last year, haven't said a word in class all year and am far behind in

56. Richard Rorty to James Rorty, November 23, 1947, RRP.
57. Richard Rorty to Winifred Raushenbush, December 15, 1947, RRP.
58. Richard Rorty to Winifred Raushenbush, April 7, 1948, RRP.
59. James Rorty to Richard Rorty, March 4, 1948, RRP.
60. Richard Rorty to James Rorty, March 6, 1948, RRP.

everything.... Perhaps the solution is just to buckle down, use the old grit, etc., etc. and get the things done. This doesn't seem to work, but I probably have not persuaded myself into it strongly enough.[61]

His father, who'd also experienced depression, warned Richard not to get caught up in it: "Watch yourself and don't lose your edge; it is too disastrous emotionally. There is always a real danger of getting into a downward spiral of health and morale in which one worsens the other; you've seen it happen to students as I remember your telling me."[62] In fact Richard did get caught up in such a spiral, and his grades suffered. He reported to his parents that spring that "the two C's" he'd received "in philosophy will stand on my record and be something of a constant drag in the future."[63] His father, expressing regret that it had been "a hard year for you," described Richard's depression as serious enough to constitute an illness and noted that their family doctor had warned him and Winifred "emphatically" that they should have "take[n]" Richard "out of school"[64] when he was in the throes of it.

Notable about this period in Rorty's undergraduate career is that through the haze of his depression, he was somehow able to formulate the aspiration to become philosopher and develop a specific plan for doing so. That his parents were intellectuals gave him decisive advantages in both respects. The first indication that Rorty was developing the ambition to become a philosopher came in May of 1948. His mother wrote to congratulate him on an outstanding natural science paper he'd written on endocrine functioning. "If you can think as well as that at 16," she observed, "you should be doing some very useful thinking at 26 and 36. Did I hear you correctly over the phone Saturday before last, and are you, as I gather, planning to do your graduate work in philosophy? You have always appeared to know what you wanted very clearly, a reassuring trait, and I trust that you will continue to do so."[65] Rorty, however, was uncertain as to the extent of his philosophical talents. In the fall of 1948 he took a course with Alan Gewirth, a former student of McKeon from Columbia whom Hutchins had also brought to Chicago. In his own work Gewirth scoured the Western philosophical tradition in search of concepts he might use for constructing a deontological ethics. The class

61. Richard Rorty to James Rorty, October 25, 1948, RRP.
62. James Rorty to Richard Rorty, October 30, 1948, RRP.
63. Richard Rorty to parents, April 6, 1949, RRP.
64. James Rorty to Richard Rorty, April 5, 1949, RRP.
65. Winifred Raushenbush to Richard Rorty, May 2, 1948, RRP.

Rorty took from Gewirth started with Descartes and ended with Kant, and even in the depths of his depression Rorty felt it was proving to be a good experience for him. He told his parents, "I have been busy writing essays, a new practice which they've put into most of the courses now. They've all been on Plato so far, since he's always the first author to be read. My philosophy course goes well, I think I'm learning something."[66] But the following spring, with the end of his bachelors program looming on the horizon and news that he'd received two Cs in philosophy earlier that year, he questioned his plan to study more philosophy. "I don't know really what they mean," he wrote, referring to his grades. "Perhaps I should give up on the idea of going into philosophy, perhaps I have just been over-lazy."[67] Unsure of what he should do with his life, he toyed with the idea of going to law school. But in the end, he told his parents he'd decided to stay on and take another year of coursework in philosophy to help him make up his mind. "When I go back to school, I can take law or philosophy; I admit law is more practical in all ways, nevertheless, if it seems alright to you, I want to take a year of philosophy, just to know what I'm dealing with. No matter what I did afterwards, this would have important permanent value."[68]

His parents had been, from the start, supportive of his plan to do graduate coursework in philosophy. In January of that year his father had written with encouraging words on Richard's plan to take a masters in philosophy, which was the Hutchins College equivalent of a major: "We were glad to get your card with news of your ... good grade in medieval philosophy. That seems to me to answer 'yes' to any question about your general plans. Obviously you can handle a philosophy major so the thing to do is to go ahead with it."[69] His mother echoed her support the following academic year, though not without warning him against the dangers of ivory towerism:

I think your path for some time, perhaps always entirely or mainly, wil. be connected with universities. This is probably the fitting place for your temperament and your gifts.... One of the problems you will at some point have to solve will be one that you are already yourself aware of: that is acquaintance and some mastery of the non-acaemic world. If you stick to universities by way of evading this problem—which is what many

66. Richard Rorty to parents, November 7, 1948, RRP.
67. Richard Rorty to parents, April 6, 1949, RRP.
68. Richard Rorty to parents, April 6, 1949, RRP.
69. James Rorty to Richard Rorty, January 7, 1949, RRP.

maybe most academicians have done, here in this country, at least—that would not be good. (In Europe the situation is I fancy somewhat different, because learning is somewhat more esteemed). I am confident that you will take this hurdle in your own good time and that you will not cramp the so far beautiful development of your life by an evasion.[70]

It is by no means inconceivable that parents who were not themselves intellectuals might be similarly encouraging if their daughter or son expressed the desire to become a philosopher; nor is it inconceivable that a young woman or man might press ahead with such a plan against parental objections or indifference—many have. But that the Rortys were themselves intellectuals and traveled in social worlds composed principally of other intellectuals probably made it more likely they would be supportive of their son's aspiration to become an intellectual too, foreswearing more practical and money-making realms like those of law or commerce that would have held greater appeal for parents located elsewhere on the class spectrum. Indeed, given the Rortys' critiques of American business and James Rorty's view that much of the regulatory apparatus of the American state serves business interests, Richard would probably have upset his parents had he decided to become a businessman or lawyer. If anything, James's view was that Richard's plan to continue with his philosophical studies right away was *too* practical—what he really needed was time to do creative work and discover himself. In June of 1949 James wrote to Richard to commend him on a fine paper he'd done on Yeats for a course taught by Allen Tate, a family friend. The paper reminded James of papers he'd written on Ibsen for his college mentor Leo Lewis; only, he said, Richard's paper was of higher quality. He counseled his son:

> When you are disposed to criticize the University of Chicago and to feel that it was unfortunate in some respects for you to have projected yourself so young into a difficult situation—there is truth in that—remember also the truth that on balance, it is probable that nothing better could have happened. You have perhaps suffered a little, but you have gained much. And you will be much stronger and better equipped for the next step, whatever it may prove to be. A little relaxation, I hope; a little chance quietly to discover yourself, possibly through a renewed attempt to release your own creative need: through writing, possibly through poetry; creative writing anyway. I regret all my diversion into journalism, etc. It

70. Winifred Raushenbush to Richard Rorty, September 30, 1949, RRP.

would have been better if I had kept, at whatever sacrifice, to the creative path.[71]

This sentiment aside, that Rorty's parents supported him when he said he wanted to study more philosophy no doubt encouraged him to do just that.

But there was another way in which his parents' occupation gave him an advantage: they could ask their intellectual friends for advice about how Richard should structure his graduate education. In light of Richard's depression, the Rortys explored the possibility that it might be better for his mental health—along with, perhaps, his intellectual development—for him not to stay on at Chicago, as he would be allowed to do perfunctorily, but instead to complete his masters coursework someplace else. Richard expressed interest in Harvard and Columbia, and James dashed off letters to his friends and acquaintances in an effort to scope out the possibilities. In early February of 1949, he asked his friend, the writer James Farrell, who had also attended the University of Chicago, whether he could ask around on Richard's behalf. Farrell, who had absorbed a considerable amount of Dewey and James in his student days, wrote to Harvard's Morton White (who, decades later, would be on the faculty of the Institute for Advanced Study for some of the time Rorty was at Princeton). That year White would publish *Social Thought in America: The Revolt against Formalism*, a critical history of the pragmatist movement and related developments in late nineteenth-century thought. "Jim Rorty's son, Richard Rorty, is at present a student at the University of Chicago," wrote Farrell, "and he intends to go on with his studies in philosophy. He is anxious to get into Harvard, and is not sure as to the possibility. Because of this, I thought I'd drop you a note to ask you whether or not you could help, and what advice you could give which would help him indirectly to get admittance. I had a long talk with Richard Rorty at Chicago when I was there recently. He is a very serious, shy, sensitive boy, and I am certain he will make a good student at Harvard."[72] A few days later, James let Richard know what he'd been up to: "Farrell sent me a carbon of his letter to Morton White of the Harvard philosophy dept.—an excellent plug for you. I have written Sidney Hook asking what he knows about Harvard, Columbia, NYU etc."[73] Richard, too, was busy "accumulating recommendations

71. James Rorty to Richard Rorty, June 6, 1949, RRP.

72. James Farrell to Morton White, February 4, 1949, RRP.

73. James Rorty to Richard Rorty, February 9, 1949, RRP.

to Harvard"[74]—something made easier by his presence at Chicago, where high-status letter writers were to be found in abundance. A few months later, Farrell wrote to Richard with White's response. White had said he couldn't be of any help because he wasn't involved with the admissions process. He suggested that Farrell write directly to Harvard's graduate school of arts and sciences. Farrell told Richard he'd be willing to do this at any point. "I'd also suggest that you write to your father," he added, "and that you arrange to get two of his friends to write letters for you," signaling his understanding that Richard could use his social networks to his advantage.[75]

In the meantime, however, James heard back from Hook. He wrote to Richard:

> I have a very cordial letter from our old friend Sidney Hook, head of the philosophy dept of NY University, whom I had written mentioning your interest in philosophy, the possibility of your transferring to Harvard, etc. The following points in his letter will interest you:
>
> 1. Harvard, Columbia, Chicago, NYU all good in philosophy. Depends upon your particular bent.
> 2. What is Dick's aptitude—mathematics and logic? Social sciences? Everything? If interests lie in mathematics and logic, youth no barrier. Otherwise maybe you're young for specialized work in philosophy.
> 3. What kind of a person are you? Especially *why* do you want to do work in philosophy.
> 4. Chances of getting a fellowship at other institutions based on Junior College degree from U of Chicago are rather remote. [76]

James suggested that Richard write Hook directly to tell him about his specific philosophical interests. There is no evidence he did. In light of Hook's opinion that Richard's chances of getting a fellowship at one of his top-pick schools were limited he began to consider other options. A few days earlier his uncle and aunt at Wisconsin had offered to host him in Madison if he wished to do graduate coursework there; they could pull strings to secure his admission to the philosophy department.[77] A few years later, applying to doctoral programs and trying to avoid being

74. Richard Rorty, postcard to parents, February 7, 1949, RRP.
75. James Rorty to Richard Rorty, March 10, 1949, RRP.
76. James Rorty to Richard Rorty, February 13, 1949, RRP.
77. See James Rorty to Richard Rorty, February 8, 1949, RRP.

drafted into the army, Richard would consider Wisconsin again as a last resort school, and his opinion about the place in 1949 was probably no different than in 1951: "Their philosophy department is absolutely worthless, but it would be so pleasant to have a small income and have to do nothing for a year except canoe around the lakes in Madison and write a little thesis. To save reputation, if I should go there, I'd have to transfer immediately to get a doctorate at some reputable institution."[78]

As well connected as Rorty's parents were, nothing other than the Wisconsin offer materialized from these contacts. The Hutchins College program was too out of sync with the rest of the American university system for other schools to know what to do with someone who had graduated at age eighteen after only three years of coursework. Richard decided to stay on at Chicago, and the experiences he underwent during his next three years there would prove formative for his later thought.

78. Richard Rorty to Winifred Raushenbush, January 12, 1951, RRP.

FOUR

M.A. in Philosophy, 1949–1952

* 1 *

When Rorty started the masters program at Chicago in 1949, he entered a philosophy department that sat in many ways at odds with national trends. In a field increasingly defined by logical positivism, Chicago maintained an eclectic orientation. Although the department had changed some since its makeover by Hutchins in the early 1930s, the appointments made then helped set the tone of the department for years to come. On the eve of Hutchins's move to Chicago, tenured department members included Edward Scriber Ames, E. A. Burtt, George Herbert Mead, Arthur Murphy, T. V. Smith, and James Tufts. Ames, Burtt, Mead, and Murphy were all supporters of Dewey. It is therefore no surprise that when Hutchins approached Tufts about the possibility of appointing the explicitly anti-Deweyan Adler, along with McKeon, Buchanan, and V. J. McGill, Tufts, after consultation with other department members, demurred.[1] Hutchins was nevertheless convinced that Adler's neo-Thomist attacks on skepticism and relativism represented the way forward for philosophy and returned to the table to ask if the department would accept the appointment of Adler alone if his position were interdisciplinary, with cross-appointments in psychology and law. The department relented, only to learn shortly thereafter that Adler had been appointed at a salary $1,000 per year higher than nearly any other department member. This so infuriated Tufts that he used it as an occasion to retire. Mead took over the chairmanship. The following year Hutchins returned to the department again, this time to press for the appointment of Buchanan

1. My discussion here draws heavily on Cook, *George Herbert Mead*, 183–94.

on terms similar to those he'd procured for Adler. It was becoming clear to members of the department that an effort was under way to radically remake it and push pragmatism out. Mead, Burtt, and Murphy retired or left the university. Three months later, Mead died.

Buchanan, in the end, went to St. Johns after only a year at Chicago, and "to appease the faculty in 1931,"[2] Hutchins made an appointment at the associate level to Mead's student Charles Morris. The other major appointments in the 1930s were to Charles Hartshorne, a young metaphysician who had done his dissertation at Harvard, who had worked as an assistant on the first edition of Peirce's collected papers, and who was appointed assistant professor; to Charner Perry and A. C. Benjamin, an ethicist and philosopher of science, respectively, who were also given junior appointments; to Werner Jaeger, a refugee classicist who would soon leave for Harvard; and to McKeon and Rudolf Carnap.

McKeon, as noted in chapter 3, came from Columbia, where he completed a dissertation in 1928 on Spinoza. At the time, Columbia was a department divided: on the one side stood Dewey, who remained steadfast in his naturalism and whose recently published book, *Experience and Nature* (1925), pushed pragmatism in an almost metaphysical direction; on the other side was Frederick Woodbridge, who, like the majority of American philosophers in the 1920s, championed realism—in his case an Aristotelian realism. While appreciating pragmatism's naturalism and theory of meaning, Woodbridge saw little value in its understanding of truth.[3] McKeon "was a graduate student in an atmosphere dominated by [this] realist-pragmatist debate."[4] He had also spent time in France studying with the neo-Thomist Étienne Gilson. McKeon's philosophical semantics might thus be seen as an attempt to "split ... the difference between realism and pragmatism,"[5] while integrating Gilson's focus on the history of philosophy. Against Deweyan pragmatism, McKeon refused to treat philosophical ideas as outgrowths of societal development. The great philosophers participate in conversations that stretch across the ages. Against the realists, however, McKeon recognized that it is neither possible nor desirable to locate a single conceptual framework that will trump all others in its approximation of the real. His insistence that each

2. Mary Ann Dzuback, 1991, *Robert M. Hutchins: Portrait of an Educator*, Chicago: University of Chicago Press, 176.

3. Frederick Woodbridge, 1929, "The Promise of Pragmatism," *Journal of Philosophy* 26:541–52.

4. Depew, *Between Pragmatism and Realism*, 35.

5. Ibid., 36.

philosophical approach makes sense in the context of the assumptions that define it was not meant to lead to relativism, but to the view that the development of philosophical semantics itself could force a bracketing of presuppositional disputes that would allow philosophers to reach dialogical understanding.[6] Given lingering opposition to the McKeon appointment in the philosophy department, when he was brought permanently from Columbia to Chicago it was as a professor of Greek.[7] He became dean of humanities a year later, formally joining the philosophy faculty in 1937.[8]

Carnap, one of the key figures in the history of analytic philosophy, had very different philosophical interests. Having received his doctorate at the University of Jena, Carnap moved to Vienna in 1926. There he became embroiled in discussions under way among such early members of the Vienna Circle as Herbert Feigl, Hans Hahn, Otto Neurath, and Moritz Schlick as to the nature of science and its implications for philosophy. Although it was the positivism of Ernst Mach that initially inspired these discussions, attention in the group soon turned toward Ludwig Wittgenstein's *Tractatus*, which would exert as great an influence on Carnap as did the thought of Gottlob Frege and Bertrand Russell. Initially embracing Wittgenstein's verifiability theory of meaning, Carnap and other members of the *Wiener Kreis* were concerned negatively to counter the metaphysical tendencies they saw as having characterized much of the history of philosophy, as well as the work of contemporary philosophers like Heidegger, on the grounds that most metaphysical statements are empirically unverifiable and hence meaningless. Positively, Carnap sought to develop a conceptual language, centered on "quantitative descriptions of definite space-time points,"[9] in terms of which all valid statements in the sciences could be expressed. He opposed the idea that the natural and social sciences were different in kind and would become one of the major organizers of the international unity of science movement. With his colleague Hans Reichenbach, then at

6. Wayne Booth, 2000, "Richard McKeon's Pluralism: The Path between Dogmatism and Relativism," pp. 213–30 in *Pluralism in Theory and Practice: Richard McKeon and American Philosophy*, Eugene Garver and Richard Buchanan, eds., Nashville: Vanderbilt University Press, 222.

7. McKeon actually spent 1934–35 at Chicago as a visiting professor of history before his permanent appointment to the faculty. See the Biographical Note to the Richard Peter McKeon Papers, University of Chicago Library.

8. Dzuback, *Robert M. Hutchins*, 176.

9. Norman Martin, 1967, "Rudolf Carnap," pp. 25–33 in *Encyclopedia of Philosophy*, Paul Edwards, ed., New York: Macmillan, 28.

the University of Berlin, Carnap founded a journal, *Erkenntnis*, devoted to positivist ideas. Hitler's rise to power, however, soon forced the migration of most members of the Vienna Circle.

Although in subsequent years pragmatism would come to see itself as opposed to logical positivism's emphasis on the distinction between analytic and synthetic statements, to its neglect of ethical and political questions, and to its reliance on symbolic logic, in the early days of the positivist movement pragmatism and positivism were often viewed as allies. Peirce's pragmatic maxim was seen as laying down comparable verificationist criteria for meaning, while pragmatism's experimentalist orientation suggested a philosophic outlook equally committed to science. At the University of Chicago, this view was championed by Morris, who proposed in 1936 that Carnap and Reichenbach be given appointments. Yet neither Adler nor Hutchins had any taste for the kind of philosophy the logical positivists produced: "While the pragmatists and the logical empiricists wished to reform philosophy by making it scientific, Hutchins and Adler fiercely resisted all things scientific in philosophy.... Were they to ascend to cultural leadership as Dewey, Morris, and the Unity of Science movement believed they should, civilization would careen into meaninglessness, and, most likely, barbarism."[10] Nevertheless, such was Carnap's international reputation—a reputation also growing within the American philosophical community—that Hutchins, not insensitive to such matters, felt compelled to accept the appointment,[11] as long as the plan to hire Reichenbach was dropped, which it was.[12] As concerns Carnap's reputation, philosophers at always-influential Harvard, including P. W. Bridgman, C. I. Lewis, Henry Sheffer, and then graduate student W. V. O. Quine, were indeed coming to regard the exiled Vienna school philosophers as crucial interlocutors, and when presentations on the school's approach were made at meetings of the American Philosophical Association (APA) in the early 1930s, they were a "*succès de scandale.*"[13] A manifesto

10. George Reisch, 2005, *How the Cold War Transformed Philosophy of Science: To the Icy Slopes of Logic,* Cambridge: Cambridge University Press, 74.

11. William McNeill, 1991, *Hutchins' University: A Memoir of the University of Chicago, 1929–1950,* Chicago: University of Chicago Press, 77.

12. Charles Hartshorne, 1991, "Some Causes of My Intellectual Growth," pp. 3–45 in *The Philosophy of Charles Hartshorne,* Library of Living Philosophers Series, vol. 20, Lewis Hahn, ed., La Salle: Open Court, 33.

13. Herbert Feigl, 1969, "The Wiener Kreis in America," pp. 630–73 in *The Intellectual Migration: Europe and America, 1930–1960,* Donald Fleming and Bernard Bailyn, eds., Cambridge: Harvard University Press, 647.

of sorts, "Logical Positivism: A New Movement in European Philosophy," published in the *Journal of Philosophy* in 1931, which described the movement as representing a "radically novel interpretation of the nature, scope and purpose of philosophy" that went beyond the "older positivism, empiricism and pragmatism" insofar as it maintained that "there are no synthetic *a priori* propositions,"[14] garnered considerable attention. So did A. J. Ayer's *Language, Truth, and Logic*, published in 1936. By the late 1930s, members of the original circle would be installed at philosophy departments around the country: Reichenbach at UCLA; Carl Hempel at Queens College, Yale, and finally Princeton; Gustav Bergmann at Iowa; Alfred Tarski at Berkeley; and Feigl at Iowa and then Minnesota. Over the next decade, the publications and teaching of the positivists, which described the mission of philosophy as that of aiding the development of science through clarification of key terms and concepts, would exert enormous influence.

McNeill notes that "when he got to Chicago, Carnap launched a vast collaborative work, intended to demonstrate the unity of science as defined in positivist terms. Morris served as coeditor."[15] In conjunction with this publication project, with which Dewey was also involved, Carnap and Morris jointly ran a colloquium "in which [they] discussed questions of methodology with scientists from various fields of science and tried to achieve a better understanding among representatives of different disciplines and greater clarity on the essential characteristics of the scientific method."[16] Although these efforts would help solidify Carnap's national and international standing, they brought little prestige at Chicago: "Despite his great reputation, Carnap had little effect on campus life at close range.... Though exiled from Prague and living in Chicago, Carnap much preferred to cultivate his connections within a circle of like-minded philosophers in Europe and paid almost no attention to local controversies."[17] This makes it sound as though the fault lay with Carnap. Abraham Kaplan, by contrast, one of Carnap's students in the late 1930s, recalls that when he arrived on campus the major division within the philosophy department was between "the Ancients and

14. Albert Blumberg and Herbert Feigl, 1931, "Logical Positivism: A New Movement in European Philosophy," *Journal of Philosophy* 28:281–96, 281–82.

15. McNeill, *Hutchins' University*, 77.

16. Rudolf Carnap, 1963, "Intellectual Autobiography," pp. 3–84 in *The Philosophy of Rudolf Carnap*, Paul Arthur Schilpp, ed., Library of Living Philosophers Series, vol. 11, La Salle: Open Court, 35.

17. McNeill, *Hutchins's University*, 78.

the Moderns," with McKeon the leading figure of the former and Carnap the leading figure of the latter. Kaplan, one of the Moderns, says that he warned his nephew, entering the university ten years later, to "Beware! Beware of the Aristotelians!" and also that he "remember[s] well … the disparity in the strength of the two sides." Carnap "had very few serious students," and "departmental fellowships were … rare for the Moderns."[18] Carnap's underdeveloped local reputation was as much a consequence of the Aristotelian commitments of the rest of the department as of his own indifference to local concerns.

And these commitments were Aristotelian, not Thomist. Despite the support of Hutchins, Adler became an increasingly marginal figure over the course of the 1940s, especially after a notorious speech in which he accused professors who resisted the truth of neo-Thomism of posing as much of a threat to civilization as Hitler. It was McKeon and his method of philosophical hermeneutics that came to command the most respect from humanists on campus, thanks in part to his willingness "to operate from within the academic hierarchy" and "influence others through a combination of intellectual persuasion and administrative action."[19] Although he was brought to Chicago as part of the neo-Thomist bandwagon, McKeon—though perhaps not an Aristotlean in the strict sense—owed more to Aristotle than to Aquinas. Aquinas, to be sure, had constructed his philosophical system around a theological reading of Aristotle. But whereas what had been important to him was the attempt to integrate Aristotelian physics and rationalism with a religious worldview, McKeon drew from Aristotle an emphasis on philosophy as a practical activity, that is, an emphasis on the nature of philosophical persuasion and rhetoric. David Depew also speculates that McKeon's philosophical semantics allowed each the variables in its taxonomy to take precisely four values because each approach to philosophy was, for him, defined by its stance in relation to Aristotle's four causes: material, formal, efficient, and final.[20] More generally, however, the divide in the philosophy department was between the majority of faculty and students who insisted that philosophical insight was a matter of erudition with respect to the history of philosophy, and those few—associated with Carnap—who thought of

---

18. Abraham Kaplan, 1991, "Rudolf Carnap," pp. 32–41 in *Remembering the University of Chicago: Teachers, Scientists, and Scholars*, Edward Shils, ed., Chicago: University of Chicago Press, 34–35.

19. McNeill, *Hutchins's University,* 79.

20. Depew, *Between Pragmatism and Realism,* 39.

philosophy as a more presentist enterprise that could measure its progress by its unwillingness to look back on bad ideas from the past.

* 2 *

In his first few quarters as a graduate student in the department, Rorty took a wide variety of courses. He wrote to his mother in September of 1949 to say, "classes begin today. I am taking medieval philosophy, ethics, & mathematics. This last course is a general introduction to calculus and advanced math in general. I am taking it because I feel that I cannot continue knowing as little . . . as I do [about mathematics] and because it will help me to understand mathematical logic."[21] Over the coming months his enthusiasm about coursework would only increase. He noted in early October that "my reading is getting quite interesting along about now. The stuff on basic ethical questions is especially good—also the logical techniques that they start out with in my mathematics course. My teachers are all fairly good, and I think that I will learn quite a bit."[22] A week later he continued in the same vein: "My studies are going reasonably well. I am especially interested in the medieval philosophy course. The whole subject fascinated me and I get considerably joy out of opening up a new author on the subject. I don't think I would want to make medieval philosophy my field, but I would like to know quite a bit more about it."[23]

It soon became clear to Rorty that his *métier* was historically oriented philosophizing. Rorty's course on medieval philosophy was not the only historically oriented class to get his attention. During his second quarter as a graduate student, he told his mother, he would be taking "Logic, European History, and Math," and of these it was the history course he was most enthusiastic about. "I shall probably be writing only one paper this quarter," he reported, with apparent satisfaction. "Something about '19th Century Interpretations of Medieval Thought'—I'm reading Henry Adams on that subject at the moment."[24] The prediction that he would enjoy the course was confirmed by his experience of it. He told his aunt, Eva Beard, in March of 1950: "I am feeling much more secure and satisfied about my work than I have before. I have just finished two interesting courses, which got me interested in the problems of a history of ideas."[25]

21. Richard Rorty to Winifred Raushenbush, September 27, 1949, RRP.
22. Richard Rorty to Winifred Raushenbush, October 5, 1949, RRP.
23. Richard Rorty to Winifred Raushenbush, October 18, 1949, RRP.
24. Richard Rorty to Winifred Raushenbush, January 11, 1950, RRP.
25. Richard Rorty to Eva Beard, March 20, 1950, RRP.

Around this time, he has said in an autobiographical piece, he became interested in books that offered sweeping histories of philosophy: Hegel's *Phenomenology of Spirit,* Whitehead's *Adventures of Ideas,* and Lovejoy's *Great Chain of Being.* If it was becoming apparent that his interests and talents lay in the history of thought, it was equally clear that they did *not* lay in the realm of logical analysis. He received a C+ on a quarterly exam he took for his mathematics class in December of 1949 and the following academic year told his parents "I have to go in now [to the department office] to find out whether I have to take a course in logic, or whether I'll be able to take something that I like."[26] Both he and his parents took his interest in and facility with intellectual history as an indication of the kind of philosophical work he should do in the future. His father was explicit. "What you can best do for us," he wrote in a letter to his son in April of 1950, "is what you have been doing: make good use of all your opportunities, discover yourself and your world, explore and choose your objectives." "The A grades from Hartshorne and Bergstrasser," he continued, referring in the latter case to a course Rorty had taken on cultural history, "seem to me to be critically important; not only will they probably assure the continuation of your scholarship; they help to define the bent of your talent and its capacity."[27]

At a time when logical positivism was winning the day in the American philosophical field, Rorty was fortunate to be in a department where historical competencies were valued. Given his growing interest in the subject, Rorty took steps to augment his set of relevant skills. One thing he did in this regard—or tried to do—was acquire linguistic skills that would permit him to better understand historical texts. He had already taken some French as an undergraduate but now aimed to learn German and Greek as well, as he told his aunt in the spring of his first year of graduate school: "I am determined to learn German this summer, with my Mother helping me.[28] Maybe I can try speaking it to you. The French accent you helped me with has been very useful. I would like to learn Greek fairly soon, also. It is getting annoying to hear my professors say loftily 'Of course, the translation cannot make clear what Aristotle meant.'"[29] He recognized that among historically minded philosophers, being able to discuss ideas in their original language was a mark of pres-

26. Richard Rorty to parents, September 29, 1950, RRP.

27. James Rorty to Richard Rorty, April 15, 1950, RRP.

28. Having grown up in a household where German was spoken frequently, Winifred was conversant in the language.

29. Richard Rorty to Eva Beard, March 20, 1950, RRP.

tige, as he noted half jokingly in a letter the following fall: "I'll be writing a paper on Plato's *Republic* this coming quarter (I intend to fill it with citations from the Greek—just to increase my self-esteem)."[30] It was with the goal in mind of becoming truly fluent in French that he formulated a plan, during his second year as a graduate student at Chicago, to spend a year studying in Paris. The plan was also motivated by two other concerns: first, although he found his courses enjoyable, he was bored and restless at having been at Chicago so long and became interested in the possibility of writing his masters thesis elsewhere, especially Harvard, or, failing that, at some European university; and second, if a scholarship for his third year of graduate work did not materialize somewhere in the United States, he would be forced to give up his student deferment from the draft. He applied again to Harvard but also began planning for a year abroad. He explained to his father why he wanted to go to Europe: "First, it's probably my last chance. I can't escape being drafted much longer, despite the present rules about graduate students, which are, from the Army's point of view, wildly impractical. Also, if I get a fellowship in this country along with my M.A., I wouldn't want to refuse it, and hence couldn't go anywhere. Second, I think it would do me good."[31]

As he contemplated this move, Richard, now nineteen years old, again relied on his parents' extensive social networks. His father wrote to various people he knew to try and find him European employment. He contacted David Saposs, for example, a labor historian who had studied under John R. Commons, who had extensive European connections, and who had written, like Rorty, on Communist infiltration of American unions. His son was considering coming to Paris, Rorty said. Could Saposs help him, perhaps in finding a job?[32] In another move, he had a friend, Frank Hannigan, editor of *Human Events*, write a letter of introduction for Richard to the political philosopher Bertrand de Jouvenel.[33] James Rorty also asked his friends about the advisability of his son's plans. Was it better, from the standpoint of his future career as a philosopher, that he use his time in Europe only to take a few courses and return to Chicago to write his masters thesis, or should he actually enroll in a European university? A letter to Richard gave the answer:

30. Richard Rorty to Eva Beard, September 21, 1950, RRP.
31. Richard Rorty to James Rorty, May 6, 1951, RRP.
32. James Rorty to David Saposs, June 3, 1951, RRP.
33. Frank Hannigan to Bertrand de Jouvenel, May 23, 1951, RRP.

Dear Dick: Talked with Dr. Jacobs, Voice [of America] script writer, NY University doctorate in philosophy under Hook. NYU couldn't get him a job; regrets he didn't go to Columbia, which can place its graduates. U of Chicago can place grads in middlewest colleges; hence he regards matriculation for MA at U of C as desirable, with arrangement for study at Sorbonne, for which credit would be given. Notes McKeon very close to Sorbonne. Not excluded you could also pick up a credit or two from Oxford and/or Cambridge, which today have more prestige than Sorbonne, tho Sorbonne still has prestige. However, MA from the Sorbonne would break your connection with U of C and its power to further careers of graduates, hence he would question this.

You probably have considered and discussed all these questions, but Jacobs is familiar with and has suffered hazards of University setup in the limited job market for professional philosophers, and his testimony may have bearing on your plans.[34]

Rorty ended up going to Paris later that summer, but stayed only two months. Perhaps following Jacobs's advice—but also homesick and having realized that his French wasn't nearly as good as he thought it was, which made auditing courses at the Sorbonne difficult[35]—he decided to return to Chicago to complete his masters. Rorty would be back in Hyde Park that fall, his French only somewhat improved and his professional trajectory in American academe uncompromised by dint of too close association with a foreign university system.

✳ 3 ✳

At the same time that he sought to hone his foreign language competencies, Rorty found his interests in the history of philosophy reinforced by his everyday experiences at Chicago. This was so because he associated himself with other Chicago students who were interested in the history of thought and among whom he could exercise his intellectual-historical faculties. Although the historically inclined McKeon occupied the most prestigious position in the philosophy department, Rorty preferred to spend his time not with other philosophy students but with students in the Committee on Social Thought, many of whom were disciples of Leo Strauss. Strauss, a political philosopher and orthodox Jew, fled his native

34. James Rorty to Richard Rorty, May 8, 1951, RRP.
35. Richard Rorty, e-mail to author, June 23, 2005.

Germany in 1932 and taught at the New School for more than a decade. He moved to Chicago as a full professor in 1949 and in a series of lectures given upon his arrival announced to those in the university community the basic themes of his thought and scholarship. As Fred Dallmayr describes it, these revolved around two issues: first, the moral character of modernity as against that of antiquity and, second, the relationship between reason and religion.[36] Modernity should be understood, according to Strauss, in terms of its anthropocentrism, its focus on interests as opposed to virtues, and its fever for change and innovation. In light of the shift in perspective modernity brings about, the meaning of such long-standing doctrines as that of natural right comes to change: whereas in antiquity natural right meant subordination to the demands of a hierarchical social order, viewed as essential to the proper functioning of the community, in modernity it comes to mean, in the context of liberalism, the right to have one's freedoms preserved in the face of threats from others. Although "Strauss presented himself not as a philosopher but as a scholar, an historian of political philosophy,"[37] he was commonly seen as sympathizing as much with the earlier as with the later conception.[38] That his own views were somewhat heretical at the time and sometimes had to be read between the lines of his historical analyses was consistent with the method for reading philosophic texts that Strauss proposed. Because there was often a "conflict between philosophy and society,"[39] philosophers may have to hide their true views and meanings so as not to offend religious authorities, patrons, and others. The task of the student of philosophy is to recover these hidden meanings through an intensive reading of the text itself. Doing so requires fluency in the original language in which the text was written, for translations often bury hidden meanings. In reading texts this way, the student is not looking backward into the past to gauge how much philosophical progress has been made but rather—precisely because Strauss saw "human nature" to be "essentially unchangeable"[40]—is searching for wisdom still applicable today,

36. Fred Dallmayr, 1994, "Leo Strauss Peregrinus," *Social Research* 61:877–906.

37. Edward Banfield, 1991, "Leo Strauss," pp. 490–501 in *Remembering the University of Chicago: Teachers, Scientists, and Scholars,* Edward Shils, ed., Chicago: University of Chicago Press, 494.

38. For a view of Strauss as being only "skeptical" toward liberalism, see Steven Smith, 2006, *Reading Leo Strauss: Politics, Philosophy, Judaism,* Chicago: University of Chicago Press.

39. Banfield, "Leo Strauss," 494.

40. Ibid., 496.

wisdom that is the subject of the great historical conversation in which all philosophers participate.

Strauss quickly gathered around him a group of students committed to his esoteric methods: "Here was a man who ... seemed to have read everything worth reading, including—especially—what was between the lines, and to have remembered it all; who seemed to have no ego that required being shown off to a captive audience; who was wholly absorbed in making clear what was often very obscure.... How could a student ... fail to be in awe of such a teacher?"[41] Among Strauss's "puppies" at Chicago during Rorty's time there were future political philosophers Allan Bloom, Victor Gourevitch, Stanley Rosen, and the classicist Seth Benardete. Rorty was friends with all of them. Typical of communication within the group was an undated letter Benardete wrote to Rorty, probably around this time. Benardete was on vacation and reported that "he was reading Plato's *Theages* and had a beautiful vision of nature in which 'omni genera mixta'—all kinds of beings were mixed."[42] Although the letter went on to address less lofty concerns, the fact that such an informal communiqué contained a high degree of engagement with classical philosophy—not to mention the fact that the letter was written in Latin, with the quotation about Plato in Greek—suggests that Rorty's friendships reinforced his identity as a student of the history of philosophy and offered him an informal setting where intellectual-historical knowledge was valued.

Rorty also found a conversation partner in Amélie Oksenberg, with whom he became friends during this time. Born in Belgium to Jewish parents from Poland, Amélie was raised on a farm in Virginia. Her father "traded in diamonds," but did so "as little as possible—only enough to finance his various philosophic experiments"; her mother had been educated as a linguist.[43] Amélie had enrolled at the University of Chicago at a young age and was, like Richard, taking graduate coursework in philosophy. Her interests, like his, lay in the history of the field, with a particular emphasis on the classics. The first hint of their having formed a relationship appears in his correspondence from 1951. Rorty's friend Charles, a graduate student at Columbia, wrote to him in February of that year to say: "Your comments about a superb young female provoke curiosity. Currently I hold the idea

41. Ibid., 497.

42. Seth Benardete to Richard Rorty, undated letter, RRP. Thanks to Adam Kissel for this translation.

43. Amélie Oksenberg Rorty, 1977, "Dependency, Individuality and Work," pp. 38–54 in *Working It Out: 23 Women Writers, Artists, Scientists, and Scholars Talk about Their Lives and Work,* Sara Ruddick and Pamela Daniels, eds., New York: Pantheon, 39.

that only intelligent and bright looking young women are worth spending time with; the other kind may be intelligent and talk cleverly, but when it comes to just the sheer sensual satisfcation of looking and admiring they fail abysmally. It is no small thing for a woman to be both beautiful and intelligent, and certainly it is a great thing if they are combined as charm."[44] Amélie would be traveling to Europe at the same time Richard did.[45] Foretelling the opposition the Oksenbergs would mount just a few years later to Amélie and Richard's marriage on the grounds of Richard's imminent induction into the army, the fact that he was not Jewish, and—as a letter from James Rorty hints[46]—the disparity of wealth between his family and Amélie's own, they disapproved of Amélie's extended European study trip, perhaps fearing contact between the two of them. By September, however, as she recounted in a letter to Richard from London, they had stopped trying to persuade her to come home.[47] Amélie would remain in Europe through the academic year while Richard labored in Chicago on his masters thesis; both would apply to the doctoral program at Yale and be accepted. Surely much of the time they spent together involved discussion of mundane matters, but that philosophical concerns too were part of their ongoing conversation, at least in this early stage in their relationship, is plain from the few surviving letters between them. In a letter from July of 1952, for example, Amélie wrote from Switzerland, where she had been studying with the existentialist Karl Jaspers. "Jaspers is heavy, pompous, dogmatic," she said. "He speaks with baroque flourishes, and I feel that each of his petals is covered with dust. He has that Germanic self-righteousness that makes me furious, and add to this, a passionate love of Hegel's *Phenomenology of Spirit*. Bah! It curdles my blood. Much rather would I bed with the logical positivists than with these vipers."[48]

* 4 *

During his time as a graduate student at Chicago, Rorty took classes from a number of professors in the department, including McKeon, Gewirth, Carnap, Manley Thompson—who had come as an assistant professor in 1949—and Hartshorne. What stands out from this list is how many of Rorty's teachers at Chicago were interested in, had previously studied,

44. "Chas M.M." to Richard Rorty, February 28, 1951, RRP.
45. "Roger" to Richard Rorty, June 25, 1951, RRP.
46. James Rorty to Amélie Oksenberg, April 12, 1954, RRP.
47. Amélie Oksenberg to Richard Rorty, September 16, 1951, RRP.
48. Amélie Oksenberg to Richard Rorty, July 7, 1952, RRP.

or felt sympathetic toward aspects of classical American pragmatism. McKeon, as noted earlier, had studied under Dewey and was sympathetic at least to pragmatism's critiques of realism. Carnap, while hardly a pragmatist, respected Morris's efforts to "combine ideas of pragmatism and logical empiricism,"[49] though "most of" the members of the Vienna circle had developed their approach "largely ignorant of American philosophy."[50] Thompson and Hartshorne, for their part, were among the country's leading scholars of Charles Peirce.

It was Hartshorne whom Rorty ultimately chose as his masters thesis advisor. In the preface to the thesis, Rorty thanks Hartshorne not just for "his kindness and assistance in regard ... to this thesis" but also for helping to shape "the direction of my work in general."[51] Hartshorne had been raised in small towns in Pennsylvania by an Episcopal minister and his wife. He attended Haverford College for two years, at his father's insistence, and while there was much affected by the lectures of Rufus Jones, a leading Quaker theologian, who encouraged him to read Josiah Royce's *The Problem of Christianity* (1913). From Royce Hartshorne took the idea—central both to pragmatism, which Royce admired in many respects, and to the neo-Hegelian idealism from which he and pragmatists like Dewey drew—that there can be no self in the absence of community, that sympathy and altruism are more natural than motives of self-interest, and that the importance of the Christian church lies in the fellowship to which it gives expression. After service in the army, where Hartshorne recalls having had the realization that the world presents itself to us in terms of feeling, not in terms of affectively neutral sense data,[52] he transferred to Harvard, where he would complete both his undergraduate and doctoral degrees. His principal teachers were Ralph Barton Perry, student and exegete of James; C. I. Lewis, who himself worked on the Peirce papers for two years while developing his own strain of conceptual pragmatism; and W. E. Hocking, an idealist and metaphysician. It was the last of these philosophical projects that held the greatest appeal for Hartshorne, whose dissertation "was full of energetic arguments for [his] then system of metaphysics, a kind of qualified spiritual monism."[53]

49. Carnap, "Intellectual Autobiography," 34.

50. Feigl, "The Wiener Kreis in America," 644.

51. Richard Rorty, 1952, "Whitehead's Use of the Concept of Potentiality," M.A. Thesis, Department of Philosophy, University of Chicago, iii.

52. Hartshorne, "Some Causes of My Intellectual Growth," 18.

53. Charles Hartshorne, 1990, *The Darkness and the Light: A Philosopher Reflects upon His Fortunate Career and Those Who Made It Possible*, Albany: State University of New York Press, 113.

A two-year postdoc in Europe permitted him to study with Heidegger and Husserl, and he returned to Harvard in 1925 as an instructor, where he would stay for three formative years. Among his duties were to grade papers for Alfred North Whitehead's metaphysics class and to assist Paul Weiss in sorting through the Peirce papers and assembling them for publication.

Whitehead—at that point an immensely popular figure both inside and outside the academy—had moved to Harvard the year before at the age of sixty-three and was making the transition from philosopher of mathematics and science to metaphysician. Against a mechanistic and materialistic view of the world, Whitehead argued that reality is composed of events and processes of becoming that coexist in unified systems he termed "organisms." Organisms acquire their reality by basing themselves on "eternal objects," akin to Platonic forms, which are grasped in moments of "prehension." This grasping is not entirely mimetic, as each process of becoming actualizes eternal objects in new and creative ways. Whitehead saw organisms as relating to and perceiving their environment through sensation. At the same time, he upheld a doctrine of metaphysical unity: the notion of organism, on his understanding, referred not just to life forms but to every aspect of reality down to atoms and molecules. This vitalist position fit squarely with the views Hartshorne had been developing independently, and Hartshorne immediately became an expositor and champion of Whitehead's metaphysics. Where Whitehead made some effort to develop the theological implications of his system, this would be one of Hartshorne's major concerns.[54] The world itself is a kind of organism for Whitehead and Hartshorne, not a mechanistic system of molecules and matter in motion, but the whole set of interdependent relationships through which existence becomes possible; and this, Hartshorne claimed, is precisely what is meant by God.[55] It was as a philosopher with strong theological interests that Hartshorne became known at Chicago, where he soon accepted a cross-appointment in the Divinity School. Such, at least, is how he was known to Rorty, who described Hartshorne to his mother in 1950 as "a famous lay theologian who was himself a pupil of Whitehead's in the 20's."[56]

54. Lewis Ford, 1991, "Hartshorne's Interpretation of Whitehead," pp. 313–37 in *The Philosophy of Charles Hartshorne*, Lewis Hahn, ed., Library of Living Philosophers Series, vol. 20, La Salle: Open Court, 313.

55. Ibid.

56. Richard Rorty to Winifred Raushenbush, January 11, 1950, RRP.

But Hartshorne was also much influenced by Peirce. While disagreeing with him in several crucial respects—for example, with the failure of his metaphysics to account for the "idea of a definite single event"[57]—he was in accord with the pragmatic view, articulated most systematically by Peirce, that "spontaneity has ultimate categorical status."[58] From his analysis of judgment, Kant had derived twelve basic categories without which experience would be impossible. Although Peirce thought highly of Kant, he did not regard these twelve categories as satisfactory and set out to develop a new understanding of judgment from which a more satisfactory set of categories could be derived. He came to the view that the relationship between the logical elements in a proposition is a relationship of signs: the subject of a proposition is a sign of its predicate. All thought, therefore, is semiotic. But if this is the case, then thinking is a specific category of consciousness, namely, that category in which signs are related to one another. The distinctive characteristic of semiosis, Peirce further argued, is that it is triadic: (1) a sign (2) stands for some object (3) to someone. A sign, Peirce would later write, is "anything which determines something else (its *interpretant*) to refer to an object to which itself refers (its *object*) in the same way, the interpretant becoming in turn a sign, and so on *ad infinitum*."[59] Because of the triadic nature of sign relations, Peirce called that category of consciousness in which thinking is carried out "Thirdness." Two other categories of consciousness are also necessary to provide the raw materials with which thought can be carried out. Peirce named these categories "Firstness" and "Secondness:" "Firstness is the monadic element of experience usually identified with feeling, secondness is the dyadic element identified with the sense of action and reaction."[60] For Peirce, Firstness, Secondness, and Thirdness are not just irreducible categories of consciousness; they are also the universal

57. Manley Thompson, 1984, "Hartshorne and Peirce: Individuals and Continuity," pp. 130–48 in *Existence and Actuality: Conversations with Charles Hartshorne*, John Cobb and Franklin Gamwell, eds., Chicago: University of Chicago Press, 138.

58. Donald Lee, 1991, "Hartshorne and Pragmatic Metaphysics," pp. 529–49 in *The Philosophy of Charles Hartshorne*, Lewis Hahn, ed., Library of Living Philosophers Series, vol. 20, La Salle: Open Court, 548.

59. Charles Peirce, [1901–5] 1991, "Sign," pp. 239–40 in *Peirce on Signs: Writings on Semiotic by Charles Sanders Peirce*, James Hoopes, ed., Chapel Hill: University of North Carolina Press, 239.

60. Nathan Houser, 1992, "Introduction," pp. ixx–xli in *The Essential Peirce: Selected Philosophical Writings*, vol. 1 (1867–93), Nathan Houser and Christian Kloesel, eds., Bloomington: Indiana University Press, xxxi.

categories into which all conceptions fall and provide the basis for on the one hand, Peirce's division of philosophy (as between phenomenology, normative inquiries, and metaphysics) and, on the other hand, for his metaphysics, which attempts to understand what kind of universe it is that could present itself in these three categories. Hartshorne did not accept this categorical scheme in its entirety,[61] but he did agree that triadic, semiotic relationships extend beyond the domain of human consciousness to form part of the world itself, as expressed by his doctrine of "panpsychism," and also that novelty and creativity inhere as potentials in every act of semiosis.

Hartshorne occupied an ambiguous position in the philosophy department at Chicago. He was hired in 1928, before Hutchins assumed control of the university, and his interest in and knowledge of Peirce fit well with the department's pragmatic orientation. Precisely for this reason, he formed part of the opposition to Hutchins's effort at remaking the department. Although interested in theological questions, he had little patience for the neo-Thomist view of God and therefore disapproved of Adler's philosophy. At the same time, while engaged with certain questions in the history of philosophy, he found himself less willing than McKeon "to allow the effort to understand the writings of past philosophers to largely crowd out philosophical understandings of nature and supernature."[62] He had also been an enthusiastic supporter of Morris's attempt to hire Carnap and Reichenbach, which did nothing to endear him to the administration. To be sure, he and Carnap agreed on few points. Hartshorne was a metaphysician, while Carnap hoped to vanquish metaphysics. Hartshorne, like Whitehead, spoke in lofty abstractions that Carnap found too vague to understand. In an autobiographical tribute to Carnap, Hartshorne recalls that "If I showed him [Carnap] a manuscript, almost all the marginal comments were 'n.c.' for 'not clear.'"[63] Nevertheless, the relations between them appear to have been cordial, and Hartshorne, for his part, was convinced that increasing the intellectual diversity of the department with Carnap's presence was all to the good.

Rorty and at least some of his fellow students, however, understood the situation differently. For them, Hartshorne's metaphysical interests stood opposed to the intellectual project of logical positivism. Rorty's

61. Charles Hartshorne, 1980, "A Revision of Peirce's Categories," *Monist* 63:277–89.

62. Hartshorne, "Some Causes of My Intellectual Growth," 32.

63. Hartshorne, no title, pp. xliii–xlv in *PSA 1970: In Memory of Rudolf Carnap*, Boston Studies in the Philosophy of Science vol. 8, Roger Buck and Robert Cohen, eds., Dordrecht: D. Reidel, xliii.

early correspondence is hardly filled with denunciations of the positivist agenda, but that he saw Hartshorne's work—and his own—as standing the ground against the positivists is clear from a letter he wrote to his mother in December of 1950. He was taking a class from Carnap and described the term paper he had written: "Finished a paper for Carnap—long, dull, of interest only to opponents of positivism. You can look at it if you like, but I can't see it interesting either you, Carnap, or anybody except the little clique of reactionary metaphysicians (the rank to which I aspire) who are trying to stop the positivist invasion. Title—'Logical Truth, Factual Truth, and the Synthetic *A Priori*.' Someone suggested as a subtitle, 'How to Square the Vienna Circle.'"[64] The paper does not survive in Rorty's files. Nevertheless, the main piece of evidence we have as to the character of Rorty's thought during his later years at Chicago—his masters thesis—is, without ever mentioning positivism, consistent with this self-described intellectual identity. Defended in 1952, the thesis was unapologetically metaphysical.

* 5 *

Its topic may have been suggested by Hartshorne. In 1948, three Whitehead specialists—Hartshorne, Victor Lowe, and A. H. Johnson—were asked to give papers on Whitehead for a special panel at the Western Division APA meetings held at Knox College in Galesburg, Illinois. Hartshorne's paper, published in 1950, identified twelve characteristics of Whitehead's thought that made him "supremely great"[65] as a metaphysician and cosmologist. These ranged from his phenomenologically sensitive empiricism to his theism to his employment, like Peirce, of a relational logic. In Hartshorne's view, however, Whitehead was not immune to criticism, particularly concerning the clarity of certain aspects of his doctrine. One of these Hartshorne singled out as in urgent need of clarification: "A difficult concept in Whitehead," he concluded the paper by noting, "is that of the Creativity, or the ultimate ground, or substantial activity. Is this a sort of God beyond God? I have some doubt whether all [Whitehead's] utterances on this topic can be reconciled."[66]

64. Richard Rorty to Winifred Raushenbush, December 16, 1950, RRP.

65. Charles Hartshorne, 1950, "Whitehead's Metaphysics," pp. 25–41 in *Whitehead and the Modern World: Science, Metaphysics, and Civilization: Three Essays on the Thought of Alfred North Whitehead*, by Victor Lowe, Charles Hartshorne, and A. H. Johnson, Boston: Beacon Press, 25.

66. Ibid., 40.

It was something very much like this topic that Rorty took up in his masters thesis. Like Hartshorne, Rorty gave Whitehead's approach high praise: "Whitehead has constructed a cosmology whose completeness of detail, and consequent adequacy of application, rank with those of the greatest of such constructions."[67] Not creativity per se, but the metaphysical category most closely related to it—potentiality—was to be the subject of Rorty's analysis. Again like Hartshorne, Rorty recognized this to be a pivot point in Whitehead's metaphysics. The question was whether Whitehead's views on potentiality were coherent across all the dimensions of his philosophy. Rorty considered in this regard Whitehead's theory of eternal objects, his theory of the eternal nature of God—according to which God as primordial nature is "the order of orderers—the arrang[er] of all eternal objects in an order among themselves"[68]—and his theory of the extensive continuum, which is the "ground of order with respect to the totality of all the actualities of the world, *qua* real potentialities."[69] With respect to the theory of eternal objects, Rorty took up the question of prehension. Eternal objects appear to be "at once absolutely determinate in respect to definiteness and absolutely indeterminate in respect to position."[70] Does the creativity that inheres in prehension, then, concern only the positioning of an eternal object on a spatiotemporal grid? Or does the notion that prehension may introduce genuine novelty into the world require that we recognize a two-way flow between the ideal and the real, with new eternal objects coming into being as a result of the creative actualization of previously constituted ones? This move away from Platonism Rorty quickly rejected on the grounds that, "by de-eternalizing eternal objects," such an approach "contaminates them with actuality."[71] Instead, he proposed an improvement to Whitehead's system according to which "a real duality of content [is] postulated within the physical pole of each actual entity, a duality of determinateness and indeterminateness. This duality is unanalyzable, for it is the ultimate postulation required by the Category of the Ultimate."[72] While still allowing prehension to involve spatiotemporal positioning, this emendation also recognized that actualities may prehend other moments of actualization in addition to eternal objects, such that creativity can introduce new forms of order without ever affecting the ideal.

As for God and primordial nature, Rorty did not advance an argument so much as note a paradox in Whitehead's system:

---

67. Rorty, "Whitehead's Use of the Concept of Potentiality," 101.
68. Ibid., 43.   70. Ibid., 34–35.   72. Ibid., 35.
69. Ibid., 61.   71. Ibid., 34.

The assertion of the reality of process is identical with the assertion of indeterminacy. Indeterminacy in actuality implies a realm of pure potentialities, in order to give meaning to the notion of novelty attained through free choice. These pure potentialities, in turn, require an orderer among themselves and a mediator between themselves and actuality. This mediator and orderer turns out to have the character of a leading thread, a determined route of progress toward a final state of process which would be the negation of indeterminacy. What is indicated by this apparent self-contradiction of the principle of process is that there is an incoherence in our theory of mediation between potentiality and actuality.[73]

Only when considered in conjunction with the notion of the extensive continuum could a solution to this paradox be found. Just as he had previously suggested a duality in the physical pole of entities, he now insisted that philosophers should "transfer ... emotions from the mental to the physical pole of actual entities—i.e., ... deny ... that subjective forms are constituted, as Whitehead says they are, by conceptual prehensions of eternal objects. Whitehead says that both the qualia which an actual entity feels, and the emotions with which it feels them, are elements in the definiteness of that actual entity. Our suggestion is that the latter are elements constitutive of the position of that entity."[74] Insofar as this move was undertaken, and the full range of freedom associated with physical prehension and positioning on the extensive continuum recognized, primordial nature would lose its power to determine the direction of the actual world-process, and the indeterminism Whitehead had been at pains to argue for would be preserved. Rorty's overall conclusion was that "freedom ... belongs to the physical pole—to real time, and to position determined by subjective form."[75] "Ideal potentiality ... is the ground of order," he concluded in a paragraph so laden with metaphysical abstraction as to boggle the mind. "Real potentiality is the ground of freedom.... It is meaningless to think of ideal potentiality as the conditioned indetermination which is real potentiality, minus the conditions. The real potentiality which is Creativity is 'actual only in virtue of its accidents'—i.e., nothing if not conditioned, nothing if not individuated."[76] Rorty hoped that "the coherence of the foundations of Whitehead's system might, perhaps, be strengthened by [his] explicit consideration of these problems."[77]

73. Ibid., 59. 75. Ibid., 100. 77. Ibid., 102.
74. Ibid., 89. 76. Ibid.

FIVE

Ph.D. at Yale, 1952–1956

∗ 1 ∗

As he worked toward the completion of his masters degree, Rorty resolved to continue on in his philosophical studies. Although his choice
of doctoral program would be fateful in terms of the kind of training he
would receive and his professional trajectory, he approached this choice,
as most graduate students do, neither with unlimited information about
which school would be best to attend nor with a sufficiently distinguished
record that his choice among schools was unconstrained. He considered
three possibilities: the philosophy departments at Harvard or Yale or staying on at Chicago and taking his degree from the Committee on Social
Thought. Remaining at Chicago was the least appealing option. His uncle
Paul Raushenbush wrote to him in June of 1951 to say, "We gather that you
don't really want to spend another year at Chicago U. In any event, we
don't believe you should. You've certainly been there long enough. A shift
would make sense."[1] His mentors in the philosophy department at Chicago probably told him it wouldn't be wise to take his Ph.D. from them, but
one of his undergraduate teachers, classicist David Grene,[2] encouraged
him to enter the Committee and promised him a scholarship if he did. Despite his shaky Greek, Rorty must have demonstrated at least some promise with classical materials. Indeed, when he was first hired at Princeton
ten years later it would be to teach ancient philosophy—though his linguistic skills would soon be judged inadequate for the task. But it was not

1. Paul Raushenbush to Richard Rorty, June 10, 1951, RRP.

2. On Grene see Todd Breyfogle, ed., 1999, *Literary Imagination, Ancient and Modern:
Essays in Honor of David Grene*, Chicago: University of Chicago Press.

yet clear that the Committee, an interdisciplinary doctoral program just getting off the ground, would be able to successfully place its graduates in teaching positions. Such, at least, was his parents' concern, and they advised Richard not to take Grene up on his offer. "We promise to tell no one at all about your conversation with Grene," his mother wrote to him in January of 1952. "The off the record offer is undeniably handsome. But if you want to teach, and have the relative security of a teaching position, then I question the Comm idea. If you wanted to go into government etc., then it might be admirable."[3] Given that they'd so frequently consulted their friends and acquaintances for advice on Richard's career, it is likely this piece of advice, too, resulted from their network contacts. There is no direct evidence to support this claim, but the Rortys did write to their friends with other questions about doctoral programs. A month after Winifred's letter to Richard, for example, Charles Walker of the Yale Institute of Human Relations wrote to James to say that he was "delighted to hear that your son Richard wants to get his doctorate in philosophy at Yale. I think we have the best department in the country."[4] Walker said he knew the dean and associate dean of the graduate school and that Richard should feel free to use his name as necessary. Because Richard did want a career in academe, he set his sights on Harvard or Yale.

The philosophy departments at Harvard and Yale presented diametrically opposed intellectual profiles—by design. The earliest reputational survey of U.S. philosophy departments, carried out in 1925, ranked Harvard first, followed by Columbia, Chicago, Cornell, and Yale. By the time of the next such study in 1957, Harvard remained in first place, with Yale, Michigan, Columbia, and Cornell rounding out the top five in descending order.[5] It speaks to the still-unsettled nature of the philosophical field at the time that two of the top departments could be so different. As the intellectual generation at Harvard that included James and Royce handed the reins over to their students around the time of the First World War— and so highly did Harvard philosophers regard themselves that they did typically hire their own—a transition was effected between two philosophical eras.[6] Under the leadership of university president A. Lawrence Lowell, privilege was granted to those academicians who "tended to

3. Winifred Raushenbush to Richard Rorty, January 29, 1952, RRP.

4. Charles Walker to James Rorty, February 20, 1952, RRP.

5. These rankings are given in Allan Cartter, 1966, *An Assessment of Quality in Graduate Education*, Washington, D.C.: American Council on Education, 29.

6. My discussion here paraphrases Bruce Kuklick, 1977, *The Rise of American Philosophy: Cambridge, Massachusetts, 1860–1930*, New Haven: Yale University Press.

think of themselves as professionals."[7] In philosophy this meant those who "promoted impersonal criteria of scholarly aptitude; their own work, often concentrating in one particular branch of philosophy, was highly and uniformly competent."[8] Vestiges of an older, more topically expansive, and more publicly oriented conception of philosophy remained in the figures of Hocking, Perry, and Whitehead, but Lewis and Henry Sheffer, logicians both, embodied the new ideals. Lewis was the more significant figure. Trained by Perry and Royce, Lewis initially defended idealism on the grounds that only it could respond effectively to Humean critiques of causality but soon moved closer to a kind of realism. Objects in the world confront us as givens presenting a minimum of order, but to understand them we must apply conceptual frameworks supplied by the mind. The frameworks we accept, however, are not logically necessary, as they were for Kant, but rather those that prove indispensable as we attempt to make sense of experience. Important though Lewis's conceptual pragmatism was in the history of philosophy, most notable about his thought for present purposes is the form it assumed. Increasingly concerned with problems in logic, Lewis not only relied heavily on symbolic logic in the writing of his philosophy but also came to believe that logic "reflected the principles of human reasoning, and that investigating the widest possible systems of order enabled us to grasp these principles."[9] This orientation characterized not only Lewis but also—and partly through his influence—younger members of the department. Classifying the specialties of those who received their doctorates at Harvard from 1893 to 1930, Bruce Kuklick finds a nearly 50 percent decline in the number of students specializing in religious and moral philosophy, a smaller drop in the number specializing in metaphysics—which remained at 31 percent during the period 1920–30—and a more than 100 percent increase in the number of students with technical orientations. As time went on it was the technically oriented students, with interests in symbolic logic, who received the best jobs.[10]

This trend toward increasing technicism continued in the 1930s and 1940s. Feigl spent the year at Harvard in 1930 and exposed students there—especially those studying empirical psychology, not yet a separate department—to the ideas of the Vienna School, as did W. V. O. Quine, who studied with Carnap in the early 1930s. Just a few years later, intellectual ties would come to be forged between members of the Harvard department like Lewis and philosophers at Oxford like A. J. Ayer, J. L.

7. Ibid., 453.   8. Ibid.   9. Ibid., 539.   10. Ibid., 476–77.

Austin, and Stuart Hampshire, who—influenced by the work of G. E. Moore, Russell, and Wittgenstein and sympathetic, in varying degrees, to the program of the logical positivists—"looked at philosophy as an activity that clarified ordinary talk and the structure of science."[11] These streams of thought converged with native currents in epistemology to result in the technical vision of philosophy promoted by many of those who taught at Harvard in the 1930s and 1940s. For them—and here Lewis and Quine were the paradigmatic figures—"symbolic logic was a tool necessary for philosophic reasoning. Although they were suspicious of any absolutistic conception of science ... [they] often elevated scientific understanding as the only kind, and indeed, with the logical empiricists, made 'the philosophy of science' a central subfield ... almost coterminous with epistemology. In focusing on the careful explication of how language was used ... analytic philosophers [as they came to be called] invented 'the philosophy of language,' another central subfield.... Although analysts did not dismiss more traditional areas of philosophy as meaningless ... by ignoring them they implied that these fields could be ignored."[12] Speculative metaphysics of the kind learned by Hartshorne under Whitehead in the late 1920s all but died out at Harvard.

In this context, philosophers in the Yale department sought to carve out a distinctive disciplinary niche by defining themselves as resistors of technicism and torchbearers for more traditional forms of philosophical inquiry, especially ethics, metaphysics, and the philosophy of religion.[13] Yale had long defined itself institutionally against Harvard as a place where higher education would serve the purpose of preserving religious and cultural orthodoxies, and in the first decades of the twentieth century the Yale philosophy department embraced this mission by hiring scholars, especially from Harvard, who had escaped the influences of James and were thus free from pragmatism's relativizing, antitraditionalist tendencies. Charles Bakewell and Wilmon Sheldon were among those brought on board under this mandate. They "saw themselves as the bearers of the

11. Bruce Kuklick, 2001, *A History of Philosophy in America, 1720–2000*, Oxford: Clarendon Press, 244.

12. Ibid., 246.

13. Here again I rely heavily on Kuklick: see Bruce Kuklick, 2004, "Philosophy at Yale in the Century after Darwin," *History of Philosophy Quarterly* 21:313–36. Peter Hare, who was a student at Yale in the 1950s, worries that this characterization of the department could lead to misunderstanding: there was no animosity toward technical strains of philosophy, he insists, "*provided that* its proponents were tolerant of systematic metaphysics and moral philosophy." E-mail to author, October 19, 2006.

tradition of Western thought that began with the Greeks, progressed through the medieval period, and culminated in the canon of Modern Philosophy. The task of these men had been to reflect on the nature and destiny of man, and present the accumulated insights to an educated public. Now philosophers in American higher education were to forward this elevated enterprise."[14]

As the influence of pragmatism gave way in the 1930s, however, to various strains of technicism, the views of Bakewell and Sheldon changed. They now saw pragmatism as an ally against those who would reduce philosophy to linguistic, conceptual, and logical analysis and, as senior faculty members and administrators, hired a new generation of scholars— some sympathetic to pragmatism—who were "determined to make New Haven stand for speculative philosophy and the sacred."[15] New ties were established to the divinity school, undergraduate education—focused on discussion of perennial philosophical problems—was reemphasized, and a department culture was institutionalized wherein "pluralism," meant to signify the value of approaching philosophy from a wide variety of perspectives, and not simply through the lens of any one approach like positivism, became enshrined as a prime academic virtue.

Brand Blanshard, a metaphysician and ethicist who had studied at Michigan, Columbia, Oxford, and Harvard, expressed the ideology of the department in an introductory chapter he wrote for *Philosophy and American Education* (1945), a volume of essays based on a series of conferences and discussions convened by the American Philosophical Association about the nature of philosophy and how it should be taught to undergraduates. There was, Blanshard reported, a widespread feeling among philosophers that the discipline had recently lost prestige, particularly among undergraduates. "Mathematics, physics, engineering, medicine— all the sciences, theoretic and applied, that have to do with the arts of war are riding high; the humanities, including philosophy, have gone into temporary eclipse."[16] This was a shame, for there were vital pedagogical functions that philosophy could be performing. Beyond the prestige philosophy had lost relative to the sciences because of the war, two disputes among American philosophers had weakened the profession. The first was the dispute between pragmatists and nonpragmatists, which Blan-

14. Kuklick, "Philosophy at Yale," 319.

15. Ibid., 320.

16. Brand Blanshard, 1945, "The Climate of Opinion," pp. 3–42 in *Philosophy in American Education: Its Tasks and Opportunities,* by Brand Blanshard, Curt Ducasse, Charles Hendel, Arthur Murphy, and Max Otto, New York: Harper and Brothers, 8.

shard framed as a disagreement between those who take an instrumental view of knowledge and those who do not.[17] Blanshard left no doubt as to where he stood in this dispute: pragmatism leads to a downplaying of metaphysics and thereby undercuts the discipline's ability to provide students with a philosophy of life resonant with their concerns about the ultimate. Nevertheless, pragmatists had at least been willing to partici-pate in discussions of such important matters with philosophers who dis-agreed with them and at the same time were to be applauded for reach-ing out to the wider public. It was a second dispute—between positivists and nonpositivists—that had been much more debilitating. On different grounds than the pragmatists, the positivists too had declared "nearly the whole of metaphysics, the central part of traditional philosophy ... to be without significance."[18] Unlike the pragmatists, they also eschewed eth-ics. Under the influence of positivism, Blanshard asserted, philosophers had ceased working on important problems, becoming encased in a nar-row professionalism "preoccupied with—well, what? With such things as the status of sense data, the meaning of meaning, the reduction of the number of primitive propositions required for deductive logic, the question of whether a priori statements are all of them, or only some of them, tautologous."[19] "Philosophy was not always thus," Blanshard con-tinued. "At the turn of the century it was still generously conceived, and was devoting itself to questions of large significance for understanding the world and for living in it."[20] Deploring the turn toward positivism, Blanshard called on philosophers to live up to the field's timeless ideals; for philosophy to once again become a profession practiced by those pos-sessing "wisdom, a breadth of experience, a sanity of practical judgment, a depth of insight into the relative values of things, [and] a serenity and clearness of view."[21] Reorienting the field in this more traditional direc-tion, which required not the advancement of a particular philosophy but dialogue among advocates of different approaches who all took seriously philosophy's historic mission, would be the self-appointed task of the Yale philosophy department.

Most of the hires made in the late 1930s, 1940s, and early 1950s were intended to promote the ideals Blanshard identified: Charles Hendel, brought to the department in 1939, was "a historian of social and po-litical thought"; Blanshard himself, hired in 1945, "defended a form of idealism in the style of Royce and Blanshard's tutor Hocking, and to this

17. Ibid., 21. 19. Ibid., 32. 21. Ibid., 40.
18. Ibid., 26. 20. Ibid.

work he added an impressive three volume exploration of metaphysics";
Paul Weiss, another 1945 hire, was a "metaphysician of the grand style";[22]
and John E. Smith, whose doctorate had been taken at Columbia and
who worked on pragmatism and the philosophy of religion, arrived in
New Haven in 1952. Other philosophers on the faculty during Rorty's
time there included F. S. C. Northrop, a generalist philosopher of science
with interests in religion and cross-cultural understanding; Carl
Hempel, the department's "token" positivist who was the replacement
for C. L. Stevenson, a positivist ethicist who had been denied tenure the
same year Blanshard and Weiss were hired; Arthur Pap, another analyst,
to whom an offer was extended after Hempel left Yale for Princeton in
1955 in light of departmental doubts as to the advisability of promoting
an analytic philosopher to the ranks of the senior faculty; Rulon Wells, a
young Peirce scholar who received his doctorate from Harvard in 1942;
and Frederic Fitch, a logician also interested in Whitehead's metaphysics, who was tenured in 1951.[23] Of these, Weiss and Wells were the most
important for Rorty's intellectual development, though the presence of
Smith in the department—for whom Rorty served as a teaching assistant for a course on pragmatism—was not irrelevant. The analytic philosopher Wilfrid Sellars, who would prove influential for Rorty's later
work, did not join the department until after Rorty had completed his
doctorate.

* 2 *

Although most Yale philosophers were Protestants—with some, like
Smith, explicitly concerned with theological questions and others making connections to prominent faculty in the Divinity School such as
Robert Calhoun and H. Richard Niebuhr, Reinhold Niebuhr's younger
brother—the department was not completely hostile to those who professed different faiths. Despite Yale's notorious anti-Semitism it did hire
Weiss, a Jew, to a tenured post—but not without considerable controversy. Weiss had been born to working-class immigrant parents in New
York City. He graduated from City College in 1927, where he studied
with Morris Cohen, Sidney Hook's mentor. Against Cohen's advice, he
went to Harvard for graduate school to work with Whitehead. Moving

22. Kuklick, "Philosophy at Yale," 320, 323.

23. See John Lango, 2002, "Fitch's Method and Whitehead's Metaphysics," *Transactions of the Charles S. Peirce Society* 38:581–603.

to Cambridge, he found, even then, that "Harvard's philosophy department...was dominated by logicians...[who] seemed to have a contempt
for the history of thought."[24] Although impressed by Whitehead—who
seemed alone in resisting the program of the logicians—and committed,
like his teacher, to working on metaphysics, Weiss was less prone than
Hartshorne to championing Whitehead's views. This was the case even
though he and Hartshorne worked closely together editing the Peirce
papers, a job Weiss agreed to take because Cohen had spoken favorably
of Peirce. Consistent with Weiss's sense that few in the Harvard philosophy department were interested in the history of the field, he reports
in his autobiography that almost no department members came to see
him and Hartshorne as they went about the task of sorting through the
thousands of manuscript pages. The same sense of being on the fringes of
the department was also communicated to him by the fact that his dissertation, a work in metaphysics titled "Logic and System," was initially
rejected by his committee. After receiving a "second-class" fellowship to
study in Europe for a year, where he heard lectures by Heidegger and Gilson, among others, Weiss took a job at Bryn Mawr, thanks to Whitehead's
recommendation.

Despite a heavy teaching load, Weiss was productive at Bryn Mawr,
publishing articles on topics ranging from ethics to Peirce to metaphysics. Many of his metaphysical claims were framed as direct challenges to
the positivists. A short discussion piece published in the *Philosophical Review* in 1934, for example, began with the assertion that "the neo-positiv-
istic challenge that metaphysics is meaningless has gone unanswered—
perhaps because the answer is so obvious."[25] Weiss claimed, as he would
elsewhere in his early work, that epistemology and ontology presuppose
one another. To know requires that we understand what kind of universe
it is that we know. Yet ontology, precisely because it cannot be known
through sense experience, will always remain mysterious. This does not
mark it as an illegitimate topic of inquiry. The most we can hope for is
to develop systematic frameworks for understanding being that are logically consistent with all we can know about it indirectly; that we cannot
attain greater certainty with regard to metaphysical issues should be no
deterrent.

24. Paul Weiss, 1995, "Lost in Thought: Alone with Others," pp. 3–45 in *The Philosophy of
Paul Weiss*, Library of Living Philosophers Series, vol. 23, Lewis Hahn, ed., Chicago: Open
Court, 9–10.

25. Paul Weiss, 1934, "Metaphysics: The Domain of Ignorance," *Philosophical Review*
43:402–6, 402.

Told that article publications alone would not get him tenure, Weiss began working on a book. His first, *Reality,* was published in 1938, and after his move to Yale in 1946 he completed three more in quick succession before Rorty, who would be his student, finished his doctorate in 1956: *Nature and Man* (1947), *Man's Freedom* (1950), and *Modes of Being* (1956).

Weiss's metaphysics went through many changes over the course of his long career, even before the publication of *Modes of Being,*[26] so offering a snapshot portrait of it is difficult. *Reality* took up the same problem Whitehead concentrated upon—that of "reconcil[ing] process and permanence"[27]—but approached it in a different way. Whereas Whitehead focused upon independent actualities that model themselves on eternal objects, Weiss claimed that being is always and intrinsically incomplete, oriented as it is toward the future it will become. At the same time, he accused Whitehead, with his Platonic emphasis, of ignoring the diversity of particular beings. This was a critique not just of Whitehead but of "the variety of process philosophies which were articulated in the early part of the twentieth century," including those of Bergson and James, whose "emphasis on process, duration, and the creative and dynamic aspects of reality" involved a "tendency to undermine the integrity, persistence and sustaining of those actualities that are capable of being creative, dynamic and free."[28] To develop a more satisfactory approach, Weiss laid out a complex, sixty-six category metaphysical scheme.

In *Modes of Being,* Weiss collapsed his earlier categorical framework, presenting his new metaphysical system in a series of propositions premised on the division of being into four distinct but related modes: Actuality, which involves "finite beings in space and time" who "complete themselves" by "striv[ing] to realize relevant, essential objectives which, in different ways, they specify out of a single common future Good";[29] Ideality, "which is the Good divorced from any exclusive reference to the particular actualities that seek to realize that good";[30] Existence, the "restless force at once ingredient in and overflowing the borders of Actualities, connecting each with

26. Andrew Reck, 1995, "The Five Ontologies of Paul Weiss," pp. 139–58 in *The Philosophy of Paul Weiss,* Library of Living Philosophers Series, vol. 23, Lewis Hahn, ed., Chicago: Open Court.

27. Ibid., 140.

28. Richard Bernstein, 1987, "Human Beings: Plurality and Togetherness," pp. 200–17 in *Creativity and Common Sense: Essays in Honor of Paul Weiss,* Thomas Krettek, ed., Albany, SUNY Press, 202–3.

29. Ibid., 212.

30. George Kimball Plochmann, 1987, "Methods and Modes: Aspects of Weissian Meta-

every other, and coming to a focus in the Ideal";[31] and God, or the principle that unites all the other modes. As he did in his earliest articles, he situated his contributions to metaphysics in relation to analytic philosophy. He noted in *Modes of Being* that the great challenge faced by thought in his day was unification in light of the growth of specialized knowledge. "It seemed for a time," he observed, "as if this challenge would be accepted in a most promising way" by "a group of well-trained, meticulous, energetic 'analytic' philosophers" who "seemed willing to take as their task the discovery of criteria and principles by means of which the efforts and outcomes of the different disciplines could be evaluated and organized."[32] "Very soon," however, "they turned themselves into another race of specialists, concentrating on the quite restricted task of clarifying the intent, methodology or usages of other men."[33] But the problem with analytic philosophy was not just that it represented an instance of promise lost. Rather, analysts sought to proscribe exactly that form of philosophical inquiry—metaphysics— that offered the greatest hope for unifying knowledge, for "only if we know what it is to be, to inquire, to know, can we recognize that we are all dealing with different phases of the same subject."[34] His own metaphysics would be an effort at overcoming this analytic constriction of vision and at presenting a comprehensive philosophical system.

The immediate occasion for Weiss's being brought to Yale from Bryn Mawr, where he'd risen to chair of the philosophy department, was that Blanshard became sick upon his arrival in New Haven. A temporary replacement was needed, and Weiss was given the job. Blanshard and Northrop took the opportunity to suggest that Weiss, who received favorable reviews from students that semester, be offered a tenured position. Dan Oren, telling the story of Weiss's move to Yale and the resistance he faced because of anti-Semitism, notes that "from an intellectual standpoint, Weiss's credentials were spectacular,"[35] but it was not simply the volume of his scholarship or where he had gone to graduate school that made him appealing. Here was a traditional metaphysician with interests in ethics, a philosopher who resisted analytic technicism and was making a national reputation for himself around this professional identity. Who better to help anchor the Yale department?

physics," pp. 15–42 in *Creativity and Common Sense: Essays in Honor of Paul Weiss*, Thomas Krettek, ed., Albany: State University of New York Press, 20.

31. Weiss, *Modes of Being*, 14.　　32. Ibid., 3.　　33. Ibid., 4.　　34. Ibid.

35. Dan Oren, 1985, *Joining the Club: A History of Jews and Yale*, New Haven: Yale University Press, 262.

Not everyone who had signed on to the department's vision, how-ever, supported the Weiss appointment. Hendel had his doubts, as did the now retired Bakewell and Sheldon. They objected not to the fact that he was Jewish per se but that his working-class and immigrant up-bringing had rendered him "a caricature of the all-knowing and pushy Jew."[36] Without questioning his intellectual abilities, they wondered how he would fit in with the rest of the refined and cultured faculty and how he would fare when faced with a classroom of undergraduates from more privileged backgrounds. Blanshard and Northrop won the debate in the department, and when it came time for the university to finalize the appointment, saner heads carried the day, not least because Yale was beginning to lose legitimacy in the national arena because of its reputa-tion for anti-Semitism. Hiring Weiss would be a way to signal that the doors to Jews at Yale were now open and to gain a first rate colleague in the process.[37] Within two years of moving to New Haven, Weiss took steps to spread more widely the department's gospel of a return to tra-ditional philosophical concerns, founding and assuming the editorship of a journal, the *Review of Metaphysics,* in 1947. Although devoted to no single metaphysical viewpoint—a memo written in 1953 identified as the philosophers to whom it wished to pay special attention those as diverse as Jaspers, Romero, Ewing, Northrop, Blanshard, and Hartshorne[38]—the journal proved an important home to thinkers, like Weiss, for whom metaphysical inquiry was philosophy itself.

* 3 *

Given the traditionalist and metaphysical orientation of the Yale depart-ment—and the close connection between Hartshorne and Weiss—it is no surprise that when Rorty applied to graduate school, he was welcomed at Yale with open arms. Harvard granted him admission as well, but not the free-ride scholarship he was able to secure from Yale.[39] The skills and knowledge he had accumulated at Chicago were simply more valuable in the Yale context. Beyond his interest in metaphysics, Rorty was a young scholar whose thought ranged widely and who was not only knowledge-able about the history of philosophy but also classically educated in the

36. Ibid., 262.   37. Ibid., 266–67.

38. Paul Weiss and Irwin Lieb, "A Report of the 6th Year from the Editor and Managing Editor," November 19, 1953, RRP.

39. Letter from Yale to Richard Rorty, March 31, 1952, RRP.

humanities as a whole. Rorty presented himself as such in his graduate school application essay. "By myself," he wrote,

> through independent work, I should like to extend my knowledge of languages, and to develop, intensively and extensively, my knowledge of the history of philosophy. In my formal program of studies, I should like to acquire a better grasp of the alternative views on the nature and content of logic, and, most of all, to learn as much as I can about the specific differences and similarities between the methods and results of the predecessors and exponents of existentialism and those of the type of philosophy which, I think, reaches its culmination in Whitehead and his successors.... Eventually ... I should like to study in Europe and gain a more thorough and immediate acquaintance with recent European developments in philosophy.[40]

This was precisely the kind of young person Yale philosophers wanted to attract. In his contribution to *Philosophy in American Education*, Hendel noted, writing of the graduate admissions process, that "the true breed of scholar is so rare that the universities engage in an unseemly competition for them by offering fellowships until the scene appears like a slave market, the schools thankfully paying cash to get the students."[41] Identifying students of this breed was difficult, but in Hendel's view a minimum condition was a liberal arts education. "No one should ever be admitted to graduate student in philosophy who has not already had a good liberal education," he wrote.[42] The reason it was imperative to bring in students with such a background was that by doing so the trend toward specialization, technicism, and the pursuit of esoteric questions and methods might be countered. "There is an apparent poverty of culture" in philosophy today, Hendel asserted. "Our scholars stick to the things in which they are trained and to the specialties into whose hands they have committed their souls. They do not read widely and for the sheer love of experience. They have little taste for the great bodies of expression, either in English or any other literature, where the feelings, thoughts, and aspirations of man are variously disclosed.... They do not realize that a 'craftsman of

40. Draft of graduate school application essay, no date, RRP.

41. Charles Hendel, 1945, "The Teachers of Philosophy and the Graduate School," pp. 252–78 in *Philosophy in American Education: Its Tasks and Opportunities*, by Brand Blanshard, Curt Ducasse, Charles Hendel, Arthur Murphy, and Max Otto, New York: Harper and Brothers, 256.

42. Ibid.

ideas' has to be also a craftsman in his own language and that philosophy for many centuries before the present age has been good literature appealing to all ages of mankind and not simply to an esoteric set."[43] Rorty was such a craftsman.

Yet Rorty was not the only Chicago student to have the kind of qualifications Hendel identified and to find them valued by New Haven philosophers. Amélie, his friends Richard Schmitt and Roger Hancock, and Richard Bernstein—with whom he'd become acquainted—were all granted admission around the same time. That Richard and Amélie were both admitted to Yale simultaneously no doubt made the scholarship offer even harder to resist, though there was enough uncertainty surrounding their relationship that Amélie could write to Richard from Europe of her decision to move to New Haven only that "I hope that you'll be more surprised than annoyed to learn that for many reasons, I shall be at Yale next year."[44] Regardless, it was clear that Rorty's parents could not afford for him to attend Harvard without a fellowship. While they could try to make him feel better about the fact that he hadn't received one by reassuring him that he might be eligible for a "Harvard junior fellowship plum . . . after completing your Yale residence,"[45] he would have to go where he was most wanted and where he would receive financial support.

* **4** *

Much less can be said about Rorty's experiences while at Yale than about his time at Chicago, for the volume of his correspondence dwindles with his arrival in New Haven. This is probably because greater maturity, his new relationship with Amélie, and his graduate workload conspired to lessen both his need and time for intimacy with his parents, who in the earlier period were his primary correspondents. Rorty has also said in autobiographical pieces that he learned less philosophy at Yale than at Chicago because he didn't spend as much time there, because the teachers weren't as good, and because he was so consumed with writing his dissertation. One thing his correspondence does make clear is that—his doubts about some of his professors aside—at the time he found the atmosphere at Yale congenial. Milton Crane, who formerly taught literature at the University of Chicago, wrote to him in November of 1952 to say, "My wife and I are delighted that you find Yale so good. My reports from other

43. Ibid., 269.
44. Amélie Rorty to Richard Rorty, July 7, 1952, RRP.
45. James Rorty to Richard Rorty, April 20, 1952, RRP.

ex-Chicagoans are that people are astonishingly pleasant at their new universities. You know, there *might* just be something odd about Chicago."[46] Similarly, Schmitt noted in a letter from December of that year: "I have not heard from you for a while except through Bob Hendrickson who reports that you are gaining a reputation at Yale of a person who has something to say. It is all to the credit of your colleagues that they realised this already."[47] Schmitt went on to note that he, too, had applied to both Yale and Harvard, though "after your glowing reports I feel very much inclined to try Yale." Another Chicago friend observed that "Yale has done you a lot of good. You sound happier and more content than I remember on this campus."[48]

What had changed to make Rorty's educational experience such a happy one as compared with his time at Chicago? One possibility is that Rorty liked Yale because it offered its graduate students a sense of historic mission: they would be the ones to put philosophy back on track, countering the pernicious influence of the analysts and restoring the field to its proper scope, range, and bearing. That Yale philosophers had come together around the mission of pluralism may have given Rorty the sense of being at the forefront of a major intellectual movement, a message reinforced by the fact that he was one of several students to work as an editorial assistant on the *Review of Metaphysics*, which promised to be the home for a revivification of philosophy.

∗ 5 ∗

As they went about trying to formulate a viable response to the analysts, Yale professors and graduate students drew on a number of intellectual resources: ancient philosophy, contemporary metaphysics, recent developments in Continental thought, and so on. Especially in light of criticisms by philosophers such as Susan Haack that Rorty's version of pragmatism is at odds with that offered by Charles Peirce, and hence inauthentic,[49] it is important to note that for Rorty, anyway, Peirce represented one such resource.[50] Peirce would play only a minor role in Rorty's dissertation—

46. Milton Crane to Richard Rorty, November 2, 1952, RRP.

47. Richard Schmitt to Richard Rorty, December 20, 1952, RRP.

48. "Mary" to Richard Rorty, May 2, 1953, RRP.

49. Susan Haack, 1998, *Manifesto of a Passionate Moderate: Unfashionable Essays*, Chicago: University of Chicago Press.

50. Also see chapter 6 for a discussion of the central role played by Peirce in Rorty's earliest published articles.

though he would gain in importance in Rorty's earliest published writings—but it is clear from Rorty's correspondence that Peirce was on his mind during his Yale years.[51] Rorty has also recalled in an interview that he talked a great deal about Peirce with his graduate school friends.[52]

Stronger evidence that Rorty was immersed in Peirce comes not just from the fact that he was working under Weiss or had previously studied with Thompson and Hartshorne but from a set of detailed notes, fourteen pages in length, that he took in a course on Peirce taught by Rulon Wells during the 1952–53 academic year.[53] The notes appear to record the content of Wells's lectures. While it is impossible to tell from the notes which of Wells's claims about Peirce Rorty found persuasive—they contain few annotations—and while the notes record scattered ideas about Peirce's philosophy rather than presenting a single, focused interpretation, they give at least some indication of the background against which Rorty's own views of Peirce might have been forged. Two things about the notes stand out. The first is the degree to which Peirce is discussed not as a historical artifact but as a subject of contemporary controversy. One of the founding myths of the recent revival of interest in American pragmatism is that the pragmatists were not discussed in major American philosophy departments in the 1950s and 1960s. An analysis of data on philosophy dissertations shows that this was not the case and that Yale was an epicenter of pragmatist activity.[54] Because Yale was a nodal point in pragmatist intellectual networks, Yale scholars who were interested in pragmatism knew and were able to situate themselves in relation to the wider community of American philosophers who were discussing the meaning and significance of pragmatist ideas. Wells did exactly that in his

51. For example, in January 1952 he wrote to his parents to say that he "came out to New Haven Saturday and drove in again to NY Monday with a friend to the [APA] meetings. I heard the Peirce papers in the morning and in the afternoon went up to Sarah Lawrence to hear aesthetics papers." Richard Rorty to parents, January 2, 1952, RRP.

52. Interview with author, December 22, 1998. Amélie Rorty, for her part, does not remember there being that much talk about Peirce at Yale.

53. In an initial draft of this chapter I assumed that the notes were from a course taught by John Smith for which Rorty was a teaching assistant (they are not labeled.) This was because several times the lecturer refers to Wells by name, and it seemed odd that Wells would refer to himself in the third person. Rorty's recollection, however, was that the notes were taken during Wells's course. Given the uncertainty, it is safer to privilege Rorty's recollection. Accordingly, I assume that when the notes refer explicitly to Wells, this is an instance of Rorty jotting down what Wells's own views were.

54. See Neil Gross, 2002, "Becoming a Pragmatist Philosopher: Status, Self-Concept, and Intellectual Choice," *American Sociological Review* 67:52–76.

presentation of Peirce—a classical pragmatist also highly respected in the analytic community for his contributions to the philosophy of science, logic, language, and so on. In his lecture from October 1, for example, Wells referred students to an article about Peirce by Weiss in the 1934 *Dictionary of American Biography,* as well as to Thomas Goudge's 1950 book *The Thought of C. S. Peirce,* and to several recent pieces in the *Journal of Philosophy.* Later lectures invoked Stowe Persons's 1947 book *Free Religion: An American Faith* to describe the religious background to Peirce's ideas,[55] while others referred to the work of Arthur Burks, who had identified tensions in Peirce's system.[56] Some of these were references to the work of Peirce exegetes or historians, but such philosophers of the moment as Quine and Schlick were also mentioned.[57] The overall message communicated by this tendency to situate Peirce in relation to the contemporary literature was that he remained a philosopher worth taking seriously—a lesson Rorty would heed in the early years of his career.

Equally striking about Wells's presentation of Peirce is its multidimensionality. Well into the course, he would sum up Peirce's "leading ideas" by saying they included synechism, empiricism, logicisim, and humanism and by noting that these elements of Peirce's thought combined to produce others. "Teleology + Synechsim gives Realism," Rorty's notes record. "Synechsim + Logicism give Architectonism, Humanism + Logicism gives the divorce of theory and practice," and "Synchism + Empiricism (observed change) + Humanism give Tychism." But this formulaic discussion was meant to summarize the detailed presentation that had come before, not substitute for it. Earlier lectures had covered everything from Peirce's opposition to the notion that mathematics is a branch of logic, to his discussion of instinct and doubt, to the distinction between Firstness, Secondness, and Thirdness, to Peirce's theory of signs and the relationship between Peirce, James, and Dewey. Whether or not this presentation, which made repeated reference to the Peirce edition edited by Hartshorne and Weiss, would satisfy contemporary Peirce scholars, it clearly characterized Peirce as a technical and systematic philosopher who had not only upended Cartesianism but fundamentally rethought

55. October 28, 1952, lecture, RRP.

56. December 17, 1952, lecture, RRP.

57. This is not surprising, as Wells was deeply interested in linguistic philosophy. See Adam Makkai and Alan Melby, eds., 1985, *Linguistics and Philosophy: Essays in Honor of Rulon S. Wells,* Amsterdam: J. Benjamins. As I suggest in later chapters, the Wells course may have provided Rorty with some of the intellectual materials he needed to build a bridge between pragmatism and the analytic tradition.

modern philosophy without abjuring ties to Kant, the Scottish common-sense realists, and others. When, later in his career, Rorty turned away from Peirce, it was not a turn born of ignorance.

* 6 *

Peirce, however, would not play a major role in Rorty's dissertation, a six-hundred-page tome on the subject of potentiality. Instead the thesis reviewed and assessed the adequacy of employment of this and related concepts in three philosophical systems: that of Aristotle; the seventeenth-century rationalists Descartes, Spinoza, and Leibniz; and the logical empiricists. This historical inquiry was to be carried out not for its own sake but with a specific end in view. Invoking McKeon, Rorty asserted in his introduction that an important distinction between philosophical schools is between those that focus on things, ideas and judgments, and words.[58] Although philosophers in any period may cleave to one of these foci, they represented, in Rorty's view, a distinct historical sequence, with the Greeks concerned primarily with things, the rationalists with ideas and judgments, and the logical empiricists with words. This schematization implicitly characterized logical empiricism as a movement of great importance in the history of philosophy, and Rorty was not hesitant to make such a characterization explicit. Logical empiricism, he noted a few pages later, "can fairly be said to be the school which at the present moment, at least in America, is most alive."[59] Yet the logical empiricists had incorrectly interpreted the fact that the movement was gaining so much ground as evidence that it could solve all major philosophical problems on its own and would fail to profit from an engagement with other approaches. The logical empiricists thus eschewed pluralism, downgraded the history of philosophy, "and ... fail[ed] to understand what other approaches may contribute."[60] This was a mistake. The reason for writing on potentiality was that, as Rorty saw it, the efforts of the logical empiricists to deal with this notion had been largely unsuccessful; greater traction on the problem could only be had through dialogue with other schools. The project thus aimed to identify an analytic Achilles' heel and to showcase the continued importance of the kind of metaphysical work that interested Rorty and his mentors. "Indeed," Rorty wrote, "one of the motives

58. Richard Rorty, 1956, "The Concept of Potentiality," Ph.D. Dissertation, Department of Philosophy, Yale University, xi.

59. Ibid., xvi.   60. Ibid.

in the choice of the topic of potentiality as the subject of this dissertation is the belief that it is in regard to this topic that the relation between the problems of logical empiricism and the problems of traditional metaphysics and epistemology may be most easily perceived."[61]

In two lengthy chapters on logical empiricism, Rorty presented the new analytic concern with language as continuous with Humean empiricism. "In Hume's empiricism," he observed, "the ultimately real entities are sense-data. Sense-data are the analogues of Aristotelian substances and Cartesian clear and distinct ideas, in the sense that all explanation must be in terms of them, whereas they themselves must be taken as the unexplained starting-points of inquiry." "In our own day," Rorty continued, "this program is being carried out in a new way.... The problem of validating Hume's claim that sense-data suffice to provide an explanatory ground of all our knowledge has become the problem of showing that everything which science and common sense wish to say can be formulated in a phenomenalistic language whose ... primitive predicates denote sense-data."[62] Some contemporary metaphysicians had reacted with disdain to this program because it "has seemed barren of any possibility of offering insight into traditional philosophical problems,"[63] but this was to fall into trap of conceiving the analytic movement to be discontinuous with prior philosophical traditions.

In using the term "logical empiricism" to describe the school that would be the major critical target of the dissertation, Rorty was neither going blithely along with the terminology that some in the analytic movement preferred nor using semantics to stretch the connection to Hume. It was, instead, a way of signaling that analytic philosophy had recently entered a new phase. In the work of thinkers like Hempel, Nelson Goodman, and Sellars, the movement had, over the last few years, undergone a "liberalization ... which has freed it from some of the more dogmatic aspects of positivism."[64] A key feature of this liberalization was "recognition that criteria of empirical significance are relative to particular conceptual frameworks."[65] It was this recognition that allowed such putatively metaphysical notions as that of potentiality to enter into analytic discussions, if only indirectly, and to not be dismissed outright on the grounds of impossibility of direct verifiability. The principal means by which potentiality had entered the analytic conversation was around a "nexus" of problems to do with certain ways in which entities might be described

61. Ibid.
62. Ibid., 400–401.
63. Ibid., 402.
64. Ibid., 412–13.
65. Ibid., 414.

by scientific discourse. This involved "the problem of the interpretation of terms designating 'dispositions'; … the difficulties involved in the analysis of counter-factual conditional sentences; and … the problems involved in distinguishing 'laws' from 'accidental generalizations.'"[66] In earlier chapters on Aristotle and the seventeenth-century rationalists, Rorty had shown that the "primary service" provided by the related notions of potentiality and possibility "was to signalize the presence of some sort of indeterminacy,"[67] and he now argued that "disposition-terms, counterfactuals, and laws"[68] serve the same purpose within the framework of logical empiricism. This is so because "disposition-terms and counterfactuals, in their actual use in inquiry, express the indeterminate character of a situation" by "express[ing] the fact that one characteristic of the situation depends upon another characteristic."[69] Laws, for their part, "refer to a determinate range of indeterminate instances; should every instance become determinate, the law would, in a sense, cease to be 'lawlike' … because we would then refer to the extension of the predicates used in statements expressing the 'law,' rather than to 'all possible' instances of the application of the predicate."[70] Rorty acknowledged a difference between the sense of indeterminacy implied by these constructions and that considered by other philosophical traditions: for earlier schools potentiality meant indeterminacy of being, whereas for the logical empiricists it meant indeterminacy of reference. That aside, the problem was that the solutions the logical empiricists had proposed for accounting for indeterminacy foundered for technical reasons having to do with the limitations of extensional, two-valued logic. More generally, relegating potentiality to a subsidiary and residual place in their philosophical system, the logical empiricists had brushed aside an inescapable philosophical category.

In arguing this brief as to the limitations of logical empiricism, Rorty did not intend to suggest that the solution to the problem of how best to account for potentiality was to abandon the analytic framework altogether and make a return to Aristotle or to rationalism. There was growing interest in neo-Aristotelianism among contemporary philosophers, he noted, especially among metaphysicians—he pointed specifically to the work of McKeon and Weiss—and their "sub-slogan" was "'Let's take potentiality seriously!'"[71] Although Rorty said he was "in sympathy" with this movement, the whole point of his discussion of Aristotle, to which he had devoted almost as much attention as he had to the logical empiricists,

66. Ibid., 415. 68. Ibid., 461. 70. Ibid., 461–62, including n. 46.
67. Ibid., 460. 69. Ibid. 71. Ibid., 566.

was to show that Aristotle's view of potentiality, centered on an "analysis of substantial change," "cannot admit that the intelligible necessity characteristic of scientific knowledge can be found in the series of changes in the accidents of a substance."[72] In light of this critique, Rorty thought that serious reconstruction of Aristotelianism would be required. Another group of scholars sought to return to Leibnizian rationalism—here Blanshard was the leading figure—but the "assertion of the existence of 'pure possibilities,'" whether in the form of "Santayana's 'essences,' Whitehead's 'eternal objects,' [or] Peirce's 'Firsts'" raised the problem that "possibilities are [thereby] made so determinate that they are indistinguishable from actualities."[73] Rather than champion any one of these approaches, Rorty held, in good McKeonesque fashion, that "positions of such breadth and flexibility as those which we have examined *cannot,* we should hold, be 'refuted.'"[74] By showing that all three faced common problems, Rorty sought to suggest only how fruitful it would be if there were more dialogue between them. The dissertation was thus written with the "aim of promoting mutual understanding between exponents of different positions, and ... of promoting possible solutions of common problems."[75]

Rorty defended his dissertation early in 1956. No evidence remains as to the nature of the defense, except that Weiss apparently thought enough of the dissertation to write potential employers on Rorty's behalf in the coming years. Likewise, we can infer that Hempel—who was on Rorty's committee—was sufficiently impressed that, several years later, when Rorty was being considered for a job at Princeton, he did nothing to block the appointment. Ineligible for any further draft deferment, Rorty entered the army and was sent in February of 1957 for basic training at Fort Dix, New Jersey. Three years earlier, in June of 1954, he and Amélie had been married, over her parents' continued objections.

72. Ibid., 548.   73. Ibid., 568–69.   74. Ibid., 564.   75. Ibid.

Wellesley College, 1958–1961

* 1 *

Paralleling his father's experiences, Rorty found his two years of military service to be emotionally trying. As noted in chapter 1, James Rorty had been to war, serving in the army ambulance corps during World War I—an experience that precipitated a series of emotional crises. By contrast, hostilities in Korea wound down in 1953, so Richard, who entered the service four years later, served only in the peacetime army. Basic training at Fort Dix was bearable. "The routine ... could well be worse," he wrote to his parents. "The cadre are relatively decent (Captain's a Negro—did I mention this?), and the hours are only rarely 4–11. Usually 5–5, with busy work (rifle cleaning and barracks scrubbing) until 10."[1] After completion of basic training, he used his philosophical education to help land an assignment with the computer development office of the army signal corps. Although the work must have been reasonably interesting for army labor, his correspondence suggests that he found the entire experience dehumanizing and at odds with his sensibilities. Rorty was a left-wing anti-Communist and intellectual with refined cultural tastes; the army—even in its most intellectual quarters—was about conservatism, discipline, bureaucracy, and violence. However much he supported the army's role in the Cold War, Rorty could not but feel that his talents and moral character were being wasted and undermined by his time in the service.[2]

After being discharged, he tried to make up for lost time professionally. Then—as now—most graduates from top departments in the hu-

1. Richard Rorty to parents, February 11, 1957, RRP (letter is misdated 1956).
2. See Amélie Rorty to Richard Rorty, undated letter (probably 1957), RRP.

manities and social sciences were not immediately reincorporated into the disciplinary elite as assistant professors, and Rorty was no exception. In this context, his first job offer—an instructorship at Wellesley College beginning in 1958 that would roll over into an assistant professorship in 1960—must have seemed a solid but not stellar achievement. Yet while not as highly valued as a post in a top graduate program, the Wellesley job would still have been regarded as one worth taking, particularly by Yale graduates, because of the college's general reputation, the high quality of the students, the insistence of student constituencies at top liberal arts schools like Wellesley that philosophy remain historically grounded and broad in reach, the college's proximity to Boston, and—perhaps—the fact that the department's chair at the time, Virginia Onderdonk, who had done her graduate work at Chicago, had been a student of the later Wittgenstein while studying abroad at Cambridge. A logician, Onderdonk incorporated symbolic logic into the department's course offerings without squeezing out other requirements such as Introduction to Classical Philosophy, Introduction to Moral Philosophy, Aesthetics, Ethical Theory, Kant, Theory of Knowledge, and Metaphysics.[3] Given its teaching orientation, the department was no hotbed of research, but it had a solid enough reputation that Amélie could, in an undated letter probably written around this time, describe a position she had applied for there as "the least likely" of all her job prospects "since it is a job that everyone would like to have"[4]—though her comment to this effect may also reflect the fact that Wellesley was a women's college and offered employment to female philosophers during a time of rampant discrimination against women in the academic labor market.

Rorty has speculated that he received the Wellesley offer because Weiss had connections there. This seems plausible. Weiss's connection was Ellen Haring, who took her Ph.D. from Radcliffe in 1959 and had come to Wellesley in 1945 as an instructor with an M.A. degree. Haring was a classicist interested in metaphysics. Her first publications, a three-part article series printed in Weiss's *Review of Metaphysics* in 1956–57 that formed the basis for her dissertation, were on the topic of "substantial form in Aristotle's metaphysics Z." By 1962, she would be writing on Rorty's masters thesis topic, Whitehead's ontology, again for Weiss's journal.[5] It is likely that Haring brokered the Rorty appointment.

3. This is a partial list of the courses offered in 1957–58 and is taken from the department's Web site: http://www.wellesley.edu/Philosophy/history.html, accessed February 9, 2007.

4. Amélie Rorty to Winifred Raushenbush, undated letter, WRC.

5. Ellen Haring, 1962, "The Ontological Principle," *Review of Metaphysics* 16:3–13.

In an autobiographical essay, Rorty forthrightly recalls that Onder-donk and Haring were helpful to "a conceited and aggressively ambitious twenty-seven-year-old."[6] Indeed, it quickly became apparent to members of the department that Rorty's stay at Wellesley would be temporary and that he would use the job as a stepping-stone to a more prestigious post. Three years after Rorty moved to Wellesley, Haring wrote to explain the dilemma the department was facing: "Beyond any doubt, Virginia [On-derdonk] and I want to keep you in the department. Indeed we intend to keep you and, of course, to see that you get tenure when the time comes for that.... There is a problem, though not an insoluble one: (1) You and some other able member of the department are apt to become eligible for our one tenure opening at about the same time. (2) College policy favors a strictly limited number of tenure-members in a department.... (3) You are practically bound to receive offers from such places as Yale and Chicago, and some offer may well be of the kind you should not reject."[7] The third of these claims raises an interesting question: what did Rorty do between 1958 and 1961 to improve his chances of getting a job in a top graduate program?

While Richard was still at Wellesley, his father wrote with words of ad-vice on how he should handle his career. James Rorty accounted for what he saw as his own failure to live up to his potential by pointing to his in-ability "despite repeated efforts to achieve the emotional and psychologi-cal stability that is necessary for the release of full energy and the avoid-ance of any kind of anxious haste including the haste to get published and praised."[8] He warned his son not to follow suit: "Despite Hook's counsel to 'publish early and often' I urge you to avoid both the haste and espe-cially the anxiety; actually you'll get farther faster if you do." Richard was successful in his early years, but it was not by following his father's advice. He was constitutionally anxious: in a letter he and Amélie sent around announcing the birth of their son Jay in July of 1961, the couple described themselves as "more scared than awed.... Isn't it after all rather naïve of us to produce a kid? Nervous and irritable types like us?"[9] He also published early and often.

6. Richard Rorty, forthcoming, "Intellectual Autobiography," in *The Philosophy of Rich-ard Rorty*, Library of Living Philosophers Series, vol. 32, Randall Auxier, ed., La Salle: Open Court.

7. Ellen Haring (name is obscured on original) to Richard Rorty, November 1, 1961, RRP.

8. James Rorty to Richard Rorty, March 19, 1961, RRP.

9. Letter to family and friends from Richard and Amélie Rorty, July 18, 1961, RRP.

∗ 2 ∗

Rorty pursued two lines of research. First, he offered himself up as a translator between analytic and nonanalytic approaches. As a scholar with broad training and interests, it would be his contribution to point out the thematic continuities and overlaps between diverse philosophical traditions, enabling philosophical investigation to reach a higher level of synthesis. In an undated grant application, probably written in the late 1960s, he noted that "most of my early work in philosophy consisted in comparisons between issues discussed by important figures in the history of philosophy and issues discussed in recent analytic philosophy.... All of these pieces ... were attempts to show that there was more continuity between contemporary movements and traditional figures than might be suspected."[10] Often he glossed these efforts as contributions to metaphilosophy. In a 1961 article he defined metaphilosophy as "the result of reflection upon [an] inconsistent triad: (1) A game in which each player is at liberty to change the rules whenever he wishes can neither be won nor lost; (2) In philosophical controversy, the terms used to state the criteria for the resolution of arguments mean different things to different philosophers...; (3) Philosophical arguments are, in fact, won or lost, for some philosophical positions do, in fact, prove weaker than others."[11] Metaphilosophy would not be mere comparison but would assess the value of competing approaches in light of an examination of the higher-order criteria that should be employed for selecting among them, thus rationalizing the resolution of philosophical controversies. More generally, the metaphilosopher would be the scholar familiar enough with competing schools and traditions to stand above the fray of disagreement on particular substantive issues and make recommendations concerning the most fruitful paths for the field to follow—a remarkably ambitious program for a young scholar to get involved with and bespeaking considerable self-confidence on Rorty's part.[12]

Rorty did not invent metaphilosophy. A half-dozen prominent articles on the topic were published in the 1960s, and a book titled *Studies in Metaphilosophy*, by Morris Lazerowitz, a philosopher at Smith College,

10. Richard Rorty, no date, "Brief Narrative Account of Previous Accomplishments," RRP.

11. Richard Rorty, 1961, "Recent Metaphilosophy," *Review of Metaphysics* 15:299–318, 299.

12. Thanks to Charles Camic for this observation.

was published in 1964. Rorty sought to jump onto this intellectual band-wagon.[13]

His attempt to establish himself as a metaphilosopher was evident in two papers written before his Princeton move: "Realism, Categories, and the 'Linguistic Turn,'" originally delivered at a conference in 1960, and "The Limits of Reduction," published in 1961. The aim of the first, published in *International Philosophical Quarterly*, was to get nonanalytic realists talking with analytic philosophers of the ordinary language variety. "Among contemporary realistic philosophers there is a tendency to see the history of philosophy from Descartes to Wittgenstein as one continuous process of garnering the wages of sin,"[14] Rorty began. The "funny thing," he continued, was that "something very much like a rediscovery of realism has taken place among linguistic analysts.... If certain writings of this school look, at first glance, more like lexicography than philosophy, a second glance will show that they are filled with devastating critiques of phenomenalism, disdainful dismissals of Humean scepticism..., violent rejections of Cartesian dualism, and even (in some cases) wholesale borrowings of Thomistic distinctions and maxims."[15] With the aim of promoting "fruitful conversation" between "traditional realists and analytic philosophers," the paper proposed to "sketch a revised map of present-day philosophical battle-lines."[16]

As part of the project of showing up the increasingly realist tendencies of ordinary language philosophy, Rorty argued there were at least two paths a philosopher could take toward recognition of the centrality of language: the Kantian one of assuming it is impossible to ever "penetrate behind a battery of epistemological categories to the thing-in-itself," and a second path that emerges "as a practical solution to a practical problem," namely, "how can we maintain a philosophic thesis about the ultimacy of some given set of categories without falling into the dilemma of self-

---

13. For discussion of the origins of the subfield, see Armen Marsoobian, 2007, "Metaphilosophy," pp. 500–501 in *American Philosophy: An Encyclopedia*, John Lachs and Robert Talisse, eds., New York: Routledge. The journal *Metaphilosophy* was started in 1970 by the philosophers Terry Bynum and William Reese. Bynum was Rorty's student at Princeton in the 1960s and found inspirational the work Rorty had done on metaphilosophy. On bandwagons in science, see Joan Fujimura, 1996, *Crafting Science: A Sociohistory of the Quest for the Genetics of Cancer*, Cambridge: Harvard University Press.

14. Richard Rorty, 1962, "Realism, Categories, and the 'Linguistic Turn,'" *International Philosophical Quarterly* 2:307–22, 307.

15. Ibid., 308–9.   16. Ibid., 309.

referential inconsistency on the one hand and circularity on the other?" "The answer," Rorty wrote, "is: by recognizing that to propose a set of categories is not to offer a description of a non-linguistic fact, but to offer a tool for getting a job done.... Those who have taken this second route toward the linguistic turn have done so *precisely to avoid* the dialectical circle involved in grounding one's metaphilosophy upon one's epistemology."[17] Philosophers who take this second, more pragmatic path are the ones most likely to embrace ordinary language assumptions—ordinary language solutions being more practical than ideal language ones—and the remarkable thing about such scholars, Rorty observed, citing the case of Gilbert Ryle, is that they have not only issued attacks on their ideal language counterparts reminiscent of nonanalytic realist attacks on reductionism but could recently be found developing "an epistemology and a metaphysics which sound remarkably like Aristotle's."[18] To the extent this is so, nonanalytic realist critiques will not apply to ordinary language philosophy, and the potential exists for fruitful dialogue between the approaches if either side were willing to engage seriously the other.

Metaphilosophy as consideration of decisional criteria was even more central to "The Limits of Reduction." Here Rorty considered what is being asserted when one philosopher accuses another of reductionism. However important such an analysis might be, though, it could not provide a final answer to the question of at what point reduction reaches its productive limit. A provisional answer might be given—Rorty's was that "reduction goes too far when it makes the construction of distinctions of level impossible"—but he held that this answer could only be true on pragmatic grounds, for with respect to this as well as all other metaphilosophical questions, "the quest for absolute neutrality, and for a categorical imperative which would bind all philosophers equally, is hopeless."[19] Rorty's hope was that recognition of this point—that the charge of reductionism only makes sense relative to some set of cognitive interests—would encourage more dialogue and the overcoming of "impasses" between various philosophic schools where "communication" is "usually marked by reciprocal accusations of verbalism."[20] It was too often the case in contemporary philosophy, he said, that "the linguistic

17. Ibid., 311, 313–14.   18. Ibid., 319.

19. Richard Rorty, 1961, "The Limits of Reductionism," pp. 100–116 in *Experience, Existence, and the Good: Essays in Honor of Paul Weiss,* Iwrin Lieb, ed., Carbondale: Southern Illinois University Press, 110–11.

20. Ibid., 116.

philosophers see their colleagues' work as verbal manipulation stupidly taken to be inquiry, whereas the nonlinguistic philosophers see the work of linguistic philosophers as verbal manipulation wickedly and deliberately put forward as a substitute for inquiry."[21] Rather than accusing one another of reductionism and using this as an excuse to talk past the other side, philosophers in both camps should begin discussing and debating the goals of philosophical inquiry and assessing the value of competing approaches relative to them. The role of the metaphilosopher would be to do the philosophical spade work necessary to engender discussion between opposing camps.

It is not hard to see why metaphilosophy appealed to Rorty, for in many respects it represented merely an extension of the approach he had taken in his dissertation. There too he sought to show that dialogue between analysts and nonanalysts would be fruitful, embracing the McKeonesque themes of dialogicity and pluralism. Where the dissertation had been largely critical of logical empiricism, however, for its failure to deal adequately with potentiality, Rorty now sided more with the analysts and sought to show that analytic philosophy could be strengthened if the best insights of other approaches were assimilated into it. Rorty, rare among philosophers for his ability to speak multiple philosophical languages, would lay the groundwork for such an assimilation.

* 3 *

The second line of argumentation Rorty pursued was to build on his knowledge of classical American pragmatism to make a case for pragmatism's centrality for the analytic project. Two interlinked developments in midcentury American philosophy must be briefly discussed in order to understand Rorty's moves in this regard: first, the increasingly pragmatic temper of analytic philosophy, irrespective of Rorty, and second, the growing influence of the later Wittgenstein.

The place to begin the first of these discussions is with a comment Rorty made to lead off one of his first published articles, "Pragmatism, Categories, and Language," which appeared in the *Philosophical Review* in 1961. "Pragmatism is getting respectable again," Rorty noted. "Some philosophers are still content to think of it as a sort of muddle-headed first approximation to logical positivism—which they think of in turn as a prelude to our own enlightened epoch. But those who have taken a

---

21. Ibid.

closer look have realized that the movement of thought involved here is more like a pendulum than like an arrow."[22] This claim seems surprising given the usual story of pragmatism's marginalization midcentury, but Rorty was not alone in making it. In the preface to her 1966 anthology, *Pragmatic Philosophy,* Amélie Rorty, then at Douglass College, also observed that some philosophers "such as.... Quine, Reichenbach, Carnap, and Putnam" offer "fairly radical adaptations and developments of some pragmatic theses" despite the fact that they "would not consider themselves as falling primarily within the pragmatic tradition."[23] Amélie credited Richard Bernstein, who had landed at Haverford after being hired by his graduate alma mater—Yale—and then denied tenure there in a much-publicized case,[24] with help in assembling the pieces that would comprise the anthology, so it is perhaps no surprise that just a few years later he echoed the same theme in his 1971 book, *Praxis and Action,* which argued, inter alia, that in the work of Quine, Sellars, and others, one could detect "pragmatic themes pervad[ing] recent contemporary Anglo-Saxon philosophy."[25]

But it was not simply within this small circle of Yale graduates that pragmatic ideas—not the entire oeuvres of Peirce, James, and Dewey, but the intermingling of certain aspects of their thought with that of contemporary analysts—were seen as gaining ground in the late 1950s and early 1960s. The most prominent expositor of this view was Harvard's Morton White, particularly in his 1956 book, *Toward Reunion in Philosophy,* which was the text Richard Rorty cited in making the point that pragmatism had come back into fashion. White had been born in New York City in 1917 and attended City College before taking his doctorate from Columbia. Trained in the Columbia naturalist tradition—despite his suspicions about some of his professors there and his simultaneous attraction to more formal approaches—he taught at the University of Pennsylvania before moving to Harvard in 1948. Like Rorty, White was possessed of a wide-ranging intellect and was interested in intellectual history. He therefore had an ambivalent attitude toward his department's

22. Richard Rorty, 1961, "Pragmatism, Categories, and Language," *Philosophical Review* 70:197–223, 197.

23. Amélie Rorty, 1966, "Preface," pp. v–vi in *Pragmatic Philosophy: An Anthology,* Amélie Rorty, ed., New York: Anchor Books, v–vi.

24. See John Delvin, 1965, "Yale Pickets Win Tenure Review," *New York Times,* March 3, 35.

25. Richard Bernstein, 1971, *Praxis and Action: Contemporary Philosophies of Human Activity,* Philadelphia: University of Pennsylvania Press, 174.

recent analytic turn, which in his view had rendered his colleagues less interested than they should be in the history of philosophy. Far from seeing the move toward logical analysis in the United States as an effect only of the importation of European and British ideas, however, he glossed it as an unintended consequence of the original pragmatist movement. "Peirce and James encouraged Harvard philosophers to seek the practical meaning of any statement," he wrote in 1957 in an essay on the present state of Harvard philosophy.[26] "By doing so, they hoped, a great deal of idle and confusing language might be eliminated as meaningless." This insistence, when combined with the ideas of the positivists, eventually "encouraged a tighter, more scientifically oriented, less monumental conception of philosophy." But the move toward rigor was not in itself to be mourned. In a celebrated essay from 1947, White described pragmatism as part of an intellectual "revolt against formalism," but by this he meant the embrace of "historicism" and "cultural organicism," not a repudiation of technical philosophical discourse. In fact, as he pointed out in his essay on Harvard philosophy, "the great Harvard philosophers were not Sunday supplement scholars; they were primarily technical thinkers working on problems that baffled their predecessors."[27] Aside from a sense of history, all that had been lost by virtue of the increasingly specialized and linguistified nature of contemporary philosophy was recognition of intrinsic connection between different branches of the field. But White thought a move was afoot that would correct this.

P. M. S. Hacker has observed that "a fundamental tenet of analytic philosophy, from its post-*Tractatus* phase onwards, was that there is a sharp distinction between philosophy and science. Philosophy in the analytic tradition from the 1920s onwards, whether or not it is conceived to be a cognitive discipline, is conceived to be a priori and hence discontinuous with, and methodologically distinct from, science. Similarly, analytic philosophy in general held that questions of meaning antecede questions of truth, and are separable from empirical questions of fact."[28] Hacker goes on to identify three more specific ideas central to the analytic program as formulated by the logical positivists and those who drew on their ideas in the United States and England. These were the analytic/synthetic distinction—the distinction between statements true because of the defini-

26. Morton White, 2005, *From a Philosophical Point of View: Selected Studies*, Princeton: Princeton University Press, 146.

27. Ibid., 144.

28. P. M. S. Hacker, 1996, *Wittgenstein's Place in Twentieth-Century Analytic Philosophy*, Oxford: Blackwell, 195.

tions of the words involved and those true as a matter of "empirical fact"; the thesis of reductionism, or the notion that "all significant empirical sentences are reducible to what is given in immediate experience"; and the thesis of "sentential verificationism," or the "claim that the unit of empirical significance is the sentence, which is confirmed or disconfirmed in experience."[29]

In the 1950s, an attack on all three theses was mounted by thinkers within the analytic movement. Most directly relevant to White's project was the work of his colleague and mentor W. V. O. Quine. Quine had been a student of Whitehead at Harvard and studied with several of the positivists in Vienna before returning to Cambridge. In *A System of Logistic* (1934) and *Mathematical Logic* (1940), he made contributions to set theory. Most important in this context, however, is his work on epistemology, as outlined in "Two Dogmas of Empiricism" (1951) and *Word and Object* (1960). Against the theses advanced by the positivists, Quine argued for a holistic empiricism, or the view that knowledge consists of a system of interrelated propositions. While observation sentences concerning discrete empirical facts can be parceled out from other kinds of propositions, scientific knowledge involves a whole array of propositions and conceptual elements, many not amenable to direct empirical scrutiny and yet constituting a crucial foundation for the rest. Moreover, any particular empirical fact can be represented in different ways in different systems of thought, and there is no standpoint outside all systems from which to arbitrate these representational disputes. For Quine, "every theory is holistic; its constituent sentences and their constituent words depend for the meanings on the character of the theory."[30]

In *Toward Reunion in Philosophy*, White counted Quine—who had helped get him the Harvard job—as foremost among those recent analytic philosophers who thus recognized the relativity of all conceptual schemes. The value of such schemes is not a matter of empirical accuracy qua correspondence with the world alone. This, according to White, had two implications. On the one hand, it meant that the preference of the positivists for a criterion of meaning that excluded traditional metaphysics was just that—a preference, one among several that philosophers might hold, and in no sense logically or empirically derivable. On the other hand, it meant that there is an intrinsically normative com-

29. Ibid.

30. Avrum Stroll, 1999, "Karl Popper and W. V. O. Quine," pp. 647–52 in *The Columbia History of Western Philosophy*, Richard Popkin, ed., New York: Columbia University Press, 651.

ponent to all inquiry in the sense that inquiry must be carried out with some practical end in view that we want to achieve and that forms the basis for our preference among conceptual schemes. But this was precisely the line pushed by the classical pragmatists. Thus it was that White could describe the present period in philosophy as an "age of decision," whereby "the tradition of the analytic movement merges with that of pragmatism."[31] It may have been the decisive contribution of analytic thought to show that philosophy must take a linguistic turn—White himself believed such a turn necessary—but the "philosopher in the age of decision" "does not simply ask whether words *are* used in a certain way ... [but] goes on to ask whether they *ought* to be used in a certain way."[32] White held that this meant no strict separation could be effected between "describing, doing, and evaluating."[33] While he disagreed with the Jamesian claim that a scientific statement that causes one moral revulsion violates pragmatic standards of truthfulness, he insisted that the pragmatic turn in contemporary analytic philosophy opened up space for metaphysics and ethics that the logical positivists had neglected and for an analysis of the interrelationships among these fields—precisely a "reunion" in philosophy.

The other development that must be mentioned as background for understanding the second prong of Rorty's early career strategy is the influence of the later Wittgenstein. Wittgenstein's *Tractatus,* as Hacker also remarks, "is characterized by a single unifying vision. The insight into the essential nature of the elementary proposition was held to yield a comprehensive account of the nature of logic and of the metaphysical structure of the world."[34] By contrast, *Philosophical Investigations,* the main parts of which were composed in the late 1940s before the volume's posthumous publication in 1953, "shattered.... this sublime vision."[35] Wittgenstein now argued for a radically revised conception of the philosophical enterprise. It makes no sense, he claimed, to think of philosophy as offering theories of anything—of knowledge, of being, of ethics, and so on. Traditional philosophy assumed that each of these domains had some essence—the true nature of knowledge, of being, of ethics—that it was philosophy's job to reveal. By contrast, Wittgenstein now held that insofar as these domains have factual content, they are the subject matter of the empirical

31. Morton White, 1956, *Toward Reunion in Philosophy,* Cambridge: Harvard University Press, 299.

32. Ibid., 19.   33. Ibid., 299.

34. Hacker, *Wittgenstein's Place in Twentieth-Century Analytic Philosophy,* 99.

35. Ibid., 99.

sciences, not philosophy. Philosophy's sole task with regard to them is to document and describe the meanings of the terms around which thought in these domains revolves; there being no essences, this descriptive task can involve no more than showing the various and sundry uses to which the terms have been put in the course of linguistic practice. As philosophy carries out this task, three things become evident: first, that many of the terms found problematic by traditional philosophers, such as "knowledge" or "time," are used relatively unproblematically by conventional language users; second, that this relatively unproblematical usage occurs despite the fact that the informal rules governing "language games" may sometimes be imprecise and vague; and third, that philosophy has often taken the form of imposing pictures, images, or metaphors on the subject matters of its inquiry that do more to generate artificial puzzles and conundrums than to resolve them. Indeed, Wittgenstein held that the imposition of such pictures and images was a key aspect of philosophy as usually practiced. By recasting philosophy as the analysis of how terms are used within particular language games—but without imagining, as some ordinary language philosophers had, that the essence of the terms could thereby be revealed—Wittgenstein hoped to avoid this problem. He therefore called for a philosophical therapeutics, hoping not that his approach would resolve long-standing philosophical controversies but that it would show that in most cases there was no controversy in need of resolution, thereby curing philosophy of some of its bad preoccupations.

The publication of *Philosophical Investigations* was a major event. Although in its wake there were numerous disputes about what Wittgenstein had been trying to say, about the logical coherence of his argument, and about the advisability of his proposals, the book commanded considerable attention. In the United States, his views were disseminated by former students like Max Black and Norman Malcolm, who "transformed the Cornell philosophy department into one of the premier philosophy schools in America and into its leading centre for Wittgenstein scholarship and the development of Wittgensteinian philosophy."[36] By 1960 several monographs about Wittgenstein's work—most focused on the *Tractatus* period, but a few on his later thought—had appeared in English, along with numerous academic articles.

As Rorty sought to do work in the late 1950s and early 1960s that would bring him to the attention of the philosophical community, he

36. Ibid., 146.

took advantage of both developments—the increasingly pragmatic temper of analytic philosophy and the growing interest in Wittgenstein—to argue for the renewed importance of classical American pragmatism and thus to make an implicit case for a positive revaluation of his own intellectual competencies.[37] This he did by suggesting there were striking affinities between Peirce, analysts like Quine, and the later Wittgenstein and by suggesting that analysts would profit by looking more closely at Peirce. Far from it being the case, as some Rorty interpreters have claimed, that Rorty's interest in pragmatism arose only after he made a break with analytic philosophy, his earliest work is characterized by a desire to harness pragmatist insights in the service of a revised conception of the analytic project.

As early as 1959, Rorty could be found arguing that contemporary analytic discourse was colored by pragmatic themes. Reviewing for the journal *Ethics* Alan Pasch's book *Experience and the Analytic* (1958), Rorty noted that there was widespread recognition in contemporary philosophy of the "dreariness of empiricism"[38] as practiced by the positivists. There were two forms of reaction possible: "the violent form assumes that 'reductionism' was a colossal blunder and points the way that leads ... to ... the *Philosophical Investigations*," where the "milder form ... advocates ... loosening up the old slogans, 'reducing' only what is usefully reducible, and paying attention to the methods of science as well as codifying its results."[39] Pasch was an advocate of the second approach. "Travers[ing] pretty much the same ground covered in successive articles by Quine, White, and Goodman," Pasch made the case that both the analytic/synthetic and the given/supplied distinction make sense only in light of certain cognitive interests. "The central theme of Pasch's 'pragmatic reconstruction,'" Rorty asserted—arguing elsewhere that the "basic themes and theses" of the book "are familiar enough from Dewey and his followers"—"is that a question is always a question within a context, that a context is always one among alternative possible contexts, and that one selects one's context to fulfill a purpose."[40] Although this might sound like "a very obvious

---

37. As far as the timing of Rorty's exposure to Wittgenstein goes, he reports in an e-mail that he "read the *Tractatus* while still at Chicago, without much comprehension. I read the Blue and Brown Books in bootlegged editions (loaned by Rulon Wells) while at Yale. I read *Philosophical Investigations* while at Wellesley." E-mail to author, February 11, 2007.

38. Richard Rorty, 1959, "Review of *Experience and the Analytic: A Reconsideration of Empiricism*," *Ethics* 70:75–77, 75.

39. Ibid., 75.   40. Ibid., 75–77.

maxim," Rorty argued that good effects would flow from recognition of its truth within the philosophical community, where too often objectivity rather than intersubjective agreement was seen as inquiry's goal.

While this review saw Rorty drawing on a basic familiarity with pragmatism to bring it in line with recent analytic currents, it was his 1961 article on "Pragmatism, Categories, and Language" that dug deeper into a reading of Peirce to make a more substantial case for the continuing relevance of pragmatism. The article's thesis was as straightforward as it was bold: "I want to suggest that Peirce's thought envisaged, and repudiated in advance, the stages in the development of empiricism which logical positivism represented, and that it came to rest in a group of insights and a philosophical mood much like those we find in the *Philosophical Investigations* and in the writings of philosophers influenced by the later Wittgenstein."[41] While the two philosophers differed in certain respects, particularly with regard to the intellectual traditions out of which they emerged, they were more alike than different: "Both are fighting against the 'Ockhamistic' prejudice that the determinate always lurks—actually, and not merely potentially—behind the indeterminate. Both recognize the sense in which we cannot break out of the cluster of things which Peirce calls Thirds and whose workings Wittgenstein calls 'logical determination' (for example, signs, words, habits, rules, meanings, games, understanding) to something more definite which will somehow replace these things."[42] Rorty was convinced by both Peirce and Wittgenstein that language cannot be transcended, that the meaning of a concept lies exclusively in its use, and that reality is indefinite.

Reading Wittgenstein in light of Peirce, Rorty went on to claim, could "help free us from preoccupation with accidents of tactics and ... direct us toward the crucial insights which generate master strategies"[43] of philosophical argumentation—strategies that, Rorty implied, lead ultimately in the direction of a rigorous ordinary language approach that could make real headway in solving or at least overcoming philosophical problems and controversies. With this argument Rorty once again positioned himself in the broadly analytic camp, seeking to transform his otherwise undervalued familiarity with alternative philosophical traditions—in this case, pragmatism—into a valuable asset.

---

41. Rorty, "Pragmatism, Categories, and Language," 197–98.
42. Ibid., 216.   43. Ibid.

* 4 *

But when, why, and how did Rorty come to think of himself more as a linguistic philosopher than as a critic of the analytic tradition? My hypothesis is that he became committed to a version of analytic philosophy around the time he defended his doctoral dissertation and entered the army and that what enabled this to occur was Rorty's encounter with the work of a philosopher—Wilfrid Sellars—who provided the symbolic materials necessary for him to begin telling a coherent story about his own transition into the analytic fold. Rorty has said that Sellars influenced him greatly and that after he read his work Sellars "quickly became my new philosophical hero, and for the next twenty years most of what I published was parasitic on his ideas."[44] As a graduate student at Yale Rorty was well aware of the growing significance of analytic thought and of the fact that the field was tending in a direction different from that initially laid out by the positivists. He recalls in his autobiography, "Even at Yale the suspicion was growing that Carnap and Quine might be riding the wave of the future. So I began looking around for analytic philosophers who were less reductionistic and less positivistic than they, less convinced that philosophy had only recently come of age."[45] Sellars was such a figure.

Wilfrid Sellars was the son of Roy Wood Sellars, a critical realist philosopher who taught for many years at the University of Michigan and who rejected pragmatism for its alleged idealism while embracing naturalism, materialism, and a theory of immediate perception. His son attended Michigan, the University of Buffalo, and then Oxford, specializing in analytic philosophy, and held positions at the universities of Iowa and Minnesota before moving to Yale in 1958, after Rorty's departure. Along with Herbert Feigl he was one of the founders, in 1950, of *Philosophical Studies,* the analytic journal, and it was in a volume coedited by Feigl, *Minnesota Studies in the Philosophy of Science, Volume I,* that his landmark essay "Empiricism and the Philosophy of Mind," originally given as a lecture at the University of London, was published in 1956, the year Rorty defended his dissertation. A naturalist himself, Sellars was also a "psychological nominalist" who denied that sensations put us in touch with universals. On his understanding, the placing of sensations and feels under the rubric of "epistemic discourse" depends on the knower's command of the linguistic practices necessary within some intersubjective community to justify

44. Richard Rorty, "Intellectual Autobiography."
45. Ibid.

claims to having had such sensations and feels. To the extent this is so, what he called the "myth of the given," central to positivist efforts to cast knowledge as a matter of inference from immediately given sense-data, is undermined. What acquires salience instead are the public, linguistic practices through which the given is constituted. Like the pragmatists, however, Sellars did not believe that debilitating skepticism would result from the impossibility of stepping out of discourse to establish firm foundations for belief. Philosophy's task was precisely to reconcile "manifest" and "scientific" "images" of the world, and if the latter lead ultimately toward a rejection of some of the paradoxes inherent in the former, philosophy has done its job.

Rorty saw in Sellars a kindred spirit. Like Rorty, "Sellars was unusual among … American philosophers of the post-World War II period, and quite different from Quine and Wittgenstein, in having a wide and deep acquaintance with the history of philosophy."[46] That "this knowledge of previous philosophers kept intruding into [Sellars's] work"[47] appealed to the historically minded Rorty, who, though drawn increasingly to the kind of technical rigor characteristic of analytic philosophy generally, wished nevertheless to find a middle road between technicism and historicism. At the same time, there seemed clear affinities between Sellars and Peirce. These centered on Peirce's claims for the semiotic nature of thought and his emphasis on the practical aspects of cognition. Furthermore, like White, Quine, and Wittgenstein, for whom Rorty also had tremendous admiration, Sellars's approach called into question the reductionism of the positivists. Unlike the later Wittgenstein, whose program for philosophy was largely deconstructive, Sellars's analysis had the added benefit of pointing the way toward new, constructive solutions to philosophical puzzles. It would not be correct to say that Rorty became a linguistic philosopher simply because he read and was influenced by Sellars. But in a context where doing philosophical work that would be seen as important at the highest levels required engaging in an analysis of language, Sellars, along with Wittgenstein, Quine, White, and others, provided Rorty with a model he could follow that did not require him to abandon the other philosophical commitments—to the reality of vagueness, the richness of intellectual history, and the valorization of intersubjectivity—he had previously held dear.

46. Richard Rorty, 1997, "Introduction," pp. 1–12 in *Empiricism and the Philosophy of Mind*, by Wilfrid Sellars, Cambridge: Harvard University Press, 3.

47. Ibid.

* 5 *

Rorty's unpublished manuscript "The Philosopher as Expert," written while he was at Wellesley and revised after he made the move to Princeton, highlights the complex "identity work"[48] he was forced to undertake to recast himself as an analyst. The manuscript may have been overdetermined by Rorty's complicated relationship to his parents. As noted previously, Rorty's parents had, from the start of his intellectual career, warned him against the dangers of academicism. Intellectual pursuits should serve practical interests, they insisted, and remain connected to real-world concerns. While supportive in a general way of his career, they now questioned whether the precise and technical philosophy to which he was increasingly drawn met these criteria. His father wrote to him in 1961, for example, just a year before suffering a mental breakdown, to say,

> thanks for sending us the reprint of your article ["Pragmatism, Categories, and Language"] in the Philosophical Review. I read it through at a sitting without difficulty and have even persuaded myself that I understood what you were talking about. Give me time and I shall yet be a philosopher; it's easier than I had thought, once one learns the terms. I realise belatedly that philosophy is concerned not so much with *what* to belief, but *how* to believe or doubt or think—at least that this is the chief present preoccupation of philosophers, the epistemological problem as I find it is called, having looked it up in the Oxford dictionary for the twentieth time.[49]

Anyone who knew James Rorty would have recognized this to be a backhanded compliment; if philosophy is not about what to believe, if someone who is well educated has to consult a reference source twenty times to understand it, of what use is it to life? In light of this criticism, lodged so close to home, "The Philosopher as Expert" might be read as an attempt to legitimate in the eyes of Rorty's parents and their friends and colleagues outside philosophy the professional orientation he was now taking on.

It was to just such an audience that the piece was addressed. Readers of the *New York Times* who come across reports from annual meetings of

48. For discussion of this concept, see David Snow and Leon Anderson, 1987, "Identity Work among the Homeless: The Verbal Construction and Avowal of Personal Identities," *American Journal of Sociology* 92:1336–71.

49. James Rorty to Richard Rorty, April 8, 1961, RRP.

the American Philosophical Association might wonder about the state of contemporary philosophy, Rorty observed. Are philosophers today concerned only with niggling problems of no interest to anybody but themselves? Such a question, Rorty suggested, might be asked with special urgency by readers of magazines like *Encounter* and *Partisan Review*—magazines not coincidentally close to his parents' orbit—for in their pages writers could often be found "dismiss[ing] ... professional philosophizing ... with a pat historical generalization: 'the absorption in linguistic trivia of recent Anglo-American philosophy,' 'the hysterical irrationalism of post-war European philosophy,' 'the fantastic divorce between fact and value which has crippled philosophy since the Renaissance,' 'the worship of mathematics which has vitiated philosophical speculation since Plato.'"[50] "Such dismissive cliches," Rorty continued, "usually picked up third hand, permit literary intellectuals to take over the role of critic and conscience of culture without bothering to find out why, or even whether, the professional philosophers have abdicated it." So what is the nature of contemporary philosophy, and is all well with it?

Rorty's answer was complex—so complex that the *Yale Review* rejected the piece for being "too languid in manner" and "simply tak[ing] too long to make its points."[51] Anticipating Thomas Kuhn's distinction between revolutionary and normal science, Rorty recognized there to be two types of philosophers: great philosophers who ask bold new questions and revolutionize philosophical discourse and lesser philosophers who work out the details, implications, internal tensions, and contradictions. Practiced by scholars of either type, philosophy is neither pure science nor pure art:

> As against science, in philosophy the criteria for being "evidence" or for being "well-founded" are themselves in question. ... But as against the arts, the totality which we're accustomed to think of as "a philosophy" is essentially incomplete once it is separated from all the *other* "philosophies." If one asks how one can break the circle of mutual understanding and appreciation formed by the professional philosophers of a given epoch, the answer is that one can appeal to the unanswered questions of philosophers of other epochs. But if one asks how one can escape from the dialogue which is the history of philosophy to a point outside it from which its

50. Richard Rorty, undated manuscript, "The Philosopher as Expert," RRP, 4.
51. Paul Pickrel to Richard Rorty, April 22, 1963, RRP.

"progress" may be gauged, there is no answer. One can't. This dialogue is autonomous.[52]

The inescapable dialogicity of the philosophical enterprise had implications for assessing the present state of the field. Although Rorty acknowledged that philosophy may fare better or worse in different historical epochs, it was in philosophy's nature that contributions to it could only be properly evaluated against the backdrop of ongoing philosophical conversation. What separates the professional from the amateur philosopher is immersion in this stream of dialogue: "Philosophers are philosophers not because they have common aims and interests (they don't), or common methods (they don't), or agree to discuss a common set of problems (they don't), or are endowed with common faculties (they aren't), but simply and solely because they are taking part in a single, continuing conversation."[53] In recent years, the nature of the conversation had drifted in an analytic and linguistic direction. The positivists, bold philosophical visionaries, had proposed the elusive notion of a "perfect language," and only as a result of the careful work done by countless lesser philosophers in their wake had the field recently come to the realization that though the focus on language was essential, a perfect language could never be constructed. Seeing in this shift a move from idealism to realism—one played out countless times before in the history of philosophy—Rorty took it as an example of the fact that "philosophies... aren't killed off, but ... are modified almost (but never entirely) beyond recognition as the dialogue continues."[54] His larger point was that insofar as the turn toward ordinary language was the collective tendency of the profession, it had to be seen as legitimate. This metaphilosophical thesis blended together elements drawn from McKeon (the focus on dialogue), Peirce (the notion of a community of inquirers and truth as a matter of ultimate convergence among them), and Wittgenstein (philosophy as a language game).

Rorty's productivity during his Wellesley years was impressive. In four years he published three substantive articles and six book reviews and had numerous additional pieces forthcoming. It was enough, given its content and quality, to make Rorty a serious candidate for a position at a better-ranked philosophy department.

52. Rorty, "The Philosopher as Expert," 16.
53. Ibid., 24.   54. Ibid., 22–23.

SEVEN

Princeton University, 1961–1965

* 1 *

In an autobiographical piece, Rorty recalls the circumstances that led to the job offer from Princeton University:

> During my third year at Wellesley, at the American Philosophical Association meetings in December of 1960, I was interviewed by Gregory Vlastos. He had recently taken over the chairmanship of the philosophy department at Princeton, and had heard about my dissertation from Blanshard. He asked me whether I thought I could "make a contribution to American philosophy" and I stoutly replied that I certainly hoped so—a response that was less the product of self-assurance than of the sense that any other answer would ruin my chances of an offer. To my very considerable surprise, Vlastos called up a few months later to offer me a visiting one-year job at Princeton, teaching Greek philosophy (and, in particular, Aristotle, leaving Vlastos himself free to concentrate on Plato). As soon as I got to Princeton in the fall of 1961 I realized that I did not know nearly enough Greek for Vlastos' purposes, and that I was probably not the man he wanted. So I assumed I would be back at Wellesley the following fall. But, again to my surprise, I was offered a three-year further appointment.[1]

This modest retelling of the story makes it sound as though Rorty was initially recruited only for his capacity to fill a short-term teaching need of the department. This is possible, but it is equally likely that Princeton had its eye on Rorty for a tenure-track job and used the short-term appointment as a way to get to know him. Such was his growing reputa-

1. Rorty, "Intellectual Autobiography."

tion in the field, however, that Princeton was not the only department to come calling.

No sooner had the visiting professorship at Princeton been converted to a tenure-track position than did other schools—Texas, Yale, and then Harvard, Johns Hopkins, and Connecticut—approach Rorty about the possibility of moving. The first was Texas. Asked to give a paper in 1962 in the University of Texas philosophy department's colloquium series, Rorty proposed the title, "Why Whitehead Is Good but Wilfrid Sellars Is Better." Charles Hartshorne had moved to Texas that year after a seven-year appointment at Emory, following his departure from Chicago, and John Silber, writing from Austin, reported to Rorty that his masters thesis advisor was scandalized by his former student's choice of topic.[2] But this was beside the point. Silber's invitation to lecture there was not born merely of a desire to hear the philosophical views of a former Yale classmate. "There is no point in denying that we should be very interested in having you join our staff," Silber wrote.[3] Having just moved from Wellesley to top-ranked Princeton, however, Rorty was in no mood to leave. Unable, for reasons of propriety, to state this in his reply, he politely rebuffed Silber's advance, while keeping his options for future mobility open. He told Silber that for the moment he had it pretty good at Princeton. "It would be a pleasure to have you as a chairman," he wrote just a week after receiving Silber's letter, "but then it's pleasant to have Vlastos as a chairman."[4] Beyond this colleagueship, Amélie had a job at nearby Douglass College. What was more, "there seems to be a reasonable chance, although no certainty, of being reappointed for a second three-year term as Assistant Professor here.... I am fairly sure that (unless I surprise myself and them by writing a worthwhile book) I shan't be promoted to tenure here, but this problem is still so remote that I don't think it necessary to worry about it.... On the whole, it seems best to sit tight, even at the cost of finding oneself jobless later, if only because if one keeps moving around one can never get any sustained work done (or at least I can't)." It can't be known whether Rorty genuinely believed he had no shot at tenure at this point or whether he was simply playing it safe in assuming he didn't, but he was careful not to burn any bridges: "As to future years, I should of course be very grateful if Texas kept me in the back of its mind. Sooner or later Princeton will tell

2. Silber wrote: "Hartshorne, you may be interested to know, did not even believe you have written such an article; he finds the very idea too preposterous." John Silber to Richard Rorty, October 25, 1962, RRP.

3. John Silber to Richard Rorty, October 10, 1962, RRP.

4. Richard Rorty to John Silber, October 17, 1962, RRP.

me to hit the road, and at that point I shall probably send out shy little mendicant letters to everybody I know. You will be receiving one."

Not a week later, Rorty received a letter from John Smith at Yale, for whom he had once served as a teaching assistant. Wrote Smith, "If you are attracted by the idea of returning to the old stand, will you let me know."[5] Smith offered Rorty an assistant professorship at a salary of $7,500 per year plus an extra $1,000 for summer research, or roughly $58,000 in 2007 dollars. Rorty's experience at Yale had been more or less positive, so it was no doubt with some genuine feeling that he replied, "I am, Lord, knows, attracted by the idea [of returning] … to the old stand."[6] But what kind of position was it to be, exactly? Smith reiterated that the offer was for an assistant professorship with the possibility of tenure, not an interim post. Although it was well known that tenure from within was unlikely at schools like Yale and Harvard, Smith assured Rorty that he would be guaranteed at least six years in New Haven before he went up. Moreover, he would soon be eligible for a Morse Fellowship, which would allow him to take a year off from teaching to devote exclusively to research. Smith made a case for Yale by appealing to the department's familiar identity as a center for pluralism: "It is our hope at the present time and even more than hope (it is a matter of policy) to preserve the plurality of outlooks and positions in the department; to keep up a staunch concern for genuine philosophical issues, to keep in touch at the same time with what is going on in the profession at large, and to avoid having the department identified with any single specialism or any one point of view which happens to be fashionable at the moment. This, as you know, has been the main drift of the department over the past two decades and I want to assure you that there is no intention of changing that line."[7] This last letter, however, crossed in the mail with one Rorty sent a day later turning Smith down on the grounds that what he wanted more than anything was to stay in one place and get work done.[8] In light of the fact that the value of his Yale education had effectively diminished in an increasingly analytic disciplinary marketplace, Rorty—though attracted to Yale's pluralism—may have been of the opinion that the job was a step down from his current one, that the prospects for tenure at Yale were even slimmer than they were at Princeton, and that Smith, with his dismissive reference to au courant philosophical movements, was betraying his own incapacities.

5. John Smith to Richard Rorty, October 22, 1962, RRP.
6. Richard Rorty to John Smith, October 25, 1962, RRP.
7. John Smith to Richard Rorty, November 15, 1962, RRP.
8. Richard Rorty to John Smith, November 16, 1962, RRP.

These points could not be expressed to Smith, who would have reacted badly to the charge that Yale was no longer at the philosophical forefront, so Rorty, a few days later, politely glossed his decision as being "either as the result of a cowardly search for security or as a result of the exercise of *phronesis*. I wish I could make up my mind how to interpret it myself."[9] Smith wanted to keep open the possibility that in future years an offer might be extended to both Richard and Amélie,[10] but nothing more came of the conversation.

The situation the following year with Hopkins and Connecticut played out in a similar manner. Rorty was approached and asked if he'd have any interest in a position—at Hopkins an assistant professorship, at Connecticut nothing less than the headship of the department. With Connecticut—at that time, as today, a lower-tier department—he rejected the offer out of hand, but at Hopkins, where his contact was with the analytic historian Maurice Mandelbaum, he at least professed interest, with the caveat that he would only consent to move if he were to be given a tenured appointment. This proved impossible, for reasons that are unclear, so he stayed on at Princeton.

With Harvard, things were different. Here was a top-ranked department whose siren call no philosopher could refuse. That philosophers in Cambridge—who just a few years earlier had refused to give Rorty even a graduate student fellowship—were now inviting him to join their ranks was a testament to how much recognition he had carved out for himself as a promising young scholar in such a short time. But there was a major catch. Just as the Princeton position began as a visiting job, so too was the Harvard offer for a visiting lectureship, with the mere possibility of rollover into an assistant professorship. At a proposed salary of $10,000, the pay was good, but there could be no future guarantees. It would only make sense for Rorty to take the position if Princeton would grant him a one-year leave, with the possibility that he could return to his old job if things didn't work out at Harvard. Princeton, bent on retaining Rorty, refused, and so it was that Rorty wrote with a heavy heart to Rogers Albritton, the Harvard chair, in 1963, striking a very different note on the question of his tenure chances at Princeton than he had with other suitors:

> I never thought the day would come when I should turn down an offer from Harvard, but it seems impossible for me to accept. The department

9. Richard Rorty to John Smith, November 19, 1962, RRP.
10. John Smith to Richard Rorty, January 2, 1963, RRP.

here at Princeton is unwilling to recommend that I be given a leave without pay in order to accept the appointment.... The department's decision, reached at a meeting of the senior members, is probably not unshakeable. If I asked for a hearing, and kicked and squealed enough, I might get them to recommend a leave to the Dean. However, considerations of both courtesy and prudence seem to work against such a move. On the side of courtesy: the department here has been very generous to me (they have, for example, just given me a huge raise) and I don't wish to seem ungrateful, even though I think that their argument about the effect of my leaving is weak. On the side of prudence: since I have some hopes of eventually being given tenure here, I don't want to queer my chances by being obstreperous and "disloyal."[11]

It's hard to know what Rorty's thoughts were while entertaining these offers, but wage bargaining wasn't far from his mind. Critics of the contemporary American academy have decried the tendency of academic superstars to extract ever-higher wages from their home institutions by getting competing offers from other schools, but the Rorty case reminds us that this is hardly a new phenomenon and that it does not occur only at the senior faculty level. A decade later, having refused yet another offer from Hopkins, Rorty would confide in his friend Milton Fisk, "I turned down the job at Hopkins, and now don't know how serious I was about it. I suppose one never does; at the time it seems like an existential crisis and a week later it seems like simply the occasion when one got a raise. Princeton doesn't even try to keep your salary up with the cost of living unless you threaten or quasi-threaten them with offers, and this makes it terribly difficult to know whether you are considering an offer, or simply pretending to yourself to consider it because you need to convince yourself that you have to go in and tell the dean that if you don't get a raise you'll leave."[12]

* 2 *

But what was the department at Princeton like? In his recent history of Princeton, James Axtell shows how the institution was transformed, over the first half of the twentieth century, from a college placing heavy emphasis on teaching and moral and religious instruction into a top-ranked

---

11. Richard Rorty to Rogers Albritton, December 2, 1963, RRP.
12. Richard Rorty to Milton Fisk, February 16, 1974, RRP.

research university. Princeton began offering graduate courses in the late 1870s under the leadership of President James McCosh, himself a philosopher, but it was not until Woodrow Wilson took over the presidency of the university in 1902 that reforms were made that helped convert it into center for research. Especially important in this regard was the raising of endowment funds, which the university used to build new facilities and lure prominent and promising faculty members. It was because of Wilson's reforms, for example, that Princeton was able to hire philosopher Norman Kemp Smith from the University of Glasgow in 1906. A key figure in the history of philosophy, Kemp Smith's commentaries on Kant, Descartes, and Hume were definitive in their day and helped establish the department's reputation for idealism and historical scholarship. Wilson faced numerous obstacles in his upgrading efforts, however, including a resistant faculty and board of overseers, competition from schools that had made the research transition earlier, and his own preference for the hybrid identity "teacher-scholars," with considerable emphasis still placed on the former. It was not until several decades later, in the wake of the Second World War, that Princeton emerged as the powerhouse research university it is today. "After the war," Axtell notes, "the self-identifying word from Nassau Hall was almost exclusively 'university' [as opposed to college]. The leading voice was that of J. Douglas Brown '19, *28, expert on industrial relations, consummate judge of talent, and [Presidents] Dodds' and Goheen's dean of the faculty (1946–1967) and simultaneously Princeton's first provost (1966–1967).... Brown spoke more and more frequently about Princeton as a 'liberal university' and a 'national university' and its faculty exclusively as 'scholar-teachers' who had an obligation to '*lead*' in the search for new knowledge."[13] Such calls might have amounted to nothing were it not for changes in the environment of American higher education that Brown and other administrators could leverage into major institutional transformations. The flow of federal research dollars into the university sector made possible new institutes and fellowships, while a lag in graduate enrollments relative to significant growth in the undergraduate population produced a demand-heavy academic labor market—a context in which higher faculty salaries, aimed at recruiting stars at the senior and junior levels, could be both justified and paid for. Whereas teaching ability had previously loomed large as a criterion by which faculty were assessed for promotion, by "the

13. James Axtell, 2006, *The Making of Princeton University*, Princeton: Princeton University Press, 88.

late 1950s, when Princeton accepted once and for all its status as a world-class research university ... its faculty reward structure ... leaned heavily, decisively, on scholarship rather than teaching."[14]

Chapter 10 argues that these and related developments in higher education in the postwar era made possible a second wave of professionalization in the American academy. This wave, I will there argue, had as one of its correlates the privileging, in the humanities and social sciences, of those approaches that claimed to be more rigorous and scientific than the rest. What Carl Schorske has called the "new rigorism in the human sciences,"[15] of which analytic philosophy is but one example, had neither its intellectual origins nor its debut as a strategy for securing disciplinary legitimacy during the period in question. Nevertheless, administrators, disciplinary entrepreneurs, and funding agencies promoting an agenda of academic professionalization routinely invoked the trope of rigor in the post–World War II period in characterizing the intellectual changes they saw as necessary to bring American humanities and social-science scholarship in line with the success of the natural sciences. Among other things, the emphasis on rigor and scientificity, variously glossed in different disciplines, offered a uniform criterion for the evaluation of intellectual products in a period of rapid institutional growth and change, serving as a common currency for a variety of academic-organizational entities increasingly concerned with their standing in national scientific and intellectual fields.

The Princeton philosophy department was not the only department on campus to be affected by these local and national developments, but affected it was. Like many other philosophy departments around the country, Princeton saw its idealist tendencies give way, in the 1910s and 1920s, to various strains of realism.[16] Although ranked sixth in the nation in a reputational survey carried out in 1925,[17] the department was not one of highest distinction in the 1930s and early 1940s, as positivism came to define the nature of the conversation, save for the presence of Walter Stace, an empiricist with interests in metaphysics and the history of philosophy, and of the department's chair, the classicist Robert Scoon.[18]

14. Ibid., 94.

15. Carl Schorske, 1997, "The New Rigorism in the Human Sciences: 1940–1960," *Daedalus* 126:289–309.

16. James Ward Smith, "The Department of Philosophy," http://etcweb.princeton.edu/CampusWWW/Companion/philosophy_department.html, accessed August 29, 2007.

17. Cartter, *Assessment of Quality in Graduate Education*, 29.

18. Smith, "The Department of Philosophy."

Only in the late 1940s and early 1950s did it attain an international reputation with the hiring, in 1947, of Walter Kaufmann, major interpreter of Nietzsche, existentialism, and the entire Continental tradition, and then, a year later, of Jacques Maritain, the French Thomist. These hires brought the department attention and were consistent with Scoon's interest in achieving a "balance" in the representation of different philosophical schools, but in an increasingly analytic climate were not enough to give much of a national reputational boost. A wave of deaths and retirements opened up new slots for senior faculty in the late 1940s and 1950s, however, and the department, eager to bolster its standing, especially in light of challenges from public research institutions like Michigan, Berkeley, and UCLA, made a series of key hires. Carl Hempel was brought from Yale in 1955; Vlastos from Cornell in 1955; the ordinary language philosopher Stuart Hampshire from London in 1963; Donald Davidson from Stanford in 1967; and the logician Dana Scott in 1969.[19] The department remained sixth-ranked on a 1957 reputational survey but by 1964 had climbed into fourth place behind Harvard, Michigan, and Yale on measures of faculty quality.[20] Measured by the perceived effectiveness of its graduate program, it was second to none. This change in reputational ranking was a function not just of senior hires but of junior ones as well, and also reflected indirectly the raids that up-and-coming departments like Pittsburgh were making on competitor schools like Yale, which was, in any case, on a downward trajectory.[21]

A sense of the Princeton department's character during Rorty's early years there can be gleaned from two pieces of correspondence, both writ-

19. Smith, "The Department of Philosophy."

20. Cartter, *Assessment of Quality in Graduate Education*, 29.

21. Brian Leiter notes: "In the 1950s, the top philosophy program in the United States was, by a wide margin, Harvard (W. V. O. Quine, an aging C. I. Lewis, Morton White, Roderick Firth, etc.), followed by some mix of Cornell (Max Black, Norman Malcom, a young John Rawls, etc.), Michigan (William Frankena, Cooper Langford, Charles Stevenson, etc.), Princeton (esp. after Carl Hempel and Gregory Vlastos moved there circa 1955), and Yale (Hempel, until he left for Princeton, but also a young Wilfrid Sellars, Brand Blanshard, Alan Anderson, Arthur Pap, etc.), and then some mix of, depending on who you asked, UCLA, Chicago, Columbia, Brown, maybe Berkeley. A decade later, say circa 1965, Harvard was still on top (Quine, Rawls, a young Putnam, Owen, etc.), but Princeton was now a powerhouse (Hempel, Vlastos, Hampshire, a young Gil Harman, a young Richard Rorty, a young Joel Feinberg, etc.), Cornell (Black, Malcolm, a young Shoemaker, etc.) and Michigan (Alston, Brandt, Frankena, Stevenson, a young Alvin Goldman, etc.) were still among the top five, with Pittsburgh (Sellars, Rescher, K. Baier, Grünbaum, etc.) closing in. Yale, after the exodus of faculty to Pittsburgh, was fading though perhaps hanging on in the

ten after Rorty had received tenure but reflective of the situation he would have encountered as an assistant professor. The first letter was penned in 1967 and addressed to Charles Gilbert, a philosopher at Swarthmore, who had written on behalf of the American Philosophical Association's Committee on Educational Policy. Rorty had become head of the graduate program, and Gilbert asked him, as he did others holding similar positions around the country, what kind of student the department tended to favor for admission. Rorty stressed that while Princeton admittees should have some background in the history of philosophy, what really mattered was that they should be familiar with and competent to participate in debates about analytic philosophy. Wrote Rorty,

> We would expect a student applying for graduate study to have had a few courses (two or three—perhaps at an introductory level) on the history of philosophy—enough to give him some familiarity with the great names. We would expect him to have had some logic—at least an elementary course in symbolic logic (propositional calculus and first-order functional calculus). We would expect him to have had several courses dealing with contemporary discussions of philosophical problems in philosophy of mind, or theory of knowledge, or ethics. In particular, we would expect him to have some familiarity with discussions of Wittgenstein, Austin, Hare and other much-discussed recent philosophers. None of these courses are necessary conditions for admission, but a student's chances of admission are substantially decreased if he seems to have had no training in one of these areas.... In general, though we sometimes deplore the increased professionalism of philosophy, and say that we ought to make sure that we don't exclude people who may need a year of graduate work to become acquainted with the questions and methods now used by analytic philosophers, we do favor candidates who are fairly thoroughly "professionalized." We admit a few students each year (say two or three out of fourteen) who come from schools where they have had little exposure to analytic philosophy and who may be expected to be a bit "lost" during their first month here—but these students are admitted in fear and trembling.[22]

---

top ten; Columbia and Chicago were hanging on too; while UCLA (Carnap, Montague, a young Kaplan, a young David Lewis etc.) and Berkeley (Feyeraband, Mates, a young Searle, a young Stroud) and perhaps Stanford (Suppes, Davidson) were now solidly in the top ten." See his discussion at http://leiterreports.typepad.com/blog/2003/10/the_us_philosop. html#more, accessed February 9, 2007.

22. Richard Rorty to Charles Gilbert, February 9, 1967, RRP.

This letter testifies to the heavily analytic identity and character of the department in the first half of the 1960s—and the degree to which an analytic orientation was equated in everyday discourse with notions of professionalism—but, written for public consumption, it said nothing about internal cleavages within the department or about which factions held the most power. A 1971 letter that Rorty wrote to Princeton president R. F. Goheen, by contrast, held nothing back. The subject was the department's chairmanship, which had recently fallen open after Vlastos's years in the position. Whom did Rorty favor as a replacement? He began by painting a picture for Goheen of the current situation. "During most of the decade I've been here, the shape and direction of the department have been determined very largely by a few senior people—Vlastos, Hempel, Hampshire, and Davidson—whose opinions were deferred to by the rest of the department because of their extraordinary distinction and, in part, because of their personal qualities,"[23] noted Rorty. "But now Hampshire and Davidson are gone," he continued—Hampshire having retired in 1970, with Davidson moving to Rockefeller University that same year— "and Vlastos and Hempel are being viewed as people who will soon be gone. Thus there is a sort of power vacuum." (In fact Vlastos did not leave Princeton until 1976, when he moved to Berkeley; Hempel retired in 1973, moving to Pittsburgh in 1977.)[24] In Rorty's view, these departures, recent and imminent, had hurt the department's reputation. "Once Hempel and Vlastos are gone, no one who is up-to-date on who's in the department would dream of ranking Princeton 'first' in distinction of philosophy faculty. If I were doing the ranking, and we didn't make any new senior appointments in the meantime, then in 1974 I would rank Princeton somewhere between tenth and fifteenth in distinction of philosophy faculty.... So, unless some really brilliant appointments are made, Princeton will by then have a good, but not a distinguished, philosophy department." Within the department different proposals had been floated for rectifying the situation, but decisive action had been stymied by the fact that the department was split along analytic versus pluralistic lines, which Rorty described as reflecting the "usual ideological differences which traditionally beset philosophy departments." "On the one hand," he said,

23. Richard Rorty to R. F. Goheen, October 22, 1971, RRP.

24. For these and many other details concerning appointments, I have relied throughout the book on Stuart Brown, Diané Collinson, and Robert Wilkinson, eds., 1996, *Biographical Dictionary of Twentieth-Century Philosophers,* London: Routledge. On Princeton appointments specifically, see http://philosophy.princeton.edu/our_history.html, accessed May 14, 2007.

there are the tough-minded technicians (e.g., Harman, Benacerraf, Grandy, Lewis, Field) who often brush aside work which doesn't seem to them in the "main stream" of current concern. Then there are more broad- and tender-minded types (e.g., Kaufman, Smith, Vlastos, me) who talk about the need for greater "balance" in the department (a phrase which these days has become a euphemism for "fewer logicians and philosophers of language.") It is not that there are clear factions (on the contrary, we are all such prima donnas that votes, though often very close, are seldom predictable as to who will be on each side), but rather that there is a persistent tension between those who want the department to keep a fairly tight focus on certain areas and those who want to spread it out and not put too many chips on certain current concerns.... As things stand, each quasi-faction has a sort of veto power, and there is not much will to compromise or make deals.[25]

Chapters 8 and 10 describe the developments and events in the late 1960s and 1970s that helped move Rorty into the "broad- and tender-minded" camp. For the moment, though, what is important to note is Rorty's assessment that the most powerful senior faculty members at the time he went up for tenure were Vlastos, Hempel, and Hampshire. Although he grouped Vlastos with the broad-minded in 1971, owing to the fact that he was a classicist, what made Vlastos's approach to Plato unique was that he sought to reconstruct ancient philosophy through an analytic lens, influenced as he was by Wittgenstein. In the introduction to one of the Plato volumes he edited, he noted: "The last three decades have witnessed a renaissance of interest in Plato among philosophers throughout the world.... Much of this new zeal for Platonic studies has been generated by the importation of techniques of logical and semantic analysis that have proved productive in contemporary philosophy. By means of these techniques we may now better understand some of the problems Plato attempted to solve.... The result has been a more vivid sense of the relevance of his thought to the concerns of present-day ontologists, epistemologists, and moralists. He has become for us less of an antique monument and more of a living presence."[26]

25. Gilbert Harman has pointed out that this discussion of the department fails to mention Thomas Nagel or Margaret Wilson. In fact, Rorty goes on to discuss both later in the letter, commenting on their suitability for the chairmanship.

26. Quoted in Donald Davidson and John Ferrari, 2004, "Gregory Vlastos," *Proceedings of the American Philosophical Society* 148:256–59, 257.

Hempel and Hampshire, for their part, were also of an analytic cast. Hempel had been a student of both Reichenbach and Carnap before the war and had been on a steep upward career trajectory since his immigration to the United States in 1937, moving from positions at City College and Queens College to Yale before taking the job at Princeton. A philosopher of science, Hempel did not cleave strictly to the logical positivist program, following Quine in rejecting the analytic/synthetic distinction and criticizing verificationism.[27] Instead he developed an analysis of the conditions under which observation sentences may be said to be confirmed and sought to place confirmation under the rubric of a "covering-law" framework for explanation. Hampshire, a moral philosopher trained at Oxford, raised questions very different from those that had concerned other analytic philosophers—about such things as the nature of the self—but did so by means of an analysis of language. A rival of A. J. Ayer, whose former wife he ended up marrying in a much-publicized scandal, Hampshire attempted to broaden analytic philosophy's frame of reference, tentatively engaging with certain thinkers in the Continental tradition, such as Maurice Merleau-Ponty, who, like him, stressed the corporeal dimension of human agency. At the end of the day, however, Hampshire still preferred a top-notch logician to a top-notch Continentalist, as illustrated by a letter Rorty wrote to him in 1969. Hampshire, out of the country at the time, was keen for the department to appoint Dana Scott, a logician who had graduated from Princeton in 1958 and held positions at Berkeley and Stanford. Rorty favored extending an offer to Herbert Marcuse. "I'm sorry I didn't answer your note about the move to appoint Scott before this," he wrote to Hampshire.[28]

We have widely different intuitions about these things. I don't have any sense of nobleness about logicians as such . . . ; if the truth were told, I'm afraid I regard them the way literary critics view the need to have a man in Anglo-Saxon in the English department. Every department needs one, but they're harmless drudges until proved otherwise. As you doubtless know from Donald [Davidson], [Stephen] Graubard turned us down for an assistant professorship in political philosophy, so now we're back on the Marcuse kick. . . . I think I have an higher opinion of him than you do; I've been

27. A. R. Lacey, 1996, "Carl Hempel," pp. 332–33 in *Biographical Dictionary of Twentieth-Century Philosophers*, Stuart Brown, Diané Collinson, and Robert Wilkinson, eds., London: Routledge.

28. Richard Rorty to Stuart Hampshire, February 3, 1969, RRP.

reading through *One-Dimensional Man* lately, and I would rank him with Ortega and Niebuhr. (Not the highest praise, no doubt, but something.)

In this context—one in which the most powerful figures in the department were committed to analytic work[29]—it would have been eminently clear to Rorty that in order to be tenurable, he would have to make a significant contribution to analytic thought. Concerns about tenure would not have been unjustified, however confident Rorty might have been in his own abilities. Although Princeton's tenure rate would decrease in the coming decades as the administration sought increasingly to ensure the quality of the senior faculty, it was nevertheless the case in the 1960s that only one in three junior professors received tenure.[30] That Rorty had received so many other job offers—not least from Harvard—no doubt reduced whatever insecurities he might have had, but the point remains that the only way he would be promoted at Princeton would be by doing work recognized as important by the analytic community. Again he pursued two broad lines of research.

* 3 *

The first involved pushing his interest in metaphilosophy in new directions. Rather than urging simply that the best insights of nonanalytic approaches be assimilated into analytic thought—an interesting exercise, and one that had helped get him the job at Princeton, but not an approach likely to earn him a reputation as an important and original contributor to the analytic project—he now used his metaphilosophical skills to consider why philosophers should become analysts in the first place. His argument to this effect was most fully developed in his introduction to *The Linguistic Turn*, the edited volume he published in 1967. It testifies to how soon after the completion of his dissertation he came to consider himself a linguistic philosopher—and how important metaphilosophy was as a tenure strategy—that he could be found pitching the book idea to publishers as early as 1962. In May of that year he wrote to the philosophy editor at Prentice-Hall, Richard Trudgen, to follow up on an earlier conversation in which he had first proposed the volume. "The

29. Princeton's national and international reputation for rigorous, technical philosophy was also enhanced by the presence on the local scene of the mathematicians and logicians Kurt Gödel at the Institute for Advanced Study and Alonzo Church in the Department of Mathematics. (Church held a joint appointment with philosophy.)

30. Axtell, *Making of Princeton University*, 98.

title of the anthology would be something like: *The Linguistic Turn: Essays in Philosophical Method*," he suggested.

> It would consist of a number of "programmatic" essays written during the last thirty years by philosophers who share the view that, in some important sense of "verbal," many traditional philosophical problems are verbal ones, and who therefore share the view that the method of philosophy involves the analysis of the language in which these problems are stated. The selection would attempt to make clear the aims and presuppositions of the various "movements" which have occurred in recent "linguistic" philosophy by reproducing, and commenting upon, various "classic" statements of aim and method and various "classic" criticisms of alternative aims and methods. It would, therefore, be a collection of essays in metaphilosophy: discussions of what philosophy has been, of what it might become, and what it must do to become what it should.[31]

The target audience for the book would be graduate students in philosophy as well as intellectuals in other disciplines who wanted to familiarize themselves with analytic thought, and the volume would be designed for seminar use. As Rorty envisioned it, the book would be taught, not as a substitute for, but in conjunction with other similar books that had recently appeared such as Antony Flew's *Essays on Logic and Language* (1951) and *Essays in Conceptual Analysis* (1956), A. J. Ayer's *Logical Positivism* (1959), and Gilbert Ryle's *The Revolution in Philosophy* (1956).

That these books had recently been published, however, led the reviewers to whom Trudgen sent the proposal to conclude that the market for analytic anthologies was saturated. A month later, he wrote to Rorty with the disappointing news that while "some of the reviewers seem to feel strongly that the book would be extremely useful and others have recommended certain changes ... one or two of them are not quite sure of its need."[32] Trudgen suggested they sit on the proposal for a year or two and then revisit it.

Having recently learned of his transition from visiting instructor to tenure-track assistant professor, however, Rorty could ill afford to wait several years for the mere possibility of a publication opportunity. So he got in touch with people he knew to see if they could intervene on his behalf. His friend Vere Chappell, who had defended a dissertation on

31. Richard Rorty to Richard Trudgen, May 30, 1962, RRP.
32. Richard Trudgen to Richard Rorty, June 27, 1962, RRP.

process philosophy at Yale in 1958 before moving to the University of Chicago, replied, probably in the fall of that year, to a letter Rorty sent bemoaning Prentice-Hall's decision. "I'm surprised at the fate of your metaphil. anthology. Would you be willing to have [University of] Chicago Press look at it? They're eager to do paperback anthologies that might have class use, and would give you the same deal that commercial publishers give. (I was talking to [University of Chicago Press Director Roger] Shugg about this very thing last week, so this is semi-official.)"[33] Beyond the chance to help a friend publish an important volume, there would be something in it for Chappell as well: "If you are willing to let Chicago look at it," he continued, "would you also be willing to send your proposal to me and let me give it to them? There's been talk about my doing some ms. procurement for them and their paying me for it. So in other words I'd write a recommendation of your proposal, give it to them, and get something for it myself—a sort of beefed up readers fee is what it would amount to. But every little bit helps."

This is exactly what Rorty did, later acknowledging Chappell in his preface for "aid[ing] this project at every step."[34] The process of securing permissions to reprint articles and drafting his long introduction took longer than initially planned. Chicago would not sign a final contract until most of the volume had been assembled and come back from peer review, and this still had not happened by 1964.[35] As late as 1965 Rorty could be found writing to scholars like Carnap, asking if he would consent to have two pieces of his, "On the Character of Philosophical Problems" and "Empiricism, Semantics, and Ontology," reprinted.[36] Carnap agreed, as did Quine and twenty-five of the other most prominent figures in analytic philosophy at the time. Nothing Sellars had published quite fit the volume, so Rorty wrote to ask if he would compose something especially for it: "I'm not asking anybody else to write something for the anthology, since there's an *embarras de richesse* in print. But I would very much like to have something of yours in it, while nothing you've so far written seems suitable.... Possibly you regard metaphilosophy as an unmanageable subject, but, as I say, I'd be delighted if you cared to air your

33. Vere Chappell to Richard Rorty, letter dated September 1 (no year), RRP.

34. Richard Rorty, [1967] 1992, "Preface," pp. i–ii in *The Linguistic Turn: Essays in Philosophical Method*, Richard Rorty, ed., Chicago: University of Chicago Press, ii.

35. Kenneth Douglas, editor at the University of Chicago Press, to Richard Rorty, November 12, 1964, RRP.

36. Richard Rorty to Rudolf Carnap, July 8, 1965, RRP.

views."[37] Sellars's response is lost, but nothing of his ended up appearing in the book.

While *The Linguistic Turn* was published too late to figure directly in his tenure case, the fact of its imminent publication may have counted in Rorty's favor. Indeed, it is only because of heightened productivity expectations today that editing an important volume does not count toward tenure in major research departments. Princeton philosophers may also have read drafts of the long introduction Rorty wrote for the book, which sought to do much more than merely summarize the ideas of his contributors. The argument he produced there for the value of linguistic analysis is telling with regard to the development of his thought. "The history of philosophy is punctuated by revolts against the practices of previous philosophers and by attempts to transform philosophy into a science,"[38] Rorty began. In light of this unceasing intellectual dynamism, it is easy to imagine that philosophy never makes progress, not least because philosophical revolutionaries often propose new criteria for evaluating success. But one standard by which the state of philosophy may be judged—here Rorty rehearsed the Peircean argument he'd made in the "Philosopher as Expert" piece—is "movement toward a contemporary consensus," and it was in light of the recent emergence of such a consensus around the position that "philosophical problems are problems which may be solved (or dissolved) either by reforming language, or by understanding more about the language we presently use" that the book aimed to "provide materials for reflection."[39] "This view," Rorty intoned, "is considered by many of its proponents to be the most important philosophical discovery of our time, and, indeed of the ages," though he acknowledged in the same breath that "by its opponents, it is interpreted as a sign of the sickness of our souls."[40] The problem is that there is little serious debate anymore between analysts and nonanalysts as to the value of their respective positions. Analysts, for their part, having reached a stage in their thought where dismissing traditional philosophical claims is no longer a major preoccupation, now justify their approach simply by pointing to the fruits of their labors, while nonanalysts refuse to accept that the benefits of linguistic analysis are so obvious. Most analysts remain ana-

37. Richard Rorty to Wilfrid Sellars, June 24, 1965, RRP.

38. Richard Rorty, [1967] 1992, "Introduction: Metaphilosophical Difficulties of Linguistic Philosophy," pp. 1–39 in *The Linguistic Turn: Essays in Philosophical Method*, Richard Rorty, ed., Chicago: University of Chicago Press, 1.

39. Ibid., 2–3.   40. Ibid., 3.

lysts because, at the end of the day, no other approach provides as clear answers to the question of "what could count as evidence for or against the truth of [philosophical] views"; because linguistic analysis *"does* seem to hold out hope for clarity on this methodological question," it alone paves the way "for eventual agreement among philosophers."[41] But the lack of explicit debate on the matter represents an unhealthy intellectual situation, and it was with the goal of getting analysts to be more clear about their metaphilosophical justifications that the essays in the book were assembled.

Rorty went on to consider two questions central to any such discussion: first, whether "the statements of linguistic philosophers about the nature of philosophy and about philosophical methods [are] actually presuppositionless," as some have claimed; and second, whether "linguistic philosophers actually have criteria for philosophical success which are clear enough to permit rational agreement?"[42] With respect to the first question, he took up and rejected in short order the answers given by Ayer and Carnap, which centered on assessments of significance, meaningfulness, and verifiability that were asserted to be matters of logic but in fact depended on certain substantive precommitments. More satisfactory was Gustav Bergmann's emphasis on ideal language; if a language could be constructed in which all nonphilosophical statements could be expressed, but in which no traditional philosophical statements could, it would suggest that philosophical questions "are questions which we ask only because, as a matter of historical fact, we speak the language we do."[43] This would not imply that philosophical questions should be dismissed; instead, Bergmann held that in his ideal language "all philosophical propositions can be reconstructed as statements about its syntax ... and interpretation."[44] On this understanding, philosophers in the past are seen as attempting, however unsatisfactorily, to "find a language in which philosophical propositions could not be stated."[45] "If there is a single crucial fact which explains the contemporary popularity of linguistic philosophy," Rorty concluded from his discussion, "it is the inability of its opponents ... to give a satisfactory answer to this question"[46] of what philosophers in the past were doing if they were not doing *this.* Moreover, Bergmann's approach is not subject to the criticism that it rests on propositions to which nonanalysts would never agree. In fact, Rorty held,

41. Ibid., 4.   42. Ibid.   43. Ibid., 7.
44. Gustav Bergmann, quoted in ibid., 6.
45. Ibid., 7.   46. Ibid., 8.

Bergmann presupposes almost nothing, arguing for the linguistic turn on "practical" rather than "theoretical grounds."

This was not to say, according to Rorty, that there is no rejoinder to Bergmann. The most significant is that advanced by idealists like Brand Blanshard, who hold that linguistic analysis constrains us to focus on words rather than the concepts those words represent. In defense of Bergmann, and against Blanshard—whose critical study of analytic philosophy he had recently skewered in a book review—Rorty mobilized Wittgenstein to argue for the thesis of "methodological nominalism," or the position that all questions about universals that can't be answered through empirical research but can be somehow answered "can be answered by answering questions about the use of linguistic expressions."[47] This thesis couldn't be definitively proven, but neither had any nonanalysts given an effective refutation of it. But Rorty claimed that one did not have to be a proponent of ideal language to benefit from Bergmann's argument, for the best ordinary language philosophers advance the same metaphilosophical position, simply regarding ordinary language as ideal and wielding common sense as their weapon, much as ideal language philosophers wield symbolic logic. That there was great controversy between constructionalists and philosophers of an ordinary language persuasion—a controversy which Rorty reviewed—did nothing to undermine the value of the turn toward language embraced by both sides.

As to the question of whether linguistic analysis offers any clear-cut criterion for philosophical success, Rorty staked out a careful position. The best way of posing this question, he claimed, was to rephrase it by asking whether linguistic analysis offers any clear criterion for determining whether particular philosophical problems should be dissolved. The criterion analysts had recently formulated was that a problem should be dissolved if it can be shown that "a *particular formulation* of . . . [it] involves a use of a linguistic expression which is sufficiently unusual to justify our asking the philosopher who offers the formulation to restate his problem in other terms."[48] Although this standard might seem "wishy-washy," in fact it is not, "for, despite their dubious metaphilosophical programs, writers like Russell, Carnap, Wittgenstein, Ryle, Austin, and a host of others have succeeded in forcing those who wish to propound the traditional problems to admit that they can no longer be put forward in the traditional formulations."[49]

47. Ibid., 11.   48. Ibid., 32.   49. Ibid., 32, 33.

In light of the value of the linguistic turn that these considerations re-vealed, what did the future hold for philosophy? Rorty forecast six possibilities. If methodological nominalism were undercut—as it might be by phenomenology—the one presupposition underlying the linguistic turn would be undermined, and analytic philosophy would cease to be important. Alternatively, this might happen at the same time that the "demand for clear-cut criteria of agreement [in philosophy] would be dropped," in which case philosophy would "cease to be an argumentative discipline, and grow closer to poetry," on the model of the later Heidegger.[50] Or philosophers might continue to insist on methodological nominalism but get rid of the demand for agreement, which would usher in a new era of system building—"the only difference being that the systems built would no longer be considered *descriptions* of the nature of things or of human consciousness, but rather *proposals* about how to talk" that would be evaluated by whether they were "new, interesting and fruitful."[51] Another alternative would be to take Wittgenstein's stance, which would lead us to "see philosophy as a cultural disease which has been cured";[52] this wouldn't put philosophers out of work but would redirect them to the task of stamping out bad philosophical ways of talking. A different future for philosophy would see it merging with the field of linguistics, which could turn out to "provide us with non-banal formulations of the neces-sary and sufficient conditions for the truth of statements, and non-banal accounts of the meaning of words."[53] Finally, in a neo-Kantian moment, philosophy might seek to identify the "necessary conditions for the pos-sibility of language itself,"[54] as proposed by scholars like P. F. Strawson. In Rorty's view, the current consensus in the field was that the last two of these possibilities were the most likely, though he expressed doubts about Strawson's proposal.

Rorty concluded with a prescient warning. Although earlier in the introduction he had described linguistic analysis as largely presupposi-tionless, he had not considered how philosophy was intertwined with culture or with historical changes in our intellectual vocabularies. But this was important, for in Rorty's view—a view he said he developed by reading philosophers such as Dewey, Hampshire, Sartre, Heidegger, and Wittgenstein—"the most important thing that has happened in philoso-phy during the last thirty years is not the linguistic turn itself, but rather

50. Ibid., 34.   52. Ibid.   54. Ibid.
51. Ibid.   53. Ibid., 35.

the beginning of a thoroughgoing rethinking of certain epistemological difficulties which have troubled philosophers since Plato and Aristotle."[55] This rethinking, centered on a repudiation of the "spectatorial account of knowledge" according to which "the mind is conceived of as a sort of 'immaterial eye,'" would, if successfully carried out, "lead to reformulations everywhere else in philosophy," calling into question the distinction between philosophy and science and rendering "most of the essays in this volume ... obsolete."[56] It is remarkable that already by the mid-1960s, when the introduction was written, Rorty foresaw the argument he would advance in *Philosophy and the Mirror of Nature*. But it is also apparent that with *The Linguistic Turn* he threw his hat in with the analysts. Much earlier in the introduction he noted appreciatively that "linguistic philosophy, over the last thirty years, has succeeded in putting the entire philosophical tradition, from Parmenides through Descartes and Hume to Bradley and Whitehead, on the defensive. It has done so by a careful and thorough scrutiny of the ways in which traditional philosophers have used language in the formulation of their problems. This achievement is sufficient to place this period among the great ages of the history of philosophy."[57] That Rorty would, a quarter-century later, recall with great embarrassment having written such a passage, describing it "as merely the attempt of a thirty-three-year-old philosopher to convince himself that he had the luck to be born at the right time—to persuade himself that the disciplinary matrix in which he happened to find himself ... was more than just one more philosophical school, one more tempest in an academic teapot,"[58] does nothing but emphasize the degree to which it expressed a conviction deeply held at the time.

∗ **4** ∗

But using metaphilosophy to develop arguments about the importance of the linguistic turn was not the only strategy Rorty pursued to win tenure. In fact, probably as a result of tenure pressure, Rorty went through a significant transition in the early 1960s: from being primarily a metaphilosopher, as he was at Wellesley, to also contributing substantively to analytic debates. In the grant application cited earlier from the late 1960s, Rorty noted that he had been working along two parallel tracks. Much

55. Ibid., 39.   56. Ibid.   57. Ibid., 33.
58. Richard Rorty, 1992, "Twenty-Five Years After," pp. 371–74 in *The Linguistic Turn: Essays in Philosophical Method*, Richard Rorty, ed., Chicago: University of Chicago Press, 371.

of his writing had been concerned with metaphilosophical matters, trying first to bring strands of nonanalytic discourse into line with analytic
concerns, later identifying the reasons that linguistic approaches should
be preferred over nonlinguistic ones. Yet he had also been at work on
another set of issues:

> In addition to these various metaphilosophical and historical pieces, I have
> done some writing on the metaphysical problem of the nature of mental
> entities—a couple of papers (one published, the other not) on mind-body
> identity and a couple of others (neither published as yet) on the so-called
> "private language problem." In these papers, I have tried to argue that one
> can simultaneously (a) reject logical behaviorism and accept the existence
> of mental entities, (b) grant that such entities might turn out to be brain-
> states, and (c) avoid the bad consequences which Cartesian epistemology
> drew from the existence of mental entities. Roughly, I have tried to show
> that one can keep the anti-Cartesian arguments advanced by Wittgenstein
> and by materialists while avoiding the counter-intuitive theses advanced
> by both schools.[59]

Where elsewhere in the application he highlighted the continuities
between these strands of his thinking, arguing that the central theme in
all was that contemporary philosophy was, in various ways, coming to
"abandon" the "Cartesian 'veil of ideas' theory," with profound implications, his studies of mind-body identity and the private-language problem—though informed by the same mix of Sellars, Wittgenstein, and
Peirce that characterized his earlier work—are best read as a distinct piece
of his oeuvre. They represent Rorty's attempt to make contributions to
analytic thought of a piece with those that other bright, young analytic
philosophers of his generation were making. They were, in other words,
part of Rorty's efforts to position himself even more squarely within the
mainstream philosophical establishment. I don't mean to imply by this
that Rorty consciously shifted gears, moving into more substantive areas out of an explicit desire to bolster his reputation as an analyst and
thus to secure more status with key senior faculty members at Princeton
who would vote on his tenure case. But it is suggestive of a connection
between his work on these topics and his interest in promotion that he
began writing some of the relevant articles only a few years before he
had to prepare his tenure file. It is also telling that he attempted to place

59. Richard Rorty, "Brief Narrative Account of Previous Accomplishments."

these pieces in prominent analytic venues and sought out the advice and opinions of trusted local analytic authorities in revising them.

His article "Mind-Body Identity, Privacy, and Categories," for example, published in the *Review of Metaphysics* in 1965, was originally submitted as a chapter for a volume edited by the Cornell analyst Max Black, titled *Philosophy in America* (1965). Intended to showcase the work of "junior colleagues" of distinction who had raised problems "both important and unsolved"[60]—problems that should, in Black's opinion, move to the center of philosophical discussion in the years to come—the volume's contributor list reads like a Who's Who of important young analytic philosophers of the day, from Bruce Aune to Stanley Cavell, Jerry Fodor to John Searle. So prestigious was the volume to be that, as Black noted with more than a hint of self-congratulation, more than 160 young philosophers had submitted pieces for consideration. Rorty was among them, but in 1963 Black rejected his contribution, no doubt in a blow to Rorty's ego.[61] No less disconcerting, given that Black and Vlastos had been close colleagues for many years, was Black's global assessment of Rorty: "Perhaps you will allow me to add that your style, which is on the whole forceful and direct, occasionally lapses into academic pomposity. I can say this without embarrassment, because I suffer from the same malady all too often." Rebounding from the rejection, Rorty had no difficulty publishing the piece in the *Review of Metaphysics*—his graduate school friend Bernstein had taken over editorship of the journal the year before from Weiss—but this was not the kind of venue he would have most preferred with an eye to tenure, though the paper would turn out to be one of his most frequently cited pieces.

He was more successful with two essays he wrote for *The Encyclopedia of Philosophy* (1967), an eight-volume attempt, published by Macmillan, to survey the entire field with nearly 1,500 contributions. The *Encyclopedia* was edited by Paul Edwards, a Viennese-born ethicist who taught for seventeen years at NYU before moving to Brooklyn College in 1966. Trained at Columbia, Edwards was an analyst and did not deny that his own "bias" and "ideological commitments" had "influenced ... [the *Encyclopedia's*] content."[62] While he did not exclude major figures and concepts associated with other approaches, he, "like the majority of my closest advisors...,

60. Max Black, 1965, "Preface," p. 9 in *Philosophy in America*, Max Black, ed., Ithaca: Cornell University Press.

61. See Max Black to Richard Rorty, November 26, 1963, RRP.

62. Paul Edwards, 1967, "Introduction," pp. ix–xiv in *The Encyclopedia of Philosophy*, vol. 1, Paul Edwards, ed., New York: Macmillan, xi.

[had] been raised in the empirical and analytic tradition of Anglo-Saxon philosophy." The *Encyclopedia* was a major analytic undertaking whose contributors included many prominent figures in analytic philosophy. Given this, and that many of the entries represented important substantive contributions in their own right and not merely pat summaries, the fact that Rorty managed to get his work published in the volume was a feather in his cap. Not surprisingly, he ran drafts of his entries by his analytic colleagues at Princeton in an attempt to make the arguments more airtight and rewrote them in accordance with the suggestions he received. In September of 1964 he wrote to Philip Cummings, one of the senior editors for the project, to say that "when I sent you a draft of my INTUITION piece on July 17, I thought I'd be sending a polished version in a few weeks. In fact, however, the criticisms which my colleagues gave of that draft were such as to make me sit down and write a substantially new piece. I've now finished polishing this, and I send a copy along as my final submission."[63] One assumes that he followed a similar procedure with his other entry, "Relations, Internal and External," though there is no direct evidence of this and no indication of what kind of advice for revision he received.

What arguments did Rorty advance as he tried his hand as a substantive analytic thinker? Characteristic of both articles in the *Encyclopedia* was the claim that contemporary analysts had fundamentally rethought a number of long-standing philosophical debates. In the piece on internal and external relations, these debates were metaphysical in nature. Are the properties that define an entity internal to it in the sense of being essentially relational or external in the sense of being nonrelational? Rorty noted that two types of answers had been given by recent philosophers. Some, connected to the idealist tradition, held that all of a thing's properties are internal. Whereas a number of philosophers in the past had thought this to be true on the grounds of self-identity, idealists like Blanshard offered a more cogent argument from causality: "If ... all true relational propositions about particulars are propositions which are true in virtue of causal relations between the particulars mentioned in these propositions, then it follows that all particulars are connected to all others by logical relations and that every such proposition would be seen (by omniscience) to entail a logical truth about every such particular."[64] By

63. Richard Rorty to Philip Cummings, September 18, 1964, RRP.

64. Richard Rorty, 1967, "Relations, Internal and External," pp. 125–33 in *The Encyclopedia of Philosophy*, vol. 7, Paul Edwards, ed., New York: Macmillan, 128.

contrast, linguistic philosophers took this view to be a nonstarter. They maintained that particulars are not internally related to other particulars because "the only entities which can be internally related to one another are *characteristics* of particulars"[65]—that is, characteristics that obtain within linguistic descriptions. Although at the conclusion of the piece Rorty issued the McKeon-inspired warning that both positions "are parts of internally consistent philosophical systems" and that "in the absence of a touchstone other than common sense, it is difficult to see how a rational choice between such systems can be made,"[66] his preference was clearly for the view that "to speak of 'logically necessary conditions for the self-identity of X' is, at best, to speak elliptically of 'logically necessary conditions for describing X as a K.' "[67] He aimed to do more than highlight the advances made on this topic by philosophers of a linguistic persuasion, however. For some analysts, he noted—like Ryle—this way of thinking about relations leads to the view that particulars are "bare" in the sense that they "could logically have *any* properties."[68] But Rorty expressed "discomfort" with this notion, which seemed at odds with common sense. He championed instead the pragmatic position recently set forth by Timothy Sprigge—a British analyst influenced by William James—who argued that internality versus externality is a matter of degree and depends on the interests of those who are talking about the entity in question. On this understanding, particulars are not "bare" because we "relativize the notion [of internal property] and say that certain properties are internal to X relative to a person S whose personal criteria for identifying X include the presence of these properties."[69] This way of proceeding avoids Aristotelian essentialism, but also the more troubling implications of logical behaviorism.

More original and important in the history of analytic philosophy was the *Review of Metaphysics* paper on identity theory, discussed in the introduction and, since 1975 alone—the first year of coverage of the Arts and Humanities Citation Index—cited some 125 times. Here—with the defense of the "disappearance form" of identity theory, soon to be renamed "eliminative materialism"—was a bold new argument that, while in certain respects merely drawing out the implications of the philosophical viewpoints toward which he felt allegiance (Wittgenstein, Sellars, etc.), was nevertheless more than an effort at arguing for them on metaphilosophical grounds. Although Black may not have liked the paper much,

65. Ibid., 129–30.   67. Ibid., 130.   69. Ibid., 131.
66. Ibid., 132.   68. Ibid.

it positioned Rorty at the center of a lively debate and seemed to many an important if controversial contribution. It cannot be known with any certainty what role the paper played, if any, in convincing members of the Princeton department to recommend him for tenure,[70] but it probably illustrated to them not simply his continued productivity but also that he was capable of engaging in analytic debates at the highest levels and of moving the discussion forward. With it, Rorty's transition from Whiteheadian metaphysician and McKeonesque historian of philosophy to mainstream analytic philosopher was complete. Among others, his mother noticed the change. She wrote to a correspondent in 1966: "Dick and Amelie keep right on climbing that ladder, careerwise. Each is editing an anthology, Amelie's is out, Dick's out shortly, Dick is vice-chairman of his dept.... Dick is gay and relaxed, Amelie beautiful, the boy is a pint sized bottle of joy and healthiness. Also, they are both changing ... Amelie took a semester off and got a grant to do a study in anthropology.... Dick has stopped being a metaphysician."[71]

70. I do not have access to Rorty's tenure file.

71. Winifred Raushenbush to "MR," November 6, 1966, WRC. I have reordered the last sentence for emphasis.

EIGHT

Princeton University, 1965–1982

* 1 *

The first few years after he received tenure in 1965 were relatively productive ones for Rorty. He published little in 1966—only a two-page encyclopedia entry on Aristotle and a review of John Boler's book *Charles Peirce and Scholastic Realism*—but the following year saw the publication of *The Linguistic Turn*, along with Rorty's entries in Paul Edwards's *The Encyclopedia of Philosophy*. By 1970, when he was promoted to full professor, several more important articles of his had appeared in print, each analytic in style and choice of subject matter. "Strawson's Objectivity Argument," for example, published in the *Review of Metaphysics* in 1970, examined critically the analytic philosopher P. F. Strawson's attempt, in his 1966 book *The Bounds of Sense*, to improve upon Kant's effort to show that "the possibility of experience somehow involves the possibility of experience of objects."[1] "Wittgenstein, Privileged Access, and Incommunicability," published in *American Philosophical Quarterly* that same year, took on philosophers like George Pitcher—one of Rorty's colleagues at Princeton—who had interpreted Wittgenstein's comments on the impossibility of private language to mean that Wittgenstein was saying that "I cannot conceive that another person feels the same sensation that I do when I feel a pain."[2] Rorty insisted this was to attribute to Wittgenstein "paradoxical" views he never held. A short piece in the *Review of Metaphysics* defended Rorty's

1. Richard Rorty, 1970, "Strawson's Objectivity Argument," *Review of Metaphysics* 24:207–44, 207.

2. George Pitcher, cited in Richard Rorty, 1970, "Wittgenstein, Privileged Access, and Incommunicability," *American Philosophical Quarterly* 7:192–205, 193.

earlier thesis of eliminative materialism against recent attacks.[3] And in "Incorrigibility as the Mark of the Mental," published in the *Journal of Philosophy*, also in 1970, Rorty took on the standard view that mentality is defined by such qualities as intentionality or intuitiveness or nonspatiality. Against this view, he argued that the only way that "mental events are unlike any other events" is that "certain knowledge claims about them cannot be overridden. We have no criteria for setting aside as mistaken first-person contemporaneous reports of thoughts and sensations."[4] This is true not as a matter of "logical possibility,"[5] but because people today tend to subscribe to what he described in a follow-up paper as a "heuristic rule that when first-person contemporaneous reports of certain states conflict with other evidence about the presence of those states, the former should override the latter."[6] It may seem strange, Rorty acknowledged, to assert that "the truth of an ontological thesis [about the mind] depends in part upon what linguistic practices are adopted by the community,"[7] but the Wittgensteinian, who does not think it possible to describe ontology except from within some linguistic practice, asserts exactly that.

Those observing Rorty's career from afar might have interpreted this spate of analytic publications, coming on the heels of *The Linguistic Turn*, as evidence that Rorty had joined the ranks of the analytic community and saw his work as of a piece with that being done by other analysts. He had indeed undergone a conversion from metaphysician to analytic philosopher, as was argued in the preceding chapter, and could often be found extolling the virtues of analytic philosophy. In the summer of 1968, for example, he was asked to attend a philosophy workshop held on the Notre Dame campus. Sponsored by the Carnegie Corporation, the workshop was designed to acquaint philosophy professors at Catholic schools with recent developments in analytic thought. Rorty helped lead the workshop, and he recommended it for future funding on the grounds that familiarizing more Catholic philosophers with the analytic tradition was a good thing.[8] Likewise, Rorty privileged as a criterion for evaluating

3. Richard Rorty, 1970, "In Defense of Eliminative Materialism," *Review of Metaphysics* 24:112–21.

4. Richard Rorty, 1970, "Incorrigibility as the Mark of the Mental," *Journal of Philosophy* 67:399–424, 413.

5. Ibid., 417.

6. Richard Rorty, 1972, "Functionalism, Machines, and Incorrigibility," *Journal of Philosophy* 69:203–20, 214–15.

7. Rorty, "Incorrigibility," 423.

8. Richard Rorty to Carnegie Corporation, September 11, 1968, RRP.

philosophical work the degree to which it evidenced "analytical intelligence," by which he meant the capacity to think through every step of an argument with complete and utter clarity. "Very sharp analytical intelligence, lots of energy and drive," he wrote in a graduate school letter of recommendation for a student he'd taught while spending a semester as a visiting professor at Catholic University in 1969.[9] "As far as I could figure out, my seminar (Wittgenstein, Sellars, Putnam, etc.) was the first time he'd come across analytical philosophy, but he took to it like a duck to water."

Nevertheless, it would be a mistake to infer that Rorty was an uncritical participant in the analytic enterprise. As the 1960s and 1970s wore on, in fact, he became increasingly disdainful of mainstream analytic philosophy, which in his view had become too closed off to insights derived from other intellectual traditions. He was particularly frustrated with members of his own department, whom he thought embodied both the best and the worst tendencies of the analytic approach.

* 2 *

In the years immediately after he received tenure, Rorty was happy enough at Princeton. In October of 1965 he declined an informal offer from Kent Bendall, a philosopher at Wesleyan, to join the department there. "Wesleyan would be a good place to be," Rorty told him, "but, all things considered, Amélie and I think we had better stay put for a while. We both have tenure now, and although there are the usual dissatisfactions with the present arrangement, things are really pretty good down here. . . . Someday, I can well imagine, we might feel bored and fed up with Princeton and Douglass, but for the time being we're both inclined to just sit back, reflect, and see how things go."[10] Rorty was not being disingenuous. Although he probably would never have taken a job at a school so much lower down in the academic hierarchy, there were many things about Princeton he found to be intellectually satisfying. It was presumably because of this satisfaction that, in 1966, he turned down a job offer from Pittsburgh, which was making its rapid ascent in the status structure of the discipline.[11] Beyond the stimulation offered by his Princeton colleagues, Rorty appreciated being at an institution with high-quality

9. Richard Rorty, letter for Thomas Russman, December 5, 1970, RRP. Russman ended up attending Princeton, from which he received his Ph.D. in 1976.

10. Richard Rorty to Kent Bendall, October 26, 1965, RRP.

11. Kurt Baier to Richard Rorty, January 25, 1966, RRP.

graduate students. He confided in his friend Milton Fisk in 1974 that one department that was courting him had "lousy graduate students, and I don't know if I could give up having hot-shot graduate students."[12] He also liked the fact that the teaching load and administrative responsibilities at Princeton were relatively light, so that, as he explained to Peter Caws in 1968, declining an invitation to join to faculty of the CUNY Graduate Center, "one gets great quantities of time to work on one's own [research].... This seems too precious to lose."[13]

But it would not be long before Rorty experienced a falling out with his department. The trouble began in the 1967–68 school year, when Rorty cotaught a seminar with Gilbert Harman called "Semantics and Metaphysics." The aim of the seminar, as Rorty explained in a letter to Sellars, was to understand better some of the issues at stake in the different metaphysical stances of Sellars, Carnap, and Quine.[14] At least initially Rorty enjoyed the experience. "Sounds like your seminar with Harman is fun," Fisk wrote to Rorty in March of 1968. "I'm sure you'll be beyond me soon on logico-linguistic lore."[15]

Yet it soon became clear that he and Harman did not see eye to eye. In an undated letter to his mother probably written around this time, Rorty recounted that "the troubles have principally been that when I came here I was taken up by the local bright young man in the department, and thought I'd found a friend and someone to talk philosophy to. However, this guy ... decided over the last few months that I just didn't have the brains he'd given me credit for; in the way of the very intelligent who don't suffer fools gladly, he let me see this pretty clearly. The let-down that came with this (the feeling that now there was *no* point in my being at Princeton—since I can't seem to talk to anybody *else* in the department) has been afflicting me."[16] Rorty did not specify that the person in question was Harman, but in the letter to Princeton president Goheen cited in chapter 7, it was Harman whom he described as "the most brilliant philosopher in the department"—adding that, though this was true, Harman had "no *phronesis* at all."[17]

12. Richard Rorty to Milton Fisk, February 16, 1974, RRP.

13. Richard Rorty to Peter Caws, March 25, 1968, RRP.

14. Richard Rorty to Wilfrid Sellars, July 13, 1967, RRP.

15. Milton Fisk to Richard Rorty, March 7, 1968, RRP.

16. Richard Rorty to Winifred Raushenbush, May 25 (no year), RRP.

17. Richard Rorty to R. F. Goheen, October 22, 1971, RRP. Harman, who has read these pages, doubts that this was a reference to him. He suspects that Rorty was referring to Paul

It was not only Harman with whom he came to have disagreements. His relationship with Gregory Vlastos—who had hired him on in the first place—also deteriorated. It is not clear exactly when this first happened, but by 1974 Rorty could be found in an intense exchange about Vlastos with Edward Lee, who had moved to La Jolla to take a job at the University of California, San Diego, after completing a dissertation at Princeton in 1964.[18]

Some of the disagreement with Vlastos stemmed from events surrounding Rorty's divorce from Amélie, as is described below. Some may have had to do with the fact that Vlastos had hired Rorty to teach Greek philosophy, which Rorty lost interest in doing. But some, surely—and what also underlay his differences with Harman—had to do with Rorty's conception of the philosophical enterprise. In notes written in 1976, Rorty observed, in the context of a discussion of Hans-Georg Gadamer, that there are two fundamentally different types of philosophers: those who are "argumentative" and those who are "emblematic." "Some philosophers, like Quine or Sellars or Godel or Gettier, show something which one can repeat. They attain an objective result. . . . Other philosophers are emblematic, and are known for a vocabulary, for having invented a new language-game, rather than having made a famous move in an old one. . . . The one sort of philosopher is associated with the notion of 'objectivity' and science-as-a-model-for-philosophy. The other is associated with the man of letters."[19] Rorty expressed the same point in the concluding chapter of *Philosophy and the Mirror of Nature,* where he glossed the difference as that between systematic and edifying philosophers. However labeled, the point is that despite his ongoing work in an analytic style, Rorty increasingly saw himself as someone who reserved the greatest respect for edifying or emblematic philosophers. While keeping up with debates on the analytic research front, he made no effort to hide the fact that he read widely in the history of philosophy and in contemporary Continental thought. Most of his colleagues in the Princeton philosophy department did not, or at least Rorty perceived that they did not, and this was the major source of his growing frustration with them.

Evidence of Rorty's philosophical range can be found throughout his papers. In the fall of 1966, one year before the publication of *The Lin-*

Benacerraf. Rorty told me that he had no specific recollection of the matter and thought either interpretation plausible.

18. Edward Lee to Richard Rorty, March 29, 1974, RRP.

19. 1976 NEH seminar notes, RRP.

guistic Turn, he taught a course on the philosophy of religion, requiring students to read theologians such as John Hick and Paul Tillich.[20] That same year he exchanged letters with a colleague at Johns Hopkins about recent lectures Paul Ricoeur had given on Edmund Husserl.[21] The year following, he wrote to the philosophy editor at Prentice-Hall to urge that he commission a new series on Continental thought. "The other addition which occurs to me," he told Alan Lesure, who'd written to ask his advice on some other book proposals, "is a volume on the cultural context of the rise of phenomenology and existentialism. This is a matter on which a lot of trash has been written (all about the French resistance, the Nazis, etc.), and on which a good book is needed. Richard Schmitt of Brown or Charles Taylor of Toronto would be good people for such a book."[22] In July of 1968 he wrote to Donald Davidson to express support for Walter Kaufmann's plan to bring in Susan Sontag the following academic year to teach a course on philosophy and literature.[23] It was noted earlier that in 1969 Rorty supported giving an appointment to Herbert Marcuse; in 1971 he exchanged manuscripts with Jürgen Habermas;[24] and in an undated letter probably written in the early 1970s he recommended to the Guggenheim Foundation that a fellowship be given to Alexander Nehamas, whose proposed project on Nietzsche would "be not only an important contribution to our understanding of Nietzsche but an important book for 'building bridges' between Anglo-Saxon and Continental philosophy. Nehamas is one of the few philosophers of his generation who can read both kinds of philosophy with equal sympathy and understanding."[25] In a similar vein, he told Ian Hacking in 1976: "I confess I dither about Derrida myself. I think he's for real, and neither a fraud nor a fad.... What I like about him is that he assimilates the later Heidegger without being frightened or defeated by him, and talks back to him as an equal. This seems to me as difficult to do as it was to talk back to Nietzsche, and I admire Derrida for it."[26]

20. Fall 1966 syllabus for Philosophy 309, RRP.

21. "Ed" to Richard Rorty, April 17, 1966, RRP.

22. Richard Rorty to Alan Lesure, September 5, 1967, RRP.

23. Richard Rorty to Donald Davidson, July 25, 1968, RRP.

24. Richard Rorty to Jürgen Habermas, June 9, 1971, RRP.

25. Undated letter of recommendation to the Guggenheim Foundation, RRP.

26. Richard Rorty to Ian Hacking, November 29, 1976, RRP. In an interview with Josh Knobe, Rorty recalls that he began reading Derrida when he joined a Princeton reading group led by literature professor Jonathan Arac. See http://www.unc.edu/~knobe/rorty.html, accessed August 27, 2007.

That Rorty allowed himself to range widely did not mean he stopped producing analytic work, but unlike some other analysts he was by no means dismissive of other philosophical traditions. He held in especially high esteem philosophers who, as he himself increasingly did, wrote in an analytic style but sought to connect up, where possible, analytic philosophy and other approaches. It was on these grounds that he evaluated favorably the work of Arthur Danto, whom he recommended for an American Philosophical Society fellowship in 1973: "Professor Danto is one of America's most distinguished philosophers, and it is good news that he is planning a book on Sartre. He is one of the few philosophers in the country who has made important contributions to analytic philosophy while also writing very sympathetic and useful studies of topics which the so-called 'analytic' tradition has customarily neglected."[27]

What he objected to increasingly about some of his analytic colleagues at Princeton was that, in his view, they had no appreciation for nonanalytic philosophy and refused to acknowledge that work in other traditions or in the history of philosophy could have value on its own terms. In 1974 Rorty wrote to his dean, Aaron Lemonick, with whom he'd recently met, to say that he'd decided to turn down a job offer from Johns Hopkins. Rorty noted: "I was glad of the occasion to talk to you, and glad that the administration is aware of where my department is heading.... Gregory [Vlastos] and I have long since reached a tacit understanding that we share no common ground and won't be discussing the issue further, but every once in a while I feel the impulse to shatter my colleagues' complacency and then I make a polemical and counterproductive speech to a department meeting about our insufferable parochialism."[28] That this parochialism, in Rorty's view, centered on the tendency to dismiss nonanalytic work is evident from the fact that one of his great hopes for the department—also expressed in the letter to Lemonick—was that it would find its way toward appointing classicist Michael Frede. Princeton did end up making an offer to Frede, and Rorty made clear, in a letter to Michael and his wife Dorothea, also a philosopher, that his main gripe with the place concerned precisely its lack of a historical and pluralistic orientation. Of the Princeton philosophy department, he said in 1974:

> It is as good as any department in the country except perhaps Pittsburgh and Harvard.... I think the bad thing about the department is that it is very pleased with itself, very snobbish, very concerned to continue to be

27. Richard Rorty to the American Philosophical Society, April 23, 1973, RRP.
28. Richard Rorty to Aaron Lemonick, January 28, 1974, RRP.

the "mainstream," the avant-garde, and all that nonsense. This is to say that it has the vices of its virtues.... I find it a bit terrifying that we keep turning out PhDs who quite seriously conceive of philosophy as a discipline in which one does not read anything written before 1970, except for the purposes of passing odd examinations. I think that a genre of philosophy is coming into existence in which, to be sure, it will be unnecessary to read further back than four years or so. But I would like our students to know that there are also other genres of philosophy.[29]

What Rorty really wanted was to be in a more broad-minded department, and this was one of the main reasons he had declined the Hopkins offer. "What finally decided us," he wrote to another correspondent, "was that when we got things into perspective Hopkins didn't look that different from Princeton—it didn't seem a big enough change, in the way that going to the West Coast, going abroad, going to a department radically different in philosophical orientation, or going to a small college, would be."[30] As he told Mandelbaum that same year, "I ought to be very sure, before finally taking off from here, that I'm going somewhere where there are people whom I want to spend the rest of my life talking to. (Or, at least, people who can tolerate listening to my particular brand of philosophy—roughly, therapeutic positivism laced with historicism and *Schwarmerei*—and can see the point of what I want to do.) ... The Hopkins department is a much more agreeable place than the Princeton department, but it is part of the same circuit and on the same wavelengths."[31] The bad thing about turning down the offer was that "I would now have to spend at least another year sitting through endless meetings with my Princeton colleagues and listening to them explain how wonderful they were, how none of the candidates we were considering appointing were really good enough for us, etc."

How did Rorty reconcile his continuing penchant for work in an analytic style with his sense of the importance of intellectual history and pluralism? He did so precisely by conceiving of himself as a "therapeutic positivist"—as someone who recognized, as many of his analytic colleagues did not, that philosophical problems are bequeathed to us by culture and that, although linguistic analysis may be essential for helping us see through some of these problems, it does so not as a method that unlocks timeless truths but simply as a technique for disposing of cultural para-

29. Richard Rorty to Michael and Dorothea Frede, October 20, 1974, RRP.
30. Richard Rorty to "Peter," July 28, 1974, RRP.
31. Richard Rorty to Maurice Mandelbaum, January 28, 1974, RRP.

doxes. This point of view, which Rorty associated with the latter Wittgenstein, ultimately took a deflationary stance with regard to analytic philosophy: it was important, but its importance was only a reflection of the artificiality of most philosophical problems in the first place. As Rorty saw it, few of his Princeton colleagues shared this attitude. Because they did not, they were inclined to take themselves too seriously, to think that the philosophical school they represented was of greater world-historical importance than it actually was, and to eschew work done in other traditions and styles.

* 3 *

Superimposed on Rorty's philosophical differences with his colleagues at Princeton were differences of a more personal nature. In a remarkable 1977 essay on her life, Amélie Rorty described the situation faced by the wives of successful academicians and other professionals:

> The lives of the women who are in the entourage of academic and professional men—lawyers, doctors, and the like—carry extra hazards. For while the wife of a postman or a grocer can respect the social value and understand the personal satisfactions of her husband's work, she knows that she could do it too.... It is not like being married to a priest or being the nurse of a great surgeon; there is nothing sacred involved. But the women who surround scholars, scientists, and politicians are in the service of men who feel entitled to demand sacrifice from their women without embarrassment. They are not doing it in their own name, but in the name of something that is supposed to transcend them all.[32]

This, she noted earlier, was a description of her own experiences. "As a young man," she said of Richard, "my husband was a person of high and austere ideals, rather rigid, very reserved, a brilliant philosopher. He was dedicated to the greater glory of God through philosophy, and to developing his self-respect."[33] So, although she was trained as a philosopher as well, Amélie resigned herself to holding a series of positions, "always within commuting distance of my husband's jobs."[34] She got some writing done during this time, but not as much as she would

32. Rorty, "Dependency, Individuality, and Work," 46–47.
33. Ibid., 40.   34. Ibid.

have liked. "The wives of intellectuals and professional men are often as highly trained as their husbands," she observed, "often as intent on their work and scholarly projects. But what typically happens is that, at a time when both are just starting to work, the man gets a better job offer than the woman; the woman follows him and takes her chances on finding something within the vicinity. There is rarely anything to match his working conditions, his stimulation; she is lucky if she finds anything at all. The common pattern is for her to languish at home, trying to work on her book or finish her thesis, all the while blaming herself for making too little progress."[35] This results in the woman being unhappy and depressed and telling herself she is a failure. "Eventually her husband will accept her account of the situation and alienate himself, finding his real life in his work or his colleagues or the young graduate students, women who are still interesting and not yet embittered."[36] In her own case, "for one reason and another and mostly for no reason at all, I decided in 1971 to take a two-year research fellowship at King's College, Cambridge. Since my husband didn't hold with this idea, it meant a divorce. So I took a divorce too."[37]

It is impossible to know whether, as this account of the failure of their marriage suggests, Amélie and Richard would have been happy had she been able to find a position in as stimulating an intellectual environment as Princeton. Whatever the causes of the divorce, the effects on Richard's daily work life were clear: beyond having to spend time negotiating the details of the divorce settlement, he grew even farther apart from many of his colleagues, whom he perceived to have sided with Amélie.

Richard Rorty had in fact met someone—the philosopher Mary Varney, who was to become his second wife—and he reported finding great happiness with her.[38] In January of 1971 he wrote to his friend Milton Fisk: "Thanks very much for your good wishes on my good fortune. It really is, I do believe, as good as I suggested. I've just come back from three weeks with the lady I referred to, and I don't think I've ever had three better weeks. I spent them out in California, which was nice in itself, and we had some marvelous days watching whales and sea lions off Point Reyes, long-billed curlews in the Bolinas lagoon, and the like. Either we have all the

---

35. Ibid., 47.   36. Ibid., 48.   37. Ibid., 41.

38. And more than that: Rorty told me in an e-mail that he came to think of Varney as his "muse—as having given me the self-confidence necessary to write as I pleased without worrying about the reaction of my audience." E-mail to author, April 17, 2007.

same tastes, or we're doing a hell of a job pretending to each other that we do."[39] The contrast with his relationship to Amélie could not have been more stark. He continued to Fisk: "I doubt that anybody—even you, who had been able to observe us two philosophical entrepreneurs from our first crude beginnings in the Yale Grad. School—could imagine the domestic scenes between Amélie and me. Marriage is, thank God, like nothing else on earth as far as bringing out the hidden seams."[40]

Rorty soon found himself ensnared in a legal battle with Amélie over ownership of their house,[41] but he was so happy with Mary that he could endure the hardship. Such was his happiness that it even tempered, for a time, his displeasure with his Princeton colleagues. He noted to Fisk: "My own life is, mortgage foreclosures and all, however, very good at the moment, because (shortly after Amélie bugged out) I fell in love with a woman who, for some odd reason, doesn't seem put off by my pedantry, paunch, and graying hair. Omnia vincit amor, to my surprise—I never really grasped the point before. As long as this lasts, I have no complaints about anything much—even mortgages and my ghastly department (which I nonetheless fret about a lot, by sheer force of habit)."[42]

But this would soon change. It's not that his relationship with Varney soured. Rather, as Rorty tells the story, Amélie was a popular figure with his colleagues, and he felt that they had remained friendly toward her, continuing to include her in their social circles, when loyalty to him would have demanded they keep their distance. This was not a problem so long as she was in Britain, but in 1974, after she returned, a major blow-up occurred. In May of that year Richard wrote an indignant letter to Paul Benacerraf: "As you know, I arrived at the department's dinner for [Hilary] Putnam to find myself [and Mary] staring at my ex-wife. Yesterday I asked George [Pitcher] and Gregory [Vlastos] what had happened, and they explained that you had invited her as one of the distinguished philosophers who were guests of the department. George promptly and decently of-

39. Richard Rorty to Milton Fisk, January 7, 1971, RRP.

40. Amélie Rorty, reading this letter thirty-five years later, recalls that emotional repression rather than domestic squabbles characterized their marriage. I found no archival evidence to suggest that fights of the kind Richard Rorty hints at here were commonplace.

41. See, for example, the letter from Richard Rorty to his divorce lawyer, September 12, 1971, RRP.

42. Richard Rorty to Milton Fisk, October 26, 1971, RRP.

fered apologies and regrets, but you will be glad to hear that Gregory thought that my wife's hurt and embarrassment were baseless."[43]

Rorty charged that anyone familiar with social conventions would have known better than to invite a man, his new wife, and his ex-wife to the same dinner party. Since he assumed Benacerraf was not ignorant of such conventions, he must have intended to cause upset. A few weeks later, Vlastos wrote to defend Benacerraf:

> Speaking for our own time (not for the Edwardian or even the pre-World War II era), I deny categorically that there is any convention which rules that A and B, once divorced from each other, can no longer be friends. On the contrary, this happens all the time, and no convention is broken when A or B, accompanied by their present spouse, go to a party given by a mutual friend or to each others' party. *A fortiori* no convention is broken if A and B are both invited to a departmental dinner for a visiting speaker. On what terms A and B will remain when divorcing is nobody else's business but theirs. They, and they alone, have the right to decide whether they are going to be friends or not. If they take the latter option, their acquaintances will naturally respect it. Thus C will not ask A and B together to his own home. That interdict does not apply to a departmental affair such as the one for Hilary. It would be highly improper if D, satisfying qualifications for invitation, were excluded merely because D does not happen to be on speaking terms with E, a member of the department, or with E's wife: the exclusion would be unfair to D and unfair to the department.[44]

Nothing more of the incident is recorded in Rorty's correspondence, but it certainly did nothing to endear his colleagues to him. Rorty has noted in an interview: "My recollection is that for the first ten years at Princeton, I was seen as one of the boys. But for the second ten years, I was seen as increasingly contrarian or difficult.... I got divorced and remarried, and because my first wife was a philosopher and a friend of my colleagues, there were problems. It was not a friendly divorce and I didn't handle it very well."[45] By the time *Philosophy and the Mirror of Nature* was published, Rorty recalls, "I was pretty much sick of my colleagues and they of me, so we didn't talk much."[46]

43. Richard Rorty to Paul Benacerraf, May 24, 1974, RRP.

44. Gregory Vlastos to Richard Rorty, June 15, 1974, RRP.

45. Richard Rorty, quoted in James Ryerson, 2000–2001, "The Quest for Uncertainty: Richard Rorty's Pragmatic Pilgrimage," *Lingua Franca* 10:42–51, 47.

46. Richard Rorty, interview with author, December 22, 1998.

* 4 *

As Rorty went about developing a historicist, therapeutic alternative to the analytic philosophy he saw being practiced by his Princeton colleagues and others, no one's work was more important to him than that of Thomas Kuhn. In a 1997 essay on Kuhn, Rorty recalled that "Carnap and others had persuaded me, in my early twenties, that philosophers should indeed try to become more 'scientific' and 'rigorous.' I was even briefly persuaded that learning symbolic logic was probably a good way of achieving this end."[47] Reading Kuhn, however, gave him a different view of things. In light of Kuhn, "I began to think of analytic philosophy as one way of doing philosophy among others, rather than as the discovery of how to set philosophy on the secure path of a science."[48] Kuhn's "sociological view," Rorty asserted, "has made people in many disciplines more relaxed about the question of whether they have a rigorous research method," and any analytic philosopher willing to take Kuhn seriously will show "an increased willingness to historicize: to grant that there is no point in dividing the history of philosophy into sense and nonsense, and to admit that even Hegel and Heidegger might have done useful philosophical work."[49]

In 1964 Kuhn left a professorship in the history of science at Berkeley to take a position at Princeton.[50] Two years earlier, *The Structure of Scientific Revolutions* had been published by the University of Chicago Press. Kuhn argued that conventional histories of science are flawed: they depict scientific accumulation as linear in nature, as one discovery or finding is layered on top of another; they fail to appreciate the degree to which a scientist's immersion in a theoretical or conceptual framework may color her or his interpretation of the data; and they do not attend to the intrinsically social nature of science, in particular the fact that scientists representing a school or approach may band together in support of one another's research. Instead, Kuhn famously proposed that the history of science is a history of alternation between different modes of knowledge production, designated normal and revolutionary science. In normal science, scientists engage in empirical research informed by an established framework or paradigm. As this research proceeds, however, anomalous

47. Rorty, *Philosophy and Social Hope*, 177–78.

48. Ibid., 178.   49. Ibid., 181–82.

50. See Lawrence Van Gelder, 1996, "Thomas Kuhn, 73; Devised Science Paradigm," *New York Times* June 19, B7.

findings—those at odds with what the established framework would predict—may accumulate. Scientists committed to the old paradigm may
not recognize these as true anomalies. But other scientists will, and some
will propose abandoning the established paradigm and converting to an
altogether different one. This represents a period of revolutionary science, as champions of the new approach battle it out against conservative
defenders of the old scientific order. Eventually the new framework may
become paradigmatic.

Kuhn's examples were drawn mostly from the history of the natural
sciences, but Rorty was quick to see the applicability of the theory to the
history of philosophy. Kuhn's ideas made no appearance in the introduction to *The Linguistic Turn* or in the bibliography of writings on philosophical method Rorty prepared for the book with Jerome Neu. But by
the late 1960s, Kuhnian ideas began to figure in Rorty's work. In October 1968, for example, Rorty submitted a fellowship application to the
American Council of Learned Societies. He proposed to take a semester
off from teaching to work on a study in the history of philosophy. The
project was not to be exclusively historical but was undertaken with the
aim of answering a more general question: "Is there any interesting way
of demarcating philosophy from other disciplines?"[51] Against the notion that philosophy's distinctiveness involves historical continuity with
regard to subject matter or method, Rorty proposed that philosophy is
built around a series of problems. He acknowledged that "one obvious
snag in any such suggestion is that Greek philosophy doesn't seem to deal
with the same problems as 17th-century philosophy, nor 17th-century
philosophy with quite the same problems as 20th-century philosophy."
Rather than attempt to impose an artificial homogeneity that would wash
away these differences or take the positivist stance of "treat[ing] all philosophy before a certain date as largely a confusion of philosophy with
other things," Rorty embraced the idea that philosophers in different eras
tend to work on different problem sets. If these problem sets could be
reconstructed, it might be possible to "relate" them "in an order of dependence" and regard this dependence as constituting philosophy's historical unity. He proposed research on seventeenth- and eighteenth-century
philosophy that would identify the key problems of the time and noted
that a recent paper of his had argued that "surmounting epistemological
scepticism became the paradigm of what it was to do philosophy in the

51. Richard Rorty, October 1968, ACLS Fellowship application, RRP.

17th and 18th centuries"—an unacknowledged reference to Kuhn and a first suggestion that he regarded the conceptual language of paradigmicity as applicable to philosophy.

In the paper to which he was referring, "Cartesian Epistemology and Changes in Ontology," published in 1970 in a volume edited by John Smith, Rorty invoked Kuhn explicitly. How should we make sense of the fact that what classical philosophers such as Plato, Spinoza, Kant, and even Whitehead said about ontology no longer seems satisfactory? We should not dismiss their views as mere error, Rorty insisted. Rather, we should understand them in light of the fact that "the ways of answering the ontological question, 'What is really real?' are very different at different epochs."[52] In the seventeenth century, ontology was usually justified by the "fact that neither science nor common sense could offer an adequate reply to the epistemological sceptic."[53] The skeptics of the time argued that knowledge rests ultimately on a base of sensation, that sensation cannot be trusted, and that we cannot therefore be certain about any of our knowledge. Cartesian philosophers responded by constructing ontological systems "deduced from sheer reflection on the nature of knowledge,"[54] and their goal was to shore up the possibility of indubitable knowledge. In our day, however, "the post-Cartesian tradition (exemplified by Wittgenstein, Austin, Sellars, Dewey, and Quine) rallies around the principle that empirical knowledge needs no foundation ... and consequently does not imagine that an exploration of how we know could lead us to conclusions which would clash with either science or common sense."[55] This bespeaks a fundamental shift in the paradigm of ontology, Rorty claimed, noting that, "As may be obvious, I am here drawing upon a terminology and outlook put forward by T. S. Kuhn."[56] Applicable though Kuhn's conceptual vocabulary was, Rorty suggested that paradigms in philosophy are different from those in science. "Scientific epochs are defined by the *solutions* they take as paradigmatic," he argued, "whereas philosophical epochs are defined by the *problems* they take as paradigmatic."[57]

"Cartesian Epistemology and Changes in Ontology," with its Kuhnian undercurrents, helped lay the groundwork for *Philosophy and the Mirror of Nature*, published nearly a decade later. Most of the writing for the book had been completed by 1974, after Rorty received a fellowship in 1973

52. Richard Rorty, 1970, "Cartesian Epistemology and Changes in Ontology," pp. 273–92 in *Contemporary American Philosophy*, John Smith, ed., New York: Humanities Press, 274.

53. Ibid., 275.   55. Ibid.   57. Ibid..
54. Ibid., 283.   56. Ibid., 275.

from the Guggenheim Foundation to support another leave. In a letter to the president of the Foundation, Rorty described the central thesis of his manuscript:

> The book attempts to present "modern day philosophy" (i.e., epistemology and metaphysics since Descartes) as a working-out of the consequences of Descartes' picture of human knowledge as an ordering of inner representations. I argue that the image of the Mind as a Mirror of Nature brought in its train the notion of the Mind as a metaphysically distinct realm of being, and thus the notion of philosophy as a discipline which centers around the questions "How can the subject get to the object (through the veil of ideas)?" and "How can man be both a Mind—an hardly understood Glassy Essence—and something material?" In other words, I argue that the notion of philosophy as constituted by epistemology and metaphysics is a relatively recent and parochial one—that without problems about the veil of ideas and the relation between mind and body which were barely formulated (and could hardly have been intelligible before Descartes) we have [no] notion of "epistemology" or "metaphysics."[58]

Philosophy and the Mirror of Nature is often described as a key text in Rorty's turn toward pragmatism, and so it was, but it is worth noting that Kuhn is cited in the book as often as Dewey. Kuhnian ideas entered in three ways. First, Rorty continued to subscribe to the belief, evident in earlier writings, that historical periods differ with regard to dominant philosophical paradigms. He used this claim to suggest that select strands of twentieth-century philosophy together marked a qualitative break with what had come before. What made "Wittgenstein, Heidegger, and Dewey" so different from earlier philosophers was that they "brought us into a period of 'revolutionary' philosophy (in the sense of Kuhn's 'revolutionary' science) by introducing maps of the terrain (viz., of the whole panorama of human activities) which simply do not include those features which previously seemed to dominate."[59] Different though their perspectives were, all three philosophers converged around the themes of historicism and antifoundationalism, and this represented a paradigm shift from the Cartesian-Kantian era. Beyond advancing the thesis of this convergence—and arguing for its importance—another aim of the book was to "trace some of the crucial stages in the transition from the campaigns of Descartes and Hobbes against 'the philosophy of the schools'

---

58. Richard Rorty to Gordon Ray, September 16, 1974, RRP.
59. Rorty, *Philosophy and the Mirror of Nature*, 6–7.

to the nineteenth century's reestablishment of philosophy as an autonomous, self-contained, 'scholastic' discipline."[60] This Rorty did by describing a series of breaks and shifts in philosophy's "frame of reference,"[61] each championed by philosophical revolutionaries who challenged the dominant paradigms of their day.

This use of Kuhn was consistent with Rorty's earliest invocations of him, but a second use was of more recent vintage. In an address to the American Philosophical Association (APA) in 1972, Rorty cited Kuhn, along with Quine, Feyerabend, and Sellars, as thinkers who had argued for the thesis of underdetermination: the notion that reality can be parsed and interpreted by science in multiple ways; that reality may therefore be underdeterminative with respect to choice between competing conceptual and theoretical frameworks; and that insofar as this is true no strict separation can be effected between theory and observation. Kuhn was mobilized to this effect in *Philosophy and the Mirror of Nature* as well. Like "such writers as Polanyi ... and Hanson," Kuhn "want[s] to drop the notion of observation altogether."[62] "The horror which greeted Quine's overthrow of the dogmas [of empiricism]," Rorty elsewhere noted, "and Kuhn's and Feyerabend's examples of the 'theory-ladenness' of observation, was a result of the fear that there might be no" sure way to "use contact with the real as the touchstone of truth."[63] Key here was the notion, upon which Kuhn had insisted, that paradigms are incommensurable. Again like Feyerabend, Kuhn had been "concerned to show that the meanings of lots of statements in the language, including lots of 'observation' statements, got changed when a new theory came along; or, at least, that granting that such change took place made more sense of the facts of the history of science than the standard textbook view which kept meanings constant and let only beliefs change."[64] Rorty claimed that Kuhn was essentially correct in this regard and that this undercut the Kantian foundationalist program.

Yet Rorty insisted that Kuhn had not seen clearly the implications of the point. Kuhn "questioned whether philosophy of science could construct an algorithm for choice among scientific theories."[65] But in making this claim, Kuhn often glossed incommensurability among paradigms as meaning that "proponents of different theories" "live in different worlds."[66] This assertion, with its idealistic assumptions, had gotten him into trouble with philosophers. What he should have said was "simply"

---

60. Ibid., 136.   62. Ibid., 225.   64. Ibid., 270.   66. Ibid., 324.
61. Ibid., 147.   63. Ibid., 269.   65. Ibid., 322.

that "no algorithm for theory choice is available."[67] To the extent this is so, the difference between epistemology and hermeneutics takes on new meaning. Epistemology, as Rorty understood it, is defined by the idea that "to be rational, to be fully human ... we need to be able to find agreement with other human beings."[68] Over the centuries, epistemology had looked for this common ground in notions as diverse as Being, the Forms, intuition, and language. Hermeneutics, by contrast, "sees the relation between various discourses as those of strands in a possible conversation, a conversation which presupposes no disciplinary matrix which unites the speakers, but where the hope of agreement is never lost so long as the conversation lasts."[69] Rorty read Kuhn as having argued that within the context of normal science, something like epistemology tends to prevail, whereas in the context of revolutionary science the only available procedures for choosing among competing paradigms are hermeneutic—they involve appeals not to neutral translation languages but to the same sorts of strategies and tactics of persuasion and understanding across difference as can be found in everyday conversation, save for a greater orientation to the values of science. Because revolutionary science is essential to scientific growth and progress, science can never be reduced to epistemology, and scientific knowledge rests ultimately on a base of conversation. Because Kuhn had offered arguments to this effect, profaning the "ideals of the Enlightenment," his work had been "greeted" with "fierce indignation," especially by "professional philosophers" sensitive to the issues involved and overinvested in the mirror of nature metaphor.[70]

This reading of Kuhn set up the third and final invocation of the book. Although philosophy, like science, tends to alternate between normal and revolutionary periods, not all philosophical revolutionaries intend that the programs they lay out should be institutionalized and treated as paradigms for further inquiry. "Constructive philosophers" such as Husserl, Russell, Descartes, and Kant are comfortable with this institutionalization. They "offer arguments,"[71] build philosophical systems designed to withstand the test of time, and measure their success by the certainty of the knowledge they generate. "Edifying philosophers," by contrast, "dread the thought that their vocabulary should ever be institutionalized."[72] They see it as their goal to shake up discourse in new and interesting ways, not to get us closer to knowledge of a world that is independent of our conversations about it—an ideal which they see as illusory—but

67. Ibid., 325.   69. Ibid., 318.   71. Ibid., 369.
68. Ibid., 316.   70. Ibid., 333.   72. Ibid.

with the aim of helping us avoid the danger that "some way in which people might come to think of themselves"[73] may become entrenched. Were this danger to materialize, "the resulting freezing-over of culture would be, in the eyes of edifying philosophers, the dehumanization of human beings."[74] Kuhn's distinction between normal and revolutionary science thus provided Rorty with a way to conceive of the difference between, on the one hand, philosophers like those mentioned above—and, implicitly, most contemporary analytic philosophers—and, on the other hand, those like Dewey, Heidegger, and Wittgenstein, whom Rorty much preferred and whose intentions were, on his account, largely deconstructive.

These references to Kuhn indicate clearly Kuhn's importance to Rorty and suggest something about the role of books like *The Structure of Scientific Revolutions* and later *The Essential Tension* (1977) in leading Rorty down the road to becoming a champion of antifoundationalism and pragmatism and a critic of mainstream analytic philosophy. More evidence of Kuhn's importance can be found in the fact that in the winter of 1976 Rorty led a workshop at Princeton, sponsored by the National Endowment for the Humanities (NEH), for eleven philosophy professors from around the country. The official title of the event was "Empiricism, Pragmatism, Historicism," but as Rorty explained to Hilary Putnam, inviting him to be a guest speaker, the real subject was "the impact of Kuhnian views of science on epistemology and philosophy generally."[75] Rorty's notes record that at their first meeting, he told attendees: "The most interesting thing in recent philosophy has been the breakup of positivism and the rise of historicism, with 'pragmatism' being roughly a name for the kind of attitude characteristic of Dewey. Phil. of science having been the name for epist., Kuhn seems to have shown that whatever philosophy of science may be, it is not positivism."[76] He went on to suggest there were

four ways to go from Kuhn: (1) Backward to the sources of Kuhn's insights in Quine and Wittgenstein, and in pragmatists and idealists before them; (2) Forward to people who want to out-Kuhn Kuhn, like Feyerabend and Will and MacIntyre and Toulmin, or expand him (as in Barnes on rationality and anthropology); (3) Forward to people who want to criticize Kuhn, and perhaps also Quine and Witt., like Putnam, Kripke, Dummett, etc. (4) Sideways to people who think that pragm. and pos. were simply naïve because they never grasped the point of Hegel—Heidegger on the roots of

73. Ibid., 377.   74. Ibid.
75. Richard Rorty to Hilary Putnam, October 26, 1976, RRP.
76. Richard Rorty, notes on NEH seminar, 1976, RRP.

the 17th-century, Habermas on the hermeneutic interpretation of culture, Foucault on the pre-classic way of reading nature as one read[s] a text.

The seminar would explore each of these pathways.

＊ **5** ＊

Why had Kuhn become so important to Rorty? Although Rorty had done a great deal of work to immerse himself in the analytic tradition, his broad training in the history of philosophy and the historicist and pluralist identities he'd absorbed during his years at Chicago and Yale made him different from other leading analytic philosophers. He had fared well as an analyst but increasingly realized that he was an odd man out in the analytic community. He therefore sought a set of arguments that would justify his move beyond analytic paradigmicity. Kuhn's theory of scientific revolutions, applied to the history of philosophy, provided such a justification. In Kuhn's account dominant paradigms always seem to their practitioners—just as analytic philosophy had initially seemed to Rorty—as the end of intellectual history, the final framework anyone will ever need to study a particular topic. Just as inevitably, Kuhn suggested, those paradigms will be transcended, and the objects of their study fundamentally rethought. This view gave Rorty much-needed perspective on recent developments in U.S. philosophy, leading him to conclude that problems he and others had identified with the analytic program represented nothing less than anomalies foretelling analytic philosophy's imminent demise. Kuhn also led Rorty to think about the ways in which analytic dominance of the field might reflect contingent social and historical circumstances more than intrinsic intellectual virtue and to believe that different intellectual traditions, glossed as competing paradigms, really do have a hard time understanding one another, much as McKeon had also taught. Like the later Wittgenstein, but in a more straightforward way, Kuhn thus provided Rorty with the symbolic resources he needed to argue his way out of mainstream analytic philosophy and into a broader conception of the philosophical enterprise.

The fact that Kuhn was Rorty's colleague at Princeton was another important factor in leading Rorty to make extensive use of *The Structure of Scientific Revolutions*, but this was not because he and Kuhn were especially close. Like many scholars at elite research universities, they were both so busy that they rarely saw one another. Writing to Maurice Mandelbaum in 1974 about his decision to turn down an offer from Johns Hopkins and remain at Princeton a few years longer, Rorty noted that though Hopkins seemed an attractive place, it was not because, as Mandelbaum had told him, there would be lots of interesting people around for him to talk to outside of the philosophy department. Rorty's experience was that he rarely saw anyone outside his department, and he doubted it would be any different at Hopkins. "For example," he noted, "I have a lot in common with Tom Kuhn"—who had a joint appointment in philosophy and the history of science—"and we reinforce each other philosophically a good deal, but I find I only see him about three times a year—for no reason except elective affinities or the lack of them, or possibly just because neither of us ever feels he has a moment free."[77]

Nor was Rorty drawn to Kuhn because Kuhn was well regarded by others in the Princeton department. In fact, as Rorty noted in the closing chapters of *Philosophy and the Mirror of Nature*, Kuhn was criticized heavily by some analytic philosophers who wished to defend more traditional conceptions of epistemology, and this included prominent figures in the Princeton department such as Carl Hempel, with whom Kuhn cotaught a course. While acknowledging that the "historic-pragmatic school" of which he saw Kuhn and Feyerabend to be a part has "opened up highly illuminating and promising new perspectives,"[78] Hempel had doubts about Kuhn's attempt to offer an "account of science" that is at once "empirical and normative."[79] Hempel did not reject Kuhn's project on a priori grounds but thought that the theoretical apparatus Kuhn used to explain theory choice was insufficiently developed to "yield prescriptions for scientific inquiry."[80] Moreover, Hempel accused Kuhn of imprecision, calling it "somewhat disturbing" that Kuhn and others like him had "made diverse pronouncements concerning the rationality or irrationality of science ... without ... giving a reasonably explicit characterization of the concept of rationality which they have in mind."[81] There is some question whether these and other considerations led Hempel and others in the Princeton department to take a negative view of Kuhn's contributions to philosophy, but Rorty believed his colleagues did look down on Kuhn. In his 1997 essay on Kuhn, he recalled "resentment over the fact that Kuhn was constantly being treated, by my fellow professors of philosophy, as at best a second-rate citizen of the philosophical community.

---

77. Richard Rorty to Maurice Mandelbaum, January 28, 1974, RRP.

78. Carl Hempel, 1979, "Scientific Rationality: Analytic vs. Pragmatic Perspectives," pp. 46–58 in *Rationality To-day*, Theodore Geraets, ed., Ottawa: University of Ottawa Press, 58.

79. Ibid., 48.   80. Ibid., 57.   81. Ibid., 50.

Sometimes he was even treated as an intruder who had no business attempting to contribute to a discipline in which he was untrained."[82]

But there was an important center in the Princeton intellectual community where Kuhn's ideas, and a historicist orientation toward intellectual history and science more generally, were taken seriously: the Institute for Advanced Study (IAS), founded in 1930. Rorty was never a member of the Institute or on its faculty. But he was an interested party in developments taking place there in the mid-1970s that put historicism front and center. These developments were tied to the institution-building agenda of economist Carl Kaysen, who had taken over the directorship of the IAS from Robert Oppenheimer. In the late 1960s, Kaysen formulated a plan to develop a School of Social Science at the Institute where scholars would bring sophisticated theoretical and methodological tools to bear on problems to do with social evolution and change.[83] He found inspirational in this regard the work of sociologist Edward Shils and passed along to Orville Brim, Jr., president of the Russell Sage Foundation—and to the head of the Carnegie Corporation, from whom he also sought funding—a piece Shils had published in the *Times Literary Supplement* in 1966 titled "Seeing It Whole," which called for more comparative-historical social science. Kaysen invited Shils, along with Erik Erikson and Seymour Martin Lipset, to become members of the new school,[84] which both Russell Sage and Carnegie—along with Ford and Sloan—ended up generously funding. It was Clifford Geertz, however, who landed the first permanent appointment, helping to lay the groundwork for the kind of "interpretive social science" for which it would become known.[85]

Other key IAS appointments from the standpoint of the Rorty story involved visitors rather than permanent faculty. As early as 1963, Kuhn had written to inquire about the possibility of an IAS affiliation were he to move from Berkeley to Princeton.[86] The affiliation was not secured until a decade later, at which point Kuhn reduced his teaching commitment at Princeton to halftime, spending the other half year writing on

82. Rorty, *Philosophy and Social Hope*, 175.

83. Carl Kaysen to Orville Brim, Jr., January 17, 1967, Director's Office, School Files, School of Social Science, IAS.

84. Kaysen to Edward Shils, August 6, 1966, Director's Office, School Files, School of Social Science, IAS.

85. See Joan Scott and Debra Keates, eds., 2001, *Schools of Thought: 25 Years of Interpretive Social Science*, Princeton: Princeton University Press.

86. Thomas Kuhn to Robert Oppenheimer, September 13, 1963, Thomas Kuhn Files, IAS.

IAS grounds. In 1975, Geertz, Kuhn, and Kaysen decided that the theme of the social science program for the following academic year should be the sociology of science. This was a topic of obvious interest to Kuhn, but it interested Geertz as well. As a result of this programmatic decision, visitors in the 1976–77 school year included sociologists of science Barry Barnes, Joseph Ben-David, Diana Crane, and Nicholas Mullins. A weekly seminar was held to discuss work in progress, and the first paper discussed was Kuhn's "Mathematical vs. Experimental Traditions in the Development of Physical Science," published in the *Journal of Interdisciplinary History* in 1976. Other seminar meetings that year considered the work of Mullins and Belver Griffith on "The Social Analysis of Cocitation Groups," Robert Kohler's work on "Medical Reform and the Establishment of Biochemistry as a Discipline, 1895–1940," Jerome Ravetz on "Laissez-Faire and Gene Splicing," and Crane on "Assessments of Theoretical Innovations in Science."

Rorty was one of several Princeton faculty members on the recipient list for notices about the seminar. Several years earlier he had become friendly with Geertz, lunching with him occasionally and sending him in 1974 a description of *Philosophy and the Mirror of Nature* that emphasized precisely his historicism and increasing doubts about the value of philosophy as currently practiced:

> Herewith a hundred words on what I'm working on: I am trying to finish a book whose themes are the Image of Knowledge as Mirror of Nature (i.e., as set of representations which may or may not be accurate), the Image of the Ghost in the Machine (Ryle's phrase for Descartes' "immaterial substance"), and the Image of Philosophy (as a discipline distinct from the arts and the sciences, devoted to struggling with the questions of the accuracy of our inner representations and the relations between the Ghost and the Machine). The moral is supposed to be that "philosophy" as a distinct discipline did not exist in antiquity or the middle ages, that it became a distinct discipline because of the rise of the other two Images in the seventeenth century, and that it would be no tragedy if it ceased to be an autonomous discipline in the future, being replaced by various forms of historical and sociological investigation on one hand, and of myth-making on the other.[87]

He read Geertz's work, in turn, and recommended several of the essays in *The Interpretation of Cultures* to his student Robert Brandom

---

87. Richard Rorty to Clifford Geertz, October 4, 1974, RRP.

in 1976, along with Ravetz's *Scientific Knowledge and Its Social Problems* (1971), which, he said, was "filled with interesting gossip about how the scientific disciplines actually do things."[88] Geertz, for his part, invited Rorty to take part in the IAS seminar: "We are going to have a seminar of some sort, I am sure, on history, sociology, and philosophy of science (we never think little around here!) because that is the concentration we have this year," Geertz wrote to Rorty in 1976. "Both Albert [Hirschman] and I would certainly be extremely pleased if you would be able to attend it. I hope in addition to the people here in that field, Arnold Thackray may be able to join us, and of course Tom Kuhn will be deeply involved."[89] That same year Rorty asked Barry Barnes to speak to his NEH seminar on Kuhn, convincing Barnes to do so despite the fact that Barnes imagined that most philosophers would react badly to his efforts to highlight the social dimensions of scientific knowledge production.[90] Rorty was quite interested in participating in the IAS seminar, as he told Kuhn that same year in response to an independent invitation from him, and the reason was that he was coming to think about the history of thought in historicist and quasi-sociological terms himself: "Thanks very much for the invitation to the potential sociology of science seminar. I should like very much to come.... I don't know that I have anything to contribute to the substance of the seminar, outside of the usual kibbitzing. But at some point I should like to see if they would be interested in some notes on the effects of professionalization on philosophy, particularly in the time of Kant and in the early twentieth century in America."[91]

Another participant in these IAS discussions about the sociology of science was Quentin Skinner. Skinner visited the IAS in 1974–75 and again from 1976–79. Skinner's landmark essay "Meaning and Understanding in the History of Ideas" asserted that the only way to pin down authorial intentionality is to reconstruct the sociointellectual context in which a text was written. His historiographic contributions were of great interest to those at the Institute, as Kaysen made clear in a memo announcing Skinner's arrival: "Skinner's interests lie in the relation between political theory and politics. He is interested in these questions both from the point of view of how one studies intellectual history in general, and con-

---

88. Richard Rorty to Robert Brandom, August 23, 1976, RRP.

89. Clifford Geertz to Richard Rorty, August 31, 1976, RRP.

90. Barry Barnes to Richard Rorty, October 20, 1976, RRP.

91. Richard Rorty to Thomas Kuhn, October 11, 1976, RRP.

cretely studying the history of political ideas in early modern Europe.... In both his methodological and historical interests, Skinner is concerned with understanding the relationship between social and political theory and social and political actions."[92]

Rorty became friends with Skinner, who was also on the recipient list for the sociology of science seminar. He shared with him not only a commitment to historicism and contextualism but also an interest in work that attempted to bridge multiple intellectual traditions. In a letter written from England, Skinner described to Rorty "the intensity of the animus" that his colleagues on the Cambridge University philosophy faculty "display against continental philosophy"[93]—something Rorty could certainly relate to, given his experiences at Princeton. "I think they've a genuine feeling," Skinner explained, "that they are dealing with a tradition which doesn't value clarity and rigour in quite the way we've been brought up, and as a result tries to get away with vatic pronouncements which, it's suspected, may often be nothing but dressed up truisms." Skinner called this "a sorry state of affairs," given that "the same issues really are being addressed" in Continental and analytic thought, and went on to comment on the virtues and problems of Habermas, Gadamer, Putnam, and Davidson.

Rorty appreciated Skinner's range and commitment to historicism, so much so that, in the years to come, he would coedit with him and J. B. Schneewind an important series with Cambridge University Press called Ideas in Context. The first volume in that series, *Philosophy in History: Essays on the Historiography of Philosophy*, was based on a series of lectures given at Johns Hopkins in 1982–83. In Rorty's contribution, he expressed his sympathies for the historiographic projects of both Skinner and Foucault, though he did not think that intellectual history should consist only of Skinnerian or Foucauldian narratives. In contrast to Skinner, Rorty argued there was no one right answer to the question of which context for an historical work should be privileged, for this "depends upon what we want to get out of thinking about the assertion."[94] And against Foucault, he denied that the lesson to be learned from nominalism and historicism is that there is no need for narratives

92. Kaysen to faculty, November 10, 1975, Quentin Skinner files, IAS.

93. Quentin Skinner to Richard Rorty, October 30 (no year), RRP.

94. Richard Rorty, 1984, "The Historiography of Philosophy: Four Genres," pp. 49–76 in *Philosophy in History: Essays on the Historiography of Philosophy*, Richard Rorty, J. B. Schneewind, and Quentin Skinner, eds., New York: Cambridge University Press, 55.

that tie together the thinkers enshrined in some disciplinary canon. "I am all for getting rid of canons which have become merely quaint," Rorty insisted, "but I do not think we can get along without canons," for it might be crucial to the continuation of a valuable form of intellectual discourse that thinkers still believe that "the intellectuals of the previous epochs of European history form a community."[95] Nevertheless, he applauded the efforts of Skinner and Foucault to undermine the approach to intellectual history Rorty termed "doxography," which assumes that philosophy is "the name of a discipline which, in all ages and places, has managed to dig down to the same deep, fundamental, questions"[96] and which aims to show what those questions are and how various thinkers have responded to them.

Skinner, for his part, has written that he was much influenced by his time at the IAS and that the climate of the day was so heavily antifoundationalist that it led him to be even more skeptical of Marxian conceptions of ideology than he was previously:

> My other main reason for being a non-Marxist is related to the positivism of Marxism, a weakness I became increasingly aware of in the seventies. During those years I was working at the Institute for Advanced Study in Princeton, and so had the amazing good fortune to be a colleague of Clifford Geertz and Thomas Kuhn. (I had the office next to Kuhn's.) They helped me to see the importance of the fact that Marx still inhabited an unduly simple world in which he felt able to speak of true consciousness and false consciousness. But in a more postmodern culture—of the kind I found myself exposed to at Princeton—in which consciousness is seen more in the nature of a construction, Marxism begins to look like a very crude way of looking at the social world. The more interesting questions seem to be about how to negotiate different constructions, since all of them might have something to be said for them.[97]

How did developments at the IAS affect Rorty's thought? There is no way to be sure, but I would venture the hypothesis that faculty and members of the IAS served as an alternative intellectual reference group for Rorty, providing him with intellectual and social support for his growing embrace of historicism and doubts about the analytic paradigm. Rorty didn't become a

---

95. Ibid., 73.   96. Ibid., 63.

97. Quentin Skinner, 2002, "Quentin Skinner," pp. 212–40 in *The New History: Confessions and Conversations*, Maria Lúcia G. Pallares-Burke, ed., Cambridge: Polity, 221.

historicist simply because he saw other prominent figures of the day insisting that the history of thought and science should be treated as a history of concrete social institutions and practices. It's true that such figures existed—not just Kuhn and Skinner and Geertz but also Feyerabend, Foucault, Habermas, Marcuse, and sociologists of science—and that Rorty read their work with interest. But he had been a historicist ever since his days at Chicago and Yale, and though it would not be until the 1970s that he saw the implication of historicism to be a calling into question of analytic paradigmicity, his earliest analytic papers, indebted to the later Wittgenstein, were more consistent with his later metaphilosophical assumptions than divergent from them. Contact with Skinner, Geertz, Kuhn, and others at the IAS did not convert him to historicism, then, but may have bolstered his confidence that the philosophical arguments he was developing on the basis of his preexisting beliefs had merit. Here were eminent and learned men who agreed with him—to the extent they considered the fate of his discipline—that philosophy's history and indeed historicity should not be ignored. While scholars like Kuhn would soon distance themselves from claims made by Rorty on their behalf, Rorty's involvement in IAS circles in the mid-1970s probably helped steel him against some of the criticisms that would be made by analytic philosophers of *Philosophy and the Mirror of Nature* and the essays in *Consequences of Pragmatism*.[98]

* 6 *

As described below, *Philosophy and the Mirror of Nature* was a successful and controversial book almost as soon as it was published. In 1979, however, the year of its release, the main controversy to occupy Rorty's attention involved not the book but the APA. The year before, Rorty had been elected president of the prestigious Eastern Division of the Association,

98. An additional factor that may be worth mentioning in this regard is Rorty's psychoanalysis. Amélie Rorty has suggested to me that Richard's psychoanalysis in the years preceding the publication of *Philosophy and the Mirror of Nature* may have given him the confidence necessary to write a book in which he would cast himself as a disciplinary provocateur. This seems plausible, but Richard denied it. As noted previously, he attributed his self-confidence instead to his happy second marriage. As for the nature of his therapy, he reported in an e-mail that "I was in treatment with Dr. Ellen Simon for obsessional neurosis from the time my father went psychotic in late 1962 until 1968 or so, with some follow-up visits in the late sixties and early seventies. Full-fledged analysis began sometime in 1963 and ended about five years later" (Richard Rorty, e-mail to author, February 11, 2007). Freud would begin to factor prominently in Rorty's work in the years following

a testament to his standing in the profession. No sooner did he take the helm than he found himself embroiled in a major challenge to the APA's leadership: the so-called pluralist revolt.

The pluralist revolt centered around the demand of nonanalytic philosophers that analysts relinquish their control of the APA and allow philosophers associated with other intellectual orientations and traditions the chance to serve in leadership capacities and present papers at the organization's annual meetings. These demands were not without justification. Throughout the 1960s and 1970s, graduate departments where analysts predominated ranked highest on reputational surveys, journals devoted to analytic work were the most well regarded, and nonanalysts felt looked down upon by their analytic colleagues. Analysts parlayed their intellectual influence into control over the APA. Between 1960 and 1979, nearly all the presidents of the Eastern Division were analytic philosophers.

Because analysts held top positions in the APA, they could appropriate for themselves one of the organization's key resources—slots for papers at the annual meetings. In a report drafted in 1979, Rorty observed that "many 'non-analytic' people feel that the chances of their papers getting on the program are so small that they don't bother to submit them.... Some such feelings may be exaggerated. But I don't think all such feelings are.... [Analytic philosophers], who make up most of the membership of the Program Committees, tend to have ... suspicions about Whiteheadians, Deweyans, or phenomenologists, not to mention bright young admirers of Deleuze or Gadamer."[99] In the eyes of many nonanalytic thinkers, this was a distressing situation.

Dissatisfaction with the APA program led nonanalysts to create their own fora for presenting papers. The 1960s and 1970s saw significant growth in the number of APA "satellite groups"—philosophical organizations devoted to specific areas of philosophy, often meeting in conjunction with the APA convention, and serving as sites for papers written in the style of or on topics of interest to group members.[100]

Consequences of Pragmatism. But Rorty said he did not begin reading Freud until after his own psychoanalysis ended—indeed, he said his therapist demanded that he not read any psychoanalytic literature.

99. Richard Rorty to members of the Eastern Division APA Executive Committee, June 15, 1979, RRP. On slots for papers as resources, see Neil Gross and Crystal Fleming, 2007, "Academic Conferences and the Making of Philosophical Knowledge," unpublished manuscript.

100. Bruce Wilshire has observed that by the late 1970s, "there were more philosophers on the sidelines than in the game.... Many fringe groups had developed: societies of metaphysics, of process studies, of phenomenology ... [and] many of these ... met at ghetto

By the late 1970s, resentment over analytic control of the APA was running high. Nonanalytic philosophers "had been sidelined for decades. Resignation and despair were deeply ingrained."[101] As the decade drew to a close, an event transpired that catalyzed these resentments and mobilized nonanalysts to collective action: an evaluation of the philosophy department of the New School for Social Research. Consistently ranked in the third tier of philosophy graduate programs on reputational surveys in the 1950s and 1960s, the New School's philosophy department in 1978 awarded eight Ph.D.'s, had some 152 graduate students enrolled in its courses, and had only three tenured or tenure-track professors on staff.[102] These professors were specialists in the American and Continental traditions and in ancient philosophy.

In an interview, Rorty—part of the team sent to evaluate the New School—described the circumstances leading to the evaluation:

> I was part of ... a project for the government of the state of New York [whose mission was] to write reports on the philosophy graduate programs in all the universities in New York State and say which were good and which were bad.... That project was a bad idea.... It suggested the need for a kind of standardization of philosophy departments. [Nonanalytic philosophers] thought that this was an assault by the analytic establishment ... against everybody who was non-establishment, and in retrospect I think they were right.[103]

The evaluation would have occasioned reaction under any circumstances, but the timing was particularly bad, for the New School's philosophy department was in a state of crisis. The dean of the graduate faculty, Joseph Greenbaum, had recently imposed a moratorium on hiring, and as a result there were too few senior faculty members to teach and advise

hours during the APA convention.... In fact, so many peripheral societies and associations developed that the APA was in danger of implosion, collapse at its core." Bruce Wilshire, 2002, *Fashionable Nihilism: A Critique of Analytic Philosophy*, Albany: State University of New York Press, 52. Wilshire's claim can be corroborated by comparing the listing of philosophical societies in the 1964–65 *Directory of American Philosophers* with the listing in the 1974–75 edition.

101. Ibid.

102. *Directory of American Philosophers*, 1978–79, vol. 9, Bowling Green: Philosophy Documentation Center, 99; *Review of Metaphysics*, 1978, 32:182.

103. Interview with author, December 22, 1998.

graduate students. In part for this reason, the decision had been made "to close the 'pipeline' of students able to advance to the Ph.D. degree,"[104] a decision that, in the opinion of Albert Hofstadter, the department's chair, had "brought about the demoralization of the faculty and students." It was in this context that the site visit of the evaluations committee, chaired by Maurice Mandelbaum, provoked such anxiety.

For his part, Rorty had no desire to see the department shut down. Although he thought a major organizational restructuring was in order—he recommended in a letter to Greenbaum that he consider hiring Alasdair MacIntyre to replace Hofstadter—the last thing he wanted was for the department to be remade in an analytic image. To the contrary: he thought the New School might play an important role in revivifying U.S. philosophy because of its connection to Continental thought:

> Speaking now as the private citizen I became when the Rating Committee's task ended last Friday, and without further reference to our Committee's report, I would like to say that the New School seems to me to have a golden opportunity to form a link between American philosophers and the exciting work which is currently going on among German philosophers.... Philosophy in America is at the exhausted tail-end of an epoch and is looking around for something to revitalize itself. All over the country, there are young people in philosophy departments who see the current controversies in Germany as raising the most interesting philosophical issues being pursued anywhere. In this situation, the New School with its tradition both of contacts with the German academic world and of concern with the relation between philosophical issues and theoretical issues within the social sciences, is just the place where one would expect to find blossoming. It would be a tragedy if this period, of all periods, were one in which philosophy died out at the New School.[105]

This, however, was not how nonanalysts perceived the intentions of the evaluations committee. Apparently unfamiliar with Rorty's recent work, they knew him only as the archanalytic editor of *The Linguistic Turn* and harbored suspicions of Mandelbaum as well. In their view, the major action of the committee was to "threaten ... to remove state recognition from the [New School] program, to effectively shut it down. One of the chief grounds was that the curriculum was too specialized."[106]

104. Albert Hofstadter to Joseph Greenbaum, October 24, 1977, RRP.
105. Richard Rorty to Joseph Greenbaum, June 10, 1977, RRP.
106. Wilshire, *Fashionable Nihilism*, 53.

For nonanalysts in the New York area, the philosophy department of the New School had an almost sacred status, whether because of the important role the school had played over the years in the intellectual life of New York City, because of the school's history as a refuge for those fleeing Nazi persecution, or because it was home, until to the mid-1970s, to such eminent thinkers as Hannah Arendt and Hans Jonas. A coalition of non-analysts quickly rallied to the New School's defense and began meeting to develop a strategy to save the department. Members of this coalition, dubbed the "Saturday Group," dispatched "letters protesting the New School plight to friends outside our immediate group. The response was gratifying. Many scores of philosophers signed these letters."[107] The Saturday Group came to concern itself with more than just the New School, however. Yale's John Smith recalls that the group soon broadened out into "a combination of philosophical discussion, exchanging of experience and common concerns and keeping tabs on what was happening in the Eastern Division of the APA, especially as regards officers and personnel on the … committees, the make-up of the annual program, and the distribution of research awards."[108]

Expanding their cause, Saturday Group members decided to hold a meeting at that year's Eastern Division APA convention in Washington, D.C., to see if there was national interest in collective action aimed at challenging analytic dominance in the profession. Rutgers philosopher Bruce Wilshire reports that "well over a hundred people"[109] attended the meeting, where a "Committee for Pluralism in Philosophy" was founded with the goal of "work[ing] for an APA which is more representative of the diversity of philosophical activity in the U.S."[110] When the meeting adjourned, "pluralist" philosophers made their way to the poorly attended business meeting of the APA. There, because of their numbers, they were able to push through a "sunshine motion" requiring that the activities of the Nominating Committee be carried out in a manner open to public scrutiny. For although the Committee was free to nominate whomever it wanted for executive positions in the organization, it was supposed to take into consideration the preferences of the membership at large as these were revealed through suggestion forms sent to all APA members.

107. Ibid., 54.

108. John Smith, memorandum to author, November 4, 1998, 2.

109. Wilshire, *Fashionable Nihilism*, 54.

110. "Committee for Pluralism," unpublished document, 1979. Files of Kenneth Stikkers, Southern Illinois University–Carbondale.

The pluralists' sunshine motion required that these suggestions be tallied and read aloud during future business meetings.

The pluralists' activities at the meeting occasioned a worried letter from Ernest Sosa of Brown, the association's secretary-treasurer, to other members of the APA's Executive Committee, which included Rorty as the new president. Philosophers had been complaining since the late 1960s that the APA had become politicized, with activists insisting that it take stands on issues of the day, but the 1978 meetings represented the "first time in several years," according to Sosa, "that caucusing was in evidence" at the business meeting.[111] Sosa expressed concern that the pluralists' sunshine motion was about more than transparency; he feared that during the 1979 meetings, pluralists might try to nominate and then elect candidates directly from the floor. He proposed that the Executive Committee consider changing the organization's by-laws to prohibit such elections and then, depending on the reaction, actually make the change the year following.

Rorty, convinced like Sosa that direct elections from the floor would be a bad idea, agreed with Sosa's plan.[112] But his intention in supporting the maneuver was not to block nonanalysts from gaining representation in the APA. In fact, he told Robert Sokolowski, "I quite agree about the justice of the complaints which [the pluralists] have made. There is, alas, an 'analytic establishment' in our discipline, and it has, off and on, done things which smack of the tyranny of the majority—not, I think, out of ill will but just out of complacency and thoughtlessness. The APA had better figure out how to get out of such bad habits."

Rorty confessed that he felt somewhat powerless to deal with the situation:

I feel a bit diffident about all this because [SUNY at Stony Brook's] Don Ihde seems, judging from the 1978 Business Meeting, the most vociferous of the people concerned about the problem. He sees me as an enemy because I sat on a committee some years back which reported on the program at Stony Brook to the N.Y. State Regents [the same committee as had evaluated the New School]. Ihde didn't like the report, and was very bitter in his criticism of the committee. (I found myself bemused by the episode, since I am unaccustomed to being viewed as the Hatchet Man of the

111. Ernest Sosa to members of the Eastern Division Executive Committee, February 23, 1979, RRP.

112. Richard Rorty to Robert Sokolowski, March 27, 1979, RRP.

Analytic Establishment. My colleagues at Princeton tend to regard me as subversive of that same establishment, being "soft" on Heidegger, Derrida, etc.) This difficulty with Ihde prevents me from doing what I would do if anyone else had spearheaded the drive at the business meeting—namely, getting together with him and talking things out.

Although he did not get in touch with Ihde, Rorty made several attempts to do something about the problem the pluralists had identified. For example, he proposed overhauling the Program Committee, which was charged with deciding which papers to accept for APA panels. He suggested that the committee be composed of philosophers representing a variety of approaches and traditions.[113] Rorty realized this change in itself would do nothing to encourage nonanalytic philosophers to send their papers to the APA for consideration, so he proposed as well that the Program Committee "get out a statement conveying that it realized that there has been this problem, that it had restructured things to avoid it, and that it trusted that in the future people would send in anything they'd written without *a priori* fears."[114]

These proposals were linked to Rorty's identity as a pluralist and historicist. Had he not thought of himself in these terms he would have no doubt resisted the pluralist movement more than he did. But his proposals were also informed by and reinforcing of his specifically Kuhnian understanding of philosophy. He tied his calls for change in the APA to the view that the field was increasingly split between philosophers representing incommensurable paradigms. Although it might be the case, as he put it in a note to Monroe Beardsley, chair of the Nominating Committee, that the Committee for Pluralism is "dominated by people whose resentment exceeds their knowledge of what's going on in the profession,"[115] the pluralists were right that the future would bring not "a softening of lines between the analytic majority and the non-analytic minority, but rather a deepening polarization based roughly on the different sorts of graduate training currently being offered. One sort (typified by Princeton and Harvard) is training people to solve problems stated in the recent literature. The other emphasizes acquaintance with historical texts. The two kinds of philosophers produced can barely talk to each other now,

---

113. Richard Rorty to members of the Eastern Division Executive Committee, June 15, 1979, RRP.

114. Richard Rorty to Robert Sokolowski, April 25, 1979, RRP.

115. Richard Rorty to Monroe Beardsley, July 10, 1979, RRP.

and will be less and less able to do so in the future."[116] Only by making room on the program for both kinds of philosophers could harmony be maintained.

Just as Rorty's self-understanding as pluralist and historicist marked him as an exception in the Princeton philosophy department, so too did it mark him as an exception in the analytic community more generally. He wished to move the association in a more pluralistic direction, but others did not. He reported in depressed tones to Sokolowski in November, just a month before the winter meetings, that "I argued at length at the APA National Board meeting that the APA's committees did not include a sufficient spectrum of philosophical points of view, but did not get much sympathy. Indeed, [some board members] were furious at me for raising the question. I am glumly inclining to the view that the Analytic Establishment's refusal to make concessions is not the result of simple thoughtlessness and self-absorption, but of active hostility toward those who refuse to acknowledge the analytic hegemony."[117]

In preparation for the 1979 APA meeting in New York City, leaders of the pluralist movement had discovered that suggestions made by the membership to the Nominating Committee "had been ignored whenever they proved unpleasant—deposited in the circular file."[118] Pluralists spread word of this through mailing lists and, as the New York City convention drew closer, announced plans for a rally to be held the night before the business meeting. Attendance at the rally was greater than the pluralists could have dreamed possible. Smith recalls that "the main ballroom of the hotel was packed" with philosophers who "expressed outrage at this disregard of their rights."[119] Speakers at the event, which drew the attention of the *New York Times,* asserted that "the American Philosophical Association ha[d] become 'a monolith' and 'intolerant,' that its programs 'neglect[ed] basic philosophic issues,' and that its leadership 'ha[d] lost contact with other philosophers.'"[120] At the business meeting the following day, Nominating Committee members—as had been their routine—announced their nominees for executive positions. Beardsley, on behalf of the committee, nominated Adolf Grünbaum of Pittsburgh for the vice presidency, a position that would roll over into the presidency

116. Richard Rorty to Ernest Sosa, July 9, 1979, RRP.

117. Richard Rorty to Robert Sokolowski, November 6, 1979, RRP.

118. Wilshire, *Fashionable Nihilism*, 55.

119. John Smith, memorandum to author, 2.

120. Thomas Lask, 1979, "Philosophical Group's Dominant View Is Criticized," *New York Times,* December 30, 23.

the following year.[121] The pluralists, invoking the sunshine motion, then demanded to know whom the membership at large had nominated, and a number of names were read out, including Smith's. Because of the sunshine motion, committee members were also forced to reveal the tallies of nomination suggestions from the membership. The chair of the committee "was ... reluctant to read the list. In a hesitant voice he began. The top achievers for each post were not those his committee had nominated."[122] That Nominating Committee members would so blatantly disregard suggestions from the membership at large, even in the face of public scrutiny, sent waves of anger rippling across the room. Prepared for such a turn of events, those affiliated with the pluralist cause then further enhanced their legitimacy as champions of democratic reform by nominating from the floor precisely those candidates who had received the largest number of votes from the membership at large and whom they had planned to nominate all along. Smith was promptly nominated in this way, along with John Lachs, Quentin Lauer, and John McDermott—other organizers of the pluralist revolt—and the matter was put to a vote. Two days earlier, at the Executive Committee meeting, Rorty's plan to announce that the APA would now be more open to nonanalytic papers had been passed, but it was not until *after* the election of executive officers at the Business Committee meeting that a vote would be taken on Sosa's proposed amendment to the by-laws that would have prevented an election from the floor. Because the pluralists had packed the room, Smith beat Grünbaum by a vote of 198 to 165. Accusations were made that some students had voted in the election and that the results were therefore invalid. The meeting was adjourned while Rorty decided what to do. The next day, he reconvened the meeting and reported, according to the minutes, "that although a check of the credentials of those present at the first session of the Business Meeting had revealed that some 56 voting cards had gone to persons not affiliated with the Eastern Division ... it had also revealed that the number of legitimate voters present (368) exceeded the vote total for each election where members were allowed one vote each."[123] Rorty declared the election valid, and Smith the winner. His ruling was challenged but sustained by a voice vote. It was within Rorty's power to

121. In fact, Beardsley had notified Grünbaum of his nomination back in November. See Monroe Beardsley to Adolf Grünbaum, November 10, 1979, RRP.

122. Wilshire, *Fashionable Nihilism*, 57.

123. Ernest Sosa, Minutes of the 1979 APA Eastern Division Business Meeting, January 14, 1980, RRP.

rule the election invalid, given irregularities in who had cast ballots; he did not so rule.

It was in the context of these tumultuous events that Rorty's presidential address at the APA meeting, "Pragmatism, Relativism, and Irrationalism," subsequently published in *Consequences of Pragmatism*, made such a splash. In most respects the piece did what most presidential addresses do: it rehashed points the speaker had made in his own recent writings, using the occasion as an opportunity to promote his own intellectual views. Whereas *Philosophy and the Mirror of Nature* had championed Dewey, Wittgenstein, and Heidegger about equally, Rorty now argued that Dewey and James were the philosophers to whom renewed attention should be paid. Some in the analytic movement regarded the pragmatists as having made important contributions inasmuch as their thought "suggested various holistic corrections of the atomistic doctrines of the early logical empiricists,"[124] but Rorty advanced the more radical interpretation that Dewey and James had been antifoundationalists to their core and rejected the vision of philosophy to which most analytic philosophers still cleaved. James and Dewey "asked us to liberate our new civilization by giving up the notion of 'grounding' our culture, our moral lives, our politics, our religious beliefs, upon 'philosophical bases.' They asked us to give up the neurotic Cartesian quest for certainty [and to] ... think of the Kantian project of grounding thought in a permanent ahistorical matrix as *reactionary*."[125] Rorty encouraged his audience to follow James and Dewey in this regard, arguing that their position followed naturally from the realization that while it might well be possible to compare particular observation sentences with the world to determine whether those sentences corresponded or not, recent work in philosophy and the history of science had revealed that there is no way to compare entire vocabularies with the world in this fashion. When it comes to choosing vocabularies, we must let practice be our guide. Particularly when it comes to moral and political philosophy, we should give up the idea that we can find the truth about how we ought to behave by approaching the world with a sufficiently "unclouded mental eye."[126] The only basis for deciding what is good in politics and morality is to converse with our fellow human beings and try to come to some kind of intersubjective agreement with them.

This was a controversial claim. But in the context of the pluralist uprising, what really got his listeners' attention was Rorty's argument that

---

124. Rorty, *Consequences of Pragmatism*, 160.

125. Ibid., 161.   126. Ibid., 165.

pragmatism's conception of philosophy implied that major changes were in order to the way philosophy was practiced in the United States. Most contemporary U.S. philosophers, Rorty argued—clearly with the analytic community in mind—subscribed to some version of the foundationalist program. They "shar[ed the] conviction that philosophers should be as much like scientists as possible,"[127] seeking out philosophical truths. The problem, from the perspective of pragmatism, was not just that their emphasis on precision and finality led them to employ technical methods that made their work impenetrable by others but also that there was little relationship between the issues they were taking up and those of real concern to the rest of the world. From this point of view, "one will tend to see the problems about which philosophers are now offering 'objective, verifiable, and clearly communicable' solutions as historical relics, left over from the Enlightenment's misguided search for the hidden essences of knowledge and morality. This is the point of view adopted by many of our fellow-intellectuals, who see us philosophy professors as caught in a time-warp, trying to live the Enlightenment over again."[128] American academic philosophy should shed its scientism, Rorty urged, reengaging with the problematics and concerns of the rest of the humanities, repudiating the quest for timeless truths, and embracing a view of philosophy as merely an attempt to move the cultural conversation forward. The fact that the sitting APA president, who had refused to stem the rising tide of dissent, was, with this address, agreeing publicly with the dissenters that something was awry with the discipline must have made Rorty—despite his doubts about the intellectual achievements of some self-described pluralists—seem something of a turncoat to other analysts.

Rorty wasn't worried, however. He believed that opening up philosophy to nonanalytic approaches and concerns was a good thing. To be sure, he doubted whether the pluralist revolt itself or his actions as APA president would have any lasting effect. Analytic philosophy was just too entrenched, he thought.[129] At the same time, he believed that any effort to shake things up in the association should be applauded. As he told Annette Baier about a month after the meeting,

> The revolt of the pluralists was interesting but exhausting. They turned out to be two hundred strong—quite enough to fling the rascals out....

127. Ibid., 170.   128. Ibid.
129. Richard Rorty to Adolf Grünbaum, February 27, 1980, RRP.

[Logician] Ruth [Barcan Marcus] was mad as a wet hen, and was chasing around the floor of the business meeting trying to get ballots invalidated to reverse the result, but I think most people felt that it wasn't that big a deal and that harmony would be restored if everybody would keep cool for the next few years. I don't think Smith was a good candidate … but I think that the pluralists were right that the Establishment has become entirely too smug—so perhaps human happiness will be slightly increased by the events of Xmastime.[130]

∗ 7 ∗

By 1980, Rorty had been dissatisfied with his colleagues at Princeton, and with the state of the American philosophy profession, for some time. He had considered moving to warmer intellectual climes many times before but now put a plan into motion to leverage the success of *Philosophy and the Mirror of Nature* into what he hoped would be a permanent move. The question was whether he would continue teaching in a philosophy department. By no means had he dismissed the thought of doing so. In 1980, for example, he contacted Barry Stroud, then chair of philosophy at Berkeley, to inquire about an opening that would soon be created by the retirement of the philosopher of language Paul Grice.[131] There was little love lost between Rorty and some of the more analytic members of the Berkeley department such as John Searle.[132] But there were others at Berkeley with whom Rorty did share interests, especially Hubert Dreyfus. In 1980, Dreyfus ran a summer institute on phenomenology and existentialism in which Rorty, along with Sellars, Searle, Arthur Danto, Rüdiger Bubner, John Haugeland, Robert Brandom, Paul Rabinow, and John Compton, were featured speakers, and over the next few years Dreyfus and Rorty would cross paths several times, with Rorty recommending Dreyfus for an NEH-sponsored seminar on Heidegger[133] and, as a reviewer for the University of Chicago Press, recommending the publication of Dreyfus's book with Rabinow,[134] *Michel Foucault: Beyond Structuralism and Hermeneutics.* Rabinow, in turn, who joined Berkeley's anthropology department in 1978, helped put Rorty in touch with Foucault, on whom Rorty wrote an

130. Richard Rorty to Annette Baier, January 17, 1980, RRP.

131. See Barry Stroud to Richard Rorty, February 13, 1980, RRP.

132. On Rorty's view of Searle, see Richard Rorty to Richard Watson, June 5, 1980, RRP.

133. Richard Rorty, recommendation letter to NEH, August 22, 1980, RRP.

134. Richard Rorty to Fran Gamwell of the University of Chicago Press, November 3, 1980, RRP.

essay in the *London Review of Books* in 1981, laying the groundwork for the many philosophical pieces he would draft on poststructuralism over the course of the 1980s and 1990s.[135] Berkeley was less keen on Rorty, however, than he was on them. Although Stroud said that he'd "enjoyed *Philosophy and the Mirror of Nature* very much," he told Rorty the department had already made a senior offer to someone else.[136]

Stroud was not the only one who'd read the book. Rorty's friends and former students wrote to apprise him of its success. Writing from Pittsburgh, for example, Brandom told Rorty in 1980, "We started our Rorty discussion group this week. Annette, Alexander, Paul and I organized it, to read your book and recent papers. About 20 graduate students are attending. A similar group is running in the HPS [History and Philosophy of Science] dept at the students' demand. I don't think I have ever seen a book as popular and influential among graduate students and young faculty as yours is. I don't believe anyone will be able to write about epistemology or the place of philosophy in culture without accepting or rebutting your account."[137] Similarly, Jonathan Lieberson, a lecturer in philosophy at Columbia and Barnard and a contributing editor to the *New York Review of Books*, wrote to say, "One cannot get off the elevator at the Phi. Dept. at Columbia without encountering a crudely made sign announcing a student reading group, entitled, 'Is Rorty Right?'"[138] Sales figures for 1979 and 1980 are not available, but evidence that interest in the book ran high right from the start is that Rorty was invited to give numerous lectures in the first two years after its publication—in California, Georgia, Iowa, Kansas, Maine, South Carolina, and Texas, to name just a few of the states to which he traveled.[139] He was invited to give so many

135. Foucault, for his part, liked *Philosophy and the Mirror of Nature* and worked to find a French translator for it. "Forgive me not to have answered you since you sent me your book," Foucault wrote in April of 1981. "I read it over with most interest. It seems to me that it raises some of the basic questions that have been neglected those past years." Michel Foucault to Richard Rorty, April 16, 1981, RRP.

136. Barry Stroud to Richard Rorty, February 13, 1980, RRP.

137. Robert Brandom to Richard Rorty, October 5, 1980, RRP.

138. Jonathan Lieberson to Richard Rorty, June 25, 1980, RRP.

139. Often these invitations were direct responses to the book; for example, in July of 1980 Rorty received a letter from Stephen Stich of the University of Maryland: "For the last six weeks a number of colleagues and I have been having weekly meetings to discuss Philosophy and the Mirror of Nature. At a recent meeting of the group it was suggested that we should try to bring you into our conversation." Stephen Stich to Richard Rorty, July 10, 1980, RRP.

talks, in fact, that he began declining invitations, less because of the time demands than because he worried about becoming repetitive. A special panel about *Philosophy and the Mirror of Nature* was organized for the 1980 APA meetings, featuring comments by Ian Hacking and Jaegwon Kim, and by 1982 the book had already been cited some fifty-eight times in articles referenced in the Arts and Humanities Citation Index and reviewed in some thirty-five academic journals and magazines in the United States and internationally.

The most important of these reviews, from the standpoint of Rorty's future mobility, was written by Quentin Skinner and published in the *New York Review of Books* in March of 1981. Where some philosophers who had reviewed the book had been critical or even dismissive of Rorty's claims, Skinner pronounced *Philosophy and the Mirror of Nature* "disturbing" and "brilliantly argued." Although he questioned whether Rorty had effectively carried off some of his points—noting, for example, that Rorty had been unclear as to what exactly edifying philosophy would entail and that he had not made the case convincingly that knowledge is nonrepresentational—his overall conclusion was that Rorty's "general view of what philosophers cannot any longer say with any confidence is developed with so much power and persuasiveness that I am well prepared to believe that my residual expressions of doubt may amount to little more than whistling to keep my philosophical spirits up."[140]

The effect of the review on Rorty's intellectual reputation—already considerable—was immediate. Rorty wrote to Skinner, his friend, to thank him for the kind words. "I am not unaware of the sheer commercial advantages which accrue to me from your review," Rorty said.

Over the weekend, believe it or not, two universities which I hadn't thought of or dealt with before called up, one to say that they had voted to offer me a job and the other to say that they wondered if I'd be interested in a sort of ad hoc chair they were thinking of cobbling together for me. Both callers started off by asking if I'd seen your review—which seems clearly to have been the stimulus to their interest. Furthermore, for a couple of weeks I have been getting reports from Yale that some people there want to fix me up with a job. Yesterday I was told that this gallant effort had been much advanced by your review—of which my supporters

140. Quentin Skinner, 1981, "The End of Philosophy?" *New York Review of Books,* March 19, 46–48, 46, 48.

are passing out copies to deans, apparently. It is amazing what intellectual sky-writing will do.[141]

In fact, Rorty had come close to taking a job the year before—at Northwestern. The philosophy department at Northwestern had in recent years carved out a niche for itself as the major American center for Continental philosophy, and Rorty, with his broad interests, would have been a perfect addition to the faculty. Beyond his extensive reading in Continental thought, he had recently spent time in Europe and was becoming personally acquainted with key figures in the field. In the winter of 1977 he spent time teaching in Frankfurt, traveling to Yugoslavia to take part in activities associated with the newly created Inter-University Center in Dubrovnik, where a group of dissident scholars had banded together in defiance of a government crackdown.[142] Rorty also spent part of the 1981–82 academic year teaching in Heidelberg. While in Germany, Rorty once again traveled behind the Iron Curtain, this time going to Prague to give a series of lectures and also arranging for Habermas to make the trip.[143]

Administrators at Northwestern tried to woo Rorty with the promise of a joint appointment—a letter from a dean there in February of 1981 offered Rorty a salary of $55,000 (about $124,000 in 2007 dollars) and an endowed chair as John C. Shaffer Professor of Philosophy and Humanities[144]—but Rorty was disinclined to accept, at least in part because he

141. Richard Rorty to Quentin Skinner, March 2, 1981, RRP. Although the *New York Review of Books* issue was dated March 19, it must have come out earlier, since Rorty's letter to Skinner precedes this publication date by two weeks. It is possible the Rorty letter is misdated.

142. In 1978 Rorty, Richard Jeffrey, and Robert Tucker wrote to the president of Princeton to ask if he could find a way to support the Center. "Our principal motive in making this proposal is the need to support Yugoslavian scholars who are under pressure from their government, and for whom the IUC is a haven. In particular, the so-called 'Belgrade Eight'—a group of philosophers and sociologists who have been discharged from their teaching positions because of their defense of academic freedom and human rights generally—are still able to use the IUC as a sanctuary. It is the only place in Yugoslavia where they may give lectures or seminars. All of us have had considerable contact over the years with these people.... Rorty took part in an IUC course last spring. We are in a position to testify that the IUC is a very valuable point of contact between liberals in Eastern Europe and scholars and students in the West." September 27, 1978, RRP.

143. See the discussion in Barbara Day, 1999, *The Velvet Philosophers*. London: Claridge Press. Thanks to Jessie Labov for pointing this out to me.

144. Rudolph Weingartner to Richard Rorty, February 23, 1981, RRP.

thought the philosophy department was in bad shape organizationally. More important, Rorty was holding out for something better—a job entirely outside the purview of philosophy. Although, as indicated above, he remained somewhat ambivalent about this, continuing to court schools like Berkeley, he told his friend Richard Watson in 1980 that on the whole he was so sick of dealing with other analytic philosophers that he wanted out of the profession altogether. Watson had asked him if he was happy at Princeton. Rorty replied,

> Am I "perfectly happy as a serious professional at Princeton?" A serious professional what? Philosopher? No. Writer? Yes. Universities permit one to read books and report what one thinks about them, and get paid for it. I'm delighted that I lucked into a university which pays me to make up stories and tell them. About "the philosophical profession" I could care less. That profession is just a concretization of a table of organization drawn up by various accidental historical forces acting upon university administrators in the nineteenth century. I should like to think that my book will be liked by people in history and literature departments, and if I could get a job in one such I should probably take it.[145]

Rorty said much the same thing to Princeton president William Bowen when Bowen asked whether there was anything Princeton could do to retain Rorty in the face of offers from Northwestern and other schools. "There isn't anything in particular which Princeton could do to make staying more attractive for me," came Rorty's reply.[146]

> The question is really whether I think another place might have a fundamentally different atmosphere, one more sympathetic to the stuff I do. Princeton has a very good philosophy department, but, alas, not one which is much use to me (except in the way of prestige). Roughly speaking, I tell historical stories and everybody else in the department analyses arguments. Most good philosophy departments want the latter rather than the former, so it may be that I shan't find any place which would be better for me. Certainly I would not expect—and have no thought of asking—that Princeton should change for my sake. The department's direction and character are clearly determined for the foreseeable future, and could not be changed even if everybody wanted to change them.

145. Richard Rorty to Richard Watson, June 5, 1980, RRP.
146. Richard Rorty to William Bowen, February 23, 1981, RRP.

The year 1982 was a good one for Rorty. In the fall of 1981 he entered into discussions with several other departments about the possibility of relocating. He was in touch with Hayden White of the University of California, Santa Cruz, for example, who sought to make a case for why a move to Santa Cruz would satisfy Rorty's demands. "I hope you will give this possibility serious consideration," wrote White, "for it would be of inestimable benefit to us if we should succeed in luring you to leave the East coast and come to these shores. Personally, I can think of no one whom I would rather have occupy the chair of Professor of Humanities which N. O. Brown has just vacated. This would give you the position which, according to David Hoy, you desire, from which you could teach literature, philosophy, history of ideas, or whatever, according to whatever interests currently impel your studies."[147] He was also approached by the philosophy department at Michigan.[148] Simultaneously Rorty began a correspondence with the literary scholar E. D. Hirsch, chair of the English department at the University of Virginia, who had been authorized to offer Rorty an interdisciplinary position. Hirsch was straight to the point: "I understand from our talk that you are interested in the kind of position that would allow you to teach on the theoretical edges of several different fields, and also to teach courses in philosophy. From the discussions I have had, I conclude that we should be able to offer you a highly interesting position that meets your requirements."[149] Rorty had been accepted for a year's stay at the Center for Advanced Study in the Behavioral Sciences in Palo Alto in 1982–83—it was while there that he would become friends with Roberto Unger, about whose social theory he would later write—and Hirsch assured him that Virginia would grant him a leave for the year.

Later that fall, Rorty received even bigger news: he woke up one morning to find that he had been awarded a MacArthur "genius grant." This opened even more possibilities for Rorty, who could use the substantial award—$244,000[150]—to supplement his income, travel, or buy off his teaching so he'd have more time to write. Virginia agreed to be accommodating. "I think that I can better your suggested pattern for the last three years of your McArthur fellowship," wrote Hirsch in the course of the negotiation. "Instead of getting paid just two-thirds of your annual salary for teaching one semester, we might as well go ahead and pay the

147. Hayden White to Richard Rorty, November 11, 1981, RRP.

148. See Richard Rorty to Peter Steiner, February 15, 1982, RRP.

149. E. D. Hirsch to Richard Rorty, September 8, 1981, RRP.

150. See Priscilla Van Tassel, 1982, "Rich but 'Embarrassing' Prize," *New York Times*, November 7, New Jersey Weekly Section, 6.

full amount. Thereafter you would be on a one-and-one schedule at full salary."[151] Rorty was delighted. In March of 1982 he told his friend, "I've now resolved my job problems by taking a job as university professor of humanities at Virginia. It's part of a scheme to teach pretty much half time for the rest of my career—combining MacArthur money with Virginia money and think-tank money to do so. But it also gets me out of the disciplinary matrix of philosophy into a non-departmental job, which is both exhilarating and vaguely frightening."[152] While the move would never have been possible had Rorty not done work of interest to a broad humanities audience, he credited the MacArthur award with giving him the confidence needed to break out of the discipline. He told the vice president of the MacArthur Foundation,

> I mentioned in a previous letter that I'd been emboldened by the MacArthur to make a kind of career change. Nothing very dramatic, since it merely involves ceasing to be a Professor of Philosophy and becoming a Professor of Humanities—and moving to Virginia from Princeton. But the effect is to take me out of the philosophical profession, and to pin my hopes for the future on becoming a sort of all-around intellectual, or man of letters, or something of the sort. This is a move which I'd contemplated before getting the MacArthur Fellowship, but which came to seem much more plausible and desirable with the Fellowship in hand. I'd been getting increasingly itchy about writing lots of stuff on what was wrong with the self-image of the Philosophical Establishment, while remaining at the heart of that Establishment myself. My colleagues here at Princeton were also increasingly itchy, needless to say. This resulted in tensions of various sorts, particularly as to whether students writing dissertations with me were "really doing philosophy." By ceasing to be a member of the philosophy department, I get out from under a lot of problems of this sort.[153]

Rorty and his wife were excited about the move. He told Skinner, "Mary and I are wondering what the future in Dixie will bring. She's very chipper about it, whereas I alternate between euphoria and anxiety in my usual way. It's like the break-up of a long-standing, chilly, marriage. One is terribly sad it's all over on Tuesdays, Thursdays, and Saturdays. On the other days one wonders what life now holds."[154]

151. E. D. Hirsch to Richard Rorty, December 14, 1981, RRP.
152. Richard Rorty to Richard Watson, March 2, 1982, RRP.
153. Richard Rorty to Gerald Freund, March 22, 1982, RRP.
154. Richard Rorty to Quentin Skinner, February 4, 1982, RRP.

The Theory of Intellectual Self-Concept

* 1 *

The historical narrative offered thus far traces the twists and turns of Richard Rorty's philosophy and career trajectory from the intellectual milieu of his parents' household to his growing dissatisfaction with the paradigm of analytic philosophy and movement back into pragmatism in the 1970s and early 1980s. In developing this narrative I have tried to stick as closely as possible to the facts, forcing no interpretation onto them for which archival research did not yield relatively unmediated support.

Beginning with this chapter, I move to a new level of analysis. The argument I now want to make is that the developments considered in chapters 1–8 reflect not Rorty's idiosyncratic and entirely contingent biographical experiences but the operation of more general social mechanisms and processes that shaped and structured his intellectual life and career. Without abandoning the standard of fidelity to the archival materials, we can construct a more theoretically informed explanation for Rorty's moves if we see him, not as a being spinning out ideas on the basis of a transhistorically rational consideration of their objective merits or as someone pushed this way and that by his personality or character, but as a social actor embedded over time in a variety of institutional settings, each imposing specific constraints on his opportunities and choices and influencing him with respect to the formation of his self-understanding, his evaluation of the worthiness of various lines of thought, and ultimately his intellectual output.

What is true of Rorty in this regard is true of all other intellectuals: they are persons no less impinged upon by social mechanisms and processes than any other. For this reason, just as historical sociologists have found it fruitful to explain past developments in the spheres of politics, religion, the economy, and culture by applying models of social structure, institutions, and individual action derived from sociological theory,[1] so too do sociologists of ideas insist that intellectual history could benefit from a generous dose of sociological insight. In this chapter and the next, I use the Rorty case to show the explanatory benefits of such a move and to think through some of the social processes salient for humanists and others working in the contemporary American academic context.

I proceed in three steps. First, I outline in this chapter the major theoretical frameworks currently available to sociologists of ideas—those of Pierre Bourdieu and Randall Collins. Without questioning that the theories they have developed offer explanatory purchase over a range of intellectual phenomena, I suggest that both frameworks are deficient in a crucial respect—their theorization, or lack thereof, of the intellectual self. To remedy this deficiency, the chapter lays out a complementary theory of how and why individual thinkers make some of the intellectual choices they do—what I call the theory of intellectual self-concept. In chapter 10, I return to the biographical record, acknowledging the importance of the kinds of factors highlighted by Bourdieu and Collins in shaping the choices Rorty made over the course of his career but also insisting that key choices cannot be understood unless processes having to do with the quest for self-concept coherence are taken into account.

* 2 *

Since the inception of the sociology of knowledge in the mid-nineteenth century, practitioners have been interested in the social origins of philosophy. In *The German Ideology*, Karl Marx and Friedrich Engels linked the idealism of the Young Hegelians to the "religious" bent of German culture, a product in their view of the state of German class relations.[2] Karl Mannheim—rejecting the class interest approach to ideology that, with *Capital*, became even more important to Marx—illustrated his alternative theorization by accounting in more historicist terms for the rise of liberalism.[3] Émile Durkheim also sought to understand the social roots

1. See Julia Adams, Elisabeth Clemens, and Ann Orloff, eds., 2005, *Remaking Modernity: Politics, History, and Sociology*, Durham: Duke University Press.

2. Karl Marx and Friedrich Engels, 1967, *The German Ideology*, New York: International Publishers.

3. Karl Mannheim [1936] 1991, *Ideology and Utopia*, London: Routledge. On Mannheim's historicism, see David Kettler and Volker Meja, 1995, *Karl Mannheim and the Crisis of Liberalism: The Secret of These New Times*, New Brunswick: Transaction.

of philosophy. Although his formal sociology of knowledge, focused on the categories of understanding, was never extended into a sociology of philosophy per se, his insistence that the viewpoints of thinkers such as Rousseau and the American pragmatists owed much to the sociocultural contexts in which they had been developed—such that the "theories of philosophers" could be "instructive as facts" because "they teach us what passes in the public mind of one particular epoch"—evinced a willingness to view the development of philosophical ideas as a social fact explicable by other social facts.[4] When, in the middle years of the twentieth century, American sociologists picked up where Mannheim and Durkheim left off and sought to move the sociology of knowledge beyond its earlier programmatic phase, they too took philosophy to be a prime object of analysis. This was the case for C. Wright Mills, who analyzed the origins of pragmatism;[5] for Talcott Parsons, who commented on the "cultural tradition[s]" and social-structural factors that are the "prerequisite of extensive [societal] development in the philosophical direction";[6] and for Alvin Gouldner, who explored the social roots of Plato's thought.[7] At about the same time, critical theorists such as Herbert Marcuse pushed the project of ideology critique in new directions, explaining philosophical developments—like the rise of ordinary language philosophy—by pointing to the social and cultural formations to which they seemed linked.[8]

This was pathbreaking scholarship. But from the vantage point of the present day, it seems flawed. Sociologists of knowledge tried to explain broad philosophical tendencies of entire societies without accounting for internal variation. They posited the existence of overarching national cultural patterns and functional requirements and linked ideational developments to them without any concern to establish empirically their existence. They eschewed the search for specific mechanisms and processes by which social factors might influence thought, resorting to such wooly explanatory notions as "consistency, harmony, coherence, unity, congru-

4. Émile Durkheim, 1974, *Sociology and Philosophy*, trans. D. F. Pocock, New York: Free Press, 76.

5. C. Wright Mills, 1964, *Sociology and Pragmatism: The Higher Learning in America*, New York: Paine-Whitman Publishers.

6. Talcott Parsons, 1951, *The Social System*, Glencoe: Free Press, 362–63.

7. Gouldner, *Enter Plato*.

8. Herbert Marcuse, 1964, *One Dimensional Man: Studies in the Ideology of Advanced Industrial Society*, Boston: Beacon Press.

ence, compatibility, [and] ... symbolic expression"[9]—types of relations said to obtain between ideas and what Robert K. Merton called their "existential base." And only rarely did they attend closely to the nature of the institutions in which philosophers and other intellectuals are housed—academies, salons, and universities—and to how those institutions might affect thinkers' everyday work lives, and through them, ideas.

On these grounds, scholars whom Charles Camic and I refer to as "new sociologists of ideas" tend to reject work carried out in the style of the old sociology of knowledge. In its place they have developed a set of more refined theoretical and analytical tools and used them to explain a wide variety of cases, many in philosophy. Camic, for example, has written on the social roots of the eighteenth-century Scottish Enlightenment, accounting for its particular blend of humanism and empiricism by pointing to distinctive patterns of socialization its exponents underwent.[10] Michèle Lamont has analyzed the institutional conditions that made possible the success that Jacques Derrida found in France and the United States in the 1970s and 1980s.[11] Martin Kusch has considered the psychologism dispute in turn of the twentieth-century German philosophy, looking to the work of sociologists of scientific knowledge for a conceptual repertoire with which to analyze the tactics and techniques philosophers use when they attempt to close philosophical controversies.[12] Pierre Bourdieu mobilized his distinctive theoretical apparatus to account for the conservatism of Martin Heidegger.[13] And Randall Collins, in *The Sociology of Philosophies*, has used his theory of "interaction ritual chains"—described below—to explain more than 2,500 years of philosophical developments, focused especially on the question of why and how some philosophers are able to secure long-term reputations for greatness.[14]

Although there are significant differences in the frameworks employed by these scholars, the most influential theorists in the area—Bourdieu and Collins—converge around an image of the intellectual world as a site for far more strategic action than is usually recognized. Focusing much of their attention on philosophers, they argue that, especially in contemporary so-

9. Robert K. Merton, 1949, *Social Theory and Social Structure: Towards the Codification of Theory and Research*, New York: Free Press, 515.

10. Camic, *Experience and Enlightenment*.

11. Lamont, "How to Become a Dominant French Philosopher."

12. Kusch, *Psychologism*.

13. Pierre Bourdieu, 1991, *The Political Ontology of Martin Heidegger*, Peter Collier, trans., Stanford: Stanford University Press.

14. Collins, *The Sociology of Philosophies*.

cieties, the philosophical arena comes to mark itself off from other spheres of cultural production, becoming a distinctive social "field" wherein professional status and prestige are bestowed primarily by other philosophers according to specifically philosophical criteria of evaluation.[15] Philosophers, Bourdieu and Collins suggest, are oriented first and foremost toward this field and have as their primary aim to obtain as much status and prestige as possible within it. Whether or not philosophers are conscious of this goal—and both Bourdieu and Collins insist that often they are not—they enact career strategies in order to achieve it, and the philosophical positions they take should be seen as components of such strategies. Genuine though their desires may be to forge correct answers to the questions that interest them, which questions they will consider important and which approaches they will take is dependent on the way that different intellectual positions have come to be hierarchically arranged in the status structure of the field, on philosophers' own positions therein, and on the kind of strategy for amassing intellectual status and finding a reputational niche they happen to be following. In general, high-status questions garner the most attention, high-status ways of approaching those questions are the methods of choice, and iconoclastic approaches represent either failures of strategic rationality or high-risk bids at accumulating prestige that aim to rearrange the structure of the field. When they occur, large-scale social changes—for example, an expansion of the resource base[16] or growing cultural conservatism[17]—shape the content of philosophical thought only indirectly, by reshuffling the intellectual and institutional positions that together compose the philosophical field, thus changing the lay of the terrain philosophers navigate in their pursuit of intellectual status.

Understanding the dynamics of intellectual fields is critical for sociologists of ideas, and chapter 10 draws on the insights of Bourdieu and Collins in order to explain aspects of Rorty's intellectual and career trajectory. But analyses of such dynamics only go so far. True, the intellectual-historical record reveals many instances when thinkers gravitate toward one intellectual position rather than another out of an interest in securing professional status and prestige. But intellectuals—like all social actors—must also be seen as bearers of identities, and the identities that are important to them and form the core of their self-reflection cannot always be reduced to concerns over where they are located in status

15. Bourdieu, *Homo Academicus*; Fritz Ringer, 1990, "The Intellectual Field, Intellectual History, and the Sociology of Knowledge," *Theory and Society* 19:269–94.

16. Wuthnow, *Communities of Discourse*.

17. Bourdieu, *The Political Ontology of Martin Heidegger*.

structures. Without rejecting the theories of Bourdieu and Collins, the sociology of ideas should find a way to take a broadened conception of identity into account.

My efforts along these lines proceed as follows. I first lay out in more detail the arguments of Bourdieu and Collins. Next, I examine a high-profile debate in the sociology of ideas between Camic on the one side and Jeffrey Alexander and Giuseppe Sciortino on the other over how to understand Parsons's foundational book *The Structure of Social Action* (1937). While much of this debate turns out to be overblown, a consideration of the arguments involved clears the way for a sharply focused critique of Bourdieu and Collins. Finally, I present my alternative theory of intellectual self-concept.

* 3 *

Pierre Bourdieu's interest in the sociology of ideas arises out of two concerns: first, an interest in understanding the role played by academics as gatekeepers into the ranks of the upper-middle class, and second, the desire to forge a "reflexive sociology"—a sociology that, taking into account the social factors that have shaped it, can work to overcome its own biases and blind spots.[18]

In the service of these interests, Bourdieu has sought to understand the intellectual universe—especially French academia—through the lens of his more general social theory.[19] At the heart of this theory lies the insistence that contemporary societies are stratified simultaneously along multiple dimensions. On Bourdieu's understanding, these dimensions revolve around "species of capital": different types of material and symbolic goods that are valued by society and confer power on their holders. Bourdieu is concerned with four species of capital: economic capital, or control over material resources; cultural capital, or the possession of socially valued forms of knowledge and taste; social capital, or, roughly, who one knows; and finally symbolic capital, or the means by which holders of other forms of capital legitimize their possession of them. Against a traditional Marxist understanding of social stratification, which would regard class as

18. Pierre Bourdieu and Loïc J. D. Wacquant, 1992, *An Invitation to Reflexive Sociology*, Chicago: University of Chicago Press.

19. Pierre Bourdieu, 1986, *Distinction: A Social Critique of the Judgment of Taste*, Richard Nice, trans., Cambridge: Harvard University Press; Pierre Bourdieu, 1990, *The Logic of Practice*, Richard Nice, trans., Stanford: Stanford University Press; Pierre Bourdieu, 1977, *Outline of a Theory of Practice*, Richard Nice, trans., Cambridge: Cambridge University Press.

primary and treat it more or less dichotomously—someone is either an owner of the means of production or not—Bourdieu insists that society be conceived of as a space in which individuals are positioned based on how much of each of the forms of capital they possess. He couples this with an agonistic vision of social relations. Individuals and groups are engaged in struggles to amass as much capital as they can, and this takes two forms. First, they try to leverage themselves into desirable social positions by using the capital already at their disposal—trying to get into the best schools, for example, or land the top job. In the course of doing so, they may attempt to convert one form of capital to another; for example, using their economic resources to send their children to schools where they will forge important social ties, thus converting economic into social capital.[20] Second, because there is an intrinsically subjective dimension to capital, especially cultural capital—certain forms of knowledge or taste are valued only because they have been socially defined as valuable—individuals and groups are engaged in constant struggles over cultural definitions.

While the fight for capital is ubiquitous, a key feature of Bourdieu's approach is the claim that such fights typically occur in delimited arenas of social activity, or fields. At least since Durkheim's *The Division of Labor* (1893)—which gave a sociological spin to phenomena previously understood only through the lens of economics—social theorists have noted that one of the characteristics of modern society is the tendency toward differentiation: as the social whole grows more complex, people become specialists in particular kinds of activities. In laying out the basic tenets of structural-functionalism, Talcott Parsons argued that those who so specialize together compose "social subsystems," consisting of coordinated sets of social roles linked to particular domains of activity.[21] Superficially, as Bourdieu has noted,[22] fields look something like subsystems—they are sites of specialization. But there are crucial differences between Bourdieu and Parsons. For one thing, Bourdieu does not subscribe to a theory of progressive social differentiation. Fields of specialized activity arise, in his view, not out of historical necessity, but out of struggle: out of the efforts of individuals and groups to secure for themselves—and wrest from other contenders—power or jurisdiction over some arena of social life. Second, what is most interesting to Bourdieu about fields is not the function they fulfill for society as a whole—though this is part of his analy-

---

20. Pierre Bourdieu and Jean-Claude Passeron, 1979, *The Inheritors: French Students and Their Relations to Culture*, Richard Nice, trans. Chicago: University of Chicago Press.

21. Parsons, *The Social System*.

22. See Bourdieu and Wacquant, *An Invitation to Reflexive Sociology*.

sis—but rather their relative autonomy from the rest of society. While fields may be shaped by developments in the economy, by the activities of the state, or by other exogenous factors, an essential characteristic is that social action within each follows a distinctive logic. As one element of this logic, in each field a different subspecies of capital becomes consecrated as the goal that participants strive to achieve, the stake over which they fight. Fields also vary in the normatively and tacitly approved means by which actors may legitimately work toward attaining these goals.

Despite their relative autonomy, however, fields stand in a complex relationship to the multidimensional social space that society represents. On the one hand, each field is positioned somewhere in this space, which is to say that each field stands in a determinate relationship to economic, cultural, social, and symbolic capital, and hence to social power. For example, the legal field is most closely linked to economic capital,[23] while the artistic field is primarily bound up with cultural capital.[24] Some fields, therefore, are sites for the exercise of more social power than others—the legal field more than the artistic field, to continue the example. On the other hand, Bourdieu regards each field itself as composing a social hierarchy, a space of positions—some of higher, some of lower value—with each position defined in relation to all the others. In the legal field there will be high- and low-prestige firms; in the artistic field, high- and low-prestige artistic styles. As participants in these fields struggle to achieve success as the field defines it, working to get themselves situated in powerful and high-status positions, they find themselves advantaged or disadvantaged by their position in the larger social hierarchy; by the amount of economic, social, and cultural capital they have at their disposal, which is mostly a function of their social background. There thus exist "relationships of homology" or correspondence between positions in a field and positions in the larger social space, and this positionality is linked to contestation over cultural definitions: differently positioned actors struggle to impose classifications and criteria of evaluation for assessing the worth of objects and persons that will advantage them relative to others.

Bourdieu mobilizes all these concepts in his analysis of the French academic field. The relative autonomy of the field from the centers of social power was not achieved until the latter half of the nineteenth century: "the professor in higher education evolves from being the dignitary ap-

23. Pierre Bourdieu, 1987, "The Force of Law: Toward a Sociology of the Juridical Field," *Hastings Law Journal* 38:814–53.

24. Pierre Bourdieu, 1993, *The Field of Cultural Production: Essays on Art and Literature*, Cambridge: Polity.

pointed by the political authorities and committed to politics, which he was in the first half of the century, to becoming a select and specialized teacher, cut off from the world of social dignitaries by a professional activity incompatible with political life."[25] Given the nature of this evolution, the academic field has come to have an ambivalent relationship to power. It is populated by those who have moderate levels of economic capital and high levels of cultural capital but much less actual power than economic or political elites. Academic intellectuals, Bourdieu says, should therefore be understood as belonging to "a 'dominated fraction' of the dominant class."[26] At the same time, academics have a crucial role to play in the reproduction of social inequality. In what Randall Collins has called "credential societies" like modern France or the United States, elites have to do more than nakedly assert their power through economic or political means if they want to reproduce their social privilege across the generations.[27] In a cultural climate that pays lip service to notions of meritocracy, they have to somehow show that they or their children are better qualified than others to occupy positions of power. One way they seek legitimacy is by amassing prestigious credentials: getting degrees from top schools, along the way picking up tastes and styles of self-presentation that help mark them as elite.[28] It is academics, Bourdieu notes, who confer these credentials and who help teach this cultural knowledge. Bourdieu does not deny that academics may also play a role in social mobility when they teach those from less privileged backgrounds. But at least in the French case, he thinks it is the more sinister role that stands out historically. In fact, he suggests, it was only because academics were willing to play this role that elites have been willing to tolerate the academic field's claims to autonomy. If professors today find themselves free to work on whatever research projects they like or design their own syllabi for courses, it is only because control over the university curriculum has been ceded over the years in a kind of quid pro quo by those who hold economic, political, and religious power.

As a result of this concession, though, the academic field *has* become relatively autonomous. Far from being a space where success is defined in

25. Bourdieu, *Homo Academicus*, 37.

26. See the discussion in David Swartz, 1997, *Culture and Power: The Sociology of Pierre Bourdieu*, Chicago: University of Chicago Press, 223.

27. Randall Collins, 1979, *The Credential Society: An Historical Sociology of Education and Stratification*, New York: Academic Press.

28. Pierre Bourdieu, 1996, *The State Nobility: Elite Schools in the Field of Power*, Lauretta Clough, trans. Oxford: Polity Press.

terms of income, academics pursue "the only officially recognized objectives in the field, that is, scientific success and specifically intellectual prestige."[29] The amassing of intellectual prestige is the aim of what Bourdieu calls "the academic habitus." A habitus, in Bourdieu's vocabulary, is a set of socially learned habits or dispositions.[30] Against theorists who think that most of social life is governed by norms, and in opposition to rational choice theory, Bourdieu argues that the mediating link between individual action and social structure consists of patterns of perception and behavior associated with the social positions people occupy—patterns that become so deeply ingrained that they come to comprise habits of which actors are barely conscious. A habitus, on Bourdieu's account, does not mechanistically determine action. Humans are knowledgeable, improvising creatures. Yet their improvisations always revolve around principles that are part and parcel of the habitus they have learned by virtue of their social position. Thus, while feeling themselves to be free agents, they usually wind up reproducing patterns of taste, aspiration, expression, and behavior that are typical for those who share their position in social space. Just as people come to have distinctive habituses as a result of their social backgrounds, so too do participants in delimited social fields, like the academic field, tend to share a habitus—and it is this sharing, and the practices to which it gives rise, that produces and reproduces the field.[31]

Bourdieu has devoted considerable attention to the academic habitus. On his understanding it has two distinctive characteristics. First, in its mostly highly developed form—which Bourdieu sees as expressed among philosophers—the academic habitus insists on and orients itself around the "disinterested" character of academic pursuits.[32] In the world of academe, theories, arguments, and empirical claims are supposed to be formulated because they represent genuine advances in knowledge, not because the authors needed to find something to argue in order to make it to the next step on the career ladder. Indeed, nothing could be more sacred in the university setting than the pursuit of "veritas," and academic vocabularies of motive always stress higher order ideals and downplay self-interest.

29. Bourdieu, *Homo Academicus*, 99.

30. Bourdieu, *The Logic of Practice*; Bourdieu, *Outline of a Theory of Practice*.

31. See the discussion in William Sewell, Jr., 1992, "A Theory of Structure: Duality, Agency, and Transformation," *American Journal of Sociology* 98:1–29.

32. Bourdieu, *Pascalian Meditations*.

But this is a ruse, for the second characteristic of the academic habitus is the tendency for academics to gravitate toward work that will in fact bring them the most intellectual prestige. Insofar as this is so, the intellectual justifications for their positions can be seen as post hoc rationalizations. The academic field, like all fields, is a social hierarchy: some positions in it are more prestigious than others. And much of academic life, according to Bourdieu, involves academics vying with one another to occupy the most prestigious slots. To do so they must behave strategically. The key to academic success is the possession of intellectual capital, a subspecies of cultural capital. Intellectual capital refers to the knowledge, skills, qualifications, and professional achievements most highly valued by those in one's discipline or area. The aspiring academic who wants to wind up in a prestigious college or university or research institute must amass as much intellectual capital as possible over the course of her or his professional career—attending a prestigious college and graduate program, choosing a well-regarded dissertation advisor, selecting a dissertation topic and approach sure to turn heads, publishing in high-status venues, making a splash with her or his books, and so on. Here, as in other fields, social inequality reproduces itself, for an academic's capacity to do this depends on her or his social background: those from more privileged backgrounds are in a better position to make all the "right" choices. Among these choices are ideational ones that thinkers make at various points in their careers: between competing research topics, paradigms, theories, methodologies, and interpretations, each of which has a certain prestige value and becomes a determining factor in the thinker's future career trajectory. Although Bourdieu distinguishes between the academic field, composed of hierarchically arranged institutional positions, and the intellectual field, consisting of similarly arranged intellectual positions, the whole point of his theory is to explain what he sees as the frequent relationships of homology between the two—relationships linked in turn to larger patterns of social inequality.

While *Homo Academicus* is Bourdieu's most well-known foray into the sociology of intellectual life, *The Political Ontology of Martin Heidegger* (1991) offers the clearest example of his sociology of ideas at work.[33] Like others who have approached Heidegger's thought through a social and historical lens, Bourdieu situates the philosopher's interest in Being in the context of the multiple crises that gripped Germany in the 1920s. Heidegger's connections to and sympathies for Nazism are well known, and Bourdieu does not fail to discuss the factors that precipitated both

33. Bourdieu, *The Political Ontology of Martin Heidegger*.

the rise of the Third Reich and the more general intellectual discourse of cultural crisis to which Heidegger's thought belongs. These factors include the real sense of "possibility"—after an attempted socialist coup in 1919—"of a Bolshevik revolution" in Germany, numerous "political assassinations," Germany's defeat in the First World War, "the occupation of the Ruhr by the French," "the galloping inflation of 1919–24," a growing "obsession with technology and the rationalization of labor," and the depression of 1929.[34] Together these helped create a "distinctive ideological mood" in the country—a mood "haunted by the 'discontents of civilization,' fascinated by war and death, and revolted by technological civilization as well as by all forms of authority."[35] The intellectual sphere, on Bourdieu's account, was also undergoing a structural crisis at the time. There were more aspiring academics than positions available. The humanities were in particularly difficult straits, for the growing prominence of the natural and social sciences drew prestige and resources away from more traditional forms of scholarship. Under these conditions, many intellectuals, including students and those on the fringes of academe, "join[ed] those who lamented the decline of Western culture or civilization."[36] Pessimistic social commentators like Oswald Spengler, author of *Decline of the West,* and Werner Sombart—who, in a revision of Max Weber's famous thesis, argued that Judaism, not Protestantism, lay behind the rise of capitalism and its erosion of traditional cultural values—became popular.

Heidegger's thought was preoccupied with similar themes. His "elaborate system" was constituted of a "series of oppositions": "taciturn silence" and "authenticity" were opposed to "verbosity," "rootedness" was opposed to "curiosity," and "the archaic, rural, pre-industrial simplicity of the peasant" was opposed to the "oversophisticated refinement of urban, Jewish 'modernity.'"[37] In valuing the former of each opposition against the latter, Heidegger participated in the broader "conservative revolution" of the time. But Bourdieu insists that the academic field is relatively autonomous and that it is the structure and composition of this field that ultimately determines the ideational moves academics make. So it was for Heidegger: "There is no doubt that it is in the philosophical field that Heidegger—and this is what makes him a philosopher—has primarily, if not exclusively staked his credit."[38] Although in certain respects a spokesperson for the conservative zeitgeist, Heidegger's academic habitus led him to articulate these themes in such a way that by doing so he would

34. Ibid., 7–8.   36. Ibid., 14.   38. Ibid., 56.
35. Ibid., 8.   37. Ibid., 49–50.

also secure prestige from other philosophers. His "prime objective," in fact, was "the creation of a new philosophical position, defined, fundamentally, in its relation to Kant or more exactly the neo-Kantians."[39] The philosophy of Edmund Husserl was also a target. For Heidegger, "the truth of phenomenology, which phenomenology is unaware of, and the truth of [Kant's] *The Critique of Pure Reason,* which the neo-Kantians have obscured, resides in the fact that 'to know, primitively, is to intuit.' Transcendental subjectivity, in as much as it transcends itself in order to create the possibility of the objectifying encounter, the opening up towards other entities, is nothing but time, whose source is in the imagination, and which thus constitutes the source of Being *qua* Being."[40]

With this argument Heidegger could appropriate Kant's prestige and intellectual authority for himself and his own philosophical project, while also quietly drawing the links between his philosophy and conservative politics: "Granting priority to philosophy over science and to intuition over judgment and concepts ... resounds in direct harmony with the displays of irrationalism that may be observed in the political field."[41] Here it was not a privileged social background that gave Heidegger the intellectual capital he needed. Rather, it was the social distance between his habitus—with its background in "the lesser rural petty bourgeoisie"—and that of the more urbane, intellectually established neo-Kantians that led him to find their approach so distasteful. At the same time, his "rising trajectory" in social space may have given Heidegger a "gift for making connections between problems which previously existed only in fragmentary form."[42] In short, we cannot understand the origins of Heidegger's thought without grasping that "he intended to mount a revolutionary philosophical coup ... an upset of power relations at the heart of the philosophical field."[43] Heidegger—like any other philosopher—was on a quest for intellectual prestige.

* 4 *

Despite their differences, Randall Collins shares with Bourdieu a willingness to explain anything and everything about an intellectual's thought and work by reference to social facts—to develop, in other words, what Collins calls a "sociology of mind." In place of the terminology of field and habitus, however, he relies on the concepts of interaction ritual chains, intellectual networks, and the intellectual attention space.

39. Ibid.   41. Ibid., 67.   43. Ibid., 46.
40. Ibid., 61.   42. Ibid., 47.

One of the recurring concerns of contemporary sociological theory, as noted in the preface, is to bring together "macro" and "micro" levels of analysis—to forge theories capable of explaining large-scale social phenomena and events that piggyback on theories of how social action unfolds at the individual level.[44] Too often in the past theories failed on this score. Thinkers such as Louis Althusser or Claude Lévi-Strauss asserted the primacy of social structures and regarded the individual as little more than an ideological construct or epiphenomenon. Bourdieu's theory is sometimes said to belong to the moment of poststructuralism in part because it tries to transcend this limitation, positing the habitus as the crucial "micro-macro link." But while Bourdieu invests the individual with knowledgeability and the capacity to improvise, the human being as a whole becomes a vanishing point in his analysis. Influenced by, among others, the phenomenologist Maurice Merleau-Ponty, Bourdieu says more about the body than do most social theorists, but the body, like the human being more generally, nevertheless ends up figuring as a tabula rasa in his account, a blank slate on which the dispositions of the habitus are written. It does not represent an independent level of reality, governed by its own laws. The laws that would be important to consider in this regard are those of psychology, so another way this criticism can be formulated is by saying, as critics like Stephen Turner have, that Bourdieu hasn't much of a theory of individual or social psychology.[45]

One advantage of Randall Collins's theory is that it is not subject to this criticism, for it builds directly on social-psychological assumptions. Only one branch of social psychology is important to him, however: the sociology of emotions. Without denying that there is significant historical variation in the way emotions are experienced and understood, Collins follows Jonathan Turner, who has tried to integrate certain findings from evolutionary psychology into sociological theory,[46] in asserting that

44. Alexander, *The Micro-Macro Link*.

45. See Stephen Turner, 1994, *The Social Theory of Practices: Tradition, Tacit Knowledge, and Presuppositions*, Chicago: University of Chicago Press. Although I still disagree with Turner's critique of the notion of social practices, I have come to agree with his objection to Bourdieu's lack of grounding in psychology. See the discussion in Neil Gross, 1998, "Review of *The Social Theory of Practices*," *Theory and Society* 27:117–27. See also his reply in Stephen Turner, 2002, *Brains/Practices/Relativism: Social Theory after Cognitive Science*, Chicago: University of Chicago Press.

46. Jonathan Turner, 2002, *Face to Face: Toward a Sociological Theory of Interpersonal Behavior*, Stanford: Stanford University Press; Jonathan Turner and Jan Stets, 2005, *The Sociology of Emotions*, Cambridge: Cambridge University Press.

there are "four primary emotions"—anger, fear, happiness, and sadness—
that "are found in all societies."[47] Collins takes it as axiomatic that a key
motive in human life is the desire to experience positively valenced emotions, which come in different forms, ranging from happiness to self-
righteous anger. Drawing from Durkheim, Collins claims that a major
source of such emotions is social solidarity. Durkheim argued that solidarity is generated during moments of "collective effervescence," when
like-minded people come together to enact rituals of group identity.[48]
Collins's insight, which he derives by marrying Durkheim's ideas to those
of his mentor, Erving Goffman, is that every face-to-face social encounter
involving two or more people is potentially a moment of collective effervescence.[49] In such encounters people can mobilize symbols held in
common—which Collins also terms "cultural capital"—to stage rituals
that affirm their collective membership in some social group.

Collins uses the term "emotional energy" to describe the emotions
that may result if encounters do end up generating solidarity. This allows him to further specify his claim that people are motivated to experience positively valenced emotions. In fact, he says, their drive is to
experience high levels of emotional energy. He calls the mix of solidarity and other positive feelings emotional energy because in his view
it is energizing—the positive affect someone receives from a solidaristic encounter gives her or him the emotional strength necessary to
get on with the difficult business of social life. If, following Goffman,
we view each encounter as an "interaction ritual," then the life of an
individual can be understood as an "interaction ritual chain" in which
stores of emotional energy—along with a person's symbolic repertoires—are potentially augmented or depleted as she proceeds along
from encounter to encounter. Collins's theory is that such chains—and
hence patterns of social interaciton—are shaped by an invariant human
propensity to be drawn toward encounters that will maximize levels of
emotional energy. Like Bourdieu, Collins recognizes that some forms of
group inclusion are more socially valuable than others. It is not just any
kind of solidarity that is energizing and leaves one feeling good about

---

47. Randall Collins, 2004, *Interaction Ritual Chains*, Princeton: Princeton University
Press, 106.

48. Émile Durkheim [1912] 1995, *The Elementary Forms of Religious Life*, Karen Fields,
trans., New York: Free Press.

49. Erving Goffman, 1959, *The Presentation of Self in Everyday Life*, Garden City: Doubleday.

oneself but particularly that stemming from inclusion in high-status groups. For this reason, the quest for solidarity is a competitive enterprise—people have to fight with others for the privilege of being let into high-status groups, a notion that gives Durkheim a Weberian twist. Just as someone may experience an augmentation of emotional energy if she is allowed into a high-status group, so may she experience a depletion of such energy if she is dominated by a higher-status other or otherwise excluded from an interaction of which she would like to be a part. Whether someone will be included or excluded depends greatly on how much and what kind of cultural capital she has at her disposal. To the extent this is so, "What I call IR [interaction ritual] chains is a model of motivation that pulls and pushes individuals from situation to situation, steered by the market-like patterns of how each participant's stock of social resources—their EE [emotional energy] and their membership symbols (or cultural capital) accumulated in previous IRs—meshes with those of each person they encounter."[50] The unifying aim of Collins's massive corpus of work has been to shed light on various features of human societies—from social inequality to occupations, from the family to geopolitics—by working up from such a microlevel theory.

As early as his 1975 book *Conflict Sociology*, Collins applied the theory of interaction ritual chains to explain the life of the mind. Intellectuals, he suggested—like all social actors—seek to maximize their levels of emotional energy and to get themselves included in the highest-status groups possible. In the intellectual sphere, this means coming up with ideas that will win the attention of other thinkers and secure for oneself a place in the intellectual elite:

> A realistic image of science, in fact, would be an open plain with men scattered throughout it, shouting: "Listen to me! Listen to me!" ... What we [sociologists of ideas] are looking for, then, are explanatory principles stating the conditions under which men can get others' attention. There are a variety of strategies and advantages: being on the field earliest and longest; saying the most original things or those that interest the greatest number of listeners; talking to a selected audience; picking arguments with others who are better known; mentioning other people's names and ideas (since everyone likes to hear himself talked about); opening up new topics for others to follow. The political aspect of this is obvious.[51]

50. Collins, *Interaction Ritual Chains*, xiv.
51. Randall Collins, 1975, *Conflict Sociology: Toward an Explanatory Science*, New York: Academic Press, 480.

The Sociology of Philosophies elaborates on this theoretical model while focusing on a more specific question: What are the sociological causes of philosophical genius? Collins maintains that it is possible to distinguish, with some measure of objectivity, between "great" and "minor" philosophers, where "intellectual greatness is [understood as] one's effect on the course of intellectual history, influencing generations downstream from one's own."[52] Looking back at the history of world philosophy, he finds that greatness is rare. Examining more than two thousand years of Chinese history, for example—the period 535 BC to 1565 AD—he identifies only twenty-five philosophers who, judging by the number of pages devoted to them in contemporary discussions, seem to have exercised significant influence on later generations.[53] On the assumption that a "philosophical generation" lasts roughly thirty years, this averages out to 0.4 great philosophers per generation for the Chinese, or one major philosopher every eighty-four years—in contrast to one major philosopher every forty-three years for the Greeks for the period 600 BC to 600 AD. The question becomes, why do a few philosophers attain greatness when others become only marginally influential, with many more failing to secure any kind of lasting reputation?

To answer this question, Collins invokes the theory of interaction ritual chains. A great philosopher, he argues, is nothing other than an intellectual who has managed to build up a chain of a particular sort. There are, as he sees it, two sociological preconditions for intellectual greatness. First, greatness requires substantial quantities of emotional energy: "'Emotional energy' describes well the surge of creative impulse that comes upon intellectuals or artists when they are doing their best work. It enables them to achieve intense periods of concentration, and charges them with the physical strength to work long periods of time. It is this feeling of creative ideas seeming to flow spontaneously that the Greeks attributed mythologically to visitations of the Muses or *daimones*."[54] Second, to become a great intellectual demands that one have access to high levels of cultural capital—more specifically, to the form of cultural capital that prominent intellectuals value: sophisticated ideas. The would-be great intellectual needs to have mastered the symbols that, when combined in a particular way, will draw other high-status intellectuals toward them,

52. Collins, *The Sociology of Philosophies*, 59.

53. Ibid., 57. The methodological problems with this operationalization of greatness should be obvious.

54. Ibid., 34.

securing the writer's reputation and inclusion in important intellectual circles. Equally important, she or he must have an intuitive feel for which symbols will produce this effect.

But what is it that allows some intellectuals to acquire such mastery, along with the requisite levels of emotional energy? Collins doesn't hesitate to answer that, holding intelligence constant, it's a matter of one's position in intellectual networks. The more one rubs elbows with great thinkers, the better one's own chances of becoming one. This is so for three reasons. First, being associated with high-status thinkers gives one a boost of emotional energy, a feeling that one is really in the thick of intellectual life. Second, high-status thinkers are in possession of the most high-status cultural capital, which they pass on to those around them. And third, because great thinkers often know other great thinkers, those in their immediate social circle are in the best position to successfully guess which combination of symbols will generate the most solidarity within the broader intellectual network.

But if intellectual success is primarily a matter of network position, why don't all intellectuals become involved in high-status networks? And why don't all those who are involved become major thinkers? Collins responds, like Bourdieu, that the intellectual field is a competitive arena. Although "the successful intellectual may welcome followers,"[55] she or he may experience a decrease in emotional energy if those followers fail to become successful themselves or demand too much of her or his time. Aspiring intellectuals thus compete with one another for the limited attention of mentors. More important, Collins claims to have discerned a great regularity in intellectual life: what he terms the "law of small numbers." "The structure of intellectual life," he writes, "is governed by a principle: the number of active schools of thought which reproduce themselves for more than one or two generations in an argumentative community is on the order of three to six."[56] If the number of active schools dips below three, intellectual rivalries—which, on Collins's account, are critical for the generation of emotional energy—will not be intense enough. And if the number exceeds six, the amount of solidarity any one system of symbols will be capable of generating will be so small—parceled out as it will be among competing schools—that no new system will be able to gain a foothold. This explains why not all students of successful intellectuals go on to become successful themselves: "The structure of the intellectual world allows only a limited

55. Ibid., 39.   56. Ibid., 81.

number of positions to receive much attention at any one time. There are only a small number of slots to be filled, and once they are filled up, there are overwhelming pressures against anyone else pressing through to the top ranks."[57]

Therefore, in order to understand why philosophers generate the ideas they do, as well as why only a handful of them go on to achieve long-term reputations, the sociologist of ideas must analyze the "intellectual attention space" at the time they were writing, taking note of the number and type of rivals they faced, of what kinds of symbols were most likely to generate solidarity given the composition of the intellectual world, and of where the philosophers were situated in various networks.[58]

In *The Sociology of Philosophies*, Collins mobilizes this theory to explain world philosophical history. A single example suffices to convey the nature of his approach. Consider his account of the rise of idealism in Germany. In his view, idealism was closely bound up with the institutionalization of the modern university. Prior to the university reforms that swept across Europe in the the nineteenth century, universities were far from being at the center of intellectual life. Instead, intellectuals sought material support through patronage arrangements or, in some cases, were able to make a living through their writing, especially as commercial publishing expanded at the end of the 1700s. Universities remained in the hands of the church, especially in Germany, and academics were accorded relatively low status. The status of German academics was further challenged in the second half of the eighteenth century when there arose a disjunction between the occupational aspirations of many young middle-class Germans and the opportunities available to them. The expansion of the Prussian state bureaucracy led many to seek university degrees as a means to securing civil service employment, but there were more aspirants than positions available, which led to a growing sense within the Sturm und Drang generation that the university system had outlived its utility. This feeling came to a head at the turn of the nineteenth century, and "during

---

57. Ibid., 75.

58. Although I stand by this rendition of Collins's argument, there is an aspect of his approach I am understating: Collins thinks that multigenerational intellectual networks are collective actors and that individual intellectuals end up acting in the interests of the networks to which they belong. While I recognize that intellectuals may see themselves as belonging to particular schools of thought and do their best to advance their schools' interests, I do not share the social-ontological assumptions necessary to understand how a network per se could be an actor.

the crisis period of the Napoleonic wars and their aftermath ... 22 of the 42 German universities were abolished."[59]

It was at this point, according to Collins, that "the status-squeezed"[60] academics sprang into action, pushing through a series of university reforms designed to wrest control over teaching and research away from the church and to vest it in the philosophical faculties; to replace vocational training with a general philosophical education, pitched as the basis for a spiritual renewal of German life; and to solidify the place of a university education in the increasingly important logic of credentialization. The idealists, especially Fichte and Schleiermacher, were advocates of these reforms. In fact, Collins maintains that idealism served as the "ideology" of university reform. Kant's critical philosophy was a "tool capable of cutting off theological and spiritualist speculation."[61] Fichte's attempt to go "beyond Kant in showing how profoundly relational the world is ... [made] Idealism not merely a limiter of the claims of religion ... but a potential conqueror of religious turf."[62] And Hegel's appropriation of Fichte's "formula [of] thesis-antithesis-synthesis"[63] made the "dialectic ... a frame within which Hegel [could] theorize every field of research, and thereby legitimize all of them as food for the philosophical faculty."[64] In this way, "the contents of Idealism supported the claim of intellectual autonomy and dominance by the philosophical faculty."[65]

But Collins does not argue that the founders of idealism developed their positions simply in order to establish the intellectual legitimacy of reform. It is true, he claims, that "Jena and Königsberg ... were traditionalist places ... where an effort to expand opportunities for philosophy students was eagerly awaited."[66] It is also true that "Kant, Herder, Fichte, Schelling, Hegel, and Hölderlin were mostly men from modest social backgrounds, who owed their chances to the expanding public school system"[67] and that "the motivation for [the creation of many of their] ... concepts came from the realistic assessment that the structure was moving in a direction favorable to a self-governing academic elite."[68] But Collins insists, like Bourdieu, that although intellectuals may be "energized by the structural opportunities opening up in the material and political world surrounding them," they always "maneuver within their

---

59. Collins, *The Sociology of Philosophies*, 642.

60. Ibid.	63. Ibid.	65. Ibid., 650.	67. Ibid.
61. Ibid., 653.	64. Ibid., 659.	66. Ibid., 649.	68. Ibid., 650.
62. Ibid., 655.			

own attention space, reshaping the tools at hand from past and current controversies internal to their own sphere."[69] To fully understand the rise of idealism, we must superimpose onto these institutional and political-economic "layers" an understanding of "the clustering of ideas and the social networks among those who produced them."[70]

Take, for example, the contrasting cases of Hegel and Schopenhauer. Both were immersed in the social networks surrounding Fichtean ideal-ism, so at an early stage of their careers both were infused with high levels of emotional energy and in possession of a large repertoire of potentially solidarity-producing symbols. But in the struggle for intellectual atten-tion, Hegel had two decisive advantages. First, Hegel, who "had a good sense for the moods of academic disciplines,"[71] involved himself in the growing "historiographic movement" that constituted "the first wave of the new academic research disciplines."[72] Hegel thus "found his place in the intellectual attention space"[73] by developing Fichtean idealism into a philosophy of history and "thereby opened a wide terrain for the intellec-tuals of the philosophical faculty to exploit."[74] Schopenhauer, by contrast, whose "earliest contacts were with conservative French émigé circles" and whose "origin was in the salon society of the wealthy rather than the Idealist milieu of pastors and tutors struggling to shape academic career paths,"[75] sought to recombine the symbols available to him by portraying history as "an endless round of battles going nowhere [and by seeing] … the Kantian sphere of ideas [as] … a higher ground, not for scientifically comprehending the empirical world, but for transcending its change."[76] This conservative position ran contrary to the reformist impulses of Prus-sian society and cut off precisely those bases of support—namely, the new disciplines of historical and social studies—that Hegel had so effectively captured. Thus "the Fichtean slot which [Hegel] preserved and extended had far more resonances and sources of alliance in the intellectual world than Schopenhauer's iconoclasm and religious pessimism."[77] Second, Hegel had a first-mover advantage. There were several different philo-sophical perspectives in the air at the time Hegel made his appearance, including "Kant's critical philosophy; the psychological-scientific real-ist version of Kant developed by Herbart and others; Fichte's dialectical Idealism; *Naturphilosophie;* aesthetic Idealism; Schleiermacher's Idealist Christianity; and … an increasingly self-consciously orthodox religios-

---

69. Ibid., 622.   72. Ibid., 657.   75. Ibid., 663.
70. Ibid.   73. Ibid., 656.   76. Ibid.
71. Ibid., 659.   74. Ibid., 657.   77. Ibid., 637.

ity."[78] Hegel, who was "located at the center of action in [this] crowded and highly competitive space ... [thus] got virtually the last attention slot available under the law of small numbers."[79] Schopenhauer, who "had very good resources and network connections," had the misfortune of coming "onto them very late" and could therefore, for structural reasons, win little attention for himself. Where Hegel was energized by the intellectual attention he received, Schopenhauer, "up against the law of small numbers," saw his emotional energy levels decline, descended into neurosis, and gave up lecturing at a relatively early age.[80] Both thinkers, in Collins's assessment, ended up doing creative work, but it was Hegel who would be remembered as the truly great philosopher, thanks to his good timing and superior strategizing.

* 5 *

The theoretical frameworks of Bourdieu and Collins have been enormously fruitful for scholars working in the sociology of ideas. Charles Camic has appropriately described *The Sociology of Philosophies* as "by any measure ... the most important contribution ever made to the 'sociology of ideas' ... the architectonic statement [of] the field ... the one work that all sociologists of ideas, novices and veterans alike, hereafter must read."[81] And Bourdieu's concepts of field and habitus have been used to analyze a range of intellectual-historical cases, from the predisciplinary history of sociology[82] to the nineteenth-century French intellectual field.[83]

Helpful though these frameworks have been in explaining a variety of intellectual phenomena, however, both leave something important out of the equation: the fact that intellectuals are bearers of identities whose contents often have little to do with their field positions but which may nevertheless influence the views they come to hold. Rather than arguing this point in the abstract, I want to ground it in a concrete empirical example by considering a specific case to which a similar critique has been

---

78. Ibid., 634.　　79. Ibid., 657.　　80. Ibid., 636.

81. Charles Camic, 2000, "Review Symposium on *the Sociology of Philosophies*," *European Journal of Social Theory* 3:95–102, 96.

82. Johan Heilbron, 1995, *The Rise of Social Theory*, Sheila Gogol, trans., Minneapolis: University of Minnesota Press.

83. John Brooks, 1998, *The Eclectic Legacy: Academic Philosophy and the Human Sciences in Nineteenth-Century France*, Newark: University of Delaware Press; Fritz Ringer, 1992, *Fields of Knowledge: French Academic Culture in Comparative Perspective, 1890–1920*, New York: Cambridge University Press.

applied. The case is Camic's influential account of an important intellectual choice made by the early Parsons; the critique is that advanced by Jeffrey Alexander and Giuseppe Sciortino. Building on Alexander and Sciortino's arguments—though rejecting them as critiques of Camic—I can then show how the critique *does* apply to Bourdieu and Collins and clear a path for my alternative theory of intellectual self-concept.

In an article published in 1992, Camic applied the theoretical insights of the new sociology of ideas to explain a move Parsons made in formulating the basic argument of *The Structure of Social Action* (1937).[84] In that book, Parsons tried to carve out a distinct problematic for the discipline of sociology. The intellectual jurisdiction of economics was well established at the time. It studied "the processes of rational acquisition of scarce means to the actor's ends by production and economic exchange, and of their rational allocation as between alternative uses."[85] Psychology's concerns were also well defined. Psychologists focused on human behavior that is "understandable with reference to the hereditary basis of personality."[86] To answer the question of what constitutes sociology's unique domain, Parsons examined the thought of a variety of European thinkers: Alfred Marshall, Vilfredo Pareto, Émile Durkheim, and Max Weber. What they had in common, he concluded, was an interest in how human action may be shaped not simply by considerations of utility or personality but also by social norms and values. This would be the subject matter of sociology: action guided by social norms, where a norm is taken to mean "a verbal description of [some] concrete course of action ... regarded as desirable, combined with an injunction to make certain future actions conform to this course."[87]

The question Camic asked was why, in formulating this argument, Parsons had "selected" as his "predecessors" Marshall, Pareto, Durkheim, and Weber, rather than any number of other social theorists. The question had been asked by others, given the influence of *The Structure of Social Action* in establishing sociology's classical canon. Gouldner, for example, wondered why Parsons devoted so little space to Marx,[88] while Donald Levine asked why Georg Simmel's sociology—widely influential in the

84. Charles Camic, 1992, "Reputation and Predecessor Selection: Parsons and the Institutionalists," *American Sociological Review* 57:421–445.

85. Talcott Parsons, 1937, *The Structure of Social Action: A Study in Social Theory with Special Reference to a Group of Recent European Writers*, New York: Free Press, 266.

86. Ibid., 769.   87. Ibid., 75.

88. Alvin Gouldner, 1970, *The Coming Crisis of Western Sociology*, New York: Basic Books.

United States in the years before Parsons came out with *The Structure of Social Action*—received few mentions in Parsons's eight-hundred page text.[89] For Camic, however, these questions could be answered easily: Marx and Simmel were excluded because their perspectives were antithetical to Parsons's own and would have complicated and interfered with his argument. But why did he exclude a prominent group of American theorists, associated with the school of institutional economics, when they had advanced a position that was consistent with Parsons's central thesis? "From Veblen onward," Camic noted, "institutionalism opposed utilitarian views of action and the social world, and in the work of the younger members of the movement … it produced an alternative that eliminated assumptions about rational, self-interested action and the atomistic-individualistic nature of society and turned instead … to the social realm of cultural values, ideal ends, moral rules, and institutional controls—paralleling *Structure* in all these respects."[90] So why had Parsons concentrated only on European theorists, ignoring the rich, homegrown alternative that institutionalism represented?

Camic's answer hinged on the notion of credibility as developed by Bruno Latour and Steve Woolgar in their 1979 book, *Laboratory Life*. Latour and Woolgar argued that scientists seek to amass reputations for doing good work not as an end in itself but because such reputations are a critical resource for future scientific investigation.[91] Parsons's major concern at the time he was writing *The Structure of Social Action,* according to Camic, was to establish his credibility as a social scientist, and this within a particular institutional environment. The newly formed Department of Sociology at Harvard had low status in relation to the Department of Economics, and as a consequence Parsons experienced "uncertainty about his prospects for promotion … —he needed the backing of the economists and other local influentials."[92] To secure this backing, Parsons, "like most serious intellectuals … sought to build an argument that was intellectually credible both to informed parties likely to encounter the argument and to himself."[93] It was this interest in establishing credibility that accounted for Parsons's exclusion of the institutionalists, for institutionalism had a bad reputation among many American academics in the 1920s and 1930s.

89. Donald Levine, 1991, "Simmel and Parsons Reconsidered," *American Journal of Sociology* 96:1097–1116.

90. Camic, "Reputation and Predecessor Selection," 430.

91. Bruno Latour and Steve Woolgar, 1979, *Laboratory Life: The Social Construction of Scientific Facts,* Beverly Hills: Sage.

92. Ibid., 435.   93. Ibid.

"Institutional economics was widely perceived as the loser in its battle against orthodox economics,"[94] and this perception was especially pronounced at Harvard, where Parsons's neoclassicist "colleagues from the ... Department of Economics ... conveyed to him the overall contemporary verdict on institutionalism."[95] By contrast, a number of the economists around Parsons thought highly of European scholars such as Pareto and Marshall. While Parsons's decision to exclude the institutionalists and include only the Europeans should not be understood as "an instrumentalist maneuver that set aside content factors in an effort to cater to the opinions of the local crowd,"[96] it was nevertheless the case that in the course of building his argument Parsons "heeded the signs, carefully engaging work of the first order that respected local authorities endorsed."[97] A strategic, though not necessarily conscious, interest in amassing credibility thus played a crucial role in the formation of Parsons's ideas and, through him, in shaping the direction of American sociology in the twentieth century.

Several years after the publication of Camic's piece, Jeffrey Alexander and Giuseppe Sciortino came out with a sharply worded reply: an article, subsequently published as a chapter in Alexander's 1998 book, *Neofunctionalism and After*, entitled "On Choosing One's Intellectual Predecessors: Why Charles Camic Is Wrong about Parsons' Early Work."[98] The article began with the recognition—certainly correct—that in advancing this argument about Parsons, Camic meant to do more than explain a single historical case. His true aim, according to Alexander and Sciortino, was to nudge scholarship on the classical and postclassical theorists in the direction of the sociology of ideas. Not just with this paper, but in other works as well, Camic appeared to be suggesting that theoretical ideas from the past should be explained sociologically rather than merely commented upon or integrated into contemporary theorization. Insofar as this was Camic's larger project, Alexander and Sciortino recognized that that "to confront Camic ... [on Parsons] means much more than confronting a particular interpretation of Parsons' biography and intellectual corpus." It meant confronting a call for "a radical reorientation" of "the historiography of social thought," and—if one's way of understanding the history of sociology is linked to one's vision for what it can and should be in the present and future—"of the meaning and identity of the discipline itself."[99]

---

94. Ibid., 433.   95. Ibid., 434.   96. Ibid., 436.   97. Ibid., 437.

98. Jeffrey Alexander (with Giuseppe Sciortino), 1998, *Neofunctionalism and After*, Malden: Blackwell.

99. Ibid., 117–18.

With the stakes set high, Alexander and Sciortino unleashed a torrent of arguments against Camic, accusing him of misinterpreting specific pieces of historical evidence and of making contradictory and ambiguous claims. But the centerpiece of their criticism consisted of an attack on the theory of social action they saw as informing his analysis. On their view, Camic's claim that reputational factors—specifically Parsons's interest in securing credibility—influenced Parsons's thought represented "an instrumentalist approach to the sociology of knowledge."[100] Where Camic had gone wrong was in offering "an implicitly behaviorist understanding of the manner in which institutional factors affect intellectual creation."[101] His model portrayed Parsons as "a reputational dope, unable to evaluate information according to his own relevance criteria, accepting automatically and unthinkingly the ideas of whoever was most prestigious in his intellectual environment at the time."[102] But on Alexander's understanding, social action is never simply caused by forces in an actor's external environment.[103] While environmental conditions can make certain courses of action more or less likely, the emergence of action is always mediated by actors' interpretations of situations, interpretations that are influenced by the idiosyncratic subjectivities they develop over the course of their lives. These subjectivities also shape actors' intentions, and it is in light of the coming together of situational interpretations and intentions that particular courses of action are embarked upon, with actors always exercising some creativity with respect to the content and form of the action sequence. Alexander and Sciortino claimed that Camic had failed to apply such an understanding to Parsons. Without denying that to a certain extent "reputation ... matter[s]" in intellectual life, they insisted that "its impacts cannot be understood simply from the perspective of exchange"—a perspective they read Camic as having taken—because "it is intellectual actors who do the exchanging, actors who have subjectivities that inform their intentions, intentions that establish criteria for choice."[104] The real reason Parsons excluded the institutionalists, they asserted, was because he had the subjectivity of a Weberian who sought "to differentiate sociology analytically, not empirically, from the other social sciences," whereas institutionalism "had argued against utilitarianism in an empirical way."[105] It was this subjectivity—along

100. Ibid., 118.   101. Ibid., 136.   102. Ibid.

103. See especially the discussion in Jeffrey Alexander, 1988, *Action and Its Environments: Toward a New Synthesis*, New York: Columbia University Press.

104. Alexander and Sciortino, *Neofunctionalism and After*, 137.

105. Ibid., 132.

with Parsons's intention *not* to write "an exhaustive survey of the contemporary literature in European or American social theory"[106]—that accounted for the selective inclusion of certain thinkers in *The Structure of Social Action*. But the historical fact of this selectivity should not, in any event, be explained in causal terms. Rather, it should be seen as an act of will stemming from "Parsons' capacity as an agent, his capacity for judging, interpreting, and processing his experience."[107] More generally, Alexander and Sciortino saw the assumptions underlying this claim to be the appropriate foundations for any glance backward at the history of theory. For only if the classical and postclassical theorists are treated as subjects with intentions can we regard them as contemporary partners in rational conversation and thereby rely on them to help carry out the function the classics are supposed to serve (according to Alexander) in a postpositivist era, namely, that of providing a common stock of symbols with which sociologists can debate and discuss competing theoretical presuppositions.[108]

Alexander and Sciortino are onto something with this critique. But their criticism applies more to Bourdieu and Collins than to Camic. Moreover, their position leads us to the threshold of a more adequate sociological conceptualization of some of the social mechanisms and processes of knowledge making in the social sciences and humanities without actually walking us through the door.

Although Alexander and Sciortino couch the point in theoretical rather than empirical terms, much research by social psychologists and others suggests that social action is typically mediated by actors' own self-understandings. There is, to be sure, considerable disagreement among theorists and researchers in different fields as to how identity and selfhood should be conceptualized and over the exact nature of the processes by which identity shapes action and vice versa. In laying out the theory of intellectual self-concept below, I indicate which of these approaches I see as most promising for the sociology of ideas. But underlying this disagreement is

---

106. Ibid., 131.   107. Ibid., 136.

108. Jeffrey Alexander, 1987, "The Centrality of the Classics," pp. 11–57 in *Social Theory Today*, Anthony Giddens and Jonathan Turner, eds., Stanford: Stanford University Press. Alexander's argument in "Centrality" stands in some tension with the position he takes in his attack on Camic. Arguing in the former against Skinnerian contextualism, he maintains, drawing on various poststructuralist sources, that authorial intentionality is evanescent and impossible to pin down historically, whereas, writing against Camic, he attempts to engage in precisely such a pinning down with respect to Parsons.

concurrence on a fundamental point: meaningful behavior, whatever its ultimate cause, tends to be filtered through—and to some extent influenced by—cognitive and affective processes in which actors' conceptualizations of themselves and their lives figure prominently. This is obviously not to say that actors never act in instrumental ways, working in some circumstances to maximize what they conceive to be their utility. It is to say, however, that instrumental action of this sort, just like every other form of social action, is mediated by interpretations of the action environment colored by actors' past experiences and self-understandings—experiences and self-understandings to which they may and often do give conscious attention. Even in moments of habituality, action rarely bypasses actors' struggles to remain oriented toward lines of their identity.

Alexander and Sciortino are right to object to any approach to the sociology of ideas that does not recognize the importance of this insight. The problem is that their objection does not apply well to Camic, as Camic himself has pointed out.[109] His 1992 article on Parsons did not take a position one way or another on the question of the ultimate action processes through which reputational considerations might have an effect on Parsons's thought. Nor is it difficult to construct a plausible model by which credibility might be influential via the medium of self-understanding.

Where their critique does have real teeth is as applied to Bourdieu and Collins, for both build their models of intellectual choice on top of fully elaborated action-theoretical frameworks that *do* fail to allow much room for identity, understood in terms of cognitive and affective self-understanding. In making this argument, I am not trying to rehearse the critique that Bourdieu and Collins privilege structure over agency. What I mean, following a charge that Alexander levels elsewhere against Bourdieu,[110] is that neither Bourdieu nor Collins has much of a theory of the self. Despite the stated interest of both in connecting up micro- and macrolevels of analysis, there is little sense in either theory of action as being shaped by actors' understandings of themselves as beings with unique histories and identities. Of course, both theorists do recognize that the practices actors engage in reflect the experiences they have had in the past. For Bourdieu this is the very meaning of habitus, and for Collins the same point is expressed with the notion that interaction rituals are linked together in long temporal chains that stretch over the life course. But Bourdieu and

---

109. See Camic's response: Charles Camic, 1996, "Alexander's Antisociology," *Sociological Theory* 14:172–86.

110. Alexander, *Fin De Siècle Social Theory*.

Collins hypothesize not only that actors' pasts shape their present and future primarily through preconscious means—Loïc Wacquant says correctly of Bourdieu that "he builds ... on Maurice Merleau-Ponty's idea of the intrinsic *corporeality of the preobjective contact between subject and world* in order to restore the body as the source of practical intentionality ... grounded in the preobjective level of experience"[111]—but also that variation in this shaping corresponds with the structure of positions in a given social field. In other words, even if individuals have selves in the Bourdieu or Collins models, those selves are posited to be significant for action only if their content reflects the individual's field position. In Bourdieu's theory, one acts in such and such a way because one has the habitus appropriate for one's location in a particular field, at the intersection of multiple fields, or in social space more generally. Likewise, in Collins's framework, the material of selfhood, such as it exists, consists only of the patterns of symbolization one has acquired by virtue of one's positioning in various networks.

But if there is a point lying dormant in the Alexander and Sciortino critique of Camic, it is that if the main action intellectuals engage in—the production of ideas—is shaped in some significant way by their understanding of their own identities, then much of this shaping is not going to revolve around their position in a field, not because field positionality is irrelevant to intellectuals but because there are so many other kinds of self-understandings that are also important to them. Browse the Web pages of faculty members at any university and you will begin to get a sense for the wide variety of self-identifications that academics go by. Most define themselves by such things as their disciplines, research interests, theoretical persuasions, and approaches, but it is not hard to find thinkers who also identify themselves in terms of their political, religious, moral, characterological, and even lifestyle preferences and tastes. The same insight can be gleaned by examining intellectual autobiographies or interviews with intellectuals conducted for the popular press. Of course, it may be the case, following Bourdieu, that each one of the specifically intellectual identities they could give (field of specialization, approach, methodology, etc.) could be mapped onto a hierarchical space of positions that, in total, would compose an intellectual field, such that each identity, or combination of identities, would carry with it a certain prestige and weight. And perhaps one could argue that the other self-understandings intellectuals could have—for example, those to do with religion, politics, and so on—

111. Bourdieu and Wacquant, *An Invitation to Reflexive Sociology,* 20.

also have a specific valence in the field. But it is not primarily in terms of their field positional significance that the latter kinds of identities, at least, have *meaning* for the actors concerned. They see them instead as core aspects of themselves, some involving commitments to ultimate values. The standard of action-theoretical adequacy upon which Alexander and Sciortino want to insist—that any action model must recognize that individuals have selves that form a crucial point of departure for their interpretations of situations, the formation of their intentions, and the eventual emergence of their lines of action—can only be met in the sociology of ideas by a theory that allows that intellectual selfhood *as it is understood by actors themselves* may shape the content of their thought. It is precisely in this regard that the theories of Bourdieu and Collins fall short. Although Michèle Lamont makes the point in somewhat different terms, and risks conflating the empirical content of intellectual selfhood with action-theoretical processes, she raises a similar issue when she criticizes Collins for failing to "make ... room for the diversity of selves found among intellectual creators."[112] Against efforts, like that of Collins, to give "a priori definitions of the self of intellectuals," Lamont "advocate[s] approaching the diversity of their selves as an empirical issue, by using an open-ended and inductive approach. I am not arguing here against Collins's notion of interaction ritual chains as it applies to the field of philosophy. Instead, I am suggesting that it needs to be supplemented by a more fully developed concept of the self that would reflect what I believe to be the diversity of cultural orientation found among culturally central and creative intellectuals."[113]

While the Alexander and Sciortino critique is helpful in leading us to this realization, it—like Lamont's words of warning—stops short of providing a set of theoretical tools that sociologists of ideas could use to analyze the full spectrum of meanings that may form the content of intellectuals' identities and the effect of these on their ideas. The theory of intellectual self-concept attempts to fill this gap.

✳ **6** ✳

Simply stated, the theory of intellectual self-concept holds that intellectuals tell themselves and others stories about who they are qua intellectuals: about their distinctive interests, dispositions, values, capacities, and tastes. These stories are typological—they involve a thinker describing

112. Lamont, "Three Questions for a Big Book," 89.
113. Ibid.

herself or himself as an intellectual of a particular type—and once they become established they may exert a powerful effect on her or his future thought, inclining the thinker to embrace certain ideas over against others. To be sure, a thinker's position in the intellectual field may form an important part of her or his intellectual self-concept, while the actions thinkers undertake to remain true to their self-concepts unfold alongside and in conjunction with other, more strategic action processes. For these reasons, the theory of intellectual self-concept is intended to be complementary to the theories of Bourdieu, Collins, and others. At the same time, the theory suggests that many of the self-concepts that come to be important to thinkers cannot be reduced down to concerns over field position and involve a broader set of self-understandings. These self-understandings, according to the theory, are key variables that help predict which choices thinkers will make in a variety of intellectual matters. Many assumptions are built into this brief statement of the theory, and my explication consists in unpacking them. This chapter discusses the social-psychological foundations of intellectual self-concept. The next chapter develops a framework for understanding where the self-concepts of particular thinkers come from and then applies the theory to Rorty's life and career.

* 7 *

The first assumption concerns the group of social actors to which the theory is intended to apply: intellectuals and, more specifically as the theory is developed in this book, philosophers. What do I mean by these terms? As Camic and I have noted, theories of intelligentsia—of the social origins of intellectuals, their political dispositions, their role in society, their tendency to antagonize the powers that be—formed a staple of the old sociology of knowledge.[114] By intellectuals sociologists of knowledge meant something specific: learned men and women—paradigmatically humanists—who were posited to share certain cognitive, cultural, and even moral characteristics. In the formulation of Edward Shils, intellectuals were those "with an unusual sensitivity to the sacred, an uncommon reflectiveness about the nature of their universe and the rules which govern their society."[115] Definitions of this sort continue to animate work

114. Camic and Gross, "The New Sociology of Ideas." Also see Charles Kurzman and Lynn Owens, 2002, "The Sociology of Intellectuals," *Annual Review of Sociology* 28:63–90.

115. Edward Shils, 1972, *The Intellectuals and the Powers and Other Essays,* Chicago: University of Chicago Press, 3.

done today on such topics as the decline of the "public intellectual" who "speaks truth to power,"[116] but most such work is at odds with the assumptions of the new sociology of ideas. This is so because new sociologists of ideas regard the efforts of knowledge producers to draw distinctions among themselves—between "heroic" public intellectuals and "mere" academics, for instance—as reflecting (among other things) strategies and tactics for amassing prestige and power in the intellectual field and beyond that should be precisely the objects of sociological study. For this reason, new sociologists of ideas prefer to define the term "intellectuals" expansively, to include all those whose occupational roles are centrally wrapped up with the formulation of knowledge claims—that is, claims about the world that are supposed to be judged in large part for their truth-value, however much there may be disagreement about what this means in different fields. In principle, the theory of intellectual self-concept applies to all intellectuals, thus defined. The modern American university is a unique institutional locale, however, imposing distinctive demands on knowledge producers who make their living there, and as I develop the theory of intellectual self-concept in this book, I intend it to help explain the intellectual choices and knowledge-making practices of American academic intellectuals specifically. The theory may have broader application, but I leave it to future research to explore how the intellectual self-concepts of journalists, scientists working in industry, and others, as well as thinkers of historical periods past and in different national contexts, may affect their ideas. In order to avoid constant repetition of the phrase "American academic intellectuals," I use the terms "intellectual" and "thinker" as shorthand for "faculty members in modern American academic settings."

But it is not just any American academics about whom I write here. Although he would eventually leave the discipline, it was in philosophy that Rorty was trained and established his career. Against all efforts to identify philosophy's defining essence—the quality that all philosophical thought shares—I define a philosopher in the modern era simply as someone who, having undergone the requisite training and credentialization and having submitted herself to the academic labor market, winds up in an occupational slot where she is paid to engage in an activity denoted as "doing philosophy," which typically involves some combination of teaching and research. The nature of this activity and its relationship to other forms of intellectual work is nothing more than a matter of collective agreement,

116. As in Edward Said, 1994, *Representations of the Intellectual*, New York: Pantheon.

negotiation, and struggle within particular historical contexts. As every definition of philosophy legitimates and privileges certain thinkers and schools over others, which definition will prevail is always at least potentially a contested matter. The task of the sociology of ideas is not to weigh in on these disputes by defining a discipline in a particular substantive way but to observe and explain them.

One thing that should be noted, however, is that in the second half of the twentieth century, philosophy has not usually been understood as an empirical science—one that gathers data about the world and attempts to formulate explanations for patterns observed therein. New sociologists of ideas no longer feel bound by the assumption that prevailed among an older generation of sociologists of knowledge like Mannheim: that the influence of social factors on thought is greatest in the humanities and the arts, somewhat less in the social sciences, and absent in the natural and mathematical sciences. Yet it must be acknowledged that knowledge-making practices *are* different in fields defined as empirical than in those defined as not. Among other things, in the former, the demand that claims advanced be consistent with the world "out there" as measured by various instruments is more important than in the latter. This has implications for the theory of intellectual self-concept. When I argue that a self-concept led Rorty in a particular philosophical direction, I have to give some indication of how he worked through the logical complexities such a move may have required, coming to view the resulting position as rational and right, but I do not have to show how the self-concept influenced his interpretation of empirical data—a more difficult problem. Because the theory is developed under these scope conditions, it can only be extended to intellectuals working in fields defined as empirical after the theoretical work is done to show how interpretations of empirical reality may impinge upon and be impinged upon by processes relating to the quest for self-concept coherence.

* 8 *

The second building block of the theory of intellectual self-concept is an approach to understanding identity. The most promising approach for the sociology of ideas combines elements from three disparate intellectual traditions.

First, from Anglo-American social psychology, which is much indebted to William James and George Herbert Mead, I borrow the assumption that among the components of selfhood is self-concept, which Morris Rosenberg defines as "the totality of the individual's thoughts and feelings having reference to himself as an object."[117] I take it as axiomatic that all social actors have self-concepts, diffuse and malleable as these may sometimes be, and that it is in light of their self-concepts that they navigate social space. I also assume, borrowing from that strain of social-psychological work on the self that attempts to tie together self-processes and theories of social roles,[118] that people have different self-concepts for different domains of social activity. On these grounds, I theorize that all actors in the intellectual arena have "intellectual self-concepts," which, to borrow Rosenberg's language, can be defined as the totality of a thinker's thoughts and feelings having reference to herself or himself as an intellectual.

What is the nature of these self-thoughts and feelings? Leaving aside until chapter 10 the matter of their experiential origin in the lives of individual thinkers and focusing soley on their internal structure, Rosenberg's approach is again useful: "It is characteristic of the human mind to classify the parts of reality that enter its experience into categories, and this applies to people as well as to other objects.... It is these categories which constitute the individual's social identity—that is, the groups, statuses, or categories to which he is socially recognized as belonging."[119] George McCall and J. L. Simmons put the point in similar terms when they note that "identification, in the generic sense, consists of placing things in terms of systematically related categories.... Once one has properly placed some thing in such a system of categories, he knows how to act toward it from the perspective of the underlying plan of action."[120] Accordingly, I argue that intellectual self-concepts serve to position thinkers in cultural taxonomies. I have already suggested that intellectual self-concepts are typological—they involve a thinker characterizing herself as an intellectual of a certain type—and insofar as this is so, they indicate where thinkers see themselves as located in terms of ideas, values, character, capacities, and so forth, in relation to other intellectuals in some more or less shared classificatory matrix.

Yet this claim still does not tell us much about the kind of thing an intellectual self-concept is. Here I would integrate a second strand of

117. Morris Rosenberg, 1979, *Conceiving the Self,* New York: Basic Books, ix.

118. George McCall and J. L. Simmons, 1966, *Identities and Interactions,* New York: Free Press; Sheldon Stryker, 1980, *Symbolic Interactionism: A Social Structural Version,* Menlo Park: Benjamin/Cummings Publishing Co.

119. Rosenberg, *Conceiving the Self,* 9–10. On this point also see Richard Jenkins, 2004, *Social Identity,* London: Routledge.

120. McCall and Simmons, *Identities and Interactions.*

theory: that which sees much of identity to be a matter of narrative. Influential contributions in this regard have been made by, among others, Jerome Bruner, James Holstein and Jaber Gubrium, George Rosenwald and Richard Ochberg, and Margaret Somers.[121] From vantage points as different as cognitive psychology, psychohistory, and symbolic interactionism, theorists have argued that "personal stories are not merely a way of telling someone (or oneself) about one's own life; they are the means by which identities may be fashioned."[122] On this understanding, self-concepts do not consist merely of static sets of categories. Rather, human beings tell themselves and others stories about their own lives, and these stories, which have an irreducibly narratological dimension, serve to organize their experiences of themselves.

To be sure, psychologists like Ulric Neisser have insisted that self-concepts properly so-called should be distinguished from life narratives; the former pertain to the self as presently experienced, whereas life stories "establish a version of the self-concept that transcends the present moment: a *temporally extended* self."[123] According to Neisser's reading of the evidence, the capacity to understand oneself as a self usually emerges in infants by the age of one, where life narratives, "along with the skills of producing them, are acquired only in the third year or later."[124] This distinction may be important to psychologists interested in developmental processes, but for sociologists of ideas it is a moot point, for we are typi-

121. Jerome Bruner, 1990, *Acts of Meaning*, Cambridge: Harvard University Press; James Holstein and Jaber Gubrium, 2000, *The Self We Live By: Narrative Identity in a Postmodern World*, New York: Oxford University Press; George Rosenwald and Richard Ochberg, eds., 1992, *Storied Lives: The Cultural Politics of Self-Understanding*, New Haven: Yale University Press; William Sewell, Jr., 1992, "Introduction: Narratives and Social Identities," *Social Science History* 16:479–88 (and see the pieces that follow); Margaret Somers, 1994, "Narrative and the Constitution of Identity: A Relational and Network Approach," *Theory and Society* 23:605–49. A similar position on narrative identity is advanced in Christian Smith, 2003, *Moral, Believing Animals: Human Personhood and Culture*, New York: Oxford University Press.

122. George Rosenwald and Richard Ochberg, 1992, "Introduction: Life Stories, Cultural Politics, and Self-Understanding," pp. 1–18 in *Storied Lives: The Cultural Politics of Self-Understanding*, George Rosenwald and Richard Ochberg, eds., New Haven: Yale University Press, 1.

123. Ulrich Neisser, 1993, "The Self Perceived," pp. 3–21 in *The Perceived Self: Ecological and Interpersonal Sources of Self-Knowledge*, Ulric Neisser, ed., Cambridge: Cambridge University Press, 5.

124. Ibid., 5.

cally interested in social actors in adolescence and beyond for whom a present self-concept must always stand in some kind of relationship to life narratives, simultaneously deriving from and feeding back into them. So I will elide the distinction and refine the definition of intellectual self-concept as follows: it refers to the stories that intellectuals tell themselves and others about who they are as intellectuals, stories that weave together the totality of their reflexive thoughts and feelings. In asserting, as I will be doing momentarily, the causal significance of these stories, I would not deny that thinkers may be called upon to produce narratives of intellectual selfhood on particular occasions: in conversations with colleagues, in autobiographical statements, at moments when they have to frame their own contributions, during job interviews, giving speeches, and so on. Each of these occasions undoubtedly imposes certain formal requirements on the narratives, lending them an artificiality that might seem to suggest their irrelevance for everyday life. But I want to suggest that the narratives generated in such moments—by the thinker and/or through processes of "reflected appraisal" whereby significant others help to clarify for her who she "really is"[125]—do in fact carry over into everyday life, not least because they usually reflect how intellectuals latently think of themselves, and thereby gain the potential to influence routine knowledge-making practices.

But how does this influence occur? It is typical for social-psychological theories of self-concept to posit a motive for action. Beyond suggesting that actors are motivated to protect the integrity of their self-concepts against efforts to "spoil" their identities and lower their self-esteem, social psychologists argue that there is a "motive to act in accordance with the self-concept and to maintain it intact in the face of potentially challenging evidence. People behave in a fashion consistent with the pictures they hold of themselves and interpret any experience contradictory to this self-picture as a threat."[126] Reviewing just some of the many empirical studies of self-concept, David Demo reports that "people selectively interact with others who see them as they see themselves . . ., actively choose roles . . . and social environments . . . that are consistent with their self-conceptions . . ., selectively attend to self-confirmatory feedback . . ., and

125. For a useful appropriation of the reflected appraisals idea—central to symbolic interactionism—see Ross Matsueda, 1992, "Reflected Appraisals, Parental Labels, and Delinquency: Specifying a Symbolic Interactionist Theory," *American Journal of Sociology* 97:1577–1611.

126. Rosenberg, *Conceiving the Self,* 57.

reinterpret, devalue, or dismiss discrepant feedback."[127] Yet while there is general agreement among social psychologists that this motive is important, there remains disagreement as to the mechanisms through which it exerts its effects. Those working in the tradition of "processual symbolic interactionism" have generally followed its founder, Herbert Blumer, in suggesting that there is considerable variation in self-concept from situation to situation and Mead in proposing that social action unfolds as a negotiation between the history of the "me" and the novelty of the "I," a negotiation whose outcome can never be known in advance.[128] "Structural interactionists," by contrast, have developed more mechanistic models, such as Peter Burke's "identity control system" approach, which likens human beings to thermostats: with their identities "set" in certain ways, actors will evaluate reflected appraisals they receive, experience distress if those reflections do not match their pregiven identity settings, and adjust their behavior so as to bring about self-concept congruence.[129]

The problem with these approaches, from the standpoint of the sociology of ideas, is that neither is prepared to shed much light on the relationship between self-concept and intellectual production. Processual symbolic interactionists, for their part, would resist the urge to explain why, in causal terms, intellectual products end up taking one form rather than another. For them indeterminacy is part of reality, and their interest would be in the fluid, idiosyncratic, and always unpredictable processes through which self-conceptions and the content of thought come to be mutually adjusted. As for the cybernetic models of structuralists like Burke, they would be hard-pressed to accommodate the complexity of action involving the manipulation of thousands of symbols into coherent and credible texts.

As an alternative to these approaches, I turn to a third strand of theory: the ego psychology of Erik Erikson. Erikson's work was much criticized by antihumanist psychologists and others in the post-1968 period,[130] but to my mind it remains a valuable and underutilized theoretical resource when stripped of some of its more hagiographic tendencies. On Erikson's

127. David Demo, 1992, "The Self-Concept over Time: Research Issues and Directions," *Annual Review of Sociology* 18:303–26.

128. For example, see the discussion in Kenneth Plummer, 1991, *Symbolic Interactionism*, Aldershot: E. Elgar.

129. Peter Burke, 1991, "Identity Processes and Social Stress," *American Sociological Review* 56:836–49; Peter Burke, 1997, "An Identity Model for Network Exchange," *American Sociological Review* 62:134–50.

130. For discussion of some of the relevant issues, see Kenneth Gergen, 2000, *The Saturated Self: Dilemmas of Identity in Contemporary Life*, New York: Basic Books.

model, all individuals, especially during the course of maturation, seek to develop identity schemes that tie together the disparate identity elements they have been endowed with by virtue of their psychosocial experience. Most people, he suggests, make do for this purpose with prefabricated "ideological systems," each "a coherent body of shared images, ideas, and ideals which, whether based on a formulated dogma, an implicit *Weltanschauung*, a highly structured world image, a political creed, or, indeed, a scientific creed, or a 'way of life,' provides for the participants a coherent, if systematically simplified, over-all orientation in space and time, in means and ends."[131] Erikson draws a contrast, however, between those who rely on such systems and "creative individuals" who reject them and can resolve identity crises "only by offering to their contemporaries a new model of resolution such as that expressed in works of art or in original deeds, and who furthermore are eager to tell us all about it in diaries, letters, and self-representations."[132] The tendency in Erikson's work is to see individuals of the latter sort as laboring under intense psychological pressures. He notes in *Young Man Luther* that "I could not conceive of a young great man in the years before he becomes a great young man without assuming that inwardly he harbors a quite inarticulate stubbornness, a secret furious inviolacy, a gathering of impressions for eventual use within some as yet dormant new configuration of thought."[133] A key purpose served by the intellectual products of "creative individuals," therefore, is to bring together in what they see as an original and seamless way the different and otherwise hard to reconcile elements of their identities, reducing these psychic tensions. In his psychohistorical studies, Erikson explored this process as it played out in the lives of such figures as Luther, William James, and George Bernard Shaw, focusing especially on adolescence, understood as the crucial period for identity formation and crisis.

Erikson's distinction between those who are creative in the development of their identity schemes and those who are not does not withstand sociological scrutiny. Reception studies in the sociology of culture,[134]

131. Erik Erikson, 1968, *Identity, Youth, and Crisis*, New York: W. W. Norton, 189–90.

132. Ibid., 134.

133. Erik Erikson, 1958, *Young Man Luther: A Study in Psychoanalysis and History*, New York: Norton.

134. The classic is Janice Radway, 1984, *Reading the Romance: Women, Patriarchy, and Popular Literature*, Chapel Hill: University of North Carolina Press. For a discussion of recent developments in thinking about cultural reception and related matters, see Jason Kaufman, 2004, "Endogenous Explanation in the Sociology of Culture," *Annual Review of Sociology* 30:335–57.

along with the "culture in action" approach that dominates the sub-field,[135] teach us to be wary of the notion that cultural products are ever appropriated by anyone in a purely mimetic fashion. At the same time, the sociology of ideas counsels against attributing intellectual creativity and greatness primarily to inborn psychological features. Despite these problems, the essential elements of Erikson's theory should be retained, for they provide a rich model for thinking about how narratives of intellectual self-concept may influence the content of an intellectual's work. Without downplaying the importance of a more strictly Eriksonian phasic model centered on the alternation between periods of identity crisis and resolution, I suggest that intellectuals are motivated to develop or attach themselves to ideas that, while counting as important contributions to their fields, also function to give expression to and tie together in a satisfying manner what they understand to be the core features of their intellectual self-concepts.[136] It is not the desire for simple self-concept consistency that forms the basis for this motivation, but the overall drive for ego coherence in an institutional and cultural environment where one's intellectual output is seen as an essential feature of oneself. This drive is satisfied not through some mechanistic process by which action is brought into line with pregiven identities but in complex moments of intellectual synthesis in which identity elements, knowledge of one's field, and intellectual vision and intention fuse. While the precise form taken by the resulting work can never be fully predicted in advance, it is likely to be significantly influenced by the elements that composed the thinker's narrative of selfhood at the time. Some intellectuals will feel compelled to be more original than others as they engage in this act of synthesis, and some will have a greater capacity and/or institutional latitude for doing so, but the same model applies to all.

The theory of intellectual self-concept can thus be restated as follows: *Thinkers tell stories to themselves and others about who they are as intellectuals. They are then strongly motivated to do intellectual work that will, inter alia, help to express and bring together the disparate elements of these stories. Everything else being equal, they will gravitate toward ideas that make this kind of synthesis possible.* This is not to deny that intellectual self-concepts can and often

---

135. See Swidler, *Talk of Love*.

136. For a similar focus on identity coherence as a motivation for social action, see Debra Friedman and Doug McAdam, 1992, "Collective Identity and Activism: Networks, Choices, and the Life of a Social Movement," pp. 156–73 in *Frontiers in Social Movement Theory*, Aldon Morris and Carol Mueller, eds., New Haven: Yale University Press, 169.

do change over time, sometimes *in response* to the development of one's own ideas, as one gains clarity into one's intellectual identity by putting thoughts down on paper and seeing where they lead. The relationship between self-concept and intellectual choice can thus be bidirectional. This is also the case because intellectual self-concept categories sometimes refer to prior ideational commitments, such as being a philosopher of mind working in the tradition of materialism. Having defined herself as a philosopher working in this tradition, a thinker may find herself motivated—and not simply for reasons of intellectual capital investment—to make further intellectual choices that are integrative with regard to the self-definition. But that intellectual self-concepts may change over time or refer back to prior intellectual choices does not change the fact that at the moment when an intellectual project gets formulated, a self-concept of a broader nature may have enough stability to shunt thought in one direction rather than another.

∗ **9** ∗

While the theory of intellectual self-concept is an identity-based model of intellectual production, it is important to emphasize that the theory departs in significant respects from so-called standpoint theories in the sociology of knowledge. Originating in the work of Marx and Mannheim, such theories, as developed by feminist scholars such as Dorothy Smith and Patricia Hill Collins, assert that thinkers who share a set of identity attributes tend to hold common worldviews, owing both to their social interests and common life experiences.[137] Such worldviews, these theorists insist, incline thinkers in particular intellectual directions. Beyond this, standpoint theorists claim that such commonalities of perspective grant to those who are endowed with them "epistemic privilege" with respect to the analysis of certain topics. The double subjugation of women of color, for example, is theorized to give scholars who have these identity attributes special access to the phenomenology of subjugation.

Leaving aside epistemic concerns, standpoint theory is problematic for at least two reasons. First, while it may be the case that thinkers who are categorized by society in a particular fashion—as women of color, for example—have narratives of intellectual self-concept that put those cat-

137. Patricia Hill Collins, 1990, *Black Feminist Thought: Knowledge, Consciousness, and the Politics of Empowerment*, Boston: Unwin Hyman; Dorothy Smith, 1990, *The Conceptual Practices of Power: A Feminist Sociology of Knowledge*, Boston: Northeastern University Press.

egorical elements front and center, this is by no means inevitable; nor is it inevitable that such thinkers will all interpret the meaning and implications of those categorical elements in the same way. Standpoint theorists are often charged with the sin of essentialism, and rightly so. For only if those categorical elements are thought of as coexisting among the many different elements of which a thinker's intellectual self-concept may be composed—and as thereby providing a polysemous springboard for intellectual synthesis rather than as generating a worldview that is deterministic with respect to the content of thought—can standpoint theory avoid the same charge of reductionism that has been leveled against Bourdieu and Collins.[138] Second, even if—as thus reformulated—standpoint theory offers some leverage in explaining the intellectual choices of certain thinkers, it will not suffice as a general theory of knowledge production. This is so because it leaves unexplained the intellectual diversity exhibited by those who share a standpoint of relative privilege. Academic philosophy in the United States, for instance, is dominated by white men—in 2001, 73 percent of philosophy faculty members in the United States were male, and 90 percent of U.S. philosophers identified themselves as white[139]—therefore attributing to them the uniform standpoint of being mouthpieces for societal "relations of ruling" does nothing to explain the diversity of intellectual positions they occupy. Identity elements do shape the content of an intellectual's thought, but the range of these elements is much wider than the range of large-scale social groupings like race, class, gender, and sexual orientation.

* 10 *

A final issue must be addressed before bringing the chapter to a close. How should sociologists of ideas operationalize the notion of intellectual self-concept? At least when it comes to historical cases, no technical methodological procedure is required. Self-concepts, by definition, are available to what Anthony Giddens calls "discursive consciousness"[140]— they exist in intellectuals' talk about themselves. To find them, one must find instances of such talk—in autobiographical statements, essays, interviews, correspondence, and so on—and then look to see how think-

138. On this point see Somers, "Narrative and the Constitution of Identity."

139. See the report on the APA's 2002 member survey, available at http://www.apa.udel.edu/apa/profession/IUSurvey/FacultyReport.pdf, accessed February 9, 2007.

140. Anthony Giddens, 1984, *The Constitution of Society: Outline of the Theory of Structuration*, Berkeley: University of California Press.

ers' stories serve to locate them in cultural taxonomies. To be sure, we must expect variation across thinkers, over the intellectual life course, and even from situation to situation in the degree to which these stories present themselves as coherent, well developed, and highly specific with respect to taxonomic location. Intellectual self-concepts may also be differently expressed in different forms of self-talk, some of which are not available to public scrutiny. A thinker's private musing about his own qualities and capacities, carried out in the "internal conversation" of the mind[141] or expressed privately to confidants or to a therapist, may or may not make its way into correspondence or diary entries and may be different from the stories of self with which the thinker is willing to go on record. Given these complexities, analysts should concentrate on those intellectual self-concepts that are the least evanescent: those that turn up again and again in different forms of self-talk, that have a high degree of coherence, and that appear to have been genuinely salient.

I noted above that self-identity is narratological in nature, and to the extent this is so, analysts might gain further traction on intellectual self-concept by considering not simply the categories of intellectual personhood around which stories of the self revolve, but also their specifically narrative dimensions—their plot structure and sequence, for example, or the vocabularies of motive from which they draw. Because of space constraints, I do not make use of this analytic strategy in chapter 10, but it is rich with possibility, for there may be systematic variation across national, historical, and disciplinary contexts in the typical narrative devices intellectuals use to tell their own stories, and such variation may be related to outcomes of interest to the sociologist of ideas.

Beyond the demand that analysts focus on self-concepts that have a high degree of coherence and stability, the one firm requirement for operationalizing intellectual self-concept is that it be captured in such a way that the explanation for intellectual choice it is intended to provide is not tautological. To this end, one should never infer an intellectual self-concept from an intellectual choice that it is being called upon to explain. For example, one would not want to infer from an intellectual's affiliation with the Marxist tradition that he views himself as a thinker sympathetic to the interests of the working class—if that self-conception is going to be used to explain his commitment to Marxism. The requirement for

---

141. See Margaret Archer, 2003, *Structure, Agency, and the Internal Conversation*, Cambridge: Cambridge University Press; Norbert Wiley, 1994, *The Semiotic Self*, Chicago: University of Chicago Press.

nontautology is one I heed in chapter 10, finding independent evidence of Rorty's intellectual self-concepts in correspondence, in autobiographical moments in essays, and elsewhere.

The core elements of the theory of intellectual self-concept have now been laid out. But what would it look like to apply the theory in a concrete empirical case, where the quest for self-concept coherence plays out at the same time that intellectuals must engage in the strategic action necessary to mount successful academic careers, and where thinkers must navigate institutional settings and disciplinary status structures that have been shaped and reshaped by larger social, institutional, and cultural forces? Answering this question requires that another theoretical concern be taken up: the origin of intellectual self-concepts in thinkers' social experiences over the life course.

TEN

Rorty Reexamined

* 1 *

In the last chapter I made a theoretical case for building into the sociology of ideas a richer understanding of intellectual selfhood and its role in shaping the knowledge claims of intellectuals than is provided by the frameworks of Bourdieu or Collins. But what would it look like to apply the theory of intellectual self-concept to a concrete empirical case? This chapter reexamines key junctures in Rorty's intellectual career, this time through the lens of the sociology of ideas. It considers Rorty's choice of masters thesis topic, his movement into analytic philosophy in the 1960s, and his break with the analytic paradigm and embrace of a pragmatist identity in the 1970s. The theories of Bourdieu and Collins shed light on the decisions Rorty made at several of these junctures. For example, Bourdieu's focus on the reproduction of social and cultural capital helps explain Rorty's early educational trajectory, while the emphasis of both theorists on the strategic dimensions of intellectual life helps make sense of Rorty's turn toward analytic philosophy after graduate school. In other instances, however, the theories are underdeterminative with respect to explaining Rorty's actions. Only if nonstrategic processes relating to the quest for intellectual self-concept coherence are also considered can Rorty's intellectual choices be more fully explained.

* 2 *

Before undertaking such an analysis, however, some additional theoretical work is required. The theory of intellectual self-concept as laid out in chapter 9 was essentially a social-psychological theory abstracted away from the larger institutional context in which academic careers unfold. But where do the intellectual self-concepts of academicians come from?

My thinking on this matter synthesizes contributions from different lines of social-scientific investigation. The first is research on the life course.[1] The proper way to conceive of human societies, many life course researchers suggest, is in terms of population flows. Each year a certain number of persons are added to the population, whether through birth or migration, and to understand their experiences as they move through their lives and across social and physical space is to understand much about the society they inhabit. Many life course researchers focus on social roles and conceive of the life course as involving a series of role transitions: from college student to full-time participant in the paid labor force, for example.

From this line of research, I borrow the idea that a fruitful way to analyze an intellectual's life is as a series of movements, not necessarily from one role to another, but across institutions and organizations—a sequence of institutional affiliations. Especially relevant for the theory of intellectual self-concept are not general institutional forms—the nineteenth-century family, for example, or the mid-twentieth-century research university—but particular instantiations of them, such as the Smith family or the Harvard University philosophy department. Institutions in this more localized sense range in scale from dyads to formal organizations, and the kinds of affiliations thinkers can have with them vary widely. A future intellectual will be raised in a particular family, may be involved with a particular religious congregation as a child, attend a particular primary and secondary school, go to a particular college or university, enter into a particular graduate program, get an academic position in a particular department, and so on. The nature and timing of this sequence depends on how the typical life course in that intellectual's society—for persons with his socioeconomic background—is structured, and which institutions he will come to be associated with is a function largely of how his attributes line up with their criteria for membership given operative matching processes. Some attributes are particularistic and tie persons to institutions automatically. Children born to a particular set of parents, to give an obvious example, meet the key criterion for entry into the institution of their family. Other attributes—assessed levels of intelligence,

1. See, for example, Janet Giele and Glen Elder, eds., 1998, *Methods of Life Course Research: Qualitative and Quantitative Approaches,* Thousand Oaks: Sage; Erin Phelps, Frank Furstenberg, and Anne Colby, eds., 2002, *Looking at Lives: American Longitudinal Studies of the Twentieth Century,* New York: Russell Sage.

for instance, or the quality of one's academic work—are more universalistic and are relevant for entry into institutions that employ more open, essentially merit-based selection processes. Within the constraints of the opportunities thinkers have to enter institutions, they often—though by no means always—have some capacity to choose among them: to go to one college rather than another, say, though predisposing cultural factors may render such choices more apparent than real.

Fundamental to the theory of intellectual self-concept is the idea that as thinkers move across the life course and are affiliated with different institutions, they may pick up from some of them identity elements that they integrate into their self-concept narratives. The notion that institutions have internal cultures is central to work in the sociology of organizations, among other subfields of the discipline,[2] but my take on it borrows most heavily from the Durkheimian tradition, which suggests that in every social group, regardless of scale, certain ideas, symbols, objects, and practices will be culturally coded as sacred and worthy of veneration, while others will be regarded as profane and deserving of scorn.[3] These codings help to indicate the cultural boundaries of the group, the lines that distinguish insiders from outsiders,[4] and they arise through complex processes of structuration, including those by which groups seek to carve out niches for themselves on the social landscape. Among the things that get marked in this way by institutions are categories of personhood.[5] Within a family of Evangelical Christians, for example, being a Republican, being pro-life, being heterosexual, being a Texan (say), and being a Dallas Cowboys fan may all be coded as more or less sacred identity elements.

What determines whether an identity element coded as sacred within an institutional setting will come to be integrated into the self-concept

2. See Joanne Martin, 2002, *Organizational Culture: Mapping the Terrain*, Thousand Oaks: Sage.

3. See, for example, Jeffrey Alexander, 2003, *The Meanings of Social Life: A Cultural Sociology*, New York: Oxford University Press.

4. Michèle Lamont and Marcel Fournier, eds., 1992, *Cultivating Differences: Symbolic Boundaries and the Making of Inequality*, Chicago: University of Chicago Press.

5 This argument is in some ways similar to the position developed by Charles Tilly with regard to inequality. (See Charles Tilly, 1998, *Durable Inequality*, Berkeley: University of California Press.) Tilly argues that inequality always involves categorical distinctions drawn among human beings and that organizations play key roles in perpetuating inequality by tying the work that they do, and the allocation of rewards and resources, to the possession of organizationally favored categories—either those that have meaning exclusively within the organization or those that originate outside it and have meaning across organizational contexts. The major difference between my approach and Tilly's—aside from his focus on

narrative of an intellectual or future intellectual who passes through it? Humans, as Harold Garfinkel noted, are not "cultural dopes,"[6] and neither are they identity sponges. Indeed, as suggested above, some of the institutional affiliations a thinker may come to have are those he consciously chooses—albeit from a constrained choice set—so that in some instances identity may determine institutional affiliation rather than the other way around. What's more, if an intellectual were to find himself in an institution that celebrated and attempted to foist on him an identity he found noxious, he could make an attempt to exit, do his best to ignore the views of those around him, or even try to change the institution. These possibilities aside, research on religious conversions, recruitment into social movements, and other group affiliation phenomena suggest there are six key factors that help predict whether the transfer of an identity from an institution to a person who comes to be affiliated with it will occur.[7] First, some institutions can engender identities by sanctioning or threatening to sanction affiliates who do not take them on. Sanctioning is not always successful at producing genuine conversions and indeed suggests an emotional climate around the institution at odds with the second predictive factor considered below: positive affect. But threats of force or exclusion from some moral community or the withholding of some valued social good can certainly incentivize the adoption of an institution's preferred identities. The second predictive factor is the presence of strong affective bonds among those who inhabit the institution.[8] More specifically, institutions that are able to cultivate positive affect between new and established members—whatever specific form this may take—are better able to break down barriers to identity change and to

---

inequality and the greater analytic weight he places on transactions and relations than on individual decision making—is that the kinds of identities I focus on are those that are in some sense optional: positionings in social, cultural, and intellectual space that all thinkers in a field could in principle take on and switch between. In contrast, most of the categories in Tilly's account are those into which people are relegated by virtue of their physiological characteristics or social background—such as gender or race—and which may be reinforced and reified by organizations but are not acquired as identities within them.

6. Harold Garfinkel, 1967, *Studies in Ethnomethodology*, Englewood Cliffs: Prentice-Hall.

7. See Sheldon Stryker, Timothy Owens, and Robert White, eds., 2000, *Self, Identity, and Social Movements*, Minneapolis: University of Minnesota Press; David Snow and Richard Machalek, 1984, "The Sociology of Conversion," *Annual Review of Sociology* 10:167–90.

8. See Lynn Lofland and Rodney Stark, 1965, "Becoming a World-Saver: A Theory of Religious Conversion," *American Sociological Review* 30:862–75.

encourage identity emulation, not least through collectively enacted attributions of charisma to key institutional figures.[9] Such affect and the identification it promotes may be enhanced by an institution's isolation from the outside world, which minimizes the pull of countervailing social ties.[10] A third factor is ideological cohesiveness. The more seamless and better integrated the elements of an institution's culture—and the more all its established members subscribe to that culture—the greater its capacity to convert initiates to its perspective, as its ability to convincingly redescribe everything through the lenses of its worldview and to rebut objections comes to seem an indicator of its strength. Fourth, institutions have more power to stamp people with their identities when those people are young. Sociologists have long observed that much cultural change takes the form of cohort replacement, as new generations exposed to radical ideas in adolescence and young adulthood make their way through the structures of society.[11] The young exhibit greater cognitive flexibility than the old, not just for physiological reasons, but also because they lack established cognitive habits for getting by in the world, and are motivated to attach themselves to new worldviews that come along and promise them cognitive control over their environments.[12] For the same reason, those who are older but who may be experiencing a crisis in terms of how well their established habits and routines are working for them—a crisis that may be reflexively understood as a turning point[13]—may prove susceptible to new identities. Fifth, drawing on Christian Smith's "subcultural identity" model of the growth of religious denominations—though focusing less than he does on group dynamics—I want to suggest that the identities treated as sacred by institutions are especially likely to be absorbed if those identities provide a way for

9. See Charles Thorpe and Steven Shapin, 2000, "Who Was J. Robert Oppenheimer? Charisma and Complex Organization," *Social Studies of Science* 30:545–90.

10. The classic study on this point was Erving Goffman's essay on total institutions. See Erving Goffman, 1961, *Asylums: Essays on the Social Situation of Mental Patients and Other Inmates,* Garden City: Anchor Books.

11. For a typical example of such an analysis, see Judith Treas, 2002, "How Cohorts, Education, and Ideology Shaped a New Sexual Revolution on American Attitudes toward Nonmarital Sex, 1972–1998," *Sociological Perspectives* 45:267–83.

12. In the language of Ann Swidler, the young live "unsettled lives." See her *Talk of Love.*

13. On turning points in the life course, see Robert Sampson and John Laub, 1993, *Crime in the Making: Pathways and Turning Points through Life,* Cambridge: Harvard University Press.

people to feel morally superior to others.[14] The anthropological drive to distinguish oneself from others in moral terms may feed into larger processes of social stratification and may be cited as ideological justification for inequality, but it is not merely a function of such processes and lends a natural advantage to institutions, such as conservative Protestant churches in the context of modern American religious pluralism, that can provide meaningful moral distinctions to those who affiliate themselves with them. Finally, institutions are in a stronger position to convert people to the identities they consider sacred if those identities are not radically incommensurate with those previously incorporated into initiates' self-concept narratives or if cultural resources are available that allow people to tell coherent stories of their transition from one identity to the other. By no means does the presence of these six factors, separately or in combination, guarantee that an identity sacralized by an institution will be stably incorporated into the self-concept narrative of a thinker or future thinker who passes through it. But I theorize that these factors make such an incorporation more likely.

To take into account the identity-formation process thinkers undergo over the life course requires a more complex conception of the relationship between thinkers and institutions than is provided by the theory of intellectual fields. Intellectual fields are indeed, as Bourdieu and Collins suggest, status hierarchies, but academic careers must not be seen simply in terms of upward or downward status trajectories. They are also histories of exposure to different identity-inculcating institutions. A sociology of ideas focused only on the dynamics of intellectual fields will not be attentive to this exposure, to the sometimes painful reconstruction of identity narratives that may occur as thinkers move across institutional locations, to the ebb and flow of institutional and cultural circumstances that may render identity elements acquired at earlier points in time more or less salient for a thinker's current positioning in a taxonomy of intellectual personhood, to the ways in which intellectual self-concept may shape professional ambitions, and to thinkers' needs to produce ideas that will be authentic and consistent with who—as a result of this accumulated exposure—they conceive themselves to be.[15]

14. See Christian Smith, 1998, *American Evangelicalism: Embattled and Thriving*, Chicago: University of Chicago Press; John Evans, 2003, "The Creation of a Distinct Subcultural Identity and Denominational Growth," *Journal for the Scientific Study of Religion* 42:467–77.

15. Although I will not develop the point here, the theory of identity formation and self-concept laid out above may have application to other domains of social life as well. One could easily imagine the political, religious, or cultural identities of nonintellectuals

* 3 *

One more preliminary step must be taken before applying the theory of intellectual self-concept to the Rorty case. Rorty's life and career unfolded against the backdrop of major changes to the American academic field over the course of the twentieth century, and understanding these changes is essential for making sense of the circumstances Rorty faced during his years at Chicago, Yale, and Princeton.

As previously noted, Carl Schorske has argued that one of the most significant events in twentieth-century American intellectual history was the rise of what he calls "the new rigorism" in the human sciences in the years following the Second World War.[16] During this time many disciplines moved from "range to rigor, from a loose engagement with a multifaceted reality historically perceived to the creation of sharp analytic tools that could promise certainty where description and speculative explanation had prevailed before."[17] Analytic philosophy, ushered in by the logical positivists and building on native tendencies in American philosophy,[18] exemplified the new rigorism. But philosophy was not the only discipline affected. Economics saw a move toward econometric modeling; the subfield of political science concerned with American politics was swept up in a wave of behavioralism; in English departments "the New Criticism achieved a clear institutional ascendancy by the 1950s," focused on the formulation of "formal and structural analytic procedures to illuminate the particularity and protect the autonomy of literary work";[19] and in sociology the increasing "centrality of measurement"[20] and statistical modeling in survey research were part of the same trend. Although many of these approaches became institutionalized, Schorske goes on to argue that by the late 1970s, rigorism came to be regarded more negatively in some fields. Increasingly there could be heard grumblings that rigorism—which was often accompanied, as David Hollinger has noted, by universalistic

---

forming in a similar way, and exerting comparable effects on social action. Specifying at the microinstitutional level the conditions under which identity transfer is most likely to occur could improve upon existing models of socialization and cultural learning.

16. Schorske, "The New Rigorism in the Human Sciences."

17. Ibid., 295.

18. See James Campbell, 2006, *A Thoughtful Profession: The Early Years of the American Philosophical Association*, Chicago: Open Court.

19. Schorske, "The New Rigorism in the Human Sciences," 301.

20. Stephen Turner and Jonathan Turner, 1990, *The Impossible Science: An Institutional Analysis of American Sociology*, Newbury Park: Sage, 105.

assumptions about "the species as a whole"[21]—had to be rejected and that the intellectual and political projects that rigorism represented were philosophically bankrupt and morally problematic. As Randall Collins and David Waller observe in an essay that glosses such claims as representing "a broad antipositivist front," opposition to rigorism encompassed a "range of positions," including "rejection of . . . the Vienna Circle's logical positivism in its most extreme formulations," "rejection of formal or quantitative methods," "rejection of the possibility of any generalized knowledge—the alternatives are to endorse localized, historically or culturally particularistic knowledge—or skepticism about any knowledge whatsoever," and "rejection of science as a political or moral evil."[22] Collins and Waller suggest that this oppositional stance was strongest in the fields of literature, history, and anthropology, more moderate in "battleground" fields like political science, sociology, and philosophy, and present not at all in mathematics, the natural sciences, economics, psychology, or linguistics. Rorty rode both of these intellectual waves, becoming caught up in the rigorism of the analytic paradigm in the 1960s and then emerging as a leading figure in the antirigorist movement of the 1970s and 1980s. What social and historical factors account for these developments in American thought, thereby laying the groundwork for some of the institutional and intellectual experiences Rorty would undergo?

My thesis is that the shift toward and then away from rigorism in the human sciences represented a shift in the nature of intellectual authority in American academic life and that this shift was caused largely by structural transformations in the American university sector. Bourdieu is right to suggest that intellectual and cultural fields are, among other things, sites of struggle over authority, over what kinds of cultural products and producers will be regarded as the most legitimate and valuable. Consistent with the positions taken by Schorske and Hollinger, I want to suggest that in the period immediately following World War II, intellectual authority in the United States, in the natural sciences as well as the humanities and social sciences, typically flowed to scientists and intellectuals who were conceived of as "experts" in their fields, where academic expertise "implied . . . the ability to make authoritative judgments and to

21. David Hollinger, 1993, "How Wide the Circle of the 'We'? American Intellectuals and the Problem of the Ethnos since World War II," *American Historical Review* 98:317–37, 318.

22. Randall Collins and David Waller, 1994, "Did Social Science Break Down in the 1970s?" pp. 15–40 in *Formal Theory in Sociology: Opportunity and Pitfall?* Jerald Hage, ed., Albany: State University of New York Press, 16, 17.

solve problems based on disciplinary training."[23] The dominance of this form of intellectual authority, which lent support to intellectual movements claiming to be more rigorous than their competitors, was linked to the ongoing professionalization of the American professoriate, and it was the temporary devaluation of the notion of intellectual expertise in the 1970s and 1980s—a function of other processes and historical developments—that rendered rigor, understood in a particular way, a less important criterion for the evaluation of work in some fields at the time.

The notion that academics are experts in some arena of knowledge who possess the technical training necessary to make progress in solving scientific problems was not new to the middle years of the twentieth century. Natural scientists and engineers had, in varying degrees, been understood as experts in this sense through much of the second half of the 1800s, and as social scientists sought to establish and legitimate their disciplines around the turn of the century—and gain support from important constituencies such as the state and private philanthropic foundations—they often portrayed themselves as producers of expert knowledge as well.[24]

In the humanities, however, a competing form of intellectual authority remained popular through the 1930s. While sometimes making recourse to notions of objectivity, humanities scholars in fields such as philosophy, literature, and art typically presented themselves as insightful interpreters of the human condition whose insights stemmed not from their methodological training but from their vast erudition. These were scholars who defined themselves as intellectuals in the classic sense of the term, as "special custodians of abstract ideas like reason and justice and truth."[25] As Lewis Coser notes, they saw their primary pedagogical mission to be that of cultivating students' aesthetic, moral, and spiritual capacities and passing on learned traditions rather than imparting technical skills or the expert knowledge obtained through the application of such skills. Although more likely than their nineteenth-century counterparts to have doctorates or other advanced degrees, to have distinct disciplinary identities, and to be producers of research as well as teachers, these scholars

23. Steven Brint, 1994, *In an Age of Experts: The Changing Role of Professionals in Politics and Public Life*, Princeton: Princeton University Press, 40.

24. Dorothy Ross, 1991, *The Origins of American Social Science*, Cambridge: Cambridge University Press.

25. Lewis Coser, 1965, *Men of Ideas: a Sociologist's View*, New York: Free Press, viii.

cleaved to a nineteenth-century vision of intellectualism "identified with the term 'culture'":[26]

> Composed of classicists and a fraction of men from such fields as English literature and the history of art, and further able to count upon philosophical idealists as somewhat standoffish allies, the advocates of culture espoused the values of the older college-trained elite, though updating those values away from a defense of Christian orthodoxy. In their view, the main aim of education continued to be the training of future leaders for the whole society, directly inculcating them with a moral viewpoint that sought to rise above materialism. The outlook of such professors remained one of cultivated generalism.... Professors of this type—and they continued to reproduce themselves in significant numbers down through the later decades—in effect embraced the role of the man of letters.[27]

The persistence of this form of intellectual authority in the humanities well into the twentieth century is perhaps best symbolized by the popularity of Western civilization curricula for undergraduates that became of renewed importance in American university life after the First World War in conjunction with the general education movement discussed in chapters 3 and 4. "These courses," Caroline Winterer notes in her history of American classicism, "were responses to several factors, most importantly the loss of the common classical core and the proliferation of electives." They "presented to students a historical sequence of the 'rise' or 'progress' of 'Western civilization' from classical antiquity (or even before) to the modern era" and "reflected a continuing commitment to linking a liberal education to the duties of citizenship."[28] Professors called on to teach such courses displayed forms of intellectual authority that bore little relation to academic expertise as it was developing in the physical, biological, and social sciences, even while battles raged among them over whether "scholarship" or "culture" should be prioritized.[29]

By the 1950s, however, the notion of academics as experts had thoroughly permeated most fields of knowledge, including the humanities.

26. Laurence Veysey, 1979, "The Plural Organized World of the Humanities," pp. 51–106 in *The Organization of Knowledge in Modern America, 1860–1920*, Alexandra Oleson, ed., Baltimore: Johns Hopkins University Press, 53.

27. Ibid., 53–54.

28. Caroline Winterer, 2002, *The Culture of Classicism: Ancient Greece and Rome in American Intellectual Life, 1780–1910*, Baltimore: Johns Hopkins University Press, 181–82.

29. Ibid., 152–78.

The training of students in classical traditions did not cease—though it would be curtailed in the following decades—but increasingly, and especially at elite research institutions, academics of all stripes advanced knowledge claims that rested on assertions of methodological or technical competence and on the assumption that the problems a field set for itself could, through the mobilization of such competence, be definitively solved.[30] This form of intellectual authority was connected to universalistic assumptions about the natural and social worlds and to the program of the new rigorism. The intellectual expert was one who could identify the universal patterns and laws operative in her or his unique domain of study and who made progress in such a pursuit by applying rigorous, formalized methods to analyze data or nonempirical material or problems. To be sure, the tendency of social scientists and humanists to strive for intellectual authority of this kind was not a uniformity, and there continued to be disagreement in many fields over presuppositional, epistemological, and methodological questions. But the scales had tipped. During this period "nominally professional occupations"—both inside and outside academe—"that could not compete as 'expert' occupations were naturally suspect.... They lacked the certainty and often the competence to solve problems in the areas in which they claimed authority."[31] This was the case within particular fields as well, as Richard Bernstein observes of philosophy, where intellectual movements that aligned themselves with the notion of academic expertise gained ground relative to those that did not or could not:

[The period following the Second World War] was a time of great confidence among professional philosophers. It was felt by the growing analytic community that "we" philosophers had "finally" discovered the conceptual tools and techniques to make progress in solving or dissolving philosophical problems.... Of course, there were pockets of resistance.... There were those who defended and practiced speculative metaphysics...,

30. For general discussions of this point see Roger Geiger, 1993, *Research and Relevant Knowledge: American Research Universities since World War II*, New York: Oxford University Press; Thomas Haskell, ed., 1984, *The Authority of Experts: Studies in History and Theory*, Bloomington: Indiana University Press; Laurence Veysey, 1988, "Higher Education as a Profession: Changes and Continuities," pp. 15–32 in *The Professions in American History*, Nathan Hatch, ed., Notre Dame: University of Notre Dame Press, 24–25. On economics see Michael Bernstein, 1990, "American Economic Expertise from the Great War to the Cold War: Some Initial Observations," *Journal of Economic History* 50:407–16. On philosophy see Kuklick, *The Rise of American Philosophy*.

31. Brint, *In an Age of Experts*, 41.

who saw greater promise in phenomenology and existentialism ... , who sought to keep the pragmatic tradition alive.... But philosophers who had not taken the analytic "linguistic turn" were clearly on the defensive.[32]

What accounts for this development and, with it, the advantage that obtained for schools and approaches that defined themselves as appropriate vehicles for thinkers and institutions in pursuit of expert knowledge? There is probably some explanatory value in the argument that American culture in the 1950s displayed high modernist tendencies that were affined with the idea of academic expertise and leant stability to the new knowledge regime.[33] High modernism's valuation of hierarchy was consistent with the distinction between the expert knower and the layman; its emphasis on purpose called for an instrumental orientation to knowledge and coded experts as crucial sources of information for policy makers; and that high modernism presupposed the possibility of a totalizing worldview boosted efforts at finding the singular paradigmatic perspective, and with it appropriate methodologies, from which certain knowledge could be derived. While such culturalist arguments have their place, alongside others that stress the symbolic power associated with science in general and physics in particular in the wake of Hiroshima and Nagasaki and the Cold War—a power so great that other disciplines were led to adopt an emulative stance centered on the figure of the scientific expert[34]—I propose a more structural explanation: the shift in intellectual authority stemmed mostly from institutional transformations. The notion of the academic as expert, and with it the embrace of universalism and the new rigorism, were effects of the ratcheting up of academic professionalization processes in the middle years of the twentieth century.

As historians and sociologists of higher education have observed, the modern American research university, organized around academic departments where researchers pursue specialized knowledge, has its origins in

32. Bernstein, *New Constellation*, 330–31.

33. Arguments to this effect can be found in David Harvey, 1989, *The Condition of Postmodernity: An Enquiry into the Origins of Cultural Change*, Oxford: Blackwell. Also see David Garland, 2001, *The Culture of Control: Crime and Social Order in Contemporary Society*, Chicago: University of Chicago Press; George Steinmetz, ed., 2005, *The Politics of Method in the Human Sciences: Positivism and Its Epistemological Others*, Durham: Duke University Press.

34. For discussion see Paul Boyer, 1985, *By the Bomb's Early Light: American Thought and Culture at the Dawn of the Atomic Age*, New York: Pantheon. On the emulation of the natural sciences see Ellen Herman, 1995, *The Romance of American Psychology: Political Culture in the Age of Experts*, Berkeley: University of California Press.

the late nineteenth century. As Christopher Jencks and David Riesman note in *The Academic Revolution,* "it was not until the 1880s that anything like a modern university really took shape in America. Perhaps the most important breakthroughs were the founding of Johns Hopkins and Clark as primarily graduate universities.... The 1890s saw further progress, with the founding of Chicago, the reform of Columbia, and the tentative acceptance of graduate work as an important activity in the leading state universities."[35] But while it is correct to trace the emergence of the institutional form of the modern American university back to this era, reflecting as it did the diffusion of organizational repertoires and epistemic cultures that had been developed in Germany several decades prior, it is a mistake to imagine, as some have, that academic professionalization was a fait accompli in the early 1900s. Professionalization in the American academy actually occurred in two phases: a phase of initial institutional reconfiguration lasting from roughly 1890 to 1920 and coinciding with a boom in the founding of disciplines and the birth of professional societies like the American Philosophical Association (APA) and the American Sociological Society (later named the American Sociological Association), and a phase of consolidation midcentury that coincides with the hegemony of academic expertise, universalism, and the new rigorism in the social sciences and humanities.[36] Although the latter phase was contingent on the former, by no means was it inevitable. Had historical circumstances been different—most notably, had there not occurred a rapid expansion of American higher education in the years following World War II—it is likely that the professionalized "disciplinary system" described by Abbott[37] would have taken a different, more fluid form and that the trope of rigor would have been less resonant.

Professionalization involved the establishment of the separate disciplines as autonomous and self-regulating enterprises. Under the auspices of professionalization, a discipline becomes "a self-governing and largely closed community of practitioners ... which determines [its own] ... standards for entry, promotion, and dismissal."[38] The rise of the professions in American society at the end of the nineteenth century was bound up

35. Christopher Jencks and David Riesman, 1968, *The Academic Revolution,* Garden City: Doubleday, 13.

36. This argument is consistent with the larger point of the Jencks and Riesman book.

37. Abbott, *Chaos of Disciplines.*

38. Louis Menand, 1997, "The Demise of Disciplinary Authority," pp. 201–19 in *What's Happened to the Humanities?* Alvin Kernan, ed., Princeton: Princeton University Press, 205.

from the start with the institution of the modern university.[39] Fields such as law and medicine could define themselves as professions only by linking up with an emerging logic of credentialization. Universities would impart specialized knowledge to those who wished to enter a profession, and the credentials thus granted could serve as a closure mechanism for regulating entry into the field and as a badge of authority that professionals could wear as they sought control over their own work processes. The academic revolution at the turn of the twentieth century was partly driven by this social logic, as colleges and universities redefined themselves as credential-granting institutions for an expanding middle class eager for professional careers.[40] Institutional decentralization in American higher education facilitated this change: it allowed as many foundings of colleges and universities as the market could bear,[41] resulting in a plethora of postsecondary educational opportunities for middle-class students, while competition among colleges and universities promoted innovation, generating a status hierarchy in which "the schools that led the reform—the original colonial colleges, the heavily endowed new private universities, and the well-supported midwestern state universities—soon set themselves apart from those who were slow to follow."[42] At the same time that colleges and universities promoted professionalization in American society as a whole, the academic disciplines themselves benefited from it. On the one hand, expansion of the higher education sector promoted disciplinarity, as "rapid growth made some sort of internal organization necessary" and as "specific disciplinary degree[s] provided a medium of exchange between particular subunits of different universities."[43] On the other hand, practitioners of the various disciplines soon began to model themselves on other professionals, starting their own national professional organizations, insisting on their autonomy from lay constituencies such as students and university administrators, attempting to regulate their own labor markets, and engaging in coordinated discussions about professional standards, responsibilities, and privileges.

Yet the project of academic professionalization, though started around the turn of the twentieth century, was not completed within the span of

39. Magali Sarfatti Larson, 1977, *The Rise of Professionalism: A Sociological Analysis*, Berkeley: University of California Press; Collins, *The Credential Society*; Brint, *In an Age of Experts*.

40. Collins, *Credential Society*, 127.

41. David Brown, 1995, *Degrees of Control: A Sociology of Educational Expansion and Occupational Credentialism*, New York: Teachers College Press.

42. Collins, *The Credential Society*, 125.

43. Abbott, *Chaos of Disciplines*, 125.

a single academic generation. Consider in this regard the requirement, often seen as an indicator of academic professionalization, that all professors hold a doctorate. Laurence Veysey notes that already by "the turn of the century the Ph.D. was usually mandatory"[44] for those seeking teaching appointments at the most prestigious American universities, but as late as 1920, the number of doctorates awarded in the United States was very small relative to the number of institutions and students, which meant that many instructors at lower-tier schools did not have a Ph.D. and that the system still included numerous professors whose doctorates had been earned in other countries.[45] This situation was symptomatic of disciplinary fields not yet in full control over their own reproduction. But it was not only with respect to the doctorate that the project of academic professionalization failed to reach full fruition at the time. Academic salaries even at elite institutions remained low throughout the 1930s in comparison with the salaries of other professionals;[46] the use of peer review to evaluate scientific and intellectual contributions on the basis of criteria of evaluation internal to disciplines was in its infancy;[47] intellectuals located outside academic settings made well-publicized bids for intellectual authority;[48] and active intervention by academic administrators and even college trustees into hiring and promotion decisions, where a candidate's stature within his discipline or his reputation in a local department might be disregarded, were not uncommon, not least because the notion of aca-

44. Laurence Veysey, 1965, *The Emergence of the American University*, Chicago: University of Chicago Press, 176.

45. Thomas Snyder, 1993, *120 Years of American Education: A Statistical Portrait*, Washington, D.C.: National Center for Education Statistics, 75. On the importance of training in German institutions for American professors, see Jurgen Herbst, 1965, *The German Historical School in American Scholarship: A Study in the Transfer of Culture*, Ithaca: Cornell University Press; Daniel Rodgers, 1998, *Atlantic Crossings: Social Politics in a Progressive Age*, Cambridge: Harvard University Press.

46. See Logan Wilson, 1942, *The Academic Man: A Study in the Sociology of a Profession*, New York: Oxford University Press. When Hutchins took the reins at Chicago, he described it as a serious problem for higher education that "more and more of our best college graduates have been dissuaded from a scholarly career by the ... feeling that there must be some connection between compensation and ability." Respect for higher learning could not be achieved, he argued, "as long as professors must carry on outside work or teach every summer to keep alive." Robert Hutchins, 1930, "The Spirit of the University of Chicago," *Journal of Higher Education* 1:5–12, 11–12.

47. Harriet Zuckerman and Robert K. Merton, 1971, "Patterns of Evaluation in Science: Institutionalization, Structure and Functions of the Referee System," *Minerva* 9:66–100.

48. Cooney, *The Rise of the New York Intellectuals*.

demic freedom, closely linked to the project of professionalization, remained new and fragile.[49]

It was not until the 1940s and 1950s that a structural opening was created that would allow academic professionalization to become fully and
securely institutionalized. This opening took the form of a vast increase
in the resources available to higher education. Veterans going to college
on the G.I. Bill swelled undergraduate enrollments, as did the increasing
tendency of middle-class youth—in the context of an expansion of white-
collar work—to seek a college degree. Enrollments were also bolstered
by influxes of foreign students, drawn in part by America's new geopoliti-
cal importance. New colleges and universities were founded to satisfy this
growing educational demand, and existing schools were expanded, creating an imbalance in the demand to supply ratio of personnel that helped
to push faculty salaries higher. Simultaneously, large amounts of money
were poured into research by the federal government, philanthropic organizations, and the business community, a trend abetted by Cold War
fears of Soviet scientific and military superiority, the promise of scientific
breakthroughs, postwar affluence, and the growing technical needs of
American capitalism.[50] The social origins and status of the professoriate
also came to change. The demand for faculty was so strong, especially
when coupled with the growing diffusion of meritocratic ideals, that in
many fields Jews and Catholics, many from working- and lower-middle-
class backgrounds, were able to push through into the ranks of academe.
With the growth of university bureaucracies and a renewed societal emphasis on credentialization, the Ph.D. became a mandatory teaching credential in even more colleges and universities, and despite the fact that
fewer professors hailed from elite backgrounds, the new prioritization
of research, combined with the increasing involvement of professors in
public policy making that was a legacy of the war and the growth of the
American state, helped to increase the professoriate's status.[51]

These developments gave an important boost to professionalizing
efforts. As the number of faculty members increased, membership in

49. See Walter Metzger, 1955, *Academic Freedom in the Age of the University*, New York:
Columbia University Press.

50. An alternative account of higher education expansion is provided by John Mey-
er and his colleagues. For a recent statement of their position, see John Meyer and Evan
Schofer, 2005, "The Worldwide Expansion of Higher Education in the Twentieth Century,"
American Sociological Review 70:898–920.

51. On these transformations see Hugh Graham and Nancy Diamond, 1997, *The Rise
of American Research Universities: Elites and Challengers in the Postward Era*, Baltimore: John

national disciplinary organizations grew. Once membership numbers surpassed critical mass levels, these organizations could take a more active role than they had previously in regulating academic labor markets and serving as vehicles by which national disciplinary communities could impose their own criteria of evaluation for academic work. At the same time, given that demand for faculty now outstripped supply, faculty members could bargain effectively with administrators for control over hiring and promotion. Increasing competition between universities was also conducive to professionalization, because "the goal of raising academic standards in appointments tended to empower elite scholars and departments over administrators, and it reduced the claim of institutional or local particularities."[52] Finally, research funding from agencies such as the National Science Foundation came to be structured around processes of peer review, which "authorized disciplinary (even subdisciplinary) autonomy and a certain distancing of academic work from society at large."[53]

Like the scientism to which an earlier generation of social scientists had been susceptible, the notion of intellectual authority as expertise, and with it claims to universal knowledge and rigorous methodological competence, constituted at heart an ideology of professionalization. Professionalizing fields assert their autonomy from lay constituencies through boundary work that marks off their jurisdiction from that of other fields and asserts that outsiders cannot—because they have not undergone the requisite training—understand what practitioners understand. The programmatic statements of the leading approaches of the time amounted to precisely such an assertion. An important assumption in these texts, some of which were written before the new rigorism came to flourish, was that what distinguishes disciplinary insiders from outsiders is technical, methodological competence, variously understood: as competence in logic in the view of philosophers such as Rudolf Carnap and Hans Reichenbach, as competence in the formal analysis of poetry in the view of literary critics such as John Crowe Ransom and Cleanth Brooks, as competence in research design and statistics in the view of sociologists like Samuel Stouffer, and so on. Neither local administrators nor politicians nor student constituencies nor unattached intellectuals, it was implied, have any such competence

Hopkins University Press; Lewis Mayhew, 1977, *Legacy of the Seventies*, San Francisco: Jossey-Bass; Christopher Lucas, 1994, *American Higher Education: A History*, New York: St. Martin's.

52. Thomas Bender, 1997, "Politics, Intellect, and the American University, 1945–1995," *Daedalus* 126:1–38, 6.

53. Ibid., 13.

and therefore have no right to interfere in—except by supporting—the professional lives of those experts that do. Humanities and social science fields in the second stage of professionalization found the notion of expertise attractive because it contained this message, because it allowed them to obtain some of the prestige associated with the obviously "rigorous" physical sciences, and because rigorism promised a kind of standardization and "commensurability"[54] at a time of rapid institutional growth and restructuring.[55] As shown in the first half of the book and below, Rorty's career was significantly affected by the way in which the academic institutions he was affiliated with responded to these developments.

Professionalized disciplines, notions of academic expertise, and rigorism in the human sciences are still with us today. But those participat-

54. On commensuration, see Wendy Espeland and Mitchell Stevens, 1998, "Commensuration as a Social Process," *Annual Review of Sociology* 24:313–43.

55. In his book *Time in the Ditch*, John McCumber argues that academic philosophy in the United States was transformed in the 1950s by McCarthy-era campaigns against intellectuals suspected of having Communist sympathies. Professors from numerous disciplines were called upon to testify before the House Un-American Activities Committee or found themselves under suspicion by local authorities, but McCumber cites evidence suggesting that "philosophy ... may be in first place in terms of the *percentage* of its practitioners who fell afoul of right-wing vigilantes." John McCumber, 2001, *Time in the Ditch: American Philosophy and the McCarthy Era*, Evanston: Northwestern University Press, 25. This fact, McCumber argues, helps to explain developments within philosophy at the time. Philosophers felt pressure to avoid becoming ensnared in McCarthy's net, and the way they sought to protect themselves, McCumber suggests, was by holding themselves out, not as thinkers immersed in the messy and controversial world of values, but as quasi-scientists pursuing objective truths by employing rigorous methods. Logical positivism, he claims, offered just such a vision of philosophy, so that "McCarthyite paranoia" helps to explain why "American philosophers were so oddly uncritical of logical positivism" (45), why it was able to sweep the discipline so quickly, and why analytic philosophy more generally came to dominate American philosophy departments. I do not doubt that McCarthyism made some American academics hesitant to publicly express their political views—particularly if those views were left of center—and that this translated into a disadvantage for intellectual perspectives that might be seen as inherently political. But it is hard to believe that McCarthyism is the most important factor accounting for the rise of the new rigorism in philosophy. On the one hand, the logical positivists had established themselves as important figures on the American philosophical scene well before McCarthy's rise to power. On the other hand, even if the political climate effectively ruled certain intellectual choices out, it is not at all clear why the kind of analytic philosophy that became popular in the 1950s would be ruled in. Why, for example, would it have provided more political cover for philosophers than systematic metaphysics or the philosophy of Charles S. Peirce, both of which saw a decline in their intellectual status at the time?

ing in the American academic field as humanists or social scientists in the 1970s and 1980s encountered an intellectual and institutional climate that looked different than it had midcentury. What factors explain the growth of antirigorist themes, particularly in the humanities, during this time?

The first such factor is intensive social-movement activity in the late 1960s and early 1970s, which penetrated the academic sphere and helped shape the intellectual tendencies of an academic generation and beyond.[56] The antiwar movement, free speech movement, black power movement, women's movement, environmental movement and other forms of contentious politics had numerous direct and indirect effects on American academic life, altering the political composition of the faculty as movement participants entered its ranks, spurring the creation of new fields of knowledge like women's studies and African American studies,[57] laying the groundwork for the establishment of multicultural curricular requirements in the 1980s and 1990s,[58] and rendering universities less hierarchical and more responsive to diverse voices and concerns. Although there is no evidence that students or professors who took part in social-movement activity in the 1960s and 1970s were invariably led by their involvements to privilege antirigorism over rigorism, these movements—often centered around college campuses—did frequently target academics and college administrators in their rhetoric, depicting them as inherently conservative and enemies of the cause, a few sympathetic intellectuals notwithstanding. Although members of the professoriate actually came to oppose the Vietnam War earlier than other groups in American society, many student and faculty activists accused their teachers and colleagues of ivory towerism and demanded not simply that they use their professional positions to denounce the war and support the antiwar cause as well as others but also that they turn their attention toward those subjects that the radicalism of the time saw as major social ills and engage intellectually in politically acceptable ways. What Jeffrey Alexander has argued with respect to the

56. On the effects on social theory, see Alan Sica and Stephen Turner, eds., 2005, *The Disobedient Generation: Social Theorists in the 1960s,* Chicago: University of Chicago Press.

57. Ellen Messer-Davidow, 2002, *Disciplining Feminism: From Social Activism to Academic Discourse,* Durham: Duke University Press; Fabio Rojas, 2007, *From Black Power to Black Studies: How a Radical Social Movement Became an Academic Discipline,* Baltimore: Johns Hopkins University Press; Mario Small, 1999, "Departmental Conditions and the Emergence of New Disciplines: Two Cases in the Legitimation of African American Studies," *Theory and Society* 28:659–707.

58. David Yamane, 2001, *Student Movements for Multiculturalism: Challenging the Curricular Color Line in Higher Education,* Baltimore: Johns Hopkins University Press.

fate of modernization theory in sociology—that its earlier construction as sacred came to be inverted in the 1960s and 1970s as social movements sprang up that "were increasingly viewed in terms of collective emancipation—peasant revolutions on a worldwide scale, black and Chicano national movements, indigenous people's rebellions, youth culture, hippies, rock music, and women's liberation"[59]—was true of the notion of academic expertise as well. Within such movements universalism was sometimes questioned and portrayed as mere ideological cover for asserting the interests of the dominant, value neutrality was denounced as a sham, and the new rigorism, in its various forms, was accused of being a tool of oppression. Intellectual choices concerning theory and epistemology were politicized in a way they had not been since the rise of radical intellectualism outside the academy in the 1930s. As historian Henry May recalls, "Sweating out the 1960s at any major American campus was an experience never to be forgotten. Not only did we live through brief periods of the actual breakdown of social order, but, more important, the *intellectual* order of the 1950s was shattered beyond repair. Detachment became cop-out, intellectuality elitism, tolerance repressive."[60] These charges had an even greater impact than they might have otherwise because there was an expansion, throughout the period, in the number of women and people of color entering higher education, as students and then as faculty members. Many of these new entrants to the intellectual arena oriented themselves toward their respective disciplinary mainstreams, but others found that their life experiences could not be easily squared with depictions of the world offered by various universalistic and rigorist paradigms, inevitably developed by white men, and went on to become producers or consumers of feminist theory, postcolonial theory, and other radical approaches that challenged the disciplinary status quo. In this climate, it is no surprise that some intellectuals—whether or not they themselves took part in social-movement activity—would find themselves in sympathy with critiques of universalism and the new rigorism, uncomfortable with the notion of the academic as expert dispensing true knowledge from on high, and would endeavor to provide elaborate philosophical justifications and rationales for such feelings. Many of the justifications and rationales for antirigorism that garnered attention were French imports, so another way to put this point is to say that social-movement activity helped to create a large

59. Alexander, *Fin de Siècle Social Theory*, 21.

60. Henry May, 1989, "Religion and American Intellectual History," pp. 12–22 in *Religion and Twentieth-Century American Intellectual Life*, Michael Lacey, ed., Cambridge: Cambridge University Press, 16.

American constituency for "French theory,"[61] despite its sometimes ambivalent politics.

But the dissatisfaction with rigorism was not simply a flower child of the 1960s. A second generative factor was labor market conditions in the 1970s. Philosophy, like many other humanities and social-science fields, experienced in that decade what Peter Novick has called an "academic depression."[62] Between 1960 and 1970, there was a threefold increase in the total number of doctorates awarded annually in the United States, and the number of masters degrees given each year more than doubled. By the early to mid-1970s, however, university sector growth slowed, and the academic labor market—especially in humanities fields—became flooded with new Ph.D.'s. Data on the labor market experiences of new philosophy Ph.D.'s from twenty selected top- and bottom-tier schools between 1962 and 1980 show that, while 1970 and 1972 seem to have been decent years, the overall trend from 1966 to 1978 is one of decline, across both tiers, in the percentage of new Ph.D.'s who were placed in academic positions at the assistant professor level within two years of receiving their degree.[63] It was not until the mid- to late 1980s that the market began to recover. In the preceding period, as the APA reported, "discouraged and demoralized jobseekers"[64] were all too common. The consequence of such an employment draught was widespread intellectual anomie as students completing their doctorates came to realize how unlikely it was they would be awarded desirable tenure-track posts. As Walter Metzger notes, graduate students were not the only ones affected:

> Although the number of academics kept increasing throughout the 1970s, the rate of increase in that decennium fell to about a third of the historic one, and 70 percent of the increment was confined to the junior and part-time ranks, the marginal zones of the profession. Rare today is the academic old hand or acolyte who cannot give personal testimony of the hardships that come when growing stops. Veteran faculty members who keep track of the purchasing power of their paychecks, of the waiting time between

61. See Lamont, "How to Become a Dominant French Philosopher"; François Cusset, 2003, *French Theory: Foucault, Derrida, Deleuze and Cie et les mutations de la vie intellectuelle aux Etats-Unis*, Paris: Decouverte.

62. Peter Novick, 1988, *That Noble Dream: The "Objectivity Question" and the American Historical Profession*, Cambridge: Cambridge University Press, 574.

63. Data available from author.

64. David Hoekema, 1989, "Special Report: Profile of APA Membership, Employment Patterns, and Doctoral Degrees," *Proceedings and Addresses of the American Philosophical Association* 62:839–53, 845–46.

promotions, of the quality of work amenities and supporting services, of their chances of getting a research project funded, can attest that the previous period of rapid expansion was attended by the furnishing of concrete benefits the next period largely snatched away.[65]

It is common for sociologists of ideas to explain the rise of intellectual movements by pointing to labor market dynamics. The typical form of such explanations is to assert that labor market conditions in a field or set of fields render it advantageous for thinkers to gravitate toward some particular intellectual pursuit, as was the case for scholars who aligned themselves with the emerging field of experimental psychology in the context of a difficult labor market for philosophers in late nineteenth-century Germany.[66] But labor market conditions may also shape the content of intellectual work in another way, by helping to support—or undermining—the legitimacy of dominant paradigms. The capacity of a paradigm to remain hegemonic and withstand challenges from competitors is a function not just of its intrinsic intellectual power but also of its ability to serve as a covering ideational framework under which normal academic careers can unfold. Just as a political regime's capacity to ensure the material well-being of its citizens is a condition for the maintenance of its legitimacy, so too do paradigms become vulnerable to attack when they are associated with dire labor market conditions. Growing dissatisfaction with rigorist approaches in the humanities and social sciences in the late 1970s and beyond must be understood in part as a consequence of such a situation, as a shortage of openings led to widespread academic underemployment, helping to foster a rebellious academic culture built around resentments toward thinkers at top-ranked institutions, who were seen as using valuation of narrow forms of intellectual competence to monopolize for themselves and their students scarce resources.

A third factor behind the growing opposition to academic authority as expertise was that academic professionalism was now securely institutionalized. In his recent book on "French theory,"[67] François Cusset observes that the various forms of antifoundationalism that emerged in the 1970s and 1980s were all characterized by a kind of intellectual playfulness—an insistence that intellectual work not take itself too seriously and that, as in Rorty's suggestion, irony be recognized as the most appropriate stance

65. Walter Metzger, 1987, "The Academic Profession in the United States," pp. 123–208 in *The Academic Profession*, Burton Clark, ed., Berkeley: University of California Press, 125.

66. Ben-David and Collins, "Social Factors in the Origins of a New Science."

67. Cusset, *French Theory*.

for those who realize that their own views and positions do not derive from some transcendental vantage point. Cusset links this playfulness to the fact that the American college and university sector is a holding tank for young adults who would otherwise flood the labor market, who are more interested in partying than in real intellectual pursuits, and whose mood comes to color all of academic life. A less simplistic explanation is that fields still struggling to fully achieve academic professionalization midcentury could ill afford to profane such notions as truth, science, and objectivity, while securely institutionalized fields two or three decades later could. One of the conditions for the growing opposition to rigorism was therefore the very institutional success it had functioned to achieve in the period prior.

Fourth and finally, some of the opposition to rigorism in the 1970s had its origin in the efflorescence of American spirituality and religiosity in the decade before. As Robert Wuthnow and Wade Clark Roof have described it, American religion then underwent a fundamental change: although traditional forms of religion hardly died off, many Americans went from being "dwellers" to "seekers."[68] Whereas many in the generation that came of age amid the nuclear anxiety of the 1950s and the destabilization of patterns of family and community living entailed by the shift to a mass society responded in a reactionary manner by "clinging to safe, respectable houses of worship in which a domesticated God could be counted on to provide reassurance," "in the 1960s many Americans, having learned that they could move around, think through their options, and select a faith that truly captured what they believed to be the truth, took the choice seriously, bargaining with their souls, seeking new spiritual guides, and rediscovering that God dwells not only in homes but also in the byways trod by pilgrims and sojourners."[69] Vatican II, the growth of denominations that blended Christian and self-help themes, and the rise of Eastern spirituality in the United States all reflected this development, which was intertwined with social-movement activity of the day—so much so that some, like Robert Bellah, could claim that "the followers of oriental religions are in a sense counterparts to and sometimes refugees from radical political groups that have been active in America since the early 60s."[70] As American religion was thus transformed—and in the

68. Robert Wuthnow, 1998, *After Heaven: Spirituality in America since the 1950s*, Berkeley: University of California Press; Wade Clark Roof, 1993, *A Generation of Seekers: The Spiritual Journeys of the Baby Boom Generation*, San Francisco: HarperSanFrancisco.

69. Wuthnow, *After Heaven*, 57.

70. Robert Bellah, 1992, *The Broken Covenant: American Civil Religion in Time of Trial*, 2nd ed., Chicago: University of Chicago Press, 156.

context of increasingly competitive markets for religious services[71]—it attained new vitality, and some of this spilled over into the academic arena.[72] As Hollinger has pointed out,[73] it is not coincidental that the growth of scientism and secularism in the American academy in the 1940s and 1950s corresponded with the mass entry of Jews and to a lesser extent Catholics into the ranks of the faculty. Keeping one's personal values and beliefs at bay by wrapping oneself in the putative neutrality of science was an important strategy these groups employed to secure legitimacy in a hostile social environment. As the 1960s and 1970s progressed, however, and anti-Semitic and anti-Catholic sentiment in the ivory tower abated—and as the importance of religious and spiritual experience was reaffirmed throughout American culture—academics representing a variety of faith traditions found themselves turning to religion and spirituality to a degree their immediate generational predecessors had not, with some seeking intellectual orientations that would allow them to loosely incorporate religious or spiritual themes into their scholarship. Many scholars of this persuasion came to doubt the value of the new rigorism, which was seen as objectifying the human being, and came to serve as an important constituency for those calling for a move away from expertise and toward either more traditional or radically revised conceptions of intellectual authority—despite the fact that some making such a call, like Rorty, were militant atheists.[74]

How did these events influence Rorty's intellectual and career trajectories? Answering this question requires that we move from a macrolevel down to a meso- and microlevel of analysis as we examine three critical junctures in Rorty's life, the institutional contexts in which these occurred, and how in each his thought was shaped by a combination of strategic and identity concerns.

71. See Rodney Stark and Roger Finke, 2000, *Acts of Faith: Explaining the Human Side of Religion*, Berkeley: University of California Press.

72. See the discussion in Conrad Cherry, Betty DeBerg, and Amanda Porterfield, 2001, *Religion on Campus*, Chapel Hill: University of North Carolina Press. For evidence that the religiosity of American college and university professors has been underestimated, see Neil Gross and Solon Simmons, forthcoming, "The Religiosity of American College and University Professors," *Sociology of Religion*. For an opposing view, see George Marsden, 1994, *The Soul of the American University: From Protestant Establishment to Established Nonbelief*, New York: Oxford University Press.

73. David Hollinger, 1996, *Science, Jews, and Secular Culture: Studies in Mid-Twentieth-Century American Intellectual History*, Princeton: Princeton University Press.

74. For evidence that spiritually inclined philosophers are more likely to become pragmatists than analysts, see Gross, "Becoming a Pragmatist Philosopher."

* **4** *

As noted in chapter 4, Rorty's masters thesis, written under the supervision of Charles Hartshorne at the University of Chicago in 1952, was a contribution to metaphysics. It examined the role played by the concept of potentiality across different domains of Whitehead's metaphysical thought. Insofar as this concept was important for Whitehead, focusing on it gave Rorty an opportunity to explicate what he saw as the key features of Whitehead's system. The thesis was intended to go beyond mere exegesis, however, and was supposed to show up some of the problems and ambiguities in Whitehead's approach, while pointing the way toward possible solutions.

Although he did not know it at the time, Rorty's choice of masters thesis topic would have an important long-term effect on his intellectual career. This was so because the decision to write on Whitehead represented a decision to practice a different kind of philosophy than was being practiced in most other top departments, where logical positivism and allied philosophical movements came to rule the day as the wave of rigorism washed over the American university. Graduate students at other schools could be found writing dissertations such as "A Semantically Complete Foundation for Logic and Mathematics" (John Myhill, Harvard, 1949), "Operationalism as an Epistemological Theory of Meaning" (Robert Dewey, Harvard, 1949), "Pragmatics and Probabilities" (James W. Oliver, Harvard, 1949), "A Study in Meaning: The Interchangeability of Expressions in Non-Extensional Contexts" (Leonard Linsky, University of California, Berkeley, 1949), or "The Role of Propositions in Philosophical Logic, with Special Reference to the Philosophy of Bertrand Russell" (Donald Kalish, University of California, Berkeley, 1949). This kind of precise analytic work was miles away from the abstract speculation of Rorty's masters thesis, and that he'd chosen to write such a thesis may have been a factor in the decision of the Harvard department not to grant him a fellowship. By contrast, as argued in chapter 5, the strategy of the Yale philosophy department for carving out a distinctive disciplinary niche was to cast itself as a holdout against the growing analytic dominance of the field, embracing the notion of pluralism and, as a central component of it, metaphysics. Paul Weiss, under whom Rorty ended up writing his dissertation, was a metaphysician who had worked closely with Hartshorne on the Peirce papers. So while Rorty's identity as an aspiring metaphysician made him look somewhat suspect in the eyes of Harvard, the same identity rendered him appealing to professors at Yale. It cannot be known with any certainty what kind of intellectual career Rorty would have had had he gone to Harvard, but it is possible that his commitment to pluralism—which ultimately fueled his critiques of the analytic paradigm—might have been less developed.[75]

As a twenty-year-old, Rorty could hardly have foreseen these kinds of path dependencies. So what led him to write on Whitehead? A Bourdieusian approach offers some leverage on the question.

First, Bourdieu helps us explain how it was that Rorty wound up getting a masters degree in philosophy at Chicago in the first place. As noted in chapter 3, Rorty's parents were not well off financially. Intellectuals may be described, however, as Bourdieu has characterized them, as dominated members of the dominant class, and the Rortys passed along those forms of wealth they did possess—their high levels of cultural and intellectual capital—to their son, while also activating their extensive social networks of writers, artists, and professors on his behalf. Chapter 3 observed several instances where this occurred. For example, Rorty had grown up in a household where facility with language was expected of everyone, where books were readily available, and where his parents engaged in efforts to teach him how to write well, all of which helped him get into the University of Chicago and do well enough there to consider a career as a philosopher. At the same time, only well-educated parents would have considered sending their child off to college at the age of fifteen, and only parents who cared more about intellectual and cultural pursuits than about material success would have preferred Chicago to other elite institutions. That Winifred Raushenbush had herself spent time at the university and become friends with several professors there meant that, once Richard moved to Hyde Park, she could use her social networks to her son's advantage, helping him navigate the tricky waters of fellowships, giving him advice on interactions with professors, and getting him invitations to dinners with faculty couples like the Redfields. Finally, the fact that Rorty's parents were intellectuals made it more likely that he

75. Rorty has said in this regard, "Had I gone to Harvard I would have gotten acquainted with analytic philosophy sooner than I did. The only representatives of that brand of philosophy at Yale were Carl Gustav ('Peter') Hempel, later a cherished colleague at Princeton. After Hempel gratefully seized the chance to escape from Yale, Arthur Pap took his place. Hempel and Pap were marginalized by the rest of the Yale department, just as the remaining non-analytic philosophers at Harvard were marginalized by Quine and his disciples. (Quine's task was made easier by C. I. Lewis' success in taking the Harvard department back to Kant, thereby nullifying the advances made by James and Royce, and setting American philosophy back by several decades.)" Rorty, "Intellectual Autobiography."

would aspire to become one himself and that they would be supportive of his aspirations, however much they might have wished he become a writer rather than a philosopher. This support was not unimportant in his decision to stay on at Chicago for the masters thesis.

Second, again following Bourdieu, it is possible that Rorty's social background predisposed him to be antagonistic to logical positivism and sympathetic to the project of metaphysics. In the first thirty years of the twentieth century, as described in chapter 1, many aspiring entrants to the intellectual arena—most notably first- and second-generation immigrants who were Jewish—found themselves relegated to positions outside the academy and sought to make up for the structural disadvantages of their class, ethnic, and religious backgrounds by becoming learned and cultivated with respect to European culture and thought—something that their own parental backgrounds sometimes prepared them for, but that more often represented a perceived deficiency that had to be overcome through intensive self-education and immersion in environments like City College. The next generation to knock at the academy's door, in the 1940s and 1950s, pursued a different strategy: they would make up for their lack of intellectual and cultural capital by honing their skills with forms of thought that were more readily available from the public education system—mathematics, statistics, logic, and so on—and that, in the context of the scientism of the Atomic Age, were defined as being of especially high symbolic value. It was members of this generation who served as carriers for the new rigorism.

Rorty's parents, children of immigrants both—though certainly not immigrants with low levels of education—had followed the strategy of the first generation of intellectual aspirants and looked disdainfully upon the second. They mounted claims to intellectual authority as broadminded and well-educated humanists and social critics rather than technicians, and passed on some of the associated symbolic repertoires to their son. Although his own generational experiences might have inclined him in a more scientistic direction, it was precisely by rejecting scientism that Richard could best defend his inherited intellectual and cultural capital against devaluation. This he did by embracing metaphysics and indirectly thumbing his nose at those who would insist, with the positivists, that metaphysics is a meaningless enterprise, that philosophy is a handmaiden to science, and that there is little value in traditional forms of philosophical or intellectual competency.

This sheds some light on Rorty's decision to become a metaphysician. But Bourdieu only gets us so far. It is possible to craft an ad hoc explanation using his theory, but Bourdieu's basic prediction—and Collins's—would be that Rorty, well endowed with cultural, intellectual, and social capital, should have gravitated toward a thesis topic likely to garner maximal attention in the philosophical field as a whole and should have been able to leverage his status as an up-and-coming member of the intellectual elite into an affiliation with a professor who could have supervised such a thesis. This probably would have entailed working with Carnap. But Rorty did no such thing, and recalls that he found Carnap "intellectually ascetic" and his views "irrefutable and unwelcome."[76]

The theory of intellectual self-concept helps us better explain the intellectual choice at hand. Rorty's time at Chicago occurred during prime identity formation years in his life course and was a period when he was making the transition from one institutional affiliation to another. The institution with which he had been most closely affiliated as a child and young adolescent—his family—had all the characteristics likely to make it a site of identity formation. Although his parents ostensibly wanted Richard to follow his own intellectual path, they were in the habit of rewarding him—positively sanctioning him—when he expressed views similar to their own, as James did when Richard wrote from Chicago to say how dissatisfied he'd been with David Riesman's recently published *The Lonely Crowd*: "Neither Winifred nor I could take Riesman & Co. I enclose carbon of my review—congratulate your friends for not taking any wooden nickels. Intellectual vessels have to be tighter than that to carry water and quench a thirst."[77] Richard was also close to his parents, so that the institution was one where strong affective bonds were present. The Rortys had developed a comprehensive and well-integrated worldview that brought together leftist politics, anti-Communism, and a social-ecological perspective, and they actively communicated this worldview to Richard through conversation, by having him read their writings, by the other books and periodicals they kept around the house, and by exposing him firsthand to their friends and family members, many of whom were of a similar mind. Furthermore, he inhabited his parents' household when he was young and impressionable and had no independently acquired identity strands that might conflict with the identity his parents sought to instill in him or any significant countervailing social ties or institutional affiliations that might have pulled him in other directions. At the same time, his parents' strident politics and rhetoric provided Richard with a

76. Ibid.

77. James Rorty to Richard Rorty, November 9, 1950, RRP.

way to differentiate himself in moral terms from the more conservative, anti-intellectual families whose children were his classmates—as well as from other liberals who did not see the dangers of Communism. For these reasons, he came to integrate the core features of his parents' identity into his own self-concept narrative and left for Chicago as someone made almost entirely in his parents' image.

When he arrived in Hyde Park, however, he entered a solidaristic and ideologically cohesive institutional environment equally primed to shape his identity. The undergraduate college at Chicago, though by no means hostile to liberal anti-Communism, was an institution in which the most sacralized identity, for both students and faculty members, was that of someone steeped in the great books of the Western tradition. Insofar as this identity was bundled with a commitment—as it was for thinkers like Adler or Strauss—to the notion that from this tradition one could extract timeless philosophical truths, it was epistemologically at odds with his parents' worldview, which owed more to pragmatism. Rorty thus faced a conflict. Would his own emerging intellectual self-concept narrative continue to stress liberal anti-Communism and social ecologism, or would he follow the teachings of his new institution, seeing one of the most important distinctions among intellectuals to be that between ancients and moderns and locating himself squarely in the camp of the former? The resistance he evidenced to the Great Books program in letters home during his freshman year show what can happen when a previously acquired identity comes into conflict with a new one a thinker is asked to take on. As he spent more time at Chicago, however, surrounding himself with friends and teachers who had identified with the institution and beginning to feel developmental pressures to separate himself from his parents, this resistance waned, and he ended up rewriting his self-concept narrative. He continued to think of himself as a liberal anti-Communist, but, under the influence of Plato, a symbolic resource in effect mobilized by the institution, he jettisoned his parents' emphasis on social ecologism and pragmatism and became a seeker of timeless philosophical truths—a young scholar who saw himself as engaged with the ideas of philosophers past as well as the most significant of the present day and who would use this engagement to find answers to the enduring questions philosophy takes up.

This self-concept was further honed when he entered the Chicago philosophy department in pursuit of a masters degree. Despite the presence of Carnap and Morris, the department, with the support of Hutchins, was a site of active resistance to the program of logical positivism and the scientization of philosophy—and the limitation of its historical scope—that it proposed to carry out. McKeon, Thompson, and Hartshorne were among those who had been critical of the positivists, and Strauss, from his position in the Committee on Social Thought, was no more sympathetic. In this context, the intellectual identity that became coded as sacred was that of someone bent on resisting positivism—someone who would do his part, as Rorty said in the letter to his parents quoted in chapter 4, to "stop the positivist invasion." This was the identity Rorty now came to weave into his self-concept narrative, and though his social background may have predisposed him to locate himself in such a position in the intellectual taxonomy, as the Bourdieusian argument above suggests, the fact that the identity was celebrated in the institutional environment he inhabited no doubt increased the likelihood he would take it on.

There were different kinds of intellectual projects that students with such a self-concept could plausibly pursue at Chicago. It would have been consistent with the identity to attack positivism directly, for example, or to show one's disdain for the positivist dismissal of ethics or the history of philosophy by working in one of these areas or even to undertake work in the pragmatist tradition with the aim of showing that Peirce and Dewey had proven that efforts to cleanly separate the analytic from the synthetic were bound to fail. Another acceptable intellectual outlet for someone who opposed positivism—and one that was more symbolically charged—was to work on metaphysics. For the positivists, traditional metaphysics represented all that was wrong with philosophy. But had their dismissal of it been too hasty? Chicago philosophers asked their students to consider the possibility that this was so. The masters-level examination given to Rorty's Chicago friend Richard Schmitt, for example, who also finished his thesis in 1952, included the following question for the metaphysics portion of the test:

> Discussions of metaphysics are extremely confused and confusing. On the one hand, this confusion is taken to be a reason why philosophers should have nothing to do with metaphysics. On the other hand it is claimed that metaphysics cannot be avoided and that things done or assumptions made by anti-metaphysical philosophers are "really" metaphysical in any case. Try to bring some clarity out of this confusion, distinguishing a) the sense, if any, in which metaphysical problems are inescapable, b) the respects, if any, in which such problems can be solved, and c) the sense or senses in which metaphysics may be avoided. Illustrate your discussion by developing the consequences, both philosophical and scientific or practical, of

taking alternative positions, and by referring to such philosophers—e.g., Plato, Aristotle, Kant, Hume, Whitehead, Dewey, Carnap—as you find illuminating as examples.[78]

In this context, one of the illocutionary meanings of pursuing research into metaphysics was that one saw little value in positivist arguments and much value in traditional forms of philosophy. While Rorty's thesis engaged only minimally with positivist critiques, the very fact that it was unapologetically metaphysical and sought to understand the ultimate nature of reality using a conceptual language and approach that flew in the face of that championed by the positivists could be interpreted by Rorty and his friends and teachers as an indication that he had not fallen for positivist evasions of real and enduring philosophical concerns. The argument I want to advance is that Rorty chose to write a thesis on metaphysics in part *in order* to express and affirm this taxonomic positioning to himself and others and to do work he would feel to be resonant with his newfound sense of intellectual identity. As for why he decided to work on metaphysics rather than pursue one of the other lines of research that would have been seen as appropriate for a young thinker with his self-concept, this was a function of several things: that his knowledge of logic was not sufficiently advanced for him to be able to attack positivism on its own terms; that his foreign language skills were limited, which would have made it difficult for him to write a thesis on the classics or on contemporary European thought under McKeon; that working on Dewey or Peirce at that point would have done too little to differentiate him from his parents; that working on Whitehead represented an opportunity to make good use of his skills at abstraction; that it was metaphysics that had come under the most fire from the positivists, so that to work in the area was to step directly into the fray; and that, in light of his value commitments, he came to see Hartshorne as something of a heroic and kindly figure working to answer the big metaphysical questions the positivists had avoided, even if his orientation was more theological than Rorty's own.[79] In all likelihood, he approached Hartshorne about the possibility of working with him, and Hartshorne suggested a specific thesis topic based on his knowledge of the Whitehead literature. Although Rorty's

78. University of Chicago, Department of Philosophy, Final Examination for the Master's Degree, Field III–Metaphysics, February 20, 1952, RRP.

79. Indeed, given Rorty's family ties to the liberal Protestant establishment, it is no surprise that he could identify easily with Hartshorne, despite his own atheism. Thanks to Peter Hare for this point.

parents knew almost nothing about Whitehead's metaphysics, the fact that Whitehead was a popular figure among literary intellectuals at the time may have made the prospect of writing about him even more appealing. To be sure, Rorty accrued some local status and credibility as a result of his decision to work on Whitehead's metaphysics—enough that Hartshorne would recommend him to Yale. But it cannot be said that he gravitated toward the topic out of a desire to maximize his status or prestige in the philosophical field as a whole. When he wrote in his graduate school application essay that "in metaphysics, my interest and study have been chiefly concentrated on modern attempts at a systematic description of reality, within the bounds of a framework which is, broadly speaking, empiricist,"[80] he was describing the direction his thought had taken as a result of his desire to do work that would be consistent with the intellectual self-concept to which he had come to cleave during his years at Chicago: that of a philosopher engaged in traditional philosophical pursuits and interested in the ultimate nature of reality, but concerned to hold the line against positivist scientization.

∗ 5 ∗

According to standard interpretations of Rorty's intellectual trajectory, Rorty started out as a hard-nosed analytic philosopher and only later came to doubt the value of the analytic program. But, as we have seen, this is wrong: his undergraduate and graduate training were in departments where, on the whole, analytic philosophy was looked on with skepticism; his masters thesis was a work of traditional metaphysics; and while his dissertation was appreciative in parts of analytic contributions, it was precisely logical empiricism's narrowness of vision and unwillingness to engage in dialogue with other approaches to which he called attention. Accounting for Rorty's intellectual trajectory thus means understanding not only why, in the 1970s, he became a critic of the analytic paradigm but also why he became a champion of it after leaving graduate school. With respect to Rorty's analytic turn, theories emphasizing the strategic nature of intellectual life offer a convincing explanation. Rorty was professionally ambitious and realized he could not get a job in a top philosophy department—much less tenure—unless he became a participant in the analytic enterprise. Much as his later work and exit from philosophy may be read as a rebellion against disciplinary authority, so should his early

80. Undated draft of graduate school application essay, RRP.

work be seen as representing a moment of conformity to disciplinary status structures.

But while status-oriented theories such as those of Bourdieu and Collins prove helpful in explaining Rorty's moves during this time, what they claim to be a general feature of all intellectual life everywhere—the tendency for intellectuals to gravitate toward work that will bring them the highest status returns—turns out to be more true of certain moments in the intellectual life course than others. Rorty, whose social background leant him a great deal of self-confidence in intellectual matters, never appears to have been genuinely worried about whether he would get tenure at Princeton, but this was because he had a well-honed sense for which lines of philosophical argumentation would play well and which wouldn't. It was this sense that led him to throw his hat in with the analysts. But this was a unique period in his career. Indeed, the broader lesson suggested by a consideration of Rorty's biography is that strategic considerations concerning professional advancement are most likely to influence the content of an academic's thought in the years when she or he is struggling to secure tenure and build an initial reputation. Of course, some graduate students are strategic with regard to their choice of graduate departments, advisors, and dissertation topics, and well-established scholars may also be much concerned with their professional reputations. But most graduate students do not know enough about the fields they are entering and the requirements for success therein to make informed strategic decisions.[81] While established scholars may and often do want to keep their names in the limelight, they risk no total loss of income, benefits, or professional identity if they fail to do so. It is younger scholars, just starting out as professors, for whom the evaluation of their work by others matters most and who are therefore more likely to adjust the content of their work in accordance with strategic considerations.[82] This is why radical intellectual innovation—except perhaps in fields like mathematics—is most likely to come, not from young scholars, but from those who are sufficiently established as to be able to take bold professional risks.

This is not to say that young academicians working toward tenure are slaves to reputation and decide automatically to work on whatever top-

81. It is likely that levels of graduate student strategicness vary over time. One has the sense that graduate students today are more strategic with regard to professional concerns than they were fifty years ago.

82. I take this to be the lesson of Camic's work on the early Parsons as well, although I emphasize more field positionality than credibility in what follows.

ics or advance whichever ideas they think will be most warmly received, either in their local environments or in the field as a whole. As Bourdieu and Collins both recognize, such choices are constrained: it would be foolish to work in an area or on a topic for which one does not have sufficient intellectual capital to do a good job, though it may sometimes be possible to move into new areas. At the same time, the theory of intellectual self-concept would suggest that the choices young scholars make will be shaped, at least at the margins, by their sense of intellectual identity. Influenced though their work products are likely to be by the desire to impress those who hold the keys to tenure, the psychic costs of a wholly instrumental orientation in which one agrees to abandon or change any or all identity and intellectual commitments as may be required by the logic of the field would be too much to bear—and would, in any event, be self-defeating, for it would suggest to others that one has no solid intellectual core. Within these constraints, however, young scholars must impress opinion leaders or decision makers in their departments, universities, and fields, or risk losing their appointments and squandering their reputations.

Although it is common, as Bourdieu has pointed out, for intellectuals to downplay their strategic orientations, there is archival evidence of Rorty's professional ambition in the early years of his career. His autobiographical recollections of having been ambitious during his time at Wellesley, along with the letter cited in chapter 6 by then colleague Ellen Haring predicting his imminent departure for more prestigious institutional climes, suggest that Rorty was indeed looking to move up to a better-ranked department. But how important was it to him to obtain status from the discipline as a whole? A comment he made in passing a few years later suggests it was extremely important. The occasion was a review of Jencks and Riesman's *The Academic Revolution*. "At the turn of the century," Rorty noted,

> the typical American professor looked to his institution, to its head, and to the community or social groups which supported it for approval, status and rewards. His position was modeled on, and his attitude copied, those of the Protestant ministry. By a series of imperceptible changes, we have now reached a point at which a professor at a large university may not remember the president's name and may have no clear notion who supports the university nor when and why it was founded. He doesn't need to know any of these things, because his career and his status barely depend upon the institution at all. They depend upon how his work looks to the manda-

rins of his professional guild—the scholars and scientists who, with luck, will read his publications and write the letters which will get him another job wherever and whenever he wants one. Further, a scholar's self-respect comes largely from the praise he receives from his peers; approval by his students, or his institution, or the community, is prized—but all that is dust and ashes if he is not "respected by his colleagues."[83]

Rorty did not flag this as an autobiographical remark, but it can certainly be read as such.

The question is whether it was Rorty's desire for "praise ... from his peers"—and for the kind of academic position that would go along with it—that led him to become a champion of linguistic philosophy, with the ultimate goal of getting a position at a top school like Princeton and then securing tenure there. The circumstantial evidence suggests the answer is yes.

On his arrival at Wellesley, Rorty's competencies were in the history of philosophy, metaphysics, and pragmatism; one section of his dissertation also saw him trying his hand at analytic-style argumentation. Given his interest in upward mobility in the field, the problem he faced was how to mobilize these competencies, doing philosophical work that would be well regarded by important philosophers elsewhere on the institutional landscape. Rorty must have realized that certain of these competencies—his knowledge of Whitehead, for example, or familiarity with metaphysics more generally—would, given the way he had deployed them at Chicago, limit his capacity to get a job offer from a top department. There were some institutions where such competencies remained highly valued—Wellesley, for one—but at most elite graduate programs, given the rise of analytic philosophy and the new rigorism, they were not. As he went about choosing topics on which to write articles, therefore, he sought ways to leverage his knowledge and intellectual skills into contributions that would be appreciated by those it was most important for him to impress: analytic philosophers who controlled assistant professor slots in top-ranked programs.

Chapter 6 identified two lines of argumentation he pursued in this regard: linking himself with the nascent subfield of metaphilosophy, where he could use his broad historical competencies and McKeonesque training to bring nonanalytic thought into dialogue with analytic thought;

83. Richard Rorty, no date, "Review of *The Academic Revolution*," RRP. I can find no evidence of this piece having appeared in print.

and showcasing the importance of classical American pragmatism for those philosophers who had already taken the linguistic turn. With the theories of Bourdieu and Collins arrayed before us, we can see these not merely as lines of argumentation Rorty happened to see as important but as career strategies, patterns of intellectual engagement designed to capitalize on his preexisting skill and knowledge base. With Bourdieu and Collins, I do not mean to suggest that Rorty sat down and calculated which philosophical arguments would take him farthest in his career. Although Alexander has charged Bourdieu's notion of "unconscious strategies" with being nonsensical, I see no problem in suggesting that Rorty had only a half-conscious awareness of what would be good to work on from the standpoint of building his reputation. Nor is my claim that Rorty failed to attend to the intrinsic philosophical merits of the arguments he was developing. Strategies for achieving academic distinction usually shape intellectual choice precisely by coloring thinkers' impressions of the intrinsic intellectual merit of various lines of thought. This is why, as sociologists of scientific knowledge have insisted, the old distinction between externalist and internalist approaches to explaining ideas doesn't hold up, for it ignores the possibility that external determinants operate through internal evaluations of intellectual worth.

The process by which these factors shaped Rorty's thought can be reconstructed by examining his recollections of the period. Chapter 6 noted that Rorty recalls a growing awareness, during his final years at Yale, of how dominant analytic philosophy was becoming in the discipline. He has written:

> During my four years at Yale I was fortunate to have Milton Fisk, Roger Hancock and Richard Schmitt as fellow graduate students and companions. I spent a lot of time exercising my dialectical abilities on these patient friends, priding myself on my McKeon-taught ability to show how any philosophical position could be rendered impregnable to criticism by redefining terms and adopting alternative first principles. Schmitt finally pointed out to me that I was turning into a monomaniacal bore, and this rebuke encouraged me to look for some more constructive way of doing philosophy. Analytic philosophy was the obvious direction in which to turn. Even at Yale the suspicion was growing that Carnap and Quine might be riding the wave of the future. So I began looking around for analytic philosophers who were less reductionistic and less positivistic than they, less convinced that philosophy had only recently come of age. This led me to the work of Sellars, whose work set me on the paths that I have spent

the rest of my life trying to clear and broaden. Sellars combined a Carnapian style (lots of numbered premises, bedecked with lots of quantifiers) both with a thorough acquaintance with the history of philosophy and with an exuberant metaphysical imagination. That mixture of logic-worship, erudition, and romance was reminiscent of Peirce, with whose writings I had spent a lot of time, hoping to discover the non-existent secret of his non-existent "System," and, in particular, to figure out what he meant by "Thirdness is real." Sellars and Peirce are alike in the diversity and richness of their talents, as well as in the cryptic character of their writings. But Sellars, unlike Peirce, preached a fairly coherent set of doctrines.[84]

Rorty's early conversion to the analytic paradigm thus took the following form: At Yale he spent a lot of time practicing his McKeonesque skills with his friends and deploying them in his dissertation. As he did so he came to realize that their symbolic value and the value of the historical knowledge that went with them was declining because of transformations in the intellectual field, a realization that was then reinforced by what he experienced as his relative professional marginalization at Wellesley. He thus became inclined to take analytic thought more seriously and to cast himself as a philosopher of high rigor. He could only make the transition to the analytic paradigm, however, after he found an analytic philosopher—Sellars—whose ideas he could see as continuous in fundamental respects with his own. Rorty's move into the analytic paradigm, in other words, was conditional upon his being able to offer a coherent and convincing narrative to himself and others about how, in undergoing such a conversion, he was not abandoning intellectual beliefs and identities previously held dear, and this required that he have the necessary symbolic resources at his disposal: the thought of Sellars, whom Rorty saw as bridging the gap between Peirce and the contemporary analytic movement. Rorty thus rewrote his intellectual self-concept in accordance with strategic demands. As he went about refashioning himself as an analyst, he did not attempt to portray himself as something he was not. His skills at symbolic logic, for example, were limited, and he did not try to make a name for himself as a logician. Instead, he capitalized on his historical training at Chicago and knowledge of Peirce to carve out a distinctive niche within the analytic community.

On his arrival at Princeton, as was argued in chapter 7, it became even more clear to Rorty that the dominant figures in the discipline—and cer-

---

84. Rorty, "Intellectual Autobiography."

tainly in his department—were analysts and that recasting himself as a linguistic philosopher had been a good move professionally. Within a few years he had received job offers from several other departments. While this no doubt reduced his concerns about getting tenure at Princeton, it likely also reinforced his understanding that the strategy he had initiated while at Wellesley—and that he was extending while at Princeton to include the advancement of a novel Wittgensteinian-Sellarsian line in the philosophy of mind—was the way to go as far as achieving professional success was concerned. He was indeed, during this phase of his career, receiving a great deal of intellectual status and perhaps even emotional energy for all the good philosophical work he was doing and appears to have read the attention as a sign that the lines of inquiry he was pursuing were the right ones. Concerned to further solidify his reputation, he made the rounds of the philosophy colloquium circuit, sent his manuscripts to leading analysts for comment, and—by editing *The Linguistic Turn*—made himself a spokesman for the analytic movement. In the absence of strategic concerns, Rorty probably would have continued to hew to a more strictly McKeonesque line, engaging with questions in the history of philosophy. Pace Bourdieu and Collins, however, processes centered on the quest for status in the intellectual field were not ubiquitous features of Rorty's intellectual experience but concentrated in a particular period of his career: the years during which he sought to establish a foothold in the discipline and secure a permanent slot in a top department.

* 6 *

Chapter 8 detailed the experiences that precipitated Rorty's break with the paradigm of analytic philosophy in the 1970s: his growing realization that he had broader intellectual interests than many other analysts; the increasingly strained relations between him and his colleagues at Princeton, partially as a result; and the intellectual and moral support for historicism he received from contact with thinkers like Thomas Kuhn and Quentin Skinner.

There are two questions about interrelated developments at this stage of Rorty's career that need to be answered. First, how should Rorty's break with the analytic paradigm be understood sociologically? And second, why, having made such a break, did he embrace the identity "pragmatist?"

With regard to the first question, both strategic and self-concept factors must be invoked. I argued above that Rorty's movement into analytic philosophy in the 1960s represented an instance of conformity to disciplinary status structures, as these had been reconfigured by the rise of the new rigorism. By the 1970s, in contrast, the emphasis on rigor lessened. In many humanities fields, rigorism came to be seen as suspect, and status flowed to those who formulated or advanced alternative paradigms. How did this affect Rorty's thought?

In terms of strategic considerations, there can be no question but that, in this context, Rorty had a strong incentive to break with the analytic paradigm and become an expositor of the view that others should do the same. Although *Philosophy and the Mirror of Nature* almost failed to be accepted for publication because one of the reviewers thought it too technical,[85] Rorty, well positioned in a variety of intellectual networks, may have been better able to anticipate what the book's reception would be. In an environment where many humanists were coming to have their doubts about the new rigorism, there would be tremendous interest in a book—particularly one written by an insider—that used "rigorous" arguments to make a case for why foundationalist versions of analytic philosophy, and by implication its cognates in other fields, were ill conceived. That Rorty may have realized there would be such interest helps explain why he was eager to write the book and, perhaps—with the idea in mind of eventually accumulating status by writing it—why he allowed himself to drift more out of an analytic orbit over the course of the 1970s.

Nevertheless, it is doubtful that status incentives alone would have been enough to cause his break with the analytic program. As is evident from the many bad reviews *Philosophy and the Mirror of Nature* received from other analytic philosophers, the arguments Rorty cited as justification for moving away from foundationalism—including those of Quine, Davidson, Kuhn, Sellars, and Wittgenstein—could be interpreted multiple ways. Where Rorty saw them calling into question the value of representationalist theories of truth, others saw them as more consistent with

85. Rorty's editor at Princeton University Press, Sanford Thatcher—a former student of his—sent Rorty a note along with the review in 1977, saying "I now have both of our readers' reports, and I confess I don't quite know what to make of them. They are diametrically opposed in the recommendations they make, and what is most puzzling is that the negative reader is the one I expected to be most positive, and vice-versa.... I am prepared to go ahead and send the manuscript out to a third reader now in order to tip the balance one way or another, positively, I hope, of course. But I hesitate to make this move until you have had a chance to respond, for what you say may affect my thinking about what sort of third reader I should be looking for." Sanford Thatcher to Richard Rorty, December 12, 1977, RRP.

revised versions of realism. Familiarity with such arguments themselves, therefore, along with the status that would accrue to thinkers who would deploy them as Rorty did, was certainly not enough to cause a philosopher to come down one way or another on the question of the value of analytic philosophy, which continued to have many defenders. Moreover, Rorty, familiar with the attitudes of his analytic colleagues at Princeton and elsewhere, must have known that while the book might be well received by Continentalists, pragmatists, and those outside academic philosophy, it would not be so received by analysts—after all, it called into question the value of the very intellectual capital in which they had invested. Had Rorty been interested in securing status in his disciplinary field, he would never have written the book. True, he can be seen as having simply shifted his orientation toward a more interdisciplinary humanities field. But it is difficult to imagine a thinker doing this, and turning his back on his own discipline, out of a desire for status alone.

In fact, it was Rorty's self-conception as a philosopher with broad intellectual and historical interests that allowed him to make the shift. This identity and the endowments of intellectual capital that went with it were a product mostly of the institutional environments to which he was exposed as a young man. I have already explained, in discussing Rorty's masters thesis, why his social background predisposed him to defend traditional forms of intellectual capital against attack, but more to the point here is that, as described above, his formative intellectual years were spent in a local institutional setting—Chicago—where ancients, not moderns, ruled the day and where students who could display mastery of the history of thought and of a wide variety of intellectual traditions were looked upon most favorably. Rorty took on the associated identity of historically minded philosopher and retained it while at Yale. Moreover, influenced while at Chicago by McKeon and the curriculum he designed, Rorty came to link his broad-minded and historical conception of philosophy to the pluralist view that the discipline is populated by scholars who take radically incommensurate approaches, a view reinforced during his time at Yale, where pluralism was the most sacralized intellectual identity and the department watchword. A scholar with such a self-conception could not hope to find the single approach that would trump all the others but would necessarily measure intellectual progress by the degree of fruitful dialogue engendered among advocates of different approaches. Although Rorty's early work—in particular, his dissertation and contributions to metaphilosophy—was informed by this perspective, he was forced over the course of the 1960s by strategic pressures into the view that, incommensurability aside, the analytic focus on language was *the* most important discovery in the field. But by the 1970s, with his tenure secure, his earlier Chicago and Yale identities returned to the fore, and as they did he began to find his colleagues at Princeton more and more narrow and started associating with others on the Princeton scene, especially at the Institute for Advanced Study, who were equally oriented toward the history of thought and committed to historicism. Increasingly Rorty turned for inspiration to those working outside academic philosophy, and as he did he came to see other broad-minded humanists such as Skinner or Foucault or Derrida as his real interlocutors and aspired to be in a department where engagement with such figures would be expected and approved of. The status that would flow from those outside academic philosophy to Rorty for having written *Philosophy and the Mirror of Nature* appealed to him, then, precisely because his intellectual self-concept was already leading him away from concern about his disciplinary standing and into a more interdisciplinary universe. This suggests one of the ways in which concerns over status and considerations of self-concept may sometimes interact, as one's self-concept shapes the nature of one's professional ambitions.[86]

Rorty's antifoundationalism was not cast in generic terms, however, but, as the 1970s and 1980s wore on, as part and parcel of the identity "pragmatist." In the introduction he wrote to *Consequences of Pragmatism*, Rorty noted that "among contemporary analytic philosophers, pragmatism is usually regarded as an outdated philosophical movement—one which flourished in the early years of this century in a rather provincial atmosphere, and which has now been either refuted or *aufgehoben*."[87] Yet Rorty insisted that for those who take the view, as he did, that "analytic philosophy culminates in Quine, the latter Wittgenstein, Sellars, and Davidson—which is to say that it transcends and cancels itself" because "these thinkers ... blur the positivist distinctions between the semantic and the pragmatic, the analytic and the synthetic, the linguistic and the empirical, theory and observation,"[88] pragmatism can be seen as neither

86. It may also be worth mentioning here Rorty's identity as a literary intellectual—as a thinker well versed in the history of literature and of the opinion that literature and poetry are profoundly important forms of human expression. It is not clear that this self-concept—which also reflected the influence of his parents—helped push him back in the direction of pragmatism, but it certainly incentivized his participation in broad humanities discussions in the 1980s and 1990s and may have facilitated the uptake of his work by scholars of literature.

87. Rorty, *Consequences of Pragmatism*, xvii.

88. Ibid., xviii.

refuted nor transcended. In fact, "the history" of analytic philosophy "has been marked by a gradual 'pragmaticization' of the original tenets of logical positivism."[89] "James and Dewey," Rorty claimed, excluding Peirce, "were not only waiting at the end of the dialectical road which analytic philosophy traveled, but are waiting at the end of the road which, for example, Foucault and Deleuze are currently traveling."[90] This was so not only in the restricted sense that they held the views of truth they did—which Rorty glossed as a tendency to deny there was anything interesting to be said about it—but also in the more expansive sense that they wished to bring about a culture in which "we see ourselves as never encountering reality *except under a chosen description*—as, in Nelson Goodman's phrase, making worlds rather than finding them."[91] Such a culture would still contain experts—philosophers and others—who solve problems, but it would be well known that their capacity to do so is contingent on the kinds of things people want to get done and on the linguistic frameworks in which they happen to be enmeshed. No one living in such a "post-philosophical culture" would imagine that a solution could be found to the problem of what *should* get done that would reflect anything more than a temporary consensus among the relevant parties nor that one might, using the appropriate procedures, somehow get around the fact that humans invariably interact with the world through the medium of culture and language. It was just such an antifoundationalist culture that James and Dewey had envisioned, and they set about drawing out its implications for politics, ethics, aesthetics, education, science, and more. This, Rorty claimed, was pragmatism's true legacy.

This was not the first time Rorty had written positively about pragmatism. As noted throughout the book, pragmatism was important to him from the earliest days of his graduate education, given its lingering presence at Chicago and Yale. His dissertation, for example, had come to an explicitly pragmatist conclusion: "our descriptions of logical empiricism's difficulties ... suggest that we need to strive for the sort of rapprochement between formal logic, semiotics, and traditional epistemology which is found in the work of Peirce."[92] Nor did Rorty's youthful interest in pragmatism end with his departure from Yale. It testifies to the extent of Rorty's interest that in the early years of his career, he reviewed, for a number of academic journals, books that either drew upon or offered commentary on pragmatism, such as Alan Pasch's *Experience and the Ana-*

89. Ibid.   90. Ibid.   91. Ibid., xxxix.
92. Rorty, "The Concept of Potentiality," 573.

lytic, Edward Moore's *American Pragmatism*, and Paul Goodman's *Utopian Essays and Practical Proposals*.[93] Rorty's positive assessment of pragmatism comes out clearly in these reviews. In one, for example, he declared that "Dewey's philosophy is the noblest and most profound statement of the aims of a democratic society."[94] Equally important, as argued in chapter 7, Rorty's early contributions to analytic thought are imprinted with the stamp of pragmatism. His interpretation of Wittgenstein may have been influenced by his reading of Peirce, as he suggested at the time.[95] More straightforwardly, Rorty had been nursing the central claim of *Philosophy and the Mirror of Nature* for at least a decade.[96] As early as the conclusion of his introduction to *The Linguistic Turn*, he announced "the beginning of a thoroughgoing rethinking of certain epistemological difficulties" stemming from "the traditional 'spectatorial' account of knowledge" that is "the common target of philosophers as different as Dewey, Hampshire, Sartre, Heidegger, and Wittgenstein."[97] If this rethinking were to prove successful, Rorty predicted, it would "lead to reformulations everywhere else in philosophy."[98] That Rorty saw his own forays into the philosophy of mind as a step in this direction becomes clear in a 1970 paper in which Rorty noted that his Wittgensteinian account of intuitions and concepts—in which these are "analyzed into dispositions to linguistic behavior"—leaves "the notion of a 'representation' ... without work to do. The notion of a Vorstellung—something in the mind which stands in place of the object to be known—thus vanishes, and with it the notion of epistemology as the discipline which investigates the internal relations between Vorstellungen."[99] In another article from the same year, he argued that the thrust of the entire "post-Cartesian tradition (exemplified by Wittgenstein, Austin, Sellars, Dewey, and Quine)" is to deny that

93. Richard Rorty, 1959, "Review of Alan Pasch's *Experience and the Analytic*," *International Journal of Ethics* 70:75–77; Richard Rorty, 1962, "Review of Edward Moore's *American Pragmatism: Peirce, James, and Dewey*," *International Journal of Ethics* 72:146–47; Richard Rorty, 1963, "Review of Paul Goodman's *Utopian Essays and Practical Proposals*," *Teachers College Record* 64:743–44.

94. Rorty, "Review of Goodman," 744.

95. Rorty, "Realism, Categories, and the 'Linguistic Turn.'"

96. He says in the preface to *Philosophy and the Mirror of Nature* that he began "thinking out [the book's] plot ... in 1969–70" (xiv).

97. Rorty, "Introduction: Metaphilosophical Difficulties of Linguistic Philosophy," *The Linguistic Turn*, 39.

98. Ibid.

99. Rorty, "Strawson's Objectivity Argument," 243.

knowledge claims could possibly have the kind of permanent grounding epistemology aims to provide.[100] Rorty thus saw many "affinities" between contemporary trends in analytic thought and pragmatism's behavioristic rendering of meaning, in which the purely representational significance of belief falls away.[101]

Nevertheless, it was not until the 1970s that Rorty became more publicly wedded to the pragmatist tradition. Increasingly he described himself as a philosopher who had taken a pragmatist turn. Why?

Again, strategic considerations were probably not irrelevant. Rorty recognized that there was growing interest throughout the humanities in antifoundationalism. He knew that pragmatism, a tradition in which he had been trained, could be interpreted as continuous with these developments and framed as a more adequate form of antifoundationalism than others because pragmatism, with its historical ties to progressivism and democracy, was not as nihilistic as its more postmodern French counterparts. Indeed, Rorty and some of his champions like Cornel West were at pains to argue such a point throughout the 1980s, and insofar as this is so there is some truth to the often advanced claim that the pragmatist revival was linked to the explosion of interest in postmodernism and poststructuralism.

I want to suggest, however, that considerations of self-concept were at least as important in leading Rorty to become a champion of pragmatism. These had to do with the increasing salience to him of the self-concept "leftist American patriot," an identity whose original meaning for him was bound up with anti-Communism but that soon came to stand opposed to the identity of cosmopolitan multiculturalist.[102] The instance of Rorty expressing this self-concept for which he is best known occurred several decades later. In 1994 Rorty published an op-ed piece in the Sunday New York Times with the provocative title "The Unpatriotic Academy."[103] Coming on a day when the lead front-page story concerned President Bill Clinton's proposal to finance key aspects of welfare reform by taxing food stamps and slashing aid to poor, elderly immigrants,[104] Rorty's focus on

100. Rorty, "Cartesian Epistemology and Changes in Ontology," 283.

101. Richard Rorty, 1971, "Review of A. J. Ayer's *The Origins of Pragmatism*," *Philosophical Review* 80:96–100, 96.

102. See the discussion in Martha Nussbaum, 1996, *For Love of Country? Debating the Limits of Patriotism*, Boston: Beacon.

103. Richard Rorty, 1994, "The Unpatriotic Academy," *New York Times*, February 13, E15.

104. Jason DeParle, 1994, "Clinton Considers Taxing Aid to Poor to Pay for Reform," *New York Times*, February 13, 1.

the politics of academic life might have seemed, at a glance, an indication of the social and political irrelevance of the American professoriate. Who cares about academic politics when millions of impoverished Americans are about to be kicked off the welfare rolls? Would it not have been better for Rorty—an avowed leftist—to use the space to denounce the whole project of welfare reform? Although such a denunciation was not specifically on Rorty's agenda that day, it was precisely the academic left's political irrelevance to which he aimed to call attention. The socioeconomic reality of the early 1990s, Rorty realized, was not a story of economic growth floating all boats but of fewer social resources being devoted to "the weakest and poorest among us." Rather than protesting the erosion of the American welfare state, however, and helping to formulate a viable progressive agenda, leftists in the American academy, Rorty charged, had become mired in discussions about the politics of difference. He recognized that groups like "women, African-Americans, gay men and lesbians" had "gotten a raw deal in our society" and acknowledged that efforts to redress their grievances "will ... help to make our country much more decent, more tolerant and more civilized." But he saw one form taken by these efforts—the program of multiculturalism—to be at odds with a revived American progressivism. This was so because multiculturalism "repudiates the idea of a national identity," depicting any commitment to common national values and ideals as an attempt to assimilate and dominate culturally the otherwise heterogeneous groups that compose American society, groups whose distinctive cultural practices multiculturalism wished to celebrate and preserve. For this reason, supporters of multiculturalism—whom Rorty claimed could be found in abundance in American ivory towers—were unwilling to embrace patriotism in any form, even a left-wing patriotism that would ground its demands for social change in the insistence that America "live up to ... [its] professed ideals" of equality and justice for all. But in practical terms this was a recipe for political failure. "An unpatriotic left has never achieved anything," Rorty asserted, suggesting that only patriotism, loosely defined in terms of national pride, is capable of mobilizing mass support for leftist goals.

The column represented neither the first nor the last time that Rorty would express the self-concept of an intellectual with leftist patriotic inclinations. The same idea, for example, animated his often-cited 1983 essay on "postmodern bourgeois liberalism."[105] There Rorty's goal had been

---

105. Richard Rorty, "Postmodern Bourgeois Liberalism," in *Objectivity, Relativism, and Truth*, 197–202.

to argue against what he saw as a recent turn in moral philosophy toward a renewed Kantian emphasis on abstract principles of morality and justice. In the real world, Rorty claimed, people rarely make decisions on the basis of such principles. Rather, they look to "historical narratives"[106] about the groups to which they belong and assess the morality of acts by examining how well they fit with their particularistic identities. Insofar as this is so, moral philosophers concerned only with abstract principles remain unable "to converse with their fellow citizens"[107] or persuade them of anything. Why does moral philosophy find itself in such a predicament? The answer, according to Rorty, is that many American intellectuals, shocked by the atrocities of the Vietnam War, had lost the sense, still present "in Dewey's day," that the United States is "a shining historical example."[108] Unable to take pride in their country, they were prone to forget how much persuasive power there is in the exhortation to do something in the name of America. Their antipatriotism "may have served a useful cathartic purpose," but it did more to "separate the intellectuals from the moral consensus of the nation ... than to alter that consensus."[109]

Rorty embraced the identity of leftist American patriot again in his 1998 book *Achieving Our Country: Leftist Thought in Twentieth-Century America*. Here too Rorty chastised the American left—especially the "cultural left" that populates the academy—for being insufficiently patriotic. "National pride is to countries what self-respect is to individuals," he wrote, "a necessary condition for self-improvement."[110] If leftist academics "find America unforgivable ... and ... unachievable," they will "step back from their country," "give cultural politics preference over real politics" and "mock the very idea that democratic institutions might once again be made to serve social justice."[111]

Where did Rorty acquire the intellectual self-concept of leftist American patriot, when did this occur, and what effects, if any, might it have had on his philosophy? My argument is that he acquired the identity from his parents, that it became reactivated in the 1970s in response to their deaths, the rise the New Left, and other historical developments, and that its effect was to renew Rorty's commitment to American pragmatism, which he saw as giving expression to the same values.

I have already characterized the institutional environment of the Rortys' household as one where identity transfer from parents to son was likely to

106. Ibid., 200.   107. Ibid., 201.   108. Ibid.   109. Ibid.
110. Rorty, *Achieving Our Country*, 3.
111. Ibid., 35–36.

occur and mentioned that leftist anti-Communism and social ecologism were the most important identities to James and Winifred. But their anti-Communism came packaged in a specific way: as leftist American patriotism. In an autobiographical section of *Achieving Our Country,* Rorty recalled that for many in his family, leftism and patriotism went hand in hand. For example, he remembered being impressed, on trips to visit his aunt and uncle, by his exposure to the social circle around the La Follette family in Madison, Wisconsin, where "American patriotism, redistributionist economics, [and] anticommunism ... went together easily and naturally."[112] His parents held similar views. Chapters 1 and 2 described how James Rorty and Winifred Raushenbush came to appreciate the freedoms and democratic potentials of American society, especially as they entered the fiercely anti-Communist stage of their lives. Without abandoning their commitment to social justice, they were—as Rorty has suggested was true for most "Deweyans" at the time—"sentimentally patriotic about America—willing to grant that it could slide into fascism at any time, but proud of its past and guardedly hopeful about its future."[113] Although neither ever wrote much about patriotism specifically, I was able to locate several text fragments suggesting this is no misrepresentation of their position. For instance, in the early years of the Depression, Winifred noted in an article in the *New York Herald Tribune* that "America still has its patriots. A patriot is one who loves his country not only for what she is but for what she may become, and who works to make her what she is not. Or, to postulate a more modern definition: A patriot is a person who is willing to make changes when changes are clearly necessary, and who recognizes that if changes are not made in time, disaster will ensue."[114] A decade later, Winifred again mobilized the theme of leftist patriotism, this time in service of the cause of improving relations between whites and African Americans. "I profoundly believe we have reached a point in American history where we will go one way or the other in respect to race relations," she was quoted as saying for an article in the *New York Post.*[115] "Either we are going to go American, which means that we do not allow ourselves to build up a caste system created by economic repressions. Or we go the way of the older, less democratic systems and evolve a caste system based on race discriminations.... I would wish that

112. Rorty, *Achieving Our Country,* 61.

113. Rorty, *Philosophy and Social Hope,* 17.

114. Winifred Raushenbush, 1933, "History of the A.F. of L.," *New York Herald Tribune,* October 15, RRP.

115. Winifred Raushenbush, quoted in Alice Davidson, 1943, "Liberty and Justice for All," *New York Post,* October 28, RRP.

America would take the right turn at this point and that we would within one generation get in the clear about race relations. What you have to do or feel is that because you are an American you want an equal opportunity for all other Americans!" James Rorty was no less prone than his wife to the view that America, whatever its problems, was a great country with a political and cultural heritage worth preserving—a heritage that pushed ultimately in the direction of equality. In 1941, for example, he gave a speech on Americanism at Julia Richmond High School in New York City. He told his audience: "It is for you to fulfill the promise and the hope of Americanism as our great forefathers conceived it. That is a task that will require all the daring, the hard energy, the idealism of your youth and beyond that all the stamina of your maturity. We have still at least eight or nine million unemployed workers. We have forty-five million malnourished people. Is this Americanism? No, these are the shameful, the unworthy things that have come upon us because of our greed and our carelessness. They are un-American, and to endure them without protest is even more un-American. They must be attacked, banished, ended."[116]

In light of this evidence and the general thrust of his parents' thought, it is a likely hypothesis that Rorty initially formed the self-concept of leftist patriot through interaction with his parents during childhood and adolescence. Not surprisingly, it was a self-concept he expressed at several points throughout his life, though never as vehemently as in the 1970s and thereafter.[117] For example, though his early writings tended to be philosophical rather than political, he could be found in 1962 extolling the virtues of democratic America. The occasion was an unusual opinion piece published in *Teachers College Record*. Part of a symposium on whether and what American high school students should be taught about Communism, Rorty's essay followed a piece by his father in which James Rorty, displaying his characteristic opposition to censorship, came down against the notion that it was better to keep students in the dark about the Soviet Union, claiming that to do so would be to mimic the "brainwashing" carried out "back of the Iron Curtain."[118] Richard, like his father,

116. James Rorty, 1941, "Americanism," Address for the American Legion Certificate School Award, Julia Richmond High School, January 30, JRC.

117. Note that for purposes of analytic clarity—since I had not yet introduced the notion of intellectual self-concept—I avoided any discussion of Rorty's adult political-intellectual identity in the biographical chapters. This should not be read as a sign of its unimportance.

118. James Rorty, 1962, "Is Teaching Communism Necessary?" *Teachers College Record* 63:559–61, 560. I referred to this piece in passing in chapter 1.

also wore the badge of a leftist Cold Warrior, declaring it a "myth" that "high economic productivity is possible only on the basis of free enterprise" and a "delusion" to think "of socialism and Stalinism. . . . [as] merely two species of the same genus."[119] Nevertheless, Rorty thought it worth noting that the political realities of the time made it impossible that an objective picture of life in the Soviet Union would ever be painted in high school textbooks. Affirming his commitment to American democratic ideals, Rorty wrote: "It is impossible for the public schools of a democratic country to educate youth in areas in which education would call into question beliefs which are central to the general tenor of political opinion. This fact is one of the built-in disadvantages of democracy, part of the price paid for its advantages."[120]

Rorty was even more explicit in his commitment to leftist American ideals in a letter he wrote to one Dr. Turner, a correspondent who had criticized the position he'd taken in *Teachers College Record*. Turner believed students should be given a course contrasting the benefits of the American way of life with the evils of Communism. Rorty responded that this was a bad idea, even though he himself was of the view that the American way of life—notwithstanding the problems of social inequality caused by free market capitalism—*was* better. "I doubt that a course concerning matters which are directly relevant to national policy and programs will be of value unless it involves rather far-ranging debate on the bases of such programs," he told Turner.[121]

> In particular, I think that students will neither be satisfied with nor will profit from such a course unless it deals with such questions as: "Is there any truth in the Communists' claim that American firms have exploited the laborpower of underdeveloped countries or have attempted to dominate the governments of such countries," "Is there any truth in their claim that the free-enterprise system has given excessive political power to individual rich men?" "Has totalitarian rule brought any advantages to the Russian peasant, which might serve to justify the horrors of the totalitarian rule which has replaced the rule of the Czars?" Unless somebody raises such questions and unless teachers are prepared to discuss them, I don't see how a course in Americanism vs. Communism can be much more than a series of pat discussions and answers. . . . Discussing such questions involves leaving

119. Richard Rorty, 1962, "Second Thoughts on Teaching Communism," *Teachers College Record* 63:562–63, 563.

120. Ibid., 563.

121. Richard Rorty to Dr. Turner, undated letter (probably 1962), RRP.

open the possibility that Communists do have strong cases to make on various topics. Since on many topics, they *do* have such strong cases, honest discussion of these topics has to admit the strength of these cases. Discussion of topics in which the Communists do have strong cases need not obscure the central fact that their triumph would be catastrophic for civilization, and, generally, the fact that, in Hocking's phrase, "our side *is* right."

It was in the 1970s and 1980s, however, that Rorty's self-concept of leftist patriot became even more pronounced. Only then did he begin mentioning it in the context of his philosophical writing and explicitly urging other intellectuals to adopt the same identity. Three factors explain the development. The first is the rise of the New Left and Rorty's reaction to it. In his work from the 1990s, Rorty often condemned the New Left for its excessive focus on cultural politics. He wasn't sympathetic to it in the 1960s or 1970s either. He was highly critical of the student movement, for example. After a sit-in at Stanford in 1968, he wrote to Vlastos, "I saw in the *Times* that Stanford decided to go along with an amnesty for the students in question. I guess I'm glad about this, but I find myself very perplexed about just what administrations should do when students resort to force. When the question came up when Nassau Hall [at Princeton] was threatened with a sit-in I agreed with [Princeton President] Goheen's view that they be given 24 hours worth of persuasion and then cleared out by the cops. I still think this is right, but every once in a while I begin to wonder whether I'm turning into a fascist."[122] Similarly, he wrote to his father in 1970, while on a visit to California, that "Stanford is under stress these days, with $10,000 worth of windows in offices broken by students who disapprove of the faculty's 390–373 decision to continue ROTC for another year.... I think that there are no more than 25 demonstrators among the 10,000 Stanford students, but ... I am really afraid that the little brats will bring on a wave of fascist repression if they keep going.... A few more ... episodes and Reagan and Nixon will be able to organize a secret police with no trouble at all."[123] Like many of the New Left activists with whom he had disagreements, Rorty held redistributionist views, but he felt that a revolution of the kind some activists were trying to foment would result in fascism, either because of the type of government it would bring about if successful, or, more likely, because of the repression

122. Richard Rorty to Gregory Vlastos, May 16, 1968, RRP.
123. Richard Rorty to James Rorty, April 14, 1970, JRC.

it would generate when it was crushed by the right. Rorty believed the best thing that could be done for progressive social change would be to slowly liberalize the public through education, and he opposed the student movement in part because it sought to disrupt this educative function. Writing to his friend Fisk in 1971, he denied that academic freedom was a bourgeois virtue:

> No, it's the best bet available for improving society. This standard bourgeois liberal view of mine has the same cynicism of all bourgeois liberal views—it says to the people on whose necks one trods that it will be better for their children's children if they keep on getting trodden upon while we educate the more intelligent of their children to understand how society works. But I believe it anyway. I honestly think that we—the parasitic priestly class which confers sacraments like BAs and PhDs—are the best agency for social change on the scene. I don't trust the aroused workers and peasants to do themselves or anybody any good. To put it still more generally, I think that nothing but a revolution in this country is going to make it possible for millions of people to lead a decent life, but I still don't want a revolution in this country—simply because I'm afraid of finding something worse when the revolution is over. So insofar as I have any thoughts on the higher learning in America they are to the effect that we pinko profs should continue swinging each successive generation a little further to the left; doing it this way requires the continuation of the same claptrap about contemplation we've always handed out, because without this *mystique* the society won't let us get away with corrupting the youth anymore.[124]

What's more, although Rorty opposed the Vietnam War, his view was that some antiwar protesters were so virulently anti-American that they failed to appreciate what was worth preserving in America's cultural heritage. In another letter to his father from Stanford, he said: "It does seem to me that the country has been led by imperceptible steps to a situation in which it is committing barbaric and inhuman acts in a hopeless cause. Despite the pessimism of the New Left, I still think America is the most decent and civilized great power the world has ever seen. But it seems painfully easy for a great power to absent-mindedly seduce itself into committing atrocious actions."[125]

124. Richard Rorty to Milton Fisk, March 20, 1971, RRP.
125. Richard Rorty to James Rorty, February 9, 1970, JRC.

Rorty's perception that patriotism was not given a positive cultural coding by New Left activists squares with the historical evidence. As Michael Kazin and Joseph McCartin note, "In a decisive break with tradition, leading activists in the protest movements of the era took issue not just with government policies but with the ideals from which those policies were supposedly drawn. Young radicals did not seek to draw attention to the distance between America's promise and its reality as much as to debunk the national creed itself as inherently reactionary and destructive. Many black, Native American, and Chicano militants viewed themselves as victims of Americanism, while white New Leftists dismissed appeals to patriotism as a smokescreen for imperialist war and the squelching of dissent."[126] The revivification of Rorty's self-concept of leftist American patriot occurred as he reacted against New Left ideas—as these became institutionalized academically—that he saw to be at odds with an identity to which he had earlier come to cleave.

The second reason the self-concept of leftist patriot became more salient for Rorty also involved exposure to political and cultural developments, for the identity became more available to intellectuals in the 1970s—which is to say it reappeared in the American intellectual-cultural repertoire—as activity around the bicentennial celebrations of 1976 heated up. As Lyn Spillman has shown,[127] the orchestration of the bicentennial differed from the centennial celebrations a century before in that the federal government was more closely involved as an agent of cultural production. Rather than promoting a vision of national identity developed at the top, however, the American Revolution Bicentennial Administration (ARBA) worked to coordinate the efforts of tens of thousands of local groups and organizations who would mount celebrations emphasizing a variety of themes. The biggest threat ARBA and local promoters faced was from residual New Left activists as well as organizers linked to the nascent multiculturalist movement, who saw the bicentennial as an opportunity to point out how far the nation had strayed from its founding ideals and how hypocritical patriotic celebrations were. Critics also worried that the bicentennial would give expression to a unified American identity that left little room for group difference. ARBA responded to this threat by inviting critics and representatives of diverse communities to

126. Michael Kazin and Joseph McCartin, eds., 2006, *Americanism: New Perspectives on the History of an Ideal,* Chapel Hill: University of North Carolina Press, 6. Also see Todd Gitlin, 2006, *The Intellectuals and the Flag,* New York: Columbia University Press.

127. Lyn Spillman, 1997, *Nation and Commemoration: Creating National Identities in the United States and Australia,* New York: Cambridge University Press.

serve on national, regional, and local boards. At the same time, many local promoters came to center their celebrations around a vision of national identity that embraced liberal political values—liberty, equality, and so on—alongside an explicit valorization of ethnic, regional, and other forms of diversity, as part of a "rhetorical strategy for representing unity across difference."[128] These tactical maneuvers were successful; they kept critics from derailing the celebrations. As John Bodnar reports, "For many Americans the weekend celebration surrounding July 4, 1976, marked an end to a period of social unrest and dissent and a renewal of American consensus and patriotism.... Millions of citizens were exposed to rituals and symbols in common. Although they were presented in an unstructured and often cluttered manner, as event after event was flashed on television screens, the dominant theme was never lost. All that was happening was being done on behalf of the nation; it was the nation, with its past, present, and future themes and symbols, that merited loyalty and respect."[129] There has been no research on how this effort at collective meaning making shaped the activities of American academicians, but the National Endowment for the Humanities, for its part, funded thirteen academic conferences in 1976 centered around bicentennial themes, and seven in 1975. These ranged from a symposium at Columbia titled "The National Purpose Reconsidered: 1776–1976" to an American Political Science Association symposium called "The United States as Model and as Polity" to a conference at the University of Pennsylvania titled "The American Revolution and 18th Century Culture" to another, held at the CUNY Graduate Center, called "Philosophy for a New Nation," which Rorty attended.[130] This scholarly activity, occurring in conjunction with more popular celebrations of American identity, may have led thinkers like Rorty to become less fearful that expressing an attachment to the particularlistic identity of American intellectual would marginalize them politically and professionally, not least because the loose conception of American identity championed by bicentennial organizers allowed discourses of patriotism to encompass thoroughgoing critiques of American society.

Third, and perhaps more significantly, Rorty may have come to embrace more publicly the self-concept of leftist American patriot in the 1970s because it was an identity he associated with his parents, both of

128. Ibid., 126.

129. John Bodnar, 1992, *Remaking America: Public Memory, Commemoration, and Patriotism in the Twentieth Century*, Princeton: Princeton University Press, 227–28.

130. "NEH-Supported International Bicentennial Conferences," 1976, *Humanities* 6, no. 1–2:8.

whom died during the decade. Championing more fervently than ever the identity of leftist patriot would be a way to honor his parents' memory. As mentioned in chapter 1, James Rorty suffered a mental breakdown in the early 1960s and passed away in 1973. Before he did, Richard wrote to tell him how much he and Winifred meant to him. In an undated letter written before his divorce he said:

> I was very glad to have gotten home the other weekend. I don't know whether when I come home like this I'm relaxed enough to show it, but your and Mother's love & kindness mean so very much to me. I wish I could indicate how much somehow, but in recent years I seem to have developed an abstractedness & superficial coldness which doesn't even let me show such things—maybe Amelie will make me better in this direction. One of the things I've always wanted to say is how very proud I am to be your son—in fact, though I'm not modest about my own qualities, I find that this is what I like best about myself & what I talk to others when I'm flattering myself. Since I was old enough to realize what people were like & how they differed & to get some idea of what was important, I've gloried in the fact that you are what you are & do the things you do. I should like someday to do something that I thought was worthy of my father's son—I'm not sure that I shall, but this is really what drives me on.[131]

There is no doubt a degree of overstatement in this letter, written as it was to bring James a sense of comfort, but Richard clearly had deep and complex feelings about his father, as he wrote to his mother after James's death. "The relations between fathers and sons are very odd,"[132] he said,

> probably odder than I realize, since Jay hasn't even hit puberty yet. I suspect it takes most of one's life to figure out who one's father was, and I am still at it. Going through his papers, trying to decide what should be kept, reading old articles by the way, and so on, I kept noticing things—tricks of style, approaches to books—which I had picked up from him. I think that after he became ill I was so terrified of somehow inheriting or acquiring his illness that I refused to recognize any of the similarities or links between us. But all this has just to be left to time. Someday I shall have a real grasp on the resemblances, and then perhaps I'll be able to see the differences properly. And perhaps then I'll see some pattern in the twists and turns of my feelings about him and my relations to him.

131. Richard Rorty to James Rorty, May 24 (no year), JRC.
132. Richard Rorty to Winifred Raushenbush, February 27 (no year), WRC.

Although Rorty's intellectual career had taken him in a different direction than his parents might have wanted him to go—toward academic philosophy rather than muckraking journalism or poetry—he could now do something they would have been proud of: calling for a progressivism framed in terms of continuity with a distinctively American cultural tradition.

As for why the self-concept of leftist American patriot led him in the direction of pragmatism, the answer is simple: beyond the fact that Dewey was also an antifoundationalist and historicist, Rorty saw him and the pragmatist tradition more generally as the philosophical expression of precisely those progressive American values he held dear. "Pragmatism," Rorty wrote in 1980, "names the chief glory of our country's intellectual tradition,"[133] a quintessentially American philosophy. On Rorty's reading, one of the best things about Dewey was that he encouraged Americans to feel good about their secular and antiauthoritarian culture, "to take pride in what America might ... make of itself,"[134] even as he proposed the reform of basic American institutions. Dewey—and James too—thus "took America seriously ... [and] threw themselves into political movements—especially anti-imperialist movements—designed to keep America true to itself, to keep it from falling back into bad old European ways."[135] Like Rorty and his parents, Dewey was also anti-Stalinist and didn't allow his zeal for helping the poor to cloud his judgment that Communism could easily become another form of totalitarianism. These characteristics of pragmatism made it a natural fit for someone with Rorty's intellectual self-concept.

In arguing that Rorty's self-concept of leftist patriot played a decisive role in leading him back into the arms of pragmatism in the 1970s and beyond—or at least into his own idiosyncratic interpretation of it—I do not mean to suggest that he lost the desire to win attention for himself in the intellectual field. But after receiving tenure at Princeton and then promotion to full professor, strategic concerns about status played a different role in his life than they had before. While he still may have wanted to be known as a prominent thinker and did his work with an eye toward finding a receptive audience, he no longer risked losing his job if he advanced

133. Rorty, "Pragmatism, Relativism, and Irrationalism," 160.

134. Rorty, *Achieving Our Country*, 16.

135. Rorty, "Truth without Correspondence to Reality," 25. On Dewey's "cosmopolitan patriotism," see Jonathan Hansen, 2003, *The Lost Promise of Patriotism: Debating American Identity, 1890–1920*, Chicago: University of Chicago Press.

philosophical arguments and engaged in forms of intellectual work that were not highly valued by his colleagues in the Princeton department or by other analytic philosophers. If anything, his goal was now to provoke and incense his Princeton colleagues. Partaking of an academic culture suffused with notions of authenticity and stressing the finitude of academic life, Rorty now felt compelled to do work that really mattered to him and that he saw as consistent with his most deeply held values and identities. Rorty's self-concept of leftist American patriot returned to salience, then, and influenced his thought, not because processes to do with self-concept are inherently more determinative of intellectual choice than those involving the pursuit of status, but because such processes may become especially important in later stages of an academic career.

Conclusion

* 1 *

Writing in the *Journal of American History* in 1980, David Hollinger declared that "'pragmatism' is a concept most American historians have proved they can get along without. Some nonhistorians may continue to believe that pragmatism is a distinctive contribution of America to modern civilization and somehow emblematic of America, but few scholarly energies are devoted to the exploration ... of this belief."[1] Hollinger acknowledged that "scrutiny of the ideas of Charles Peirce, William James, and John Dewey goes forward as industriously as ever" but indicated that by this he had in mind editorial projects aimed at compiling the collected writings of pragmatism's founding triumvirate, along with strictly exegetical studies, rather than efforts to reinsert pragmatism into contemporary intellectual discourse. He concluded his survey of pragmatism's place in American intellectual history by suggesting that its future lay with thinkers like Richard Rorty, but this did not stop him from taking as his central problematic the question of the "vanishing pragmatist" in a variety of contemporary humanities and social-science fields.

Surveying the intellectual scene for the same journal sixteen years later, James Kloppenberg wrote that "pragmatism today is not only alive and well, it is ubiquitous. References to pragmatism occur with dizzying frequency from philosophy to social science, from the study of literature to that of ethnicity, from feminism to legal theory."[2] Synopsizing the positions advanced by thinkers as diverse as Richard Bernstein, Stanley Fish, Jürgen Habermas, Richard Poirier, Hilary Putnam, Margaret Radin, Richard Rorty,

1. David Hollinger, 1980, "The Problem of Pragmatism in American History," *Journal of American History* 67:88–107, 88–89.

2. James Kloppenberg, 1996, "Pragmatism: An Old Name for Some New Ways of Thinking?" *Journal of American History* 83:100–138, 100–101.

Cornel West, and Joan Williams, who had all made important contributions to pragmatist thought in the 1980s and early 1990s, Kloppenberg predicted that what he dubbed "the new linguistic pragmatism," focused on "the instability of meanings, the particularity of personal identities, and the creative genius of artists over rational deliberation," would "continue to attract attention from many disciplines" in the years to come.[3]

Kloppenberg was not alone in concluding that a major interdisciplinary revival of interest in classical American pragmatism had taken place in the years since the publication of Hollinger's 1980 article. Philosopher Robert Hollinger, for example, writing with David Depew, opened the introductory essay to their 1999 collection, *Pragmatism: From Progressivism to Postmodernism,* with the claim that "pragmatism has become popular again."[4] Morris Dickstein, introducing a series of pieces on neopragmatism originally presented at an interdisciplinary conference on the topic held at CUNY in 1995, likewise noted that "the revival of pragmatism has excited enormous interest and controversy in the intellectual community over the past two decades.... Pragmatism has become a key point of reference around which contemporary debates in social thought, law, and literary theory as well as philosophy have been unfolded."[5] Already in his 1989 book *The American Evasion of Philosophy,* West spoke of the "decline and resurgence of American pragmatism,"[6] while philosophers Sandra Rosenthal, Carl Hausman, and Douglas Anderson, editing another volume a decade later, asserted the tradition's "contemporary vitality."[7] The assessment that pragmatism was renascent even made its way into nonacademic discourse, thanks to Louis Menand's breakout bestseller *The Metaphysical Club,* which noted that "once the Cold War ended," the classical pragmatists "began to be studied and debated with a seriousness and intensity, both in the United States and in other countries, that they had not attracted for forty years."[8]

3. Ibid., 137.

4. Robert Hollinger and David Depew, 1999, "Introduction," pp. 1–18 in *Pragmatism: From Progressivism to Postmodernism,* Robert Hollinger and David Depew, eds., Westport: Praeger, xiii.

5. Morris Dickstein, 1998, "Introduction: Pragmatism Then and Now," pp. 1–18 in *The Revival of Pragmatism: New Essays on Social Thought, Law, and Culture,* Morris Dickstein, ed., Durham: Duke University Press, 1.

6. West, *American Evasion of Philosophy,* 182.

7. Sandra Rosenthal, Carl Hausman, and Douglas Anderson, eds., 1999, *Classical American Pragmatism: Its Contemporary Vitality,* Urbana: University of Illinois Press.

8. Louis Menand, 2001, *The Metaphysical Club,* New York: Farrar, Straus and Giroux, 441.

Nor did these conclusions represent misconstruals of the intellectual-historical evidence. Consider, as one indicator of the pragmatist revival, the volume of writing on Dewey. A comprehensive bibliography shows that English-language Dewey scholarship grew dramatically between 1900 and 1939.[9] That growth slowed between 1940 and 1979 but since then has rebounded. Between 1996 and 2004, more than 150 books were published with "Dewey" as a title word.[10] When considered in light of the overall expansion of scholarly output that took place during the same period, these figures do not indicate a mass flocking to pragmatist ideas. But while they might not demonstrate that a growing proportion of intellectuals has become interested in pragmatism—and, indeed, more fine-grained research into one field, philosophy, suggests this is not the case[11]—the fact that there was a takeoff in pragmatist scholarship in a number of fields in the 1980s and 1990s, combined with the fact that among the contributors to this enterprise were some of the most highly regarded figures in American and European intellectual life, clearly indicates that as the twentieth century drew to a close pragmatism was at the center of the "intellectual attention space"[12] in a way it had not been since it first attained popularity in the work of James and Dewey.

9. Barbara Levine, ed., 1996, *Works about John Dewey*, 1886–1995, Carbondale: Southern Illinois University Press.

10. This figure is based on a search of the Harvard library holdings.

11. My research suggests that the proportion of U.S. philosophers who write dissertations concerned with pragmatism has actually decreased over time. Approximately 9 percent of U.S. philosophy dissertations in the 1950s were concerned with pragmatism, as compared with 8 percent in the 1960s, 6 percent in the 1970s, 5 percent in the 1980s, and 5 percent in the 1990s. To obtain these figures I used John Shook's bibliography of pragmatist dissertations (listed at www.pragmatism.org), retaining only those written in U.S. philosophy departments, and then compared them with figures on Ph.D. production in U.S. philosophy departments given in the Digest of Education Statistics and on the APA's Web site. This is a slightly different method of counting than I used in "Becoming a Pragmatist Philosopher," where I relied on dissertation listings in *The Review of Metaphysics*, but Shook's knowledge of the secondary literature on pragmatism is greater than mine, and he is in a better position to know whether a dissertation that mentions Peirce, James, Dewey, or Mead in its title is substantially concerned with pragmatism or whether another that doesn't is. In any case, the percentage figure for the first half of the 1990s that I came up with was the same using both methods. Shook himself gives a different percentage at www. pragmatism.org, but this is because his count includes nonphilosophy dissertations, as well as dissertations written in Canada.

12. Collins, *The Sociology of Philosophies*.

From the earliest days of the pragmatist revival, Rorty occupied an ambiguous position in the community of scholars interested in pragmatism. On the one hand, he was universally acknowledged to have played a major role in drawing the attention of the world intellectual community back to pragmatism following its eclipse from the intellectual limelight in the 1950s and 1960s. The fame he won for himself with *Philosophy and the Mirror of Nature* and *Consequences of Pragmatism* he gave back to pragmatism a hundredfold—to Dewey in particular—always insisting that his own philosophy was merely a restatement in more contemporary philosophical terms of Dewey's own. On the other hand, many scholars of pragmatism claimed he was giving the tradition a bad name. They charged him with misrepresenting its core ideas and associating it with a kind of loose relativism much at odds with the seriousness with which the classical pragmatists regarded the enterprise of inquiry. Rorty's ambivalent status in the pragmatist community is well symbolized by two events that took place in 1995. At the CUNY pragmatism conference organized by Dickstein, Rorty—one of the attendees—was a venerated figure, hailed as a mover and shaker behind the revival. At the annual meeting that year of the Society for the Advancement of American Philosophy, by contrast—the main pragmatist scholarly organization—attendees were treated one night after dinner to a half-serious, half-comedic skit in which philosopher-actors depicting Peirce and Rorty staged a debate, using snippets from the writings of both thinkers to form the dialogue. The humor was to be found in the contrast between the careful, serious, and rigorous thinking of Peirce and Rorty's self-consciously lighthearted and ironic philosophical style. The message of the performance was clear: Peirce is the real pragmatist, Rorty an attention-grabbing interloper who has distorted the meaning of the pragmatist tradition.[13]

Nor, as I indicated in the introduction, was it only pragmatists who objected to Rorty's philosophy. It is scarcely an exaggeration to say that one could not be taken seriously as an intellectual in the 1990s without forming some kind of opinion as to Rorty's views. While Rorty had his champions and defenders, more numerous were his critics, who accused him of all manner of intellectual sins.[14]

It is not my intention, in the concluding pages of this book, to shift gears and broach the question of the cultural and institutional conditions

13. A version of the Peirce-Rorty conversation is republished in Haack, *Manifesto of a Passionate Moderate.*

14. See, for example, the essays in Robert Brandom, ed., 2000, *Rorty and His Critics,* Oxford: Blackwell; Herman Saatkamp, ed., 1995, *Rorty and Pragmatism: The Philosopher Responds*

for Rorty's national and international prominence in the closing decades of the twentieth century, to consider why his work provoked such fury, or to assess his causal contribution to the pragmatist revival. These are important questions, but they go beyond the scope of this study, focused as it is on the social processes and mechanisms that influence the development rather than the diffusion of intellectuals' ideas. Instead, in keeping with the goal of making an empirically grounded theoretical contribution to the new sociology of ideas, I want to draw the book to a close by going over once again ground covered in earlier chapters, this time with an eye toward pulling out the general propositions concerning knowledge making in the contemporary American humanities that are suggested by a consideration of the Rorty case.

* 2 *

As indicated in chapters 1 and 2, the story of Richard Rorty is not a story of the self-made intellectual man but rather one of class reproduction. James Rorty and Winifred Raushenbush were both intellectuals—not academics, but freelance writers who were also involved as activists in the political struggles of their day. James Rorty was a poet and muckraking journalist whose articles and books from the 1920s, 1930s, and 1940s lambasted American capitalism for its many failings. Raushenbush, who trained under the sociologist Robert Park, was less prolific than her husband but wrote articles, pamphlets, and book reviews on major social problems, while maintaining a lifelong interest in fashion. Both gravitated in a Communist orbit early in their lives, but later joined the ranks of the Trotskyist New York left. By the 1950s, Rorty and Raushenbush had become vigorously anti-Communist, not following other New York intellectuals who, in opposing Stalin, had come to appreciate capitalism's virtues, but nevertheless insisting that liberal politics—focused on a redistribution of wealth, control of runaway corporations, and the granting of rights to oppressed minorities—must in no way impede the other basic freedoms America gives to its citizens, and which they now saw as our nation's greatest contribution to civilization.

As a child, as was argued in chapter 3, Richard Rorty soaked up many of his parents' values, ideas, and skills. He learned from them that to be a left-wing anti-Communist is to be politically virtuous, that intellectual and artistic pursuits have great merit, and that the best intellectual work is not artificially separated off from life but carried out in the service of practical aims. He also learned how to write with clarity, gravity, and verve and, through interactions with his parents' friends and extended family—many of whom were also intellectuals—how to talk about ideas and politics. Seen by his parents as intellectually precocious, he was sent at the age of fifteen to study the great books of the Western tradition in the so-called Hutchins College of the University of Chicago. Although he continued to profit from his parents' social position, taking advantage of their social networks to seek advice and emotional support, he soon became enamored of the view that inquiry must seek out not contingent truths of the kind his parents favored—his father, influenced indirectly by Dewey, held the view that social reform should always be provisional and experimental—but rather absolute truths about the human condition of the kind discussed by the great philosophers across the ages.

With his parents' support, as described in chapter 4, Rorty decided to continue on at Chicago for a masters degree in philosophy. With neither the inspiration to study classic texts in the esoteric manner of Leo Strauss—a popular professor among his friends—nor sufficient mastery of Greek or Latin as would have been required to work under Richard McKeon—by whose pluralistic conception of philosophy he was nevertheless much impressed—Rorty came under the influence of the metaphysician Charles Hartshorne. Rorty's thesis on Alfred North Whitehead's metaphysics remained distant enough from his parents' intellectual concerns that it would be a project all his own, while it simultaneously expressed his opposition to the narrowing of philosophical horizons proposed by the logical positivists, who were looked on with skepticism in the Chicago milieu, despite the presence of Carnap.

A broadly trained and classically educated humanist, Rorty soon discovered, as described in chapter 5, that when he went to apply to doctoral programs in philosophy, the intellectual capital he had acquired at Chicago was not universally valued. Activating again his parents' social networks, from which he learned that it would be unwise, from the standpoint of his future academic career, to pursue a doctorate in a European university, he decided to apply to Harvard and Yale. The Harvard philosophy department at the time was identifying itself with positivism and other technical strains of philosophy and was not sufficiently interested in Rorty to offer him a scholarship. Yale, by contrast, seeking to carve out a disciplinary niche as a department that would resist technicism, appreciated his classical training and familiarity with metaphysics. He moved to New Haven and ended up writing a dissertation under Paul Weiss, a former colleague of Hartshorne. The dissertation mobilized the pluralistic perspective he had acquired from McKeon to make a case for bringing analytic contributions to the study of potentiality into dialogue with nonanalytic contributions.

It was a fine dissertation, and after he finished service in the peacetime army, Rorty relied on Weiss's network contacts to help him secure a teaching post at Wellesley. As chapter 6 noted, however, Rorty was professionally ambitious and realized that if he wanted to wind up teaching in a top-ranked philosophy graduate program, he would not only have to publish extensively but also do work that would bring him more into the center of the disciplinary conversation, which was tending in an analytic direction. Jumping on the emerging bandwagon of metaphilosophy, Rorty leveraged his knowledge of the history of philosophy into several articles that expanded on the call he'd issued in his dissertation for analytic thought to be brought into dialogue with nonanalytic thought. Inspired by the work of Ludwig Wittgenstein and Wilfrid Sellars, he became a convert to the analytic tradition, while also drawing on his familiarity with classical American pragmatism, especially as he had learned it from his professors at Yale, to argue that there were important overlaps between Peirce and Wittgenstein.

Rorty's productivity was impressive, and what had been a temporary position at Princeton—where analytic philosophy had come to rule the roost, as described in chapter 7—was soon converted into a tenure-track post. Aware that only by making an important contribution to analytic thought would he be promoted, Rorty began fashioning a novel approach to the philosophy of mind that stitched together ideas from Wittgenstein, Sellars, Peirce, and others. At the same time, he set about editing an anthology of writings on the linguistic turn that would demonstrate in metaphilosophical terms the value of the analytic perspective.

These efforts proved successful, and Rorty was tenured at Princeton. Throughout the late 1960s and early 1970s, as described in chapter 8, he continued to make analytic contributions and participate in analytic debates. Increasingly, however, he felt alienated. He came to dislike many of his colleagues, whom he felt had a narrow conception of the philosophical enterprise and little appreciation for the history of thought or contemporary nonanalytic contributions. These tensions were exacerbated by a messy divorce from his first wife, a philosopher whom many of his colleagues liked. Rorty formulated a long-range plan to leave the department and move into more interdisciplinary climes. He began to read extensively the work of nonanalytic thinkers for whom his colleagues had little appreciation, such as Derrida and Foucault, and forged friendships—around the Institute for Advanced Study and elsewhere—with other wide-ranging humanists. Moving from his grievances with his local colleagues to an attack on the analytic paradigm as a whole, he composed a book manuscript in which he now cast the work of Wittgenstein, Quine, Kuhn, Heidegger, Dewey, and others as calling into question philosophy's self-image—subscribed to by many analysts—as the discipline that securely grounds knowledge claims made in other fields by establishing firm philosophical foundations for them. There can be no such foundations, Rorty argued. What's more, the best philosophy is not that which rigorously argues for this or that view of knowledge or mind or the good, as was typical of analytic philosophy, but that which is akin to poetry, pushing thought along in new and interesting directions by offering novel vocabularies for conceiving of the world that appeal because of their capacity for redescription. Rorty made a case for knowledge that would not have the illusion of firm and unquestionable foundations and claimed that the views he was developing had been articulated originally by the classical American pragmatists. *Philosophy and the Mirror of Nature* brought Rorty an incredible amount of attention, and he used this to catapult himself into an interdisciplinary professorship at the University of Virginia, where he would be free to study and teach and write whatever he wanted without having to contend with analytic naysayers.

Chapter 9 began the task of reexamining Rorty's intellectual and career moves through the lens of the sociology of ideas. To this end, I laid out the central theoretical claims of Bourdieu and Collins. I argued that, while both theorists highlight processes and mechanisms that may influence academicians as they go about developing their ideas and making names for themselves among their contemporaries, neither pays sufficient attention to the possibility that the choices thinkers make at critical junctures between competing ideas may also be influenced by the intellectual self-concepts to which they subscribe: the narratives of intellectual selfhood they recount to themselves and others that characterize them as thinkers of such and such a sort.

Chapter 10 examined three such junctures—Rorty's decision to write a masters thesis on Whitehead, his movement into analytic philosophy in the 1960s, and his break with the analytic paradigm and public identification with pragmatism in the 1970s. Rorty's quest for intellectual status and prestige was an important factor influencing all three of these intellectual choices, but considerations of intellectual self-concept were also important in two of them. On the whole, however, strategic concerns were more determinative of the content of his work in the early, post-doctoral phase of his career, while concerns relating to the desire to remain true to his intellectual self-concept—in particular, the self-concept of leftist American patriot that he acquired from his parents and that was reactivated in the 1970s—became more important later on.

* 3 *

The aim of this study was to develop, by means of an immersion in the Rorty case, a theoretical understanding of some of the social mechanisms and processes that influence the thought and careers of contemporary American academicians in the humanities and social sciences. It should now be possible to identify the theoretical propositions to have emerged from this analysis. In keeping with the synthetic orientation of the book, not all of the propositions that follow stem exclusively from the theory of intellectual self-concept; some are restatements or respecifications of ideas found in Bourdieu and Collins, or elsewhere, such as in Camic's work on Parsons. All, however, are propositions for which I found prima facie support in the course of my investigation (though in listing them below I have sometimes added important qualifications and details that go beyond the evidentiary support available in the Rorty case). The propositions are not intended to reflect universal social laws of intellectual life—I doubt any such laws exist—but simply to capture general tendencies within contemporary American academe. Whether and how the propositions would apply in other national or historical contexts remains an open question.

1. Students whose parents have high levels of intellectual and cultural capital are more likely to formulate the aspiration to become a professor.[15]
2. Students whose parents have high levels of intellectual and cultural capital are more likely to engage in the kind of activity as undergraduates—writing original papers, forging close relationships with faculty, attending colleges and universities that are feeder schools for graduate study, and immersing themselves in conversation with other students

15. On the relationship between cultural capital and the likelihood of graduate school attendance, see Paul DiMaggio and John Mohr, 1985, "Cultural Capital, Educational Attainment, and Marital Selection," *American Journal of Sociology* 90:1231–61.

who are aspiring professors—that will help get them into top graduate departments.

3. Graduate departments seek out distinctive identities for themselves based on the present composition of their faculties, perceptions of opportunities for amassing institutional prestige given the nature of the intellectual field, the availability of local institutional resources, and the need to satisfy local institutional exigencies. Given their standing in the field, departments tend to recruit the best graduate students they can whose interests and aptitudes square with these identities.

4. Students whose parents have high levels of intellectual and cultural capital are in a better position to effectively utilize social networks to gain information on which graduate departments they would best fit into, on which it would be best for them to attend from the standpoint of their long-term career interests, and in general on how they should go about pursuing an academic career.

5. The intellectual self-concept narratives of incoming graduate students will tend to be composed of elements derived from and given a positive moral coding in the various institutional environments in which they have been immersed over the course of their lives: those of their families, their churches, the social movements with which they may have been involved, and so on. These self-concepts, which may or may not also reflect the endowments of intellectual or cultural capital the students have acquired, form the basis for their initial understanding of their intellectual interests and goals. A thinker is more likely to pick up self-concept elements from her immersion in an institutional environment if that environment sanctions noncompliance, is a site of positive affect, displays a coherent worldview, is one to which the thinker is exposed when she is young, and offers her an identity that allows her to feel a sense of moral superiority without being radically incommensurate with previously acquired identity strands.

6. Once admitted to graduate departments, students will seek advisors whom they perceive to have a good fit with their nascent intellectual self-concepts. Students must compete for advisors, however, as Bourdieu has noted. Going beyond the evidence from the Rorty case, I suggest that, holding constant the fact that students seek advisors whom they see as intellectually compatible, advisors whose sponsorship would be maximally beneficial in terms of career interests tend to be approached by the most students. Those students who demonstrate the greatest potential—defined according to different criteria of evaluation in different departmental settings—will be most likely to be taken on board. Like most markets, the market for advisors is

characterized by imperfect information and behavioral deviation from perfect rationality, as students may mistake an advisor's local status and network power for status in the wider intellectual field (something Rorty appears to have done in the case of both Hartshorne and Weiss) or prioritize self-concept fit over strategic considerations.

7. What courses a student takes in graduate school is a function of departmental requirements, of what courses happen to be on offer that year given the makeup of the faculty at the university, and of how well particular electives fit with students' interests. The ideas and texts that students master in these courses contribute to their endowments of intellectual capital and may also shape their intellectual self-concepts, while students may forge important network connections outside the formal advisor-advisee relationship if they impress their professors. Much intellectual innovation, as Abbott has argued,[16] involves importing ideas from one subfield or discipline into another subfield or discipline. Insofar as this is so, students who take unusual courses in graduate school may be more likely later on to do what will be seen as innovative work, as was the case for Rorty, whose study of Peirce under Rulon Wells set him up to write a series of articles on the similarities between Peirce and Wittgenstein, anticipating the argument he would develop two decades later about the relationship between Dewey and Wittgenstein.

8. The selection of a thesis topic typically involves a negotiation between students and their advisors. Students attach themselves to topics that they see as consistent with their intellectual self-concepts, that they perceive as best enabling them to utilize the endowments of intellectual capital at their disposal, and—if applicable—for which they can receive funding. Advisors push students to find topics that will be regarded as important in the intellectual field or that they themselves view as important and on which they believe the student can make a real contribution. (There is no direct evidence of such negotiation in the Rorty case, but evidence presented in chapter 4 suggests that Hartshorne may have had a hand in the selection of Rorty's masters thesis topic.) The thesis finally decided upon will be an attempt to satisfy all these exigencies and must conform to an advisor's standard of excellence. But advisors vary in their orientations toward strategic concerns, in their capacity to predict how well a particular thesis will play in the wider intellectual field, and in how much conformity they demand of their students. Some advisors, intent on building a school, will insist that their students take up the topics and approaches around which they have made their own reputations; others will allow greater

16. Abbott, *Chaos of Disciplines.*

originality. Indeed, beyond individual variation in this regard, whether advisors tend toward a collectivist or individualist orientation in their dealings with students is an important feature of "epistemic culture"[17] and may vary systematically between fields, subfields, and institutions. Students also vary in how stubborn they are in sticking with topics or approaches that deviate from those preferred by their advisors.

9. Everything else being equal, students whose parents have high levels of intellectual and cultural capital will tend to write dissertations that are viewed as satisfying all the exigencies specified in proposition 8 and that will therefore be regarded as works of high quality. This will be particularly the case if students decide to work in areas that are continuous with the endowments of intellectual capital they have received from their parents—for example, students whose parents speak French and who decide to do work on France. However, such students may also face pressures to differentiate themselves from their parents—that is, to cleave to intellectual self-concepts that locate them in some other corner of intellectual taxonomic space than that occupied by their parents—and may as a result choose to work in more far-flung areas.

10. As students near the completion of their dissertations or shortly thereafter, they enter the academic job market. This market is segmented. The exact nature of the segmentation varies from field to field and over time, but generally speaking it distinguishes between some students who are seen as elite, others who are seen as capable but not stellar, and still others—typically participating in more regional markets—who are seen more as teachers than researchers. The designation of a student as a participant in one of these market segments is a complex process and depends upon the perceived quality of her graduate institution, the prestige of her advisor, how extensive are the advisor's network contacts, and the perceived quality and importance of the dissertation and other evidence suggestive of future productivity, along with the student's ambitions. Signaling processes may also be at play—if one elite school ends up considering a student seriously for a job, word of this may lead another elite school to do the same. Generally speaking, as sociologists of science working in the tradition of Robert K. Merton have long argued, academic life involves a circulation of elites, as those who are seen as the best students of professors at elite departments are offered assistant professor slots at other elite schools and as other, less favored students take up their predesignated place in the academic hierarchy, with many—particularly in underfunded humanities fields

17. Karin Knorr Cetina, 1999, *Epistemic Cultures: How the Sciences Make Knowledge*, Cambridge: Harvard University Press.

where Ph.D. overproduction is common—never finding tenure-track posts. Whether a student will wind up with a job offer at a particular school is a function of the existence of network ties between her advisor or graduate institution and powerful figures in the department[18] and of the degree to which others in that department—in particular, those on the recruitment committee—perceive a fit between the student and local institutional interests, such as building up strengths in a research area, enhancing or maintaining a particular kind of departmental reputation, or filling a curricular gap. There is a great deal of contingency in this process, but it is not random.

11. Given the relatively small number of assistant professor slots that open up each year in elite departments and the relatively large number of Ph.D.'s such departments produce, it is inevitable that a significant number of young academicians will experience downward mobility with their first jobs, winding up with lower-status positions than they may have hoped to obtain. The majority of such persons end up adjusting their expectations downward and come to live more or less productive and happy lives at second- or third-tier institutions, either taking advantage of local opportunities to become star researchers or finding meaning in the hybrid role of teacher-researcher, in the day-to-day administration of their college or university, or in their family lives or religion or political pursuits. Some, however, will formulate a plan to move up to a higher-status job after a few years and may decide that a significant retooling of their intellectual skill set and ramping up of their productivity is required. Individuals in such a position are especially likely to put considerations of self-concept aside in the making of their intellectual choices or at least to relegate them to a secondary place and may make an effort to reinvent themselves along the lines they see as maximizing their opportunities for upward mobility, given the composition of the intellectual field.

12. Except in departments where the tenure process involves little more than a rubber stamp, it is in the nature of tenure as an institution that young academics seeking promotion will do their work in a manner that they believe is likely to impress local decision makers. Those who fail to do so—because they are incapable, because they do not agree with or respect the views of their senior colleagues, or because they do not have a proper fix on which senior colleagues' views will carry the day—risk tenure denial. This is not to say that young academics choose

18. On the importance of such ties for the prestige structures of academic disciplines, see Val Burris, 2004, "The Academic Caste System: Prestige Hierarchies in PhD Exchange Networks," *American Sociological Review* 69:239–64.

their topics and approaches in a wholly instrumental fashion or seek simply to reproduce and recapitulate the perspectives of the professors who hold power in their departments. Neither strategy would be successful, for most senior professors want their junior colleagues to have their own autonomous and indeed creative intellectual agendas and programs and to be different than they are topically, theoretically, or methodologically, thereby increasing the intellectual breadth of the department (the exception is departments that aim to be centers for some particular intellectual school). Nevertheless, junior professors seeking tenure must find a way to bring their otherwise original work into line with the views and criteria of evaluation of key department members. To this end, they can often be found reading and citing books and articles that their senior colleagues have mentioned to them as important, trying to stake out ground in debates that their colleagues have flagged as central, framing their arguments in terms familiar to other department members, employing methodologies that are locally respected, and sharing their work in progress with their colleagues in the hope of getting comments that will help them avoid objections down the line. But senior colleagues are not the only arbiters of tenure. Those seeking promotion must also compile letters from outside scholars commenting on the quality of their work and reputation in the field. Sometimes junior professors have considerable say as to who these external letter writers are—but usually not. In either case, they must attempt to anticipate the nature of these evaluations and do what they can in their written work to assure themselves of a positive review. In all these ways, the process of gaining tenure necessitates a significant amount of conformism on the part of young professors, even if it simultaneously demands that they evidence some originality (the expectation and meaning of originality may also vary between departments and institutions—while scholars at elite institutions may face more intense tenure pressures as concerns both the quantity and quality of scholarship, such institutions may also expect and reward more creativity and risk taking.[19]) Those who, from the beginning of their graduate school days, find themselves at the center of their disciplinary mainstreams may not experience demands for conformity as troubling. In contrast, those whose endowments of intellectual capital or self-concept lead them to deviate significantly from dominant disciplinary or local expectations may experience such demands as restrictions on their creativity and pine for the day when they have tenure and can let the

---

19. See Michèle Lamont, Josh Guetzkow, and Grégoire Mallard, 2002, "What Is Originality in the Social Sciences and Humanities?" *American Sociological Review* 69:190–212.

muses take them where they may. Some of these persons may develop resentment toward their senior colleagues or the disciplinary mainstream—unexpressed as this must remain for the moment—and such resentment may fuel involvement later on with intellectual movements that aim to upend the disciplinary status quo. Alternatively, some intellectual heretics may assimilate—particularly if their departmental homes are ideologically cohesive and if the ideas and perspectives their senior colleagues insist on foisting upon them provide a sense of meaningful identity. After an initial period of resistance, such persons may make a virtue of necessity and rewrite their intellectual self-concepts in line with local expectations—something that often requires the availability of a text that allows the young thinkers to tell coherent stories of their transition from one approach to another. As for what kinds of approaches and topics will be approved of by senior members of a department, this is a function of who those members happen to be, as this has been determined by prior recruitment and retention processes—themselves shaped by larger social and institutional forces—and by the current collective sense of departmental identity. The intellectual output of young academics is significantly influenced by these factors, though their involvement with "invisible colleges"[20] consisting of their former advisors and other scholars who work in similar areas may serve as a counterbalance to local pressures—particularly if invisible college members have higher status in the field than do their local colleagues, and can provide assurances of a job elsewhere if tenure is denied or effectively pressure locals into granting tenure. Note that the institution of tenure promotes conformity and hence reproduces intellectual fields whether or not a young academic is consciously worried about tenure. There is probably less such worry among academics from higher social class backgrounds, who are both more self-assured and better protected should their academic careers fail to pan out. Yet part of this self-assurance comes, as it did in the Rorty case, from an intuitive knowledge of what is required to be tenurable, and such knowledge can and does influence the content of intellectual work.

13. Professors who are granted tenure may still be much concerned with their standing and reputation in their discipline and subfield, may be actively involved with their national disciplinary associations in part out of the hope that this will keep their name in the spotlight, may desire to move up to more prestigious institutional locations, and may select projects and even form their ideas with an eye toward making an intellectual splash. Yet most will also find themselves subject to a culture

20. See Crane, *Invisible Colleges.*

of academic authenticity that encourages them, now that their jobs are secure, to do work they feel to be consistent with their deepest held intellectual self-concepts, even if this risks violating dominant disciplinary standards. Sometimes taking such a risk can result in significant status returns, anticipated or unanticipated, as happens when established academics, following the lead of their self-concepts, end up producing work that successfully challenges disciplinary orthodoxies, as was true in the Rorty case. This possibility aside, processes relating to the quest for self-concept coherence may come to be as determinative of intellectual content as strategic concerns in later phases of an academic career. To understand a thinker's intellectual self-concept at key decision junctures, especially posttenure, is thus to have important information for explaining the lines of thought she or he is likely to pursue next.

* **4** *

I noted in the preface that sociological theory should be relatively autonomous from empirical research. Although theory can make real strides only when it is freed from the requirement of having to simultaneously amass systematic empirical support for its claims, those claims should be grounded in the theorist's intimate familiarity with the empirical phenomenon under consideration and must ultimately be subjected to further empirical scrutiny. What are the next steps for the theory I have developed in the course of this case study?

The most obvious is that the lives and careers of many humanists and social scientists should be examined systematically to determine whether there is empirical support for the propositions listed above. Scholars who work on the sociology of intellectual life tend to have a distaste for quantitative research on intellectuals, which is seen as flattening out complex ideas. But such distaste is unjustified. Quantitative research on intellectuals—for example, surveys of members of an academic discipline or systematic content analysis of journal articles—can never substitute for intellectual-historical work designed to flesh out ideas and contexts, but it is not intended to do so. What it is suited for is examining, across a large number of cases, whether theorized associations between social factors and the formulation and advancement of particular ideas actually obtain. There is no reason why such work should not be done. For example, there is no reason why affiliation with an intellectual approach such as Marxism—a potential dependent variable—cannot be measured by asking academic survey respondents about the degree to which they identify with Marxism in the same way that survey researchers ask routinely about religious or political party affiliation, and there is no reason why intellectual and cultural capital, other features of thinkers' social backgrounds, or intellectual self-concept—potential independent variables—could not also be operationalized and measured using the tools of survey research. I have done some of this research myself already, fielding a nationally representative survey of U.S. philosophers and finding that, at the stage where philosophy students make choices about their dissertations, considerations of self-concept are significant—holding strategic concerns constant—in predicting whether a student will affiliate herself or himself with the pragmatist, analytic, or Continental traditions.[21] But more of this sort of work needs to be carried out, examining academicians in different national contexts, in different disciplinary fields, at different career stages, and in making different kinds of choices, while using better measures than those I employed as well as both longitudinal and cross-sectional data. With respect to propositions derived from the Rorty case, it would be particularly important—given that he eventually became an intellectual superstar—to verify that the processes that seem to have shaped and structured his life and career are generalizable at the very least to other philosophers, if not to other humanists and social scientists, and not unique to him or to those at the top of their fields. Historical quantitative studies that would code academicians from years past on relevant variables are also in order, though here gaps in the historical record—combined with selection effects whereby the most information tends to be available about those thinkers whom history regards as the most important—would pose problems. I am not suggesting that all empirical research in the new sociology of ideas employ quantitative methods, but only such methods can establish whether the propositions that emerge from individual case studies hold true for large numbers of knowledge producers and thus have at least a minimum level of generality.

In addition to quantitative research, however, we need many more case studies. These case studies should examine the mechanisms and processes I've focused on here, as well as those identified by other theorists, and offer such theoretical corrections, refinements, and additions as might be suggested by varying the historical, national, institutional, or disciplinary context or the social background of the thinker under consideration. Case study research could focus on individual thinkers, as I have done, or examine different units of analysis such as academic departments or small

21. Gross, "Becoming a Pragmatist Philosopher."

groups of scholars or broader intellectual movements, attending to the relationship between the logic of individual action and the dynamics of higher order social aggregations. Some such work should be interview based or ethnographic and attempt to capture operative mechanisms as well as the social practices of knowledge making as they happen in real time. Regardless of methodology, the key requirement of these case studies is that they be carried out in dialogue with other work in the new sociology of ideas and with the explicit aim of theory building and refinement. To be sure, there is already an enormous case study literature on intellectual life, produced by intellectual historians, biographers, historians of science, and others. Yet most such work, at least when it concerns the humanities and social sciences, is inattentive to the kinds of sociological concerns I've problematized in this book; puts the explanatory emphasis on personality or intentionality or on broad cultural or political-economic factors whose exact linkage to ideas remains wooly and underspecified; adopts a hagiographic or condemnatory tone that may obscure more than it reveals; and fails to see what it has in common with all other studies of intellectuals. What gains could be made, by contrast, if everyone who studied intellectual life had as *one* of her or his goals to understand the social mechanisms and processes that thinkers encounter as they go about formulating their ideas and staging their careers? Under such a banner, scholars working on diverse figures—on the Soviet semiologist Yuri Lotman, say, and the historian Richard Hofstadter, to mention the subjects of two recent books[22]— could find common ground in the sociological comparisons they could leverage and in what these might reveal about the processes of knowledge making operative in different historical and institutional settings and across settings. Little by little, as sociologists of ideas worked side by side with intellectual historians to produce case studies that would result in better, more explanatory theories—at the same time that systematic empirical research was under way to test them—the development by thinkers of new ideas would stop seeming to be a miraculous, inexplicable act of genius or an expression of the zeitgeist or a simplistic manifestation of class interests and would start appearing for what it is: a more or less predictable outcome of the work lives and other quotidian social experiences of those fortunate enough to occupy the relatively limited number of occupational slots society sets aside for those deemed intellectuals.

22. See Andreas Schönle, ed, 2006, *Lotman and Cultural Studies: Encounters and Extensions*, Madison: University of Wisconsin Press; David Brown, 2006, *Richard Hofstadter: An Intellectual Biography*, Chicago: University of Chicago Press.

Index